WASHINGTON, D.C.

THE COMPLETE GUIDE
1994–1995 EDITION

WASHINGTON, D.C

THE COMPLETE GUIDE
1994–1995 EDITION

JUDY DUFFIELD

WILLIAM KRAMER

CYNTHIA SHEPPARD

VINTAGE BOOKS

A Division of Random House, Inc.

NEW YORK

Vintage Books Edition, January 1994

Text copyright © 1982, 1987, 1988, 1991, 1992, 1993, 1994 by
Judy Duffield, William Kramer, Cynthia Sheppard

Maps copyright © 1991, 1994 by Robert Bull Design

Library of Congress Cataloging in Publication Data
Duffield, Judy, 1946–
Washington, D.C., the complete guide.
Includes index.
1. Washington (D.C.)—Description—1981– —
Guide-books. I. Kramer, William, 1946– .
II. Sheppard, Cynthia, 1955– . III. Title.
F192.3.D8   1987   917.53'044   88-40339
ISBN 0-679-75017-7

Subway map courtesy of
Washington Metropolitan Area Transit Authority

Book design by Robert Bull Design

Manufactured in the United States of America

10 9 8 7 6 5 4 3 2 1

CONTENTS

9

OTHER D.C. AREAS · 172

10

SUBURBAN VIRGINIA · 178

11

NEARBY MARYLAND · 202

12

A SHORT HISTORY OF WASHINGTON · 214

13

ENTERTAINMENT · 225

CONTENTS ■ ix

20

WASHINGTON ON THE RUN:
ONE-, TWO- AND THREE-DAY TOURS AND SPECIALIZED TOURS · 319

Day One . . . Day Two . . . Day Three . . . Major Attractions Arranged by
Interest Area

21

DINING · 325

Capitol Hill/Southwest . . . Georgetown/Foggy Bottom/West End . . .
Downtown . . . Chinatown . . . Northwest . . . Suburban Maryland . . .
Northern Virginia . . . Restaurants by Cuisine

22

HOTELS · 346

Bed & Breakfasts . . . Hotel Listings . . . Budget (Under $60) . . . Moderate
($60–$100) . . . Expensive ($100–$150) . . . Luxury ($150–$200) . . . Super-
Luxury (Over $200)

CALENDAR OF ANNUAL EVENTS · 363

INDEX · 369

INTRODUCTION

Washington, D.C.: The Complete Guide has one simple purpose: to be the visitor's most useful and usable guidebook to the nation's capital. As we wrote this book, we assumed that almost every sightseeing venture is dominated by one factor: time—or, rather, less than enough of it to see and enjoy all the places you may have traveled miles to visit. Our purpose is to help you make the best use of your time, and so make your Washington experience as trouble-free, relaxed, and rewarding as possible.

The authors, all natives or longtime residents and fans of the District, have concentrated on the basic questions facing all tourists: what to see; when to see it; how to get there and back. Beyond these, we also responded to concerns that other guidebooks tend to overlook: is there a place to eat? are there special accommodations for groups? is the site accessible to people with disabilities? and, if you plan ahead, can extra features and services be made available? We have employed a simple but extensive set of graphic symbols for ready reference. An explanation of these symbols follows in the next chapter.

While the *Guide* may be most useful to visitors to Washington, the information it contains will also introduce new residents to the delights (and pitfalls) of the area. And we trust that with our help even old Washington hands will be able to discover new aspects of their city.

The book is organized in straightforward fashion: we have divided the city into distinct geographical sections, starting where *you* are most likely to start—at the Mall, that grassy expanse stretching between the U.S. Capitol and the Lincoln Memorial, around whose borders are many of the principal attractions of "Federal Washington." After the Mall, we present the other parts of the city: Capitol Hill, Downtown, Georgetown/Foggy Bottom/The West End, Northwest, other areas of interest in the city, suburban Virginia and nearby

Maryland. Each area is briefly introduced; the site reports for the area are then presented alphabetically. For each site you will find our set of symbols for quick reference, a short description of particular points of interest and other useful information, including major exhibitions. Each section concludes with a brief note on places to grab a quick bite.

The remainder of the *Guide* consists of short chapters designed to make your visit more rewarding. We have included suggestions for one-, two- and three-day tours; a dining section by location and type of cuisine; a directory of local hotels and motels in an easy-to-read listing indicating price ranges and services; a description of recreation and sports opportunities in the area; details of Washington's myriad shopping opportunities and art galleries; a chapter on entertainment—for those who still have the strength—and an overview of Washington's history and people. Because Washington beckons countless families, we include a chapter on touring with children.

To the out-of-town driver, Washington streets and traffic circles are confusing, at best. It's easy to lose your way or your good humor as you try to navigate around the District. Public transportation in Washington is the best alternative to the private automobile, and may even be preferable. Each site description in the *Guide* keys you to public transportation possibilities and advises you on the parking situation in the site's vicinity. We also devote a chapter to "Getting To and Around Town," which details Washington's excellent public-transport systems, cracks the code on the many and various street signs you'll encounter and tells you what to do if your car gets towed (the District police's ticketing and towing divisions are the nation's most efficient).

For people with limited mobility, touring many places is virtually impossible. Our nation's capital, however, responded with unusual speed and thoroughness to the laws of the early 1970s that directed public facilities to provide access for those who have physical disabilities or other problems of mobility. Every major tourist attraction is accessible; in addition, special services are available in many places. We make clear, in the site reports and in Chapter 18, how people with disabilities can take full advantage of the treasures of the city with the least trouble and unnecessary expenditure of energy and time. We tell you, for example, which entrances to use and how to arrange for special tours.

Many of you will be introduced to Washington in a group. Logistics for a large group are complex and subject to breakdown—and the consequences can be dismaying. One bad hotel, one inedible meal, one wrong turn and the entire trip can turn sour. So, in a separate chapter we examine the problems of traveling and sightseeing as a group, and recommend how to make it through your trip without losing your patience—or a member of your ensemble.

International visitors can be beset with the same problems as well as the unique difficulties of currency exchange, language, etc.; we offer advice and resources in a chapter aimed at their needs.

Our own touring, both here and elsewhere, has made it clear that too much information can often be worse than not enough. We have tried to strike a balance: we include the information that is practical to have in advance, and we direct those who want to read more to worthwhile printed material. We have also included a chapter of planning tips for before you hit town and for each day you're here.

A caveat: nothing stands still. While we have made every effort to provide accurate information, the hours, prices, services and events described in the following pages are current only as of publication. We suggest checking essential facts before setting off into the wilds of Washington to make sure the day's schedule will turn out as planned.

If you discover anything has changed or anything new that we've missed, please let us know. We'd appreciate your contributions for the next edition; send them to us at Vintage Books.

Washington is a city of almost limitless resources. We have lived here for many years, yet the experience of writing this book has uncovered many new features of the city for us. We love it here and do our best to make sure you will, too. Do note that the urban ills of drugs and violent crime are largely restricted to areas where tourists have no reason to go, but let common sense prevail: stay on well-lighted and well-traveled thoroughfares after dark, and leave situations that make you uneasy. We hope the *Guide* will serve to open doors for you and give you pleasure for the moment, memories to take away and the desire to come back again and again. If this *Guide* makes it easier for you to draw from the well of over 200 years of our country's rich history and to navigate through the modern reality of a busy urban area, we will have done our job. Happy touring!

WASHINGTON, D.C.

THE COMPLETE GUIDE
1994–1995 EDITION

1

HOW TO USE

THIS BOOK

The essence of this *Guide* is the geographical presentation of the special attractions Washington has to offer. Each city section is briefly introduced to give you a sense of its flavor, tone and history. Each section concludes with a listing of where to grab a bite while you're touring. The core of each section, and of the entire *Guide,* is the site reports. To help you make best use of your time, we have devised the following format for the site descriptions to give you basic information in a bold, easy-to-read manner. Please bear in mind that Virginia and Maryland area codes must be used when calling from the District, even though the calls are local.

SITE'S NAME   **Phone Number**
(An official name, if different, may appear in parentheses)
Street Address
A mailing address, if different, will appear beneath.
Hours: For some Washington sites, these differ from summer to winter.
   Unless otherwise specified, summer hours are in effect from
   Memorial Day until Labor Day.
Price of Admission   (Most are free)

 Metro. Washington's subway system. The nearest subway stop
   to the site is noted (the subway line is given in parentheses). If
   the route from the subway to the site isn't obvious, brief walking
   instructions are provided.

Bus system. If a Metro stop isn't convenient, the buses that pass the site are listed. Since we don't know your point of origin on Metrobus routes, you should call Metrobus at (202) 637-7000 to find out which bus or buses can take you from your starting point to the site. The Metrobus TDD number for those who are hearing-impaired is (202) 638-3780.

 Taxis. We note the street or streets nearest the site where you can hail a taxi most easily. In some cases a building entrance is listed if it is a place where cabs congregate to wait for fares. A taxi zone map appears in Chapter 2, "Getting To and Around Town."

 Parking. The parking situation in the neighborhood of the site is described. In addition, driving directions from the city to suburban sites are given.

 Food. We note if food is available on the premises of the site, and the hours of availability if they differ radically from those of the site. Most places will close their eating establishments at least a half hour before general closing time. We also let you know if picnicking is possible.

 Kids. We point out a site's particular appeal to children and list any exhibits or services that are especially for kids.

 Groups. Included here are special arrangements that can or should be made when you're taking a group to the site.

 Impaired Mobility. We note if a site is *accessible*—that is, if it can be entered and toured, without assistance, by a person in a wheelchair. "Accessible" also means that there are phones and rest rooms designed for use by people in wheelchairs. The most accessible entrance to the site will be noted, if other than the main entrance. If the site has *limited access* we detail the limitations. If the site is *inaccessible* to a person in a wheelchair without assistance, but on-site assistance is available, we provide a phone number to request this service.

 Impaired Vision. Any special provisions that are made for blind or visually impaired people are indicated here.

 Impaired Hearing. Special provisions made for visitors who are hearing-impaired or deaf are noted, as well as material that can help the nonhearing person enjoy a site more fully. A TDD or TTY phone number is provided if available at the site.

Advance Planning. Here we let you know about any special benefits available if you make arrangements in advance of your visit to the site. If your visit is in the busy spring or summer months, you will always do well to write ahead. We'd like to mention here that very often your representatives in Congress can arrange special tours for you if you advise them of your visit far enough in advance. We note in the site reports if special tours for constituents are provided on a regular basis. In addition, members of Congress often have printed information they can send to help you plan your trip.

A note to those who have flexibility in timing their visit: consider Washington's weather. Summer can be beastly with high temperatures, high humidity and pollution inversions. Spring and fall are sublime; be advised, though, that the city is clogged with tourists during Easter week and at the end of the school year when kids are on class trips. Winter is not without its cold and rainy periods, but, since it's the quietest tourist season, Washington's points of interest are more accessible at this time of year. See Chapter 15, "Outdoor Washington/Sports," for a month-by-month temperature guide.

Tours. We conclude by noting the times when scheduled tours of the site are conducted.

2

GETTING TO
AND AROUND TOWN

YOUR ARRIVAL IN WASHINGTON

Some 20 million visitors come to Washington each year, making it one of the most visited destinations in the country and making tourism the city's second-largest industry (after the federal government). So you can expect lots of Washingtonians to be looking out for you, whether your visit is for business or pleasure.

Getting to Washington and getting around once you're here can be much easier if you take a little time to familiarize yourself with the city and its various means of transport.

By Air

If you're flying to Washington, you'll land in one of the three area airports: Washington National, Baltimore-Washington International or Dulles International.

National Airport is the most convenient to the city, since it's just three miles from the White House, across the Potomac River in Virginia. A Depression-era facility, National is undergoing massive renovation and expansion. From National, you can take the Metro, Washington's modern and efficient subway system, and you'll be downtown in just a few minutes. Taxis are plentiful; expect to pay about $12–$15 (not including tip) to get downtown. Major hotels, including the Capital and Washington Hiltons and the Sheraton Washington, are served by Washington Flyer buses via the downtown terminal at 1517 K St., NW every half hour for $8 one-way or $14 round trip. There is also bus service between National and the other airports.

Baltimore-Washington International Airport (BWI) is about 45 minutes from downtown Washington. There is bus service between BWI and the downtown terminal at 1517 K Street, NW, every hour and a half starting at 7 A.M. for $14 one way or $25 round trip. In addition, buses to National via the Washington Flyer operate from 1517 K Street, NW. Call Airport Connection at (301) 441-2345 for information. Amtrak trains run between Union Station and BWI about every two hours, six times daily. The one-way fare is approximately $10. Call Amtrak at (800) 872-7245. While the airport is about two miles from the BWI train station, there are free shuttle buses operating according to the train's schedule. Taxi fare is approximately $45–$50 between BWI and 1517 K Street, NW.

Dulles International Airport is about one hour from the White House. Buses run to Dulles from 1517 K Street, NW (Washington Flyer, (703) 685-1400) every half-hour starting from 5:20 A.M. and cost $16 one way or $26 round trip, cash only. Taxi rides to town are expensive—about $35. Washington Flyer cabs are available at Dulles. All have meters; credit card cabs can be requested. For information, call (703) 528-4400 or (703) 661-8230.

By Train

Amtrak, the national railway passenger system serving 500 cities, conveniently operates out of Union Station on Capitol Hill, at 1st Street and Massachusetts Avenue, NE (see site report for Union Station). The grand, newly refurbished station is now a huge shopping, eating and entertainment complex, offering the full spectrum of products and services. Amtrak also serves Washington at the Capital Beltway station in New Carrollton, Maryland (Route 495 Beltway, Exit 19B West to Route 50, then follow signs). Amtrak can be reached at (800) 872-7245.

MARC is Maryland's commuter rail system which operates from Union Station to Baltimore and BWI Airport; call (800) 325-RAIL. The Virginia Railway Express offers Virginia commuters two routes connecting to Metrorail, from Manassas and Fredericksburg. Call (703) 836-6072 for information.

THE WASHINGTON AREA

to Pennsylvania Turnpike

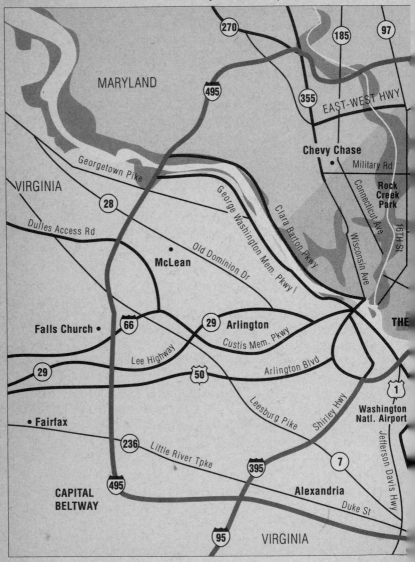

to Baltimore, Philadelphia, and New York

By Bus

Washington is well served by bus routes, although the station is not located in the best of neighborhoods. Greyhound-Trailways—(301) 565-2662—is at 1105 1st Street, NE (1st and L streets, NE).

By Car

There are as many routes into the District as there are roads. The *Guide* provides a map of major routes from all directions, but come prepared with a good, up-to-date road map of your own.

Washington is conveniently located along the eastern seaboard and is only a four-hour drive from New York. Its mid-Atlantic location makes for convenient day trips and weekend getaways to the historic cities and countrysides of Virginia, Maryland, West Virginia, Pennsylvania and Delaware.

The Capital Beltway is an expressway that circles the city and has interchanges with all major approach routes. The eastern portion of the Beltway is part of I-95, the major artery linking the District with Baltimore, Maryland, to the north and Richmond, Virginia, to the south. The rest of the Beltway is numbered I-495.

U.S. 1 and the Baltimore-Washington Parkway (Route 295) approach the city from the north; U.S. 50, Route 4 and Route 5 come from eastern and southern Maryland. Leading into the city from the south, via Alexandria and Arlington, Virginia, are U.S. 1 and I-395.

To the north, I-270 links metropolitan Washington with I-70 at Frederick, Maryland. To the west, I-66 and U.S. 50 connect with the Virginia part of I-495 on approach to Washington.

GETTING AROUND TOWN

Washington has the reputation of being a difficult city to get around in. That reputation is largely undeserved—the city does have a rational plan to it.

The basic layout is simple. The city is divided into four sections: Northeast, Northwest, Southeast and Southwest, usually denoted by initials—NE, NW, SE and SW. The dividing lines are North Capitol Street, South Capitol Street, East Capitol Street and the Mall, radiating like the spokes of a wheel from the Capitol. North-south streets are numbers; east-west streets are letters in alphabetical order (there are no J, X, Y or Z streets). When the city planners ran out of letters, they gave the streets two-syllable names (e.g., Calvert Street) in alphabetical order, and followed them with three-syllable names (e.g., Cathedral Street), reaching out to the Washington-Maryland border in upper Northwest and Northeast. Diagonal thoroughfares, designated "Avenues," are named for various states. Circles and squares occur at the intersection of diagonal avenues and numbered and lettered streets.

Be careful to check the quadrant indicators—500 C Street can be found in four different locations as 5th and C streets intersect in NW, NE, SE and SW. The street number will help you figure out what the crossroad is. For example, The White House, at 1600 Pennsylvania Avenue, NW, is at 16th and Pennsylvania; 1990 K Street, NW, is between 19th and 20th streets; and 510 7th Street, NW, is found between E and F streets—that is, between the fifth and sixth letters of the alphabet.

Driving here is not for the faint of heart or for a navigator who wants to observe the passing street scene. Fortunately, the area is served by quite reliable mass transit—a fleet of Metrobuses and a sleek Metrorail system. Taxis are reasonable in cost and plentiful in most parts of the city. The District's small scale makes this a good walking city, and we recommend as much touring on foot as your legs will take.

Metrorail

The "Metro," Washington's modern, five-line subway system, is speedy, quiet and well designed. We strongly endorse Metro as the most efficient and pleasant way to get about town. In fact, even if you drive to Washington, you may want to leave your car at a special Metro station and then do your touring. Its one major drawback for short-term visitors is cost; it can be an expensive proposition for a family—but so, too, can downtown parking, especially if you run afoul of DC's aggressively enforced meters. One possible solution is the daily unlimited rail travel pass, available for $5, and good for travel anytime after the end of the morning rush–9:30 A.M. to system closing. At $20 for a family of four, it may be $5–$10 more than all-day parking in a downtown lot, but the pass allows for great flexibility. One-day passes are available for purchase at the Metro Center station, Pentagon City and Ballston Mall Transit stores, and at some area grocery stores.

The *Guide*'s maps indicate stations with a big "M," and there's a handy system map in this book. Best of all, each of our site reports includes directions on how to get there by Metrorail. The stations are safe and well located, and Metro is easy to use once you learn how.

You'll recognize Metro stations around town by the bronze pillar with an illuminated "M" at the top; the station name is posted at the entrance. Nearly all of the tracks are underground, and the stations have both escalators and elevators (see Chapter 18, "Tips for Visitors with Disabilities," for station entrances with elevators).

Each station displays a stylized map of the various train lines, which are identified by five different colors, plus you'll find an overview of the system with the area streets and landmarks above it. If your destination is on another train line, the map shows where to transfer from one line to another.

Metrorail currently runs Monday to Friday from 5:30 A.M. to midnight, Saturday from 8 A.M. to midnight and Sunday from 8 A.M. to midnight. On major holidays, the system runs on a weekend schedule. During rush hour, trains are spaced 3 to 6 minutes apart, and they run every 10 minutes other times.

Fares, which are posted in each station, vary according to the length of your trip, as well as time of day. You can ask for help or get various brochures from the information booth in any station.

Metrobus

While speeding along underground on Metrorail is almost sure to get you there faster, riding a bus allows you to see the streetscape and how portions of the city interrelate. Red, white and blue Metrobuses plod along metropolitan area streets, following nearly 400 basic routes. You can ride for a basic fare of $1.00 within the District, and more for trips into the suburbs or during rush hour. Metrobus stops, usually located before street intersections, display red, white and blue striped signs and indicate the routes served.

Fares are exact change only, or you can buy bus tokens at Metro Center (12th and F streets, NW), the Pentagon Concourse or at any of the eight Metrobus garages.

If your trip requires changing to another route, you should tell the driver your destination when you board, pay your whole fare on the first bus and ask for a transfer. Each transfer is punched to indicate the zone and time; transfers are free and good for up to two hours. Should your trip require using both Metrobus and Metrorail, you can get a transfer from rail to bus for a free bus ride in Washington and a discount of 20¢ in Maryland and 35¢ in Virginia; oddly enough, there is a charge for transfers in the other direction.

If you'll be here for a considerable time and expect to use Metrobus often, call Metro at (202) 637-7000 for general information and details on special fares, the Metro Flash Pass.

Metrobus will mail you information on specific routes if you call (202) 637-7000, or write to Washington Metropolitan Transit Authority, 600 5th Street, NW, Washington, D.C. 20001. Hearing-impaired people should call the Metro TDD at (202) 638-3780.

Sightseeing Tours

Tourmobile, a National Park Service concessionaire, provides an opportunity to see the major sites easily, inexpensively and at your own pace. The Tourmobile offers a respite to the foot-weary visitor. The basic, narrated tour, which costs about $8.50 for adults and $4 for children (ages 3–11), will take you around all the Mall sites, Kennedy Center, Arlington Cemetery Visitors' Center, the White House, the Capitol, and Union Station. The service runs from 9 A.M. to 6:30 P.M., June 15 through Labor Day, and 9:30 A.M. to 4:30 P.M. during the rest of the year.

You can get off at any site, look around as you like and reboard another bus later in the day for no extra charge. Readers of the *Guide* have complained, however, about waiting times between buses. Tickets purchased after 2 P.M. in winter and after 4 P.M. in summer are good for the next day, at a price of $10.50 for adults and $5 for children. Or, if you prefer a quick and restful tour, stay on the Tourmobile you first board, listen to the narration and watch the sights, and land back at your starting point 90 minutes later. While the route officially begins at the East Front of the Capitol, you can simply look for the Tourmobile Shuttle Bus sign at any of the sites included, buy a ticket from the driver and start your excursion, or purchase tickets at ticket booths along the Mall.

Tourmobile also offers a complete Arlington Cemetery tour, which includes stops at the President John F. Kennedy and Senator Robert F. Kennedy gravesites, the Tomb of the Unknowns (Changing of the Guard) and Arlington House. This leg of the journey costs an additional $2.75 for adults and $1.25 for children and operates from 8:30 A.M. until 6:30 P.M. A combination Washington–Arlington Cemetery ticket is $8.50 adults, $4 children. An excursion to Mount Vernon includes a trip through historic Old Town, Alexandria, and this costs about $16.50 for adults and $8 for children, which includes the admission fee to the plantation. Call Tourmobile for this tour's schedule since it varies throughout the year. An excursion to the historic home of abolitionist Frederick Douglass leaves daily at 10 A.M. from Arlington Cemetery. The round trip fare is $5 for adults, $2.50 for children. The trip lasts 2½ hours. A two-day ticket, good for all three of the tours, costs around $25.50 for adults and $12.50 for children. Watch for promotional discount coupons at various tourism outlets. Groups of 20 or more are eligible for a discount, too. To listen to a tape recording about the Tourmobile, call (202) 554-7950. Group information is available at (202) 488-5218.

Parking for Tourmobile is available at Arlington Cemetery, for a fee.

Old Town Trolley Tours offers a narrated two-hour tour aboard old-fashioned, all-weather trolleylike buses. The 16-stop tour includes Capitol Hill, the Smithsonian, Arlington National Cemetery, Dupont Circle, Embassy Row, Georgetown and the Washington National Cathedral; it stops at some major hotels as well as tourist sites. You can stay aboard the trolley for the full two hours, or you may get off to sightsee and reboard another trolley later for no extra charge. Trolleys run every 30 minutes from 9 A.M. to the last full tour at 4 P.M. Call to check for extended summer hours. Fares are adults $15; children ages 5–12 $7; children under 5 free with adult. AAA members receive a $1 discount. Call (301) 985-3020 for details.

A variety of other tour services are listed in the District of Columbia Yellow Pages. (If you're coming as a group, many other tour services are available if you plan in advance. See Chapter 17.) Here are a few you may want to call for further information and comparative shopping:

Gray Line Tours offers a variety of different tours. On the all-day deluxe tour you'll see all the major Washington and Arlington sites; it costs about $36 for adults and $18 for children. "Washington After Dark" is a three-hour tour of the major sites, available late-March through October; it costs about $20 for adults and $10 for children. There are also excursions to outlying sites, such as Mount Vernon, Annapolis, Charlottesville, and Colonial Williamsburg, as well as other tailored tours in town. Gray Line is located at Union Station,

Bus Level, 50 Massachusetts Avenue, NE, Washington, D.C. 20002; the phone number is (202) 289-1995.

City Sights Tours offers specialized tours of black, Hispanic and Jewish interest, as well as a full line of general tours on a prearranged basis for groups. City Sights can be reached at 2025 I Street, NW, Suite 721, Washington, D.C. 20006; (202) 785-4700.

City Sights also offers a variety of deluxe tours for individuals or groups; reservations are a must.

Tours are also offered by the following:

All About Town leads complete guided tour of Washington, with accompanying lecture, via air-conditioned coaches. Free pickup at major downtown hotels. Call (202) 393-3696 for information.

A Scandal Tour of Washington is a motorcoach tour of the sites that have made Washington the scandal capital of the world. The 90-minute tour is hosted by the Gross National Product, a comedy troupe. Tours are given Saturday at 1 P.M., departing from the Washington Hilton, 1919 Connecticut Avenue, NW. Tours are $27 per person. Call (301) 587-4291 for information and reservations.

Wheels Across Washington offers horse-and-carriage tours from April through November, departing from the Willard Inter-Continental Hotel, 14th Street and Pennsylvania Avenue, NW. Operation depends on weather and cost depends on number of people. Call (1-703) 752-4763 for details.

Capitol Entertainment Services offers groups a variety of guided tours of the monuments and memorials, black history points of interest and educational sites. Call (202) 636-9203 for information.

Taxicabs

Taxis in Washington are relatively inexpensive and easy to hail, although the system can be rather confusing (see Zone Map, pages 16–17). The fare is based on a zone system, with a basic charge of $2.80 for travel within a single sub-zone (e.g., the entire trip is within zone 1B—see map p. 17) and $3.20 across a single zone (e.g., from 1B to 1C). To give you some idea, a single zone charge buys you a ride between the Capitol and Downtown (a system rumored to exist in order to allow congresspeople a Downtown lunch at minimal transportation cost). The zone system can be tricky for the consumer, though; before paying, even veteran travelers often ask the driver exactly what zones they traversed. To cloud the picture more, there's

SELECTED SITES BY TAXICAB ZONE

ZONE 1A

Bureau of Engraving and Printing	1A
Constitution Hall	1A
Corcoran Gallery of Art	1A
The Ellipse	1A
Holocaust Museum	1A
Interior Department Museum	1A
Lafayette Square	1A
Metro Center Metrorail Stop	1A
Museum of Modern Art	
of Latin America	1A
National Aquarium	1A
National Theater	1A
Organiz. of Ame. States	
(Pan Amer. Un.)	1A
Freer Gallery of Art	1A
National Museum of American History	1A
Renwick Gallery	1A
State Department	1A
Washington Monument	1A
Washington Visitor Information Center	1A
The White House	1A

ZONE 1B

Bethune Museum-Archives	1B
B'Nai B'rith Museum	1B
National Archives	1B
National Building Museum	1B
National Geographic Society	1B
Phillips Collection	1B

ZONE 1C

D.C. Convention Center	1C
National Museum of Women in the Arts	1C
Washington, D.C. Convention and Visitors Association	1C

ZONE 1D

Arts and Industries Building	1D
Ford's Theater	1D
Friendship Arch in Chinatown	1D
L'Enfant Plaza Metrorail Stop	1D
Mall Ice Skating Rink	1D
National Gallery of Art	1D
Old Post Office Pavilion	1D
Hirshhorn Museum and Sculpture Garden	1D
House Office Buildings	1D
Library of Congress	1D
National Air and Space Museum	1D
National Museum of African Art	1D
National Museum of American Art	1D
National Museum of Natural History	1D
National Portrait Gallery	1D
Senate Office Buildings	1D
Smithsonian Information Center	1D
Smithsonian Institution Building	1D
U.S. Botanic Garden	1D
U.S. Capitol	1D
U.S. Supreme Court	1D

ZONE 2

Capital Children's Museum	2C
Dumbarton Oaks	2A
Folger Shakespeare Library	2D
John F. Kennedy Center for the Performing Arts	2A
State Department (Diplomatic Reception Rooms)	2A
Textile Museum	2A
Tidal Basin	2E
Vietnam Veterans Memorial	2E
Washington National Cathedral	2A
Washington Navy Yard	2D

ZONE 3

Frederick Douglass House	3G
Jefferson Memorial	3H
Lincoln Memorial	3H
National Arboretum	3D
RFK Stadium	3E
U.S. Naval Observatory	3A
The National Zoo	3B

TAXI CAB ZONE MAP

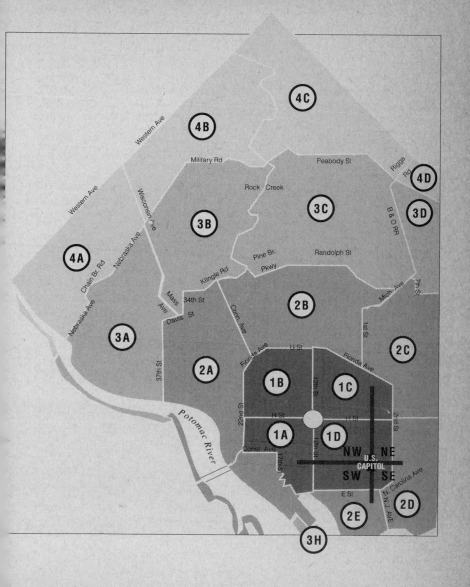

an additional $1.25 charge for travel companions, as well as a $1 rush-hour surcharge and a $1.50 surcharge for a radio-dispatched cab. Taxis licensed only in Maryland or Virginia cannot transport passengers between points within the District. Taxis are permitted to pick up additional passengers headed for different destinations, but the driver must first obtain the original passenger's permission, and it cannot result in more than a five-block diversion.

The Taxicab Commission publishes a pamphlet, "The Consumer Guide to Taxicabs," which is available for a small charge by calling (202) 767-8380.

For further information, or to file a complaint, contact the District of Columbia Taxicab Commission, 2041 Martin Luther King, Jr., Avenue, SE, Washington, D.C. 20020; (202) 767-8380.

To track lost items left in cabs, call the Police Property Bureau at (202) 767-7586.

Driving in the District

Best of luck to the visitor who expects to drive and enjoy sightseeing, too. While many come to Washington by car, smart visitors use their wits—and now this *Guide*—to plan convenient and inexpensive excursions around town. In general, the traffic, poorly marked routes and scarce parking combine to make driving here a frustrating experience. Also, if you use a map, make sure it's up-to-date. Route numbers and even Beltway exit numbers have been known to change. If you want to brave it, please read through the rest of this section to familiarize yourself with the common practices as well as the idiosyncrasies here.

For starters, rush hour brings more chaos than just impatient drivers caught in snarled traffic. Many one-way streets, and some lanes of others, change direction during rush hour, weekdays 6:30 to 9 A.M. and 4 to 6:30 P.M.

Many Metrorail stations offer inexpensive parking, for $1.50 to $2.50, on a first-come, first-served basis. We strongly recommend that visitors, especially those staying outside the city, leave their cars behind at one of the many suburban stations with parking lots.

Most metered parking spaces have a two-hour maximum, although many in Downtown are limited to one hour or even a half hour. Along Independence Avenue by the Mall you can park for three hours. If you're even luckier, you might find free, all-day parking in West

Potomac Park along Ohio Drive, south of the Lincoln Memorial. If you opt for the convenience of commercial parking lots and garages, you are warned: they are expensive—often $10–$15 per day in prime Downtown and other Northwest areas. In the evening many lots are discounted to just a few dollars.

Police and other officials do indeed ticket cars (to the tune of 6,000 a day), so this is no town for carelessness (D.C. has the most efficient parking-control system in the country). Fines start at $15 for an expired meter. Creative, illegal parking can get expensive: $50 fine for parking in a bus zone or within 20 feet of a bus stop; $50 for obstructing a crosswalk, illegal parking in a handicapped zone or double parking; $20 for parking within 5 feet of a driveway or alley or for exceeding two hours in a residential parking permit area. Also note that there's a movement afoot to raise the fines. The Bureau of Traffic Adjudication, Cashiers Office, is located at 65 K Street, NE, and the telephone number is (202) 727-5000. You can settle fines by paying cash or with a personal check, money order, VISA or MasterCard. The office is open Monday to Friday, 8:30 A.M. to 7 P.M., and on Saturday, 8:30 A.M. to noon.

If your car is towed, call (202) 727-5000 for information on its retrieval.

Car Rentals

Various car-rental companies are located at the airports, in town and throughout the suburbs. Many of them offer courtesy transportation to and from nearby airports and Metro stations. You may also want to compare any special discounts such as three-day, holiday or weekend rates when you call these or other companies.

Agency Rent-A-Car: 1-800-321-1972
Alamo Rent-A-Car: 1-800-327-9633
Avis: 1-800-831-2847
Budget Rent-A-Car: 1-800-527-0700; (703) 920-3360
Dollar Rent-A-Car: 1-800-800-4000
Enterprise Rent-A-Car: 1-800-325-8007
Hertz: 1-800-654-3131
National Car Rental: 1-800-227-7362
Sears: 1-800-527-0700
Thrifty Rent-A-Car: 1-800-367-2277; (202) 783-0400

Transportation Numbers

Metrobus and Metrorail:

Bus and Metrorail information	(202) 637-7000
Complaints and suggestions	(202) 637-1328
Bulk purchase of farecards	(202) 962-1590
Information on Flash Passes, Senior Citizen Discounts, Sales Outlet locations	(202) 637-7000
Lost and found	(202) 962-1195
Traffic and parking information	(202) 727-5000
TDD	(202) 638-3780
Police emergency	(202) 962-1289
Department of Traffic Adjudication	(202) 727-5000

Railroads

Amtrak	1-800-USA-RAIL
Commuter (Baltimore, WV)	1-800-325-RAIL

3

PLANNING

AHEAD

Advance planning can help ensure that your visit to Washington will be especially rewarding. Try to plan your activities as soon as you know you're coming. Some of the more popular tours that require reservations get booked up months in advance for the busy spring season. If you are traveling in a group, are requesting special tours or are visiting from abroad, it is essential to make arrangements even further in advance (see the "On the Town with Children," "Advice to Groups," "Tips for Visitors with Disabilities" and "A Welcome to International Visitors" chapters for specific tips). *Once you're in Washington, make daily plans, remembering to call ahead to double-check hours and events before you schedule your activities around them.* This chapter presents some additional planning hints that we hope will make your visit run smoothly and with a great measure of enjoyment.

BEFORE YOU ARRIVE

A variety of organizations will mail you information to help you plan activities in advance. When time allows, it's best to write to them well ahead of your trip, particularly if your visit is between Easter and Labor Day or if you need special arrangements. Individual site reports also contain advice on advance planning, so it's a good idea to study them before you get to town. If you want to go to the theater, you should write ahead for tickets.

Many museums, galleries and other locations will send you free calendars of events (see individual site reports for addresses).

There are a number of useful resource centers from which you can obtain information to help you plan your visit. They are:

* The Washington, D.C., Convention and Visitors Association, 1212 New York Avenue, NW, Suite 600, Washington, D.C. 20005, (202) 789-7000.
* Alexandria Convention and Visitors Bureau, 221 King Street, Alexandria, VA 22314, (703) 838-4200; maps, brochures, calendar of events, dining/shopping guide, free parking passes.
* Baltimore Area Visitors and Information Center, 300 W. Pratt Street, Baltimore, MD 21202, (410) 837-4636; the office publishes "Quick City" with city information, plus offers brochures on tourist sites, lodgings, and restaurants.
* Virginia Division of Tourism, 1021 East Cary Street, 14th Floor, Richmond, VA 23219, (804) 786-4484.
* Maryland Office of Tourist Development, 217 East Redwood Street, Baltimore, MD 21202, (800) 543-1036; will send calendar of events, travel guide and a state highway map.

Capitol Reservations and Washington, D.C., Accommodations are centralized hotel booking agencies for individuals, families and groups, often at reduced rates. (See Chapter 22, "Hotels," for phones and addresses.)

Your representative or senator may be able to reserve a place for you on various special tours of the Capitol, White House, FBI Building and government agencies (see site reports). You should call his or her local office well in advance of your visit and see if the staff can arrange tours for you. Your members of Congress can also provide bounteous brochures on particular sites that may be of interest to you.

FIRST MOVES

When you arrive in the nation's capital, you'll find your bearings a lot more quickly if you become familiar with Washington's staple sources of information. Complement this *Guide* with the vast amount of free literature widely available. Reading the *Washington Post* and the *Washington Times* any day can provide great orientation. Every Friday, the *Post* contains a wonderful supplement, called "Weekend," which highlights special events. On Thursday, the *Post* lists notable community events in "This Week." Also, take note of the *Post*'s official listings on weekdays, generally at the bottom of a page in Section A. Here you'll find the day's Supreme Court schedule and what the House, the Senate and their committees have on the agenda. The *Washington Times* publishes a supplement on Thursdays called "Washington Weekend." In addition to theater, music and movie listings, the section has a restaurant and dining guide and hints on inexpensive family fun. The daily edition includes "Capital Agenda," which lists all of the day's official events around town. *Washingtonian,* an excellent local monthly magazine, highlights events in "Where and When."

Other helpful publications for visitors are:

Visitor's Guide ($4.95). Comprehensive, 144-page guide to museums, shopping areas, restaurants and neighborhoods. Published by: C & P Telephone, 6701 Democracy Blvd., 9th Fl., Bethesda, MD 20817, (301) 493-3258.

Washington Flyer Magazine (free at airports; charge for subscription). Bimonthly magazine geared toward business travelers and affluent tourists. Only airport magazine in the country. Contains travel features, calendars of events and Metro system instructions in five languages. Published by: Ackerley Communications, 11 Canal Center Plaza, Suite 111, Alexandria, VA 22314, (703) 739-9292.

Where Magazine (free). A monthly city magazine featuring entertainment, dining and nightlife, shopping, museums and attractions. Available at hotels. Published by: Key Publishers, Inc., 1625 K St., NW, Suite 1290, Washington, D.C. 20006, (202) 463-4550.

The Yellow Pages, "Washington, D.C. Showcase" (in the C & P Yellow Pages). A 40-page color insert detailing a plethora of local events, places to go and area services. Comprehensive maps and listings. Especially helpful are the seating charts for local theaters, arenas and stadiums.

If you find a live event—theater, music or dance—that interests you, you will want to check with Ticketplace, (202) 842-5387, a service offering half-price tickets to most live attractions in town. Half-price tickets are for that day's performances only, and must be paid for in cash. Full-price tickets are also available for future performances with credit cards.

As mentioned previously, a good first stop is the Washington,

D.C., Convention and Visitors Association, where you can collect a variety of brochures. To listen to their tape recording of things to do, call (202) 737-8866 anytime. We are great fans of the new Smithsonian Information Center. Here you'll find a dazzling array of information to make your capital touring a breeze. (See site report, Chapter 4, "The Mall.")

Once in town, although almost all the telephone calls you'll make to sites for information will be local, you will still need to dial an area code if it's different from where you are. The *Guide* provides the area code in case you're calling from out of town; note that the Washington area code is 202, suburban Maryland is 301 and suburban Virginia is 703.

We want to stress the importance of calling ahead for all your stops to double-check hours, exhibits and, for restaurants and shops, their very existence.

NUMBERS TO HELP YOU PLAN YOUR ACTIVITIES—OR JUST FOR FUN

The area code for all of the following numbers is (202), unless otherwise noted.

*Audubon Voice of Naturalist	(301) 652-1088
*Congressional Proceedings (up-to-minute)	
House, Democratic	225-1600
House, Republican	225-7430
Senate, Democratic	224-8541
Senate, Republican	224-8601
Congressional Switchboard	224-3121
*Dial-A-Museum (Smithsonian Information)	357-2020
*Dial-A-Park	619-7275
*Dial-A-Story	638-5717
*National Archives Events	501-5000
National Park Service, Office of Public Affairs	619-7222
*Old Town Trolley	(301) 985-3020
*Sampler of Week's Events	737-8866
Smithsonian	357-2700

* Tape recordings

*Smithsonian Skywatcher's Report   357-2000
*Time   844-1111
*Tourmobile   554-7950
*Weather   936-1212
  White House Switchboard   456-1414

4

THE MALL

The Mall is the heart of our nation's capital and, with good cause, the focus of every tourist's visit to Washington. An elegant stretch of open space extending for two miles from the U.S. Capitol to the Lincoln Memorial, the Mall is flanked by the White House, the Jefferson Memorial, the myriad of museums that compose the Smithsonian Institution and numerous government agencies. Its focal point—indeed, the pinnacle of the city—is the Washington Monument. As the tallest edifice in the city, the monument provides a spectacular view of Washington and its surrounding communities.

The Mall reflects the basic plan drawn up by Pierre L'Enfant in 1791 for the new city of Washington. L'Enfant viewed the Mall as a dramatic span of land that would visually join the "Congress House" on Jenkins Hill to the parklike banks of the Potomac River. The central avenue would be flanked by trees, academies and other sites of learning and entertainment, as well as by a grand canal to supply merchants' needs.

Unfortunately, after only one year, L'Enfant was fired from his post as city planner. While Pennsylvania Avenue flourished and became a bustling commercial strip during the years that followed, the Mall lay bare except for the financially unsuccessful Washington Canal and a scattering of shacks and shanties. At the outset of the Civil War in 1860, the Mall was still a rough-hewn place: lumber and coal yards dotted its northern border, and the Washington Monument sat, stalled by the war, at only one-fourth its final height. The Smithsonian Institution was housed in its only building, the Castle. The

"National Museum" (Arts and Industries Building) was added in 1881 to accommodate the centennial exhibits from the nation's first world's fair in Philadelphia.

At last, in 1900, Senator James McMillan of Michigan, chairman of the Senate District Committee, appointed a panel of leading architects and planners to study the park needs of the District of Columbia. The McMillan Plan of 1902 made sweeping proposals that called for the implementation of many of L'Enfant's original ideas. A railroad was removed from the Mall to a new terminal, Union Station; the Botanic Garden's conservatory was moved from the Mall's center to its southeastern edge; and approval was given for the construction of yet another museum building, which opened in 1911 (National Museum of Natural History).

Since then, museums have gradually filled the Mall's flanks along its eastern end, land has been reclaimed from the Potomac on which to build presidential memorials on its western and southern borders, streets have been transformed into tree-lined walkways, and gardens have been created to fill a pocket, a block, or several acres. To conserve scarce space, museum designers have turned their attention underground; the Smithsonian Quadrangle, which includes the National Museum of African Art, the Arthur M. Sackler Gallery, and the S. Dillon Ripley Center, is almost entirely below the Mall. Only the entrance pavilions are on the surface, nestled in the lovely Enid A. Haupt Garden behind the Smithsonian's Castle. New museums are in the design stage: the National Museum of the American Indian and the National Museum of African Americans should both take their places on the Mall around the turn of the century. Far from a static row of memorials and museums, the Mall is alive and lively, a microcosm of the nation's past and present.

Today, the Mall not only serves tourists, but entices lunchtime joggers from surrounding offices. On weekends, it attracts recreation seekers from throughout the region who come to bike, picnic, fly kites and play baseball, rugby, volleyball, cricket and polo on its many fields. For a nominal fee, rides on an antique carousel can be enjoyed in front of the Arts and Industries Building. At night, a drive around the Mall can be quite spectacular, since the museums and monuments are flooded with light.

The Cherry Blossom Festival, complete with parade, is held annually, sometime from mid-March to mid-April, depending on the trees'

THE MALL

Start your tour at the new Smithsonian Information Center in the
Smithsonian Institution Building (The Castle). It features two
orientation theaters providing an overview of the Smithsonian;
interactive touch-screen programs on the museums; scale models
of Washington's monumental core with Braille labels; and
electronic wall maps with interactive touch-screen programs
highlighting popular attractions throughout Washington.

⭐ Smithsonian Institution Information Center
  in Smithsonian Institution Building.

1. Arts and Industries Building
2. Bureau of Engraving and Printing
3. Constitution Gardens
4. Freer Gallery of Art

GEORGETOWN (see p. 134-135)
DOWNTOWN

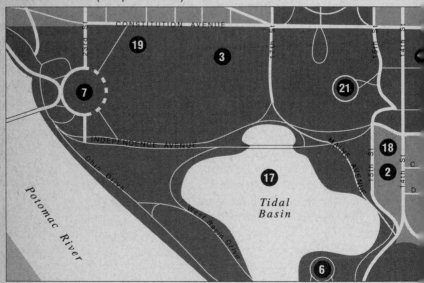

5. Hirshhorn Museum and Sculpture Garden
6. Jefferson Memorial
7. Lincoln Memorial
8. National Air and Space Museum
9. National Archives and Records Service
10. National Gallery of Art - East Building
11. National Gallery of Art - West Building
12. National Museum of African Art
13. National Museum of American History
14. National Museum of Natural History
15. S. Dillon Ripley Center
16. Arthur M. Sackler Gallery
17. Tidal Basin
18. U.S. Holocaust Memorial Museum
19. Vietnam Veterans Memorial
20. Voice of America
21. Washington Monument

(see p. 90-91)

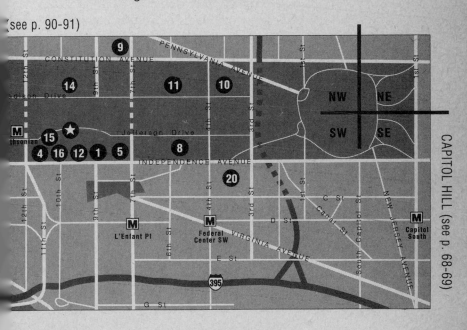

CAPITOL HILL (see p. 68-69)

"schedule." The festival celebrates the blooming of the breathtaking Yoshino and Akebono Japanese cherry trees that surround the Tidal Basin.

Since 1967, the Festival of American Folklife has drawn working people, craftspeople, dancers and musicians from across the country and around the world to exhibit and share their traditional ways. During the festival the Mall comes alive with the smells of regional cooking and the sounds of traditional music, be it Cajun, Gospel, Native American or Chicago blues. The festival is held the last weekend in June and the first weekend in July. Also on July 4, a wonderful fireworks display takes place on the Mall; it's certainly among the finest pyrotechnical performances in the country. The fireworks follow a free open-air concert given by the National Symphony Orchestra on the west terrace of the Capitol. Similar concerts are also performed on the weekends of Memorial Day and Labor Day.

In recent times the Mall has functioned as the meeting ground for Americans expressing concern about issues of national interest. In the 1960s and 1970s, many civil rights, antipoverty, and antiwar rallies were held along the Mall; later, thousands of farmers organized to drive their tractors along its bordering streets to the Capitol. Hostages and military personnel have been welcomed home after conflicts overseas. Abortion rights opponents and proponents, as well as gay rights advocates, have all used the Mall as their arena of expression.

THE SMITHSONIAN INSTITUTION

The Mall is home to the Smithsonian Institution, the largest museum complex in the world; it is composed of the following:

- Arts and Industries Building
- Freer Gallery of Art
- Hirshhorn Museum and Sculpture Garden
- National Air and Space Museum
- National Museum of African Art
- National Museum of American History
- National Museum of Natural History
- Arthur M. Sackler Gallery
- Smithsonian Institution Building (the Castle), housing the Smithsonian Information Center

In other parts of the city the Smithsonian encompasses

• Anacostia Museum
• National Museum of American Art
• National Portrait Gallery
• National Postal Museum
• National Zoo
• Renwick Gallery

Separately administered are

• John F. Kennedy Center for the Performing Arts
• National Gallery of Art

Under this vast umbrella, the Smithsonian carries out its goal: "the increase and diffusion of knowledge." The institution preserves and displays the nation's treasures, sponsors research, publishes a vast array of periodicals, and tackles countless other tasks. For more in-depth information on this grand complex, we highly recommend the *Official Guide to the Smithsonian,* on sale in all the museums and galleries for $4.95. This guide is available in Braille, on cassette tape and as a talking-book tape (this version must be played on special equipment that is furnished free by the Library of Congress).

Call (202) 357-2020 for "Dial-A-Museum," a daily announcement of new exhibits and special events. **The Smithsonian usually has extended summer hours; please check the museums for their current schedule.**

The Smithsonian museum shops are attractions worth visiting in their own right: they offer a vast and appealing selection of articles keyed to the museum in which the shop is housed.

TOURING THE MALL

We advise everyone to begin their visit at the Smithsonian Information Center, an extremely helpful resource housed in the Smithsonian Institution Building, known as the Castle (see site report, page 56). The center constitutes a high-tech orientation to Washington's attractions on and off the Mall. Become acquainted with the city through

the center's theaters, electronic wall maps, brochures, interactive videodisc stations, and a scale Mall model with Braille labels . . . and its helpful volunteer staff, too.

Where you begin your actual touring of the Mall depends on your own interests. The site descriptions that follow will give you a good idea of what each site offers, including such planning essentials as tour times, ticket requirements and eating facilities. A familiarity with the site reports should eliminate some of the running back and forth that can take the enjoyment out of sightseeing.

Numerous ways exist to get you to and around the Mall. Street parking is difficult, but the Metro subway system has several stops in the area. In addition, the Mall is served extensively by Tourmobile and Old Town Trolleys (discussed in Chapter 2, "Getting To and Around Town").

Smithsonian museums each have a few wheelchairs available for public use on a first-come, first-served basis.

ARTS AND INDUSTRIES BUILDING   (202) 357-2700
900 Jefferson Drive, SW 20560
Hours: 10 A.M.–5:30 P.M. daily
Closed Christmas
Free Admission

M Smithsonian stop (orange and blue lines); use Mall exit.

Jefferson Drive or Independence Avenue.

P Competitive parking on the Mall or Independence Avenue.

Recommended. The Discovery Theater is a great resource for children. (Adults will enjoy the presentations, too!) The theater presents month-long residences from October to June (sometimes in July) by troupes ranging from puppetry to pantomime. Performances are 10 and 11:30 A.M. Tuesday–Friday and 1 and 3 P.M. Saturday and Sunday. Tickets are $4 for adults and $3.50 for kids. Call the box office at (202) 357-1500.

Group rates for the Discovery Theater are available for 10 or more; call (202) 357-1500 for information and reservations.

Fully accessible. Use the Victorian Garden entrance on the building's west side.

Special tours can be arranged by calling (202) 357-1502.

 Tours in sign language can be arranged in advance by calling (202) 357-2700 or TDD (202) 357-1729 at least 48 hours in advance. Sign language and oral interpretation of Discovery Theater performances are available upon request; call (202) 357-1697, TDD (202) 357-1929 or TTY (202) 357-1500.

 Docents (occasionally garbed in Victorian costume) conduct tours on an irregular schedule.

The Arts and Industries Building will whisk you back over 100 years to the Philadelphia Centennial of 1876. The four exhibit halls of the museum display steam motors and Victorian whimsy; a highlight is a 42-foot model of the naval cruiser *Antietam,* which was a steam-powered sloop of war.

Construction of the building, which was designed by Adolph Cluss, commenced in 1879, making this the second oldest of the Smithsonian Mall museums. In 1881, President Garfield's inaugural ball was held here. The body of the Smithsonian's technological and aeronautic displays was exhibited in this building until the 1960s and 1970s, when other museums absorbed them. Closed in 1975, the Arts and Industries Building was totally renovated; it reopened with the continuing Centennial exhibit in 1976. A Victorian Horticultural Extravaganza is on the second floor, and a lovely fountain flows beneath the main rotunda. The recently opened Experimental Gallery (south wing) presents exhibitions from around the world.

The museum gift shop is a delight, offering books, records, stationery, jewelry, soaps, old-fashioned dolls and glass jars and special toys for kids. The museum puts out a mail-order catalog three times a year; many of the mail-order items are displayed in the shop. For a copy of the catalog write: Smithsonian Mail Order, P.O.B. 199, Washington, D.C. 20560.

BUREAU OF ENGRAVING AND PRINTING (202) 874-3019
14th and C streets, SW 20228
Hours: 9 A.M.–2:30 P.M. weekdays
        Closed legal holidays
Free Admission

M Smithsonian stop (orange and blue lines); use Independence Avenue exit.

🚗 Independence Avenue, Raoul Wallenberg Place.

P Very difficult street parking.

👫 Recommended.

♿ Accessible. A wheelchair will be supplied if requested.

👂 No special services available. Introductory video is captioned, and there are written explanations throughout the tour.

A Guided VIP tours at 8 A.M. are available through your members of Congress. Write well in advance of your trip to make arrangements.

T Self-guided tours are given from 9 A.M. to 2 P.M. Monday to Friday. From June through August, you must obtain tickets with assigned times from the ticket booth on Raoul Wallenberg Place. There is a limit of 50 tickets per person. The booth opens at 8 A.M.; on most days, tickets have all been distributed by 11:30 A.M.

This very popular tour begins with a five-minute explanatory video, "The Buck Starts Here," which traces the history of the bureau from its 1862 beginning with six employees to its current status as the largest producer of currency, security documents and stamps in the world, employing 2,300 in a 27-acre facility. The only other U.S. currency printing facility is in Ft. Worth.

During the tour you watch millions of dollars being printed in sheets, cut, and bundled for distribution. The tour concludes in the Visitors Center, where uncaptioned video monitors provide further explanations of functions performed by the bureau. A small sales area offers T-shirts, shredded money, stamps, seals, and uncut currency.

FREER GALLERY OF ART   (202) 357-2700
1200 Jefferson Drive, SW 20560
Hours: 10 A.M.–5:30 P.M. daily
          Closed Christmas
Free Admission

Smithsonian stop (blue and orange lines).

 Independence Avenue or Jefferson Drive.

 Competitive parking on the Mall and Independence Avenue.

 Recommended for older kids interested in art. Write to the Education Department four weeks in advance to arrange school tours.

 Write at least four weeks in advance to arrange for a group tour.

 Accessible. Use Independence Avenue entrance to access elevator to exhibits. Guards can provide a wheelchair for use in the museum.

 Brochures in large type are available at the information desk.

 Sign language and oral interpreters can be arranged by calling (202) 357-4880, ext. 245, or TDD (202) 786-2374 one week in advance.

 Highlight tours of the museum are offered daily; tours of specific exhibits are also often offered. For further information, check the information desk or call (202) 357-3200.

The Freer Gallery of Art is one of the most frequently overlooked members of the Smithsonian Institution, yet it contains an internationally renowned collection of Asian and late nineteenth- and early twentieth-century American art. Opened in 1923 as the first Smithsonian museum for fine arts, the Freer was designed by Charles A. Platt to resemble a Florentine palace, which Charles Lang Freer considered appropriate for the display of his collections. Recently renovated, the gallery accomplishes this task splendidly.

Freer assembled the most important collection of the works of the American expatriate artist, James A. McNeill Whistler, including the Peacock Room, designed in its entirety by the artist. Under Whistler's guidance, Freer extended his American holdings to include paintings by John Singer Sargent, Thomas Wilmer Dewing, Abbott Handerson Thayer and Dwight William Tryon.

Freer expanded his collection to include works from Asia, which he found to be harmonious with his previous purchases. Not content to buy through galleries, Freer traveled extensively through the Orient in search of masterpieces, acquiring painting, sculpture, pottery, lacquerware, metalwork, manuscripts, and screens from China, Japan, Korea, India, Iran, Egypt, and Syria. Before his death, he gave to the nation both his grand accumulation of art and the building in which to house it, with the proviso that nothing could be added to his American collection. The Asian art has been supplemented; the Gallery's holdings now surpass 27,000 works, only a small portion of which can be exhibited at any time.

The Freer shares a library with the Arthur M. Sackler Gallery, with which it is connected by underground galleries; the reading room is open from 10 A.M. to 5 P.M., Monday–Friday, except federal holidays. Call (202) 357–4880 to make arrangements to see the archives and slide library. Also in conjunction with the Sackler, the Freer offers films, lectures, and programs; for their calendar of events, write to Office of Public Affairs, Arthur M. Sackler Gallery/Freer Gallery of Art, Smithsonian Institution, Washington, DC 20560.

The Freer's small gift shop sells some attractive and unusual gift items as well as fine quality postcards, reproductions, and posters.

HIRSHHORN MUSEUM AND SCULPTURE GARDEN

(202) 357-1618

Independence Avenue at 8th Street, SW 20560
Hours: 10 A.M.–5:30 P.M. daily
       Sculpture Garden: 7:30 A.M.–dusk daily
       Closed Christmas
Free Admission

 L'Enfant Plaza stop (Smithsonian Museums exit; blue, orange, green and yellow lines).

 Independence Avenue.

 Competitive parking on Mall.

Recommended. On Saturdays—except in the summer—at 11 A.M., animated films are presented for kids; special tours for groups of children can be arranged by writing or calling (202) 357-3235. No strollers are permitted in the museum; they can be checked, and the museum will issue you a backpack for carrying your baby.

Group tours can be arranged by calling the education department at (202) 357-3235.

 Fully accessible; Sculpture Garden is accessible from the Mall.

 Call (202) 357-3235 in advance to arrange a touching tour of sculpture; approximately 30 pieces are involved.

 Call (202) 357-3235 (voice and TDD) to make arrangements for a signed tour. Two weeks' notice is required.

 Guided tours are given at 10:30 A.M., noon and 1:30 P.M., Monday–Saturday, 12:30 P.M. on Sunday. Tours are often given for special exhibits; call the museum at (202) 357-3235 to see if a special tour will be conducted while you're in town.

The Hirshhorn Museum and Sculpture Garden was originally built to house the collection of approximately 6,000 pieces of twentieth-century and late nineteenth-century paintings and sculpture donated to the Smithsonian by financier Joseph Hirshhorn. Since its opening in 1974, the museum's collection has more than doubled through Mr. Hirshhorn's bequest, as well as other gifts and purchases by the museum.

Designed by Gordon Bunshaft, the four-story cylindrical building surrounds an inner courtyard. The inner galleries of the museum, which look out on the courtyard, display the museum's indoor sculptures. Sculpture is also displayed outdoors on the plaza around the building and in the sunken sculpture garden across Jefferson Drive. The sculpture collection has many works by European artists, and the paintings and drawings exhibited in the windowless outer galleries are the work of both Americans and Europeans. Exhibits change often because space limitations allow only a small part of the collection to be shown at one time.

Among the sculptors represented in the Hirshhorn are Auguste Rodin, Henry Moore, David Smith, Magdalena Jetelova, Claes Oldenburg, Martin Puryear and William Tucker. The painting collection includes pieces from most of the major movements in modern American art: representatives of the early twentieth-century Ash Can School's seamy realism; works of the pioneer modernists, including Georgia O'Keeffe and John Marin; a large collection of the work of the abstract expressionists who dominated the 1940s and 1950s, such as Pollock, Rothko and de Kooning; and more recent pieces by artists from both here and abroad who are working in genres that are still being defined. Watch for the ongoing "Directions" and WORKS exhibitions of experimental art. Upcoming major exhibitions at the Hirshhorn include video artist Gary Hill, opening in February 1994; Sue Coe, beginning in March 1994; Bruce Nauman, opening in November 1994; Irish artist Sean Scully, beginning in July 1995; and Stephan Balkenhol, a young German artist who produces sculptures from tree trunks, in October 1995.

The Hirshhorn has a museum shop on the entrance level that sells books, posters and cards related to the collection, as well as some gift items.

From time to time the museum sponsors special lectures and shows films; for information, call (202) 357-2700. In addition, occasional concerts by the twentieth-century Consort are given in the Hirshhorn auditorium. Tickets range from $7 to $10, with discounts available to students, senior citizens and groups. Call (202) 357-3030 for information.

JEFFERSON MEMORIAL AND　　　　　　　**(202) 426-6841**
TIDAL BASIN
West Potomac Park
Mailing Address: National Park Service, Mall Operations
　　　　　　　　　900 Ohio Drive, SW 20242
Hours: Always open; park ranger available from 8 A.M. to midnight,
　　　　　except Christmas
Free Admission

M Smithsonian stop (blue and orange lines). This entails a *long* walk along the Mall and around the Tidal Basin.

13's, 50, V4, V6; Tourmobile.

Independence Avenue or Raoul Wallenberg Place

P Parking is available at the memorial and by the paddle boat concession; it's difficult during the Cherry Blossom Festival and on summer weekends.

Paddle boat concession sells hot dogs, burgers, etc.

Recommended.

 To arrange a tour, call (202) 426-6841 well in advance of your visit.

 Accessible.

 Special "touch" tours can be arranged in advance by calling (202) 426-6841. Braille maps are available for reference.

 Sign language tours can be arranged by calling (202) 426-6841 at least 48 hours in advance.

 Interpretations are given upon request when staffers are available.

Dedicated in 1943, 200 years after Jefferson's birth, the Jefferson Memorial is one of the loveliest memorials in Washington—or beyond, for that matter. The 19-foot bronze statue of our third President, sculpted by Rudulph Evans, stands beneath a simple rotunda inscribed with some of his most compelling words from the Declaration of Independence, the Virginia Statute of Religious Freedom and other works.

Jefferson was not only a president; he served as George Washington's secretary of state, drafted the Declaration of Independence, founded the University of Virginia and was an inventor, botanist and architect. The memorial design by John Russell Pope incorporates several favorite architectural motifs used by Jefferson in his own designs—rotunda and column.

A small shop on the chamber level of the memorial sells postcards, film and related memorabilia; there is a bookshop on the lower level.

When the Jefferson Memorial was built, its site was reclaimed from the Potomac River; what remains of the river's presence is the Tidal Basin. Connected by a small channel, the river and basin are, indeed, tidal in nature.

The western edge of the basin is bordered by over 600 Yoshino and Akebono cherry trees, a gift from Japan in 1912. The U.S. was able to return the favor by sending cuttings back to Japan after its native trees in Tokyo had suffered irreparable damage from pollution. When in full bloom, the trees are breathtaking—but so is the bumper-to-bumper traffic. Walk around the basin, or avoid the crush by driving out to Kenwood, Maryland, northwest of the District line, for a less crowded yet dazzling display of cherry trees decked out in their best blossoms (see Chapter 15, "Outdoor Washington/Sports").

The Cherry Blossom Festival is held annually around bloom time—sometime from mid-March to mid-April. The festival includes a parade and other festivities.

To the east of the Tidal Basin are the "floral libraries." Some 10,000 tulips usually bloom the first week in April; annuals add a bright spot to the area in summer and fall. A paddle boat concession is also on the east side of the basin. Open from April through October, 10 A.M.–7 P.M. (shorter hours in spring and fall), the concession rents boats for between $7 and $14 per hour. Each boat must have at least one person over 16 years old.

LINCOLN MEMORIAL (202) 426-6841
West end of Mall
Mailing Address: National Park Service, Mall Operations,
900 Ohio Drive, SW 20242
Hours: Always open; park ranger available from 8 A.M. to midnight, except Christmas
Free Admission

 Foggy Bottom—George Washington University stop (orange and blue lines). Walk down 23rd Street.

 Constitution Avenue or Independence Avenue.

 Competitive parking in West Potomac Park; follow signs for Ohio Drive. Don't try to drive here during rush hour; you'll most assuredly wind up in Virginia since the roadway design is demonic.

 Snacks are available at a nearby kiosk. Since the museum cafeterias are on the other end of the Mall, we suggest you take a picnic if you intend to eat around the time you plan to see this memorial.

 Recommended; although there are lots of stairs, an elevator is available.

 Special tours can be arranged in advance by calling (202) 426-6841. Resources are limited, so call well in advance.

 Accessible. The memorial (via elevator) and rest room are accessible to those in wheelchairs; special parking has been set aside for handicapped people. There is no telephone.

Special "touch" tours can be arranged in advance by calling (202) 426-6841.

 Signing tours can be arranged by calling (202) 426-6841 at least 48 hours in advance.

 Interpretive talks are given upon request when staff are available.

Many find this the most human and inspiring of memorials. A weary, pensive Lincoln sits, his large hands resting on his chair arms as he gazes down the Mall toward the Washington Monument. The 19-foot marble statue, sculpted by Daniel Chester French, is flanked by the inspirational Gettysburg Address on the south wall and the Second Inaugural Address on the north wall.

The memorial, designed by Henry Bacon in the classic Greek manner, was completed in 1922 on reclaimed swampland. The view from the back of the memorial—across the Potomac River along the majestic Memorial Bridge to Arlington National Cemetery—is almost as lovely as the Mall panorama afforded by the front view. On clear days, Lincoln's statue is, indeed, reflected in the pool below. Short interpretative talks are given by park rangers throughout the year. A free, informative pamphlet is available at the site. There is also a bookshop on the chamber level.

NATIONAL AIR AND SPACE MUSEUM   (202) 357-2700
6th Street and Independence Avenue, SW 20560
Hours: 10 A.M.–5:30 P.M. daily
        Closed Christmas
Free Admission

 L'Enfant Plaza stop (blue, orange, yellow and green lines). Walk north on 7th Street to Independence Avenue.

 Independence Avenue.

 Competitive street and Mall parking.

 Cafeteria and restaurant. Flightline is a first-rate cafeteria offering a wide range of fresh foods, from subs and pizza to hot entrees. The Wright Place is a restaurant with a more ambitious menu, a solace for the foot-weary tourist. Both are enclosed in an enormous glass addition to the museum, which, at the east end, offers a grand view of the Capitol.

Highly recommended. This is heaven for most kids. The educational services department offers a variety of demonstrations, educational programs and activities for families, students, teachers and groups of young people; for information, call (202) 357-1400. A baby service station next to Gallery 107 offers a comfortable place to change or nurse babies.

Group tours can be arranged by calling (202) 357-1400 two to six weeks in advance. Group reservations can be made for IMAX films by calling the same number at least two weeks in advance.

Fully accessible. Wheelchairs are available from the coat check attendant on the first floor. Space has been set aside in the theater and planetarium for wheelchairs.

Tours that allow people with visual disabilities to touch models and artifacts can be arranged by calling (202) 357-1400 or writing the educational services department. Guide materials are available in large print and recorded form at the information desk. Braille and cassette editions of the booklet ''Celebrating the National Air and Space Museum'' may be purchased in the museum shop.

Tours with an interpreter can be arranged by calling (202) 357-1400 or TTY (202) 357-1696. Arrange for use of a loop-amplification system on docent-led tours by calling the same numbers. Stereo headphones are provided for 50 seats in the Langley Theater and 10 seats in the Einstein Planetarium. A public telephone with amplification is available in the south lobby.

Guided tours leave from the tour desk in Gallery 100 on the first floor at 10:15 A.M. and 1 P.M. daily. The tour guides are well-versed in their subject—a few are pilots (2 hours).

The National Air and Space Museum, which opened in 1976, is the most popular museum in the world, drawing about nine million visitors annually. The huge building, designed by Gyo Obata, covers several blocks of the Mall and houses 23 galleries that focus on differing aspects of air and space exploration and travel. While the museum displays many of the world's most famous aircraft, rockets, and missiles, it is not just a repository of historically significant artifacts. Air and Space houses a multimedia extravaganza with slide shows, do-it-yourself consoles, a how-to-fly training school and many other devices visitors can interact with to feel a part of the show.

In the Milestones of Flight gallery at the museum's entrance, such prizes as the Wright brothers' 1903 "Flyer" and Lindbergh's "Spirit of St. Louis" are suspended from the ceiling; the Apollo 11 command module and the Viking Lander are also displayed. Suspended above the Independence Avenue lobby is "Voyager," the aircraft that flew around the world without stopping or refueling in 1986. Other galleries explore the topics of stars, early flight, rocketry and space flights, sea-air operations, and exploring the planets, to name a few.

"Beyond the Limits: Flight Enters the Computer Age" is a state-of-the-art exhibit that depicts the computer revolution in aviation and space. The exhibit area includes many interactive displays and illustrates computer applications in design, aerodynamics, manufacture, flight simulation and testing and air and space operations.

The newest display, "Where Next, Columbus?" uses interactive multimedia programs, feature films, a three-dimensional star map, models and displays to portray the many technical and physiological challenges that must be overcome before humans can cross vast distances of space or exist on other planets.

The museum also houses the Samuel P. Langley Theater, showing IMAX films on a five-story-high screen with exhilarating results. Several wonderful films are shown on a regular basis: "The Dream Is Alive," "Blue Planet," "Living Planet," and "To Fly." After-hours screenings of IMAX special features are presented on most evenings. Entrance to films and the Albert Einstein Planetarium costs the same—$3.25 for adults and $2 for children, students and seniors. Find out the schedule for these movies and shows when you enter the museum. It's smart to buy your tickets early because shows sell out; call (202) 357-1686 for the schedule, or check a daily newspaper.

The Air and Space Museum gift shops sell a large variety of items, including kites, models, posters, T-shirts, freeze-dried "astronaut" ice cream and books. The museum also has a large library and archives for historical aerospace research, open 10 A.M.–4 P.M., Monday–Friday. Call (202) 357-3133 for information on its use or to arrange a tour.

The Paul E. Garber Preservation, Restoration and Storage Facility, about a half-hour's drive away in Suitland, Maryland, is the site of the museum's restoration workshop. You can reserve a space on their tour by calling (202) 357-1400.

NATIONAL ARCHIVES AND RECORDS SERVICE

(202) 501-5000
(recorded information)

Constitution Avenue at 8th Street, NW 20408
(visitors)
8th Street and Pennsylvania Avenue, NW 20408
(research and special tours)

Hours: Exhibition Hall: April 1–Labor Day   10 A.M.–9 P.M. daily
September–March   10 A.M.–5:30 P.M. daily
Closed Christmas
Research Room: 8:45 A.M.–9:45 P.M. weekdays
8:45 A.M.–5 P.M. Saturdays
Closed Holidays

Free Admission

Ⓜ Archives-Navy Memorial stop (yellow and green lines).

🚗 Constitution Avenue or Pennsylvania Avenue.

Ⓟ Competitive parking on the Mall.

🍽 Snack bar on premises.

👫 Recommended. School tours and workshops can be arranged by calling (202) 501-5205 or writing the Tour Office, National Archives, NE, Room G-8, Washington, D.C. 20408.

A 90-minute Behind the Scenes tour through the working areas of the archives can be arranged by writing or calling (202) 501-5205.

♿ Fully accessible. Use the special entrance on Pennsylvania Avenue.

The National Archives is responsible for preserving, and making available for reference, all those records of the United States government that are considered permanently valuable. Within the building are 21 floors of storerooms, library stacks and offices, most of which are never open to the public. The files are available to researchers, however, and contain such historic items as all the treaties the government has signed with American Indian tribes over the years, every law enacted by Congress since the nation began and Gerald Ford's pardon of Richard Nixon.

The archives' Exhibition Hall, on the Constitution Avenue side of the building, has a permanent display of the Declaration of Independence, the Constitution and the Bill of Rights. Great efforts have been made to preserve these documents; at night or in emergencies their helium-filled cases are automatically lowered into a vault. A 1297 version of the Magna Carta, on loan from H. Ross Perot, is also on display in Exhibition Hall. A gallery behind the hall has changing exhibits from the archives' massive collection, including photographs and other nonwritten materials. Exhibits on display in 1994 and 1995 will include "The Face of War," "Powers of Persuasion" and "Saving Our Sources."

On the Pennsylvania Avenue side of the building you'll find the archives' research rooms. If you're interested in researching your family background or a specific piece of American history, this is the place to go. When you enter, pick up a pamphlet that describes available records; a staff member will show you how to use them. In addition, two exhibits are helpful to beginning researchers: "What Is the National Archives?" and "Reeling Through History."

The Watergate tapes are available for the public at the archives' facility on the University of Maryland campus in College Park, MD.

The National Archives offers an extensive program of lectures, presentations, and films—call (202) 501-5000 for a recording that lists these programs. Pick up a calendar of events at the Pennsylvania Avenue entrance or from a guard, or write or call the Public Relations office at (202) 501-5525.

The archives has a gift shop that sells reproductions of the documents on display as well as some posters, cards, mugs, T-shirts, sweatshirts, tote bags and the like.

NATIONAL GALLERY OF ART   (202) 737-4215

Constitution Avenue, between 4th and 7th Streets, NW 20565
Hours: 10 A.M.–5 P.M. Monday–Saturday
       11 A.M.–6 P.M. Sunday
       Closed Christmas and New Year's
Free Admission

 Archives-Navy Memorial stop (yellow and green lines) or Judiciary Square (red line).
 Constitution Avenue or East Building entrance on 4th Street.

Competitive parking on Mall.

On premises. Concourse Buffet (10 A.M.–3 P.M. Monday–Friday, 10 A.M.–4 P.M. Saturday, 11 A.M.–4 P.M. Sunday) and the Cascade Expresso Bar (12–4:30 P.M. Monday–Saturday, noon–5:30 P.M. Sunday) are on the concourse level; the food is tasty and reasonably priced. As you eat, you can watch a waterfall cascade from the Mall. This is one of the best eating bets in town. The Terrace Café (11:30 A.M.–3 P.M. Monday–Saturday, noon–4 P.M. Sunday) on the second floor of the East Building has more expensive meals, but a lovely view of the Mall; it's the perfect place for coffee and a pastry. A café in the garden court of the West Building serves light fare (11 A.M.–3 P.M. Monday–Friday, 11:30 A.M.–4 P.M. Saturday, and noon–6:30 P.M. Sunday).

East Building recommended. This would be a good museum in which to introduce a child to artworks. It's an interesting space, and many of the exhibits are small enough to be managed by a child. One permanent exhibition of metal sculpture is particularly appealing. Strollers are available at the main entrances. West Building not recommended for young children unless they have a particular interest in art, but fine for ages 10 and up. A guide on the permanent collections for families with children is available in the gift shop. Family programs are offered throughout the year; check the calendar of events to see what's on while you're in town.

Tours of both the permanent collection and some special exhibits are available for groups of 15 or more. Arrangements can be made by contacting the education office at least four weeks in advance at (202) 737-4215.

Fully accessible. For the West Building, use the Constitution Avenue entrance at 6th Street; the East Building has a ramp at the main entrance at 4th Street and Constitution Avenue. Wheelchairs are also available at entrances for use in the galleries.

Special hands-on tours of sculpture can be arranged by writing the tour office or calling (202) 842-6247 at least three weeks in advance.

Call (202) 842-6247 to arrange for special tours at least four weeks in advance.

For foreign-language tours, contact the education department at (202) 842-6247 at least three weeks in advance. Regularly scheduled foreign-language tours in French, Spanish or German

are offered Tuesday at noon in the rotunda of the West Building.
Check to see which language will be offered.

T Introductory tour of the West Building collections is given at
10:30 A.M. and 12:30 and 2:30 P.M. Monday–Saturday, and at
12:30, 2:30, and 4:30 P.M. Sunday (West Building rotunda).
Introduction to the East Building collections is given 11:30 A.M.
and 1:30 P.M. Monday–Saturday and 11:30 A.M. and 1:30 and
3:30 P.M. Sunday (East Building ground floor information desk).
During the winter a 50-minute Tour of the Week, focusing on a
specific style of painting on exhibition, is offered at 1 P.M.
Tuesday–Saturday and 2:30 P.M. Sunday. The gallery also offers
tours of special exhibits or periods of art history; check the
calendar of events at the information desks. You can also rent a
recorded tour of the gallery at this location.

The National Gallery of Art is one of the world's premier collections
of Western art, encompassing masterpieces from the thirteenth
through the twentieth centuries. Housed in two radically different
buildings that face each other across National Gallery Plaza (4th
Street) and connected by an underground concourse, the collection is
displayed in over a hundred galleries that cover several acres. While
the experience is magnificent, it can be daunting; pace yourself.

The original West Building displays art ranging from the thirteenth
century through the early twentieth century, while the East Building
concentrates on twentieth-century paintings and sculptures, with
changing exhibitions that may focus on art from other eras.

Both buildings and the kernel of the collection were given to the
nation by the Mellon family. Over 150 other donors have generously
added to the outstanding assemblage of masterpieces. While the gallery is operated with federal funds, all art purchases are privately
financed.

West Building

Designed by John Russell Pope, who also conceived the Jefferson
Memorial and the National Archives, the West Building opened to
the public in 1941. A massive marble structure—one of the world's
largest—the museum has an interior that is both rich and majestic.
From the central rotunda, sculpture halls stretch to the east and west;
several layers of small galleries branch from the halls. The artwork
is generally grouped chronologically by country of origin and includes

pieces from France, Italy, Spain, Germany, England, Holland and the United States. Maps are available at the entrances to guide you through the many galleries.

The collection of Italian art is one of the best outside of Europe, including works by Raphael, Titian and Bernini, to name just a few of the most famous, as well as the only work by Leonardo da Vinci in North America. The Chester Dale collection of nineteenth- and early twentieth-century French painting that includes works by all the major Impressionist painters is one of the most popular sections of the gallery. Major special exhibitions are an important ongoing part of the gallery's program as well.

East Building

The soaring East Building of the National Gallery of Art, opened in 1978, is a work of art in its own right. Designed by I. M. Pei and Partners, the building—two triangular interlocking forms—makes spectacular use of the trapezoidal plot of land on which the gallery sits. The quarry from which the marble was taken in the 1930s for the West Building was reopened to supply the same stone for this new East Building. The smaller triangular form houses administrative offices; the larger encompasses the galleries where works of the permanent collection of twentieth-century art and temporary exhibits of works from any era are displayed.

As its designer hoped it would be, this museum is a "place to be." Many of the craftspeople who worked on the building received awards for their fine contributions. While every detail was tended to, the building is not prissy—it's inviting and exciting, offering bold internal vistas and intimate galleries.

Many works of art were commissioned especially for the East Wing. A Henry Moore sculpture greets you at the entrance; in the central atrium you encounter two enormous pieces—a tapestry by Joan Miró and a mobile by Alexander Calder. Sculptures by Noguchi, Caro, Rosati and Smith can be found inside and outside the building.

Programs, Events, and Shops

The National Gallery offers a wide array of programs of interest to both the art scholar and the casual viewer, ranging from lectures, fellowships, workshops and symposia to films and concerts. Access to the extensive slide and print libraries as well as photographic and gallery archives is available to scholars. For details, request a copy of the "Guide to Resources and Programs" from the education office at (202) 842-6247.

On Sundays, art history lectures are given at 4 P.M. in the West Building auditorium by visiting experts or by staff members. On Sunday evenings at 7 P.M. (except from late June to September) free classical music concerts are given in the West Building's East Garden Court; seats to the popular concerts become available at 6 P.M. Documentary films on artists represented in the gallery are shown at 12:30 P.M. Wednesday–Saturday and 1:00 P.M. Sunday; feature, fiction and independent films are shown at 2:00 P.M. Saturday and 6:00 P.M. Sunday. All films are shown in the East Building Auditorium. These ongoing events are open to the public on a first-come, first-served basis. A monthly calendar of events, which details the special events at the gallery, can be picked up at the information desks.

The major museum shops are located on the ground floor of the West Building and the concourse level connecting the two buildings; a wide variety of fine art-related objects, books and posters are offered. In addition, temporary sales areas are often set up on the mezzanine and concourse levels to sell catalogs, posters, and postcards related to particular exhibits.

NATIONAL MUSEUM OF AFRICAN ART (202) 357-4600
950 Independence Avenue, SW 20560
Hours: 10 A.M.–5:30 P.M. daily
   Closed Christmas
Free Admission

M Smithsonian stop (blue and orange lines).

Independence Avenue.

P Competitive parking on the Mall and Independence Avenue.

Recommended. Special tours can be arranged by calling (202) 357-4600, ext. 222, at least one month in advance.

Groups tours can be arranged by calling (202) 357-4600, ext. 222, at least one month in advance.

Fully accessible.

Sign language and oral interpreters are available for tours, lectures and other educational programs; call (202) 357-4600, ext. 222, or TDD (202) 357-4814, to make arrangements. Several open-captioned videos are available for viewing; the auditorium is equipped with an assistive listening system.

 Guided tours are offered at 1:30 P.M. Monday–Friday and 11 A.M. and 1 and 3 P.M. Saturday–Sunday.

Founded in 1964 as a private educational institution, the National Museum of African Art became part of the Smithsonian Institution in 1979. Until its move to the Mall in 1987, it occupied a house once owned by Frederick Douglass, the famous abolitionist, writer and former slave.

In it sumptuous new underground quarters in the Smithsonian Quadrangle, the museum displays a selection of its 6,000-object collection of African art, one of the finest in the world. Permanent exhibitions include traditional court art from Benin, the art of the personal object, and pottery as a woman's art in central Africa.

The museum hosts a number of international exhibitions, as well. In 1994, two exhibits will be "The Face of the Spirits: Masks from the Zaire Basin" and "Beaded Splendor: Beadwork in Africa."

In addition to exhibition facilities, the museum is equipped with public education rooms for classes, workshops and presentations; offices for visiting scholars; an art research library; an art conservation laboratory; and the Eliot Elisofon Archives, with more than 150,000 color slides, 70,000 black-and-white photographs and 50 feature films. The library and archives are open to interested students and scholars by appointment.

The museum shop stocks fine reproductions of African jewelry, sculpture, textiles, games for adults and children, and books of interest to the general public and scholars.

NATIONAL MUSEUM OF AMERICAN HISTORY   **(202) 357-3129**
Constitution Avenue at 14th Street, NW 20565
Hours: 10 A.M.–5:30 P.M. daily
     Closed Christmas
Free Admission

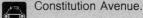 Federal Triangle stop (blue and orange lines).

Constitution Avenue.

P Competitive parking on the Mall.

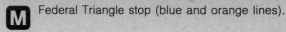 Food on premises. A cafeteria and snack bar are located in the basement; they are open from 10 A.M. to 5 P.M. An old-fashioned ice-cream parlor serves up luscious concoctions on the first floor from 11 A.M. to 4 P.M.

Recommended. During school months, Discovery Corners invite participation in the Spirit of '76 and Electricity. Children can handle the clothes and equipment of a Revolutionary War soldier, experiment with electrical paraphernalia and examine prosthetics and other aids for handicapped people. Discovery Corners are open daily except Monday from 11:30 A.M. to 3 P.M. To arrange a group tour, call (202) 357-1481.

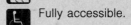 Fully accessible.

Tours for the blind and vision-impaired can be arranged in advance by calling (202) 357-1481. A large-print edition of the museum brochure with floor plans is available at the information desks.

Tours are conducted in sign language on Sundays at 11 A.M. Other tours can be arranged in advance by calling TDD (202) 357-1729. Auditorium is equipped with loop-amplification system.

T The museum offers tours starting from both the Mall and Constitution Avenue entrances. Three different tours—Highlights, A Nation of Nations and Ceremonial Court—are offered Monday–Saturday, 10 and 11 A.M. and 1 P.M., and Sunday at 11 A.M. and 1 P.M. A variety of additional walk-in tours is given from October to May; call (202) 357-2700 to find out these tour schedules, which are determined anew each year. An Information Age tour is available as well; call (202) 357-1481 at least four weeks in advance to make arrangements.

The original Star-Spangled Banner that inspired Francis Scott Key to pen our national anthem, the very desk on which Jefferson wrote the Declaration of Independence, Alexander Graham Bell's telephone, Eli Whitney's cotton gin, the gowns of the First Ladies of our nation—these and other essential items of our heritage are displayed in the National Museum of American History. This is the official repository of the American people and their accomplishments in science, technology, politics, home life, armed forces and communications.

The ground floor houses machinery from railroad locomotives to computers to tunnel-digging devices. A wonderful permanent exhibition, "Information Age: People, Information and Technology," is not to be missed. It traces the history of information technologies, from the telegraph to the computer, exploring how interactions of people, information and technology moved us into the Information Age.

The exhibits on the second floor focus on the people of our nation, our lives in our homes, our communities and the world beyond. The continuing connections among American Indian, Hispanic, African-American and Anglo-American cultures in New Mexico are the focus of the exhibit "American Encounters."

The third-floor exhibits run the gamut from musical instruments to instruments of war. In addition, pieces of one of the world's most extensive collections of ceramics are on display.

The Dibner Library of the History of Science and Technology and other facilities are available for research; call (202) 357-2414 to make arrangements.

The museum has a gift shop, with postcards, slides and memorabilia, but it also operates a transplanted nineteenth-century country store and post office that can postmark your letters with a unique Smithsonian seal. The Smithsonian Bookstore (202-357-1784) is in this museum, with an extensive range of books on American history and other subjects.

NATIONAL MUSEUM OF NATURAL   (202) 786-2950
HISTORY
Constitution Avenue at 10th Street, NW 20560
Hours: 10 A.M.–5:30 P.M. daily
　　　Closed Christmas
Free Admission

 Federal Triangle or Smithsonian stop (blue and orange lines); Archives-Navy Memorial stop (yellow and green lines).
 Constitution Avenue.

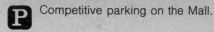 Competitive parking on the Mall.

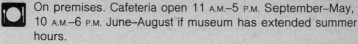 On premises. Cafeteria open 11 A.M.–5 P.M. September–May, 10 A.M.–6 P.M. June–August if museum has extended summer hours.

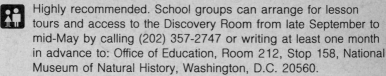 Highly recommended. School groups can arrange for lesson tours and access to the Discovery Room from late September to mid-May by calling (202) 357-2747 or writing at least one month in advance to: Office of Education, Room 212, Stop 158, National Museum of Natural History, Washington, D.C. 20560.

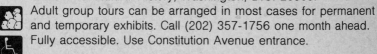 Adult group tours can be arranged in most cases for permanent and temporary exhibits. Call (202) 357-1756 one month ahead.

Fully accessible. Use Constitution Avenue entrance.

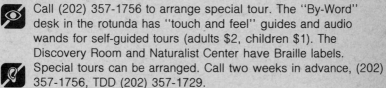 Call (202) 357-1756 to arrange special tour. The "By-Word" desk in the rotunda has "touch and feel" guides and audio wands for self-guided tours (adults $2, children $1). The Discovery Room and Naturalist Center have Braille labels.

Special tours can be arranged. Call two weeks in advance, (202) 357-1756, TDD (202) 357-1729.

Tours of the museum's highlights are given daily at 10:30 A.M. and 1:30 P.M. from mid-September to June. You can rent audio wands for self-guided tours in English and Spanish.

The Museum of Natural History is a wonderfully complex institution. Both a research center and a museum, Natural History provides laboratory space to a wealth of scientists and displays exhibits as diverse as a Neanderthal burial ceremony and a working beehive. Follow the colorful banners from the rotunda to Fossils, Mammals, Birds, Bones, Geology of the Earth, and you discover fantastic worlds. The staff and volunteers here are extremely helpful. Stop by the information desk in the rotunda if you have questions or need help.

The ground floor, accessed from Constitution Avenue or the elevator or escalator from the rotunda, is usually devoted to special exhibits. Always interesting, and sometimes spectacular, the special exhibits are worth seeing.

On the first floor, from the rotunda you can head toward the paleontology exhibit, "Fossils: The History of Life," which includes recently remodeled and expanded exhibits of early life, dinosaurs and the chain of life forms spanning millions of years. "The Earliest

Traces of Life" features a film on the origin of the first living cells, the oldest fossil evidence of life and a spectacular mural of a 3.5-billion-year-old shoreline. In May 1990, "Life in the Ancient Seas" opened; it contains a 120-foot mural with life-size prehistoric animals swimming underwater.

Sea Life Hall contains a living coral reef and many inhabitants. A 92-foot model of a blue whale dominates the exhibit hall. Beyond the marine exhibits are thousands of specimens of birds, sea life, reptiles, amphibians and mammals. Also on this floor are exhibits of African, Asian, Pacific, Eskimo and Indian cultures.

The second floor houses the minerals and gems, the most famous of which is the Hope Diamond, once owned by Mrs. Evalyn Walsh McLean, a Washington socialite. Don't be too dazzled by the Hope; there are many more beautiful and fabulous gems in the collection. This gallery is due for renovation but "Hope and Friends," an exhibit of some of the more spectacular samples of the collection, will be on display elsewhere in the museum. Other exhibits on the second floor include "Earth, Moon and Meteorites," "Prehistoric North American Cultures," "South America: Continent and Culture," "Western Civilization: Origins and Traditions," "Bones," and "Reptiles."

Two rooms of special note: the Discovery Room and the Insect Zoo. The Discovery Room (first floor) is designed for children of all ages. It is stocked with a wealth of items, such as elephant tusks, arrowheads, petrified wood and coral, all of which are available for hands-on study. It also has a dress-up corner where kids can try on costumes from all over the world. The Discovery Room is open from noon to 2:30 P.M. Monday to Thursday, and 10:30 A.M. to 3:30 P.M. Friday to Sunday. On weekends, holidays and other busy days, free tickets must be picked up at the information desk in the rotunda so that the room does not become overcrowded.

The Insect Zoo (second floor) is another treat for everyone, but especially kids. It combines traditional exhibits of live insects, dioramas of prehistoric insects, a working beehive and talks and demonstrations by museum staff. When you arrive, the Zoo's giant cockroaches might be out for handling, or the tarantula might be getting his monthly meal.

Finally, we want to mention the Naturalist Center. Each department of the museum has contributed some part of its collection to be used by the serious amateur naturalist or collector. Six major areas are represented: rocks and minerals, invertebrate zoology, insects, plants, vertebrate zoology and anthropology. You may bring in specimens in any of these areas for identification. The center is open to adults and children 12 and over, Monday to Saturday 10:30 A.M. to 4 P.M. and Sunday noon to 5 P.M. You must call (202) 357-2804 or (202) 357-1503, or write ahead, for admission. Groups are limited to six. A library, audiovisual room and laboratory are part of the Center. Two temporary exhibitions on display in the 1994–95 period are "Spiders" and "Sacred Mountains."

The museum's gift shops are excellent. The main shop is on the first floor, by the cafeteria. Books, projects, toys, minerals and gems as well as many other items are available. Two small annexes have opened on the second floor. One sells dinosaur theme items while the other focuses on minerals. Fridays at noon, the museum offers a one-hour film/lecture series in Baird Auditorium (loop-amplification system for hearing-impaired). Check at the information desk for seasonal schedule.

———————

ARTHUR M. SACKLER GALLERY   **(202) 357-2700**
1050 Independence Avenue, SW 20560
Hours: 10 A.M.–5:30 P.M. daily
          Closed Christmas
Free Admission

M   Smithsonian stop (blue and orange lines).

Independence Avenue or Jefferson Drive.

P   Competitive parking on the Mall and Independence Avenue.

Write four weeks in advance to arrange school tours.

Write four weeks in advance to arrange group tours.

Fully accessible.

A brochure with large type is available at the information desk.

Sign language and oral interpreters can be arranged by calling (202) 357-4880, ext. 245, or TTY (202) 786-2374 one week in advance.

Highlight tours of the museum are offered daily; tours of specific exhibits are also often available. Check the information desk or call (202) 357-3200 for times.

The spirit and diversity of Asia's cultures are celebrated in 5,000 years of magnificent art at the Arthur M. Sackler Gallery. The gallery consists of an entrance pavilion in the Smithsonian Quadrangle and three floors below ground for exhibitions and public programs.

The growing permanent collection is based on the nearly 1,000 masterworks of Asian and Near Eastern art donated by Dr. Arthur M. Sackler, a New York psychiatrist and medical publisher. The Sackler collection includes many important twentieth-century Chinese paintings, representing a major new area of Smithsonian scholarship and exhibition. It also includes many Chinese bronzes, jades and paintings, as well as excellent examples of Chinese lacquerware and ceremonial objects in silver, gold and bronze from the ancient Near East. Objects on display span the ages, from 3000 B.C. into the twentieth century.

Exhibitions include major international shows, often enhanced by public programs and scholarly presentations. A few that are continuing indefinitely include "Luxury Arts of the Silk Route Empires," "Metalwork and Ceramics from Ancient Iran," and "Monsters, Myths, and Minerals." The Vever Collection of Islamic Art of the Book is the focus of changing exhibitions held in two small first-floor galleries.

A lovely museum shop offers books, antiques, jewelry, reproductions, cards and gifts related to the collection.

The Sackler shares a library and sponsors a variety of public programs with the Freer Gallery; see that site report for details.

SMITHSONIAN INSTITUTION BUILDING   (202) 357-2700
(The Castle—Smithsonian Information Center)
1000 Jefferson Drive, SW 20560
Hours: 9 A.M.–5:30 P.M. daily
      Closed Christmas
Free Admission

Smithsonian stop (orange and blue lines); use Mall exit.

 Independence Avenue or Jefferson Drive.

 Competitive parking on the Mall.

 Recommended. Lots of interactive displays.

 Great place to meet and plan your day.

 Accessible. Ramp on west side of front entrance.

 A map for visually impaired visitors is available for reference at the information desk. Center has a model of the Mall with Braille labels.

 An open-captioned video is shown continuously to explain the Smithsonian's many offerings. Visitor Information TTY is (202) 357-1729.

 Walk-in tours are given 10:15 A.M. Friday, 10:15 and 11 A.M. Saturday, and 11 A.M. Sunday. On the first Saturday of the month, the 11 A.M. tour will be in Spanish or bilingual.

The Smithsonian Institution Building, more commonly known as the Castle, is the Smithsonian's original building. Designed by architect James Renwick, the Castle opened to the public in 1855. Today it houses the Smithsonian Information Center, the Woodrow Wilson International Center for Scholars and administrative offices. The center offers a wealth of useful and well-presented information, including

- Two orientation theaters that feature a 20-minute video overview of the Smithsonian. One theater is equipped with an audio loop and open-captioned video.
- Two models of Washington's monumental core that include scale renderings of the Smithsonian museums, Washington's monuments, memorials and federal buildings.
- Two electronic wall maps of the city; visitors can illuminate some 70 attractions in the nation's capital.
- The "capital attractions" interactive "touch-screen" programs, which provide information on more than 100 popular tourist destinations.

- The Smithsonian interactive "touch-screen" programs available in six languages, which feature information on each museum, including highlights, tours and demonstrations, special features, attractions for children, location, hours, transportation and visitor services. Information is also available on new and popular exhibits in the museums.
- Four-sided backlit display cases that feature general information on each Smithsonian museum and the National Zoo, as well as the planned National Museum of the American Indian.
- Scrolling screen monitors that list daily events.
- Volunteer information specialists who can answer your questions between 9 A.M. and 4 P.M. daily.

The Castle also harbors the crypt of the Smithsonian's English benefactor, James Smithson. In his will, Smithson provided for the establishment of an institution bearing his name "for the increase and diffusion of knowledge" in the United States, a country he had never even visited. Though Smithson's money arrived in 1838, Congress did not agree to accept it until eight years later, when they finally set Renwick to work designing this building.

The 4.2-acre Enid A. Haupt Garden, located on the south side of the Castle, is the ground-level focus of the Smithsonian Quadrangle, a complex housing the underground Arthur M. Sackler Gallery, the National Museum of African Art and the S. Dillon Ripley Center. The parklike area features exquisite trees, plants and flowers, as well as a Victorian embroidery parterre, period garden furniture, Chinese moongates, and many fountains and pools.

UNITED STATES HOLOCAUST MEMORIAL MUSEUM
100 Raoul Wallenberg Place, SW 20024-2150
Hours: 10 A.M.–5:30 P.M. daily
Closed Christmas and Yom Kippur
Free Admission

 Smithsonian stop (orange and blue lines); use Independence Avenue and 12th Street exit, which is one block from the museum's 14th Street entrance.

 Independence Avenue, 14th Street, or Raoul Wallenberg Place.

Extremely competitive parking on Independence Avenue.

 A small café, located in the museum's adjacent administrative center, is open to the public from 9 A.M. to 4 P.M. and offers light Jewish delicacies, such as bagels, knishes, blintzes and matzoh ball soup.

 Recommended for children 11 and up who have been prepared for the exhibit. A special exhibition, "Daniel's Story: Remember the Children," is designed specifically for visitors eight years and older and their families. A special "Guide for Families" is available at the information desk or by mail to help prepare kids to view this very powerful exhibit.

 To arrange a group tour, write to the Museum Schéduler at least one month in advance.

 Fully accessible.

 This is a very visually oriented museum. Request a docent through the visitor services staff to accompany you on the tour.

 No special services offered, but all exhibits have explanatory text and monitors, and films are captioned.

T No scheduled tours. A brochure for a self-guided architecture tour is available at the information desk.

This powerful museum memorializes the six million Jews and the millions of others who were systematically annihilated by the Nazis during World War II. The museum views its primary missión as one of informing visitors about the Holocaust, remembering all those who suffered, and inspiring the contemplation of moral implications of one's actions as well as one's responsibilities as a world citizen.

Unlike the exhibits in most museums, the exhibits here are presented in a linear fashion; they are chronological, and the visitor is funneled through them all. The building, designed by James Freed, is an integral part of the exhibits, emphasizing and reiterating themes on both literal and symbolic levels. Allow a minimum of three hours for your tour.

The exhibit begins on the fourth floor by documenting the early Nazi years and the ominous increase of anti-Jewish propaganda and restrictions that stripped Jews of their livelihood and citizenship. The third floor traces the progress of Hitler's "final solution"—the portraits of all the people of a town obliterated; a cattle car used to transport Jews, homosexuals, political dissidents, and Gypsies to concentration camps; shoes taken from the dead; battered food bowls and uniforms of camp prisoners; and other grim scenes of life and death in the concentration camps and ghettos. Floor two records the stories of survivors and rescuers and houses a multimedia learning center, which has over 20 computers to enable visitors to access articles, maps, videotaped testimonies, and music of the period. The Hall of Remembrance, designed as a place of contemplation and ceremony, is also on the second floor.

Films, lectures, and musical programs will be presented on a regular basis in the museum's theater and auditorium; check the information desk for a calendar of events. Teachers' guides and lesson plans are available from the Educational Outreach Department. The museum shop offers a selection of books and other materials related to the Holocaust.

Although on federal land, the museum has been funded by private donations. Membership forms are available at the information desk.

VIETNAM VETERANS MEMORIAL (202) 634-1568
21st Street and Constitution Avenue, NW (south side)
Mailing Address: National Park Service, Mall Operations,
900 Ohio Drive, SW 20242
Hours: Always open; park ranger available from 8 A.M. to midnight,
except Christmas
Free Admission

Ⓜ Foggy Bottom-GWU stop (orange and blue lines); walk seven blocks down 23rd Street.

🚗 Constitution Avenue or Independence Avenue.

Ⓟ Competitive parking in West Potomac Park and Constitution Avenue.

🍴 Snacks are available at a nearby kiosk. Since the museum cafeterias are at the other end of the Mall, we suggest you take a picnic if you intend to eat around the time you plan to see this memorial.

👪 Recommended; a visit to the memorial is a good way to inform children about the war.

👥 National Park Service staff will gladly talk with visitors on an impromptu basis.

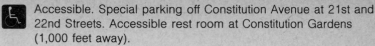 Accessible. Special parking off Constitution Avenue at 21st and 22nd Streets. Accessible rest room at Constitution Gardens (1,000 feet away).

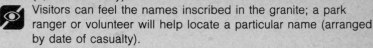 Visitors can feel the names inscribed in the granite; a park ranger or volunteer will help locate a particular name (arranged by date of casualty).

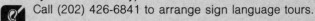 Call (202) 426-6841 to arrange sign language tours.

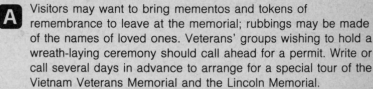 Visitors may want to bring mementos and tokens of remembrance to leave at the memorial; rubbings may be made of the names of loved ones. Veterans' groups wishing to hold a wreath-laying ceremony should call ahead for a permit. Write or call several days in advance to arrange for a special tour of the Vietnam Veterans Memorial and the Lincoln Memorial.

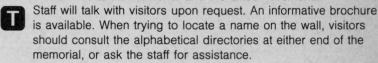 Staff will talk with visitors upon request. An informative brochure is available. When trying to locate a name on the wall, visitors should consult the alphabetical directories at either end of the memorial, or ask the staff for assistance.

The Vietnam Veterans Memorial is a tribute to the more than 58,000 men and women who died in service related to the Vietnam War and to those who fought and survived. It is a conscious attempt to separate the question of political and military policies that governed the conduct of that war from the men and women who served.

Authorized by act of Congress in 1980, the memorial is the design of Maya Lin, winner of a national design competition. Ms. Lin was, at that time, a 21-year-old architecture student at Yale University. The memorial was dedicated November 13, 1982, as the capstone of a weekend of events memorializing the survivors—as well as the dead—of the Vietnam War. The memorial serves as an act of national reconciliation in relation to the most controversial war America has fought.

It is no surprise, then, that the memorial design was, itself, controversial. Many observers saw the design as a negative political statement. Two polished black granite walls, V-shaped, inscribed with the names of the dead, half-buried in the ground, reflect the faces of the viewers. Clearly, this is not a traditional, soaring, white marble tribute. The memorial is, on the contrary, an intensely personal and powerful experience in which each visitor is confronted with the names of the scores of thousands of victims of the war. Few come away unaffected.

Despite the controversy, the memorial was built as designed, with the later addition of Frederick Hart's heroic sculpture of three male soldiers and Glenna Goodacre's bronze of three women in fatigues with a wounded male colleague, which are set up and away from the memorial. The sculptures and memorial complement each other. All funds for the memorial were raised through private contributions.

Many visitors come to the memorial with the express desire of finding the name of a friend or relative and leaving a token of remembrance. Mementos are not thrown away; the National Park Service saves all of them. Names are inscribed in chronological order by the date of casualty, and alphabetically within date order. Next to each name is a diamond sign (confirmed death) or plus sign (unconfirmed, missing or unaccounted for). Visitors are permitted to make rubbings of names. See the park rangers for assistance.

WASHINGTON MONUMENT   (202) 426-6839
Constitution Avenue at 16th Street, NW
Mailing Address: National Park Service, Mall Operations,
              900 Ohio Drive, SW 20242
Hours: April–Labor Day   8 A.M.–midnight daily (check first)
        September–March   9 A.M.–5 P.M. daily
        Closed July 4, Christmas and during lightning storms
Free Admission

  Smithsonian or Federal Triangle stop (orange and blue lines).

 Constitution Avenue or 15th Street, NW.

 Parking lot at 16th Street and Constitution Avenue; parking on the Mall. Both are likely to be very crowded during daylight hours.

None on premises. A kiosk near 15th Street sells snacks; street vendors across from the monument are on either side of the Ellipse.

 Recommended. Kids will enjoy the elevator ride and the view. There's lots of running room on the grounds.

 Groups of 20 can arrange to take a "step tour" by calling (202) 426-6841 (see Tours below).

 Fully accessible. Accessible rest room and phones at the bottom of the hill.

Call (202) 426-6841 48 hours in advance to make arrangements for a tour designed for those who are visually impaired.

 Call (202) 426-6841 48 hours in advance to make arrangements for a tour in sign language.

 Stair tours are dependent on staff availability. Call (202) 426-6841.

 For those who can't bear not walking the stairs, the National Park Service conducts walking-down "step tours" for 20 people at a time weekends at 10 A.M. and 2 P.M., staff permitting. You'll see the 193 carved memorial stones given in the nineteenth century by private citizens, societies, states and nations. Call (202) 426-6841 the day of your visit to verify it's offered.

Pierre L'Enfant's idea of an equestrian statue to honor George Washington was long forgotten in 1847 when architect Robert Mills drew up his plans for an elaborate pseudo-Greek temple to serve as the Washington Monument. During the course of construction, Mills' design was honed down to the austere marble and granite obelisk we have today. The cornerstone of the monument to our first President was laid in 1848, but quarrels over construction and lack of private funds to support the project slowed work down; the Civil War finally halted it completely. When building resumed in 1880 with government funds and the War Department's Corps of Engineers in charge, the new marble came from a different part of the same Maryland quarry—you can see the color change about one fourth of the way up the monument's side.

The Washington Monument stands 555 feet 5⅛ inches high and looms far above the rest of the city (since 1899, there has been a 90-foot limit on the height of buildings in Washington). When the monument opened in 1888, a steam-driven elevator took 10 minutes to reach the top. It is said that because the contraption was not considered entirely safe, only men were allowed to ride; women and children had to walk so their lives would not be endangered.

Generations of Americans have prided themselves on their ability to climb the 897 steps to the top of the Washington Monument. Unfortunately, in recent years the National Park Service has had to close general access to the stairs because the trip proved too strenuous for many who attempted it, and because some of the memorial stones that line the stairs had been vandalized over the years and needed to be restored. (A special walking-down tour is offered for small groups—see the key.) Today you can ride the elevator to the top and take a look at the city spread out below. The view is especially lovely on summer nights. On summer days and holidays, the wait for the elevator is from 40 to 50 minutes. A free informative pamphlet is available at the site.

Each year on the Fourth of July, Washington's big fireworks display is launched from the monument grounds. From time to time the grounds are used for various other events, such as kite-flying contests, concerts and boomerang exhibitions. One snowy winter the monument was even turned into a giant sundial by plowing the grounds around it to mark the hours. The service bands perform at the Sylvan Theater at 8 P.M. in season: Sunday, Marine Corps; Tuesday, Army; Thursday, Navy; Friday, Air Force. The Army Old Guard performs a Twilight Tattoo on Wednesdays at 7 P.M. on the Ellipse in July and August. Check the newspaper to see if anything is planned during your visit.

WORTH NOTING

Constitution Gardens, on the Mall between the Washington Monument and the Vietnam Memorial. Dedicated in 1976, the gardens provide urban respite in the form of almost 50 acres of rolling lawn, complete with a six-acre lake and over 5,000 trees. A memorial to the signers of the Declaration of Independence is on the lake's small island.

S. Dillon Ripley Center, 1100 Jefferson Drive, SW 20560, (202) 357-2700. Part of the underground Smithsonian Quadrangle, the center displays temporary exhibits of various art forms in its intimate space. The gallery ends with a soaring trompe l'oeil by Richard Haas, which visually breaks through the ground over the viewer's head to reveal the Castle above.

Voice of America, 330 Independence Avenue, SW 20547, (202) 619-3919. The Voice of America, the radio network of the U.S. Information Agency, broadcasts shows in 43 languages that are beamed all over the globe. A free 45-minute guided tour begins with a video and proceeds to fishbowl peeks into several broadcast studios as well as the

central newsroom and control room. Tours are given weekdays at
8:40, 9:40 and 10:40 A.M. and 1:40 and 2:40 P.M.

RESTAURANTS ON THE MALL

The absolute best bet for eating on the Mall is the cafeteria at the
National Gallery of Art. The food is fresh, reasonable, attractive and
varied (*every* member of the family can find something here), and the
setting, for a cafeteria, is quite elegant—you can watch water cascade
from the Mall down a sculptured waterfall.

The Air and Space Museum has a splendid new cafeteria and
restaurant, both enclosed in a glass addition with an impressive view
of the Capitol from the east side.

The Mall is the perfect place for picnics—if you aren't seeking
solitude, that is—so if you can, bring your own food. In addition,
street vendors selling a variety of foods cluster in front of the National
Air and Space Museum on Independence Avenue, along the sides of
the Ellipse across from the Washington Monument and in front of the
Natural History and American History museums on Constitution
Avenue. Refreshment kiosks are scattered along the Mall itself in
warm weather.

If you are on the south side of the Mall, consider the L'Enfant
Plaza complex, two blocks south of the Mall between 7th and 9th
Streets, SW. On the hotel's main floor are several rather expensive
restaurants; the shopping mall below offers deli and snacks during
business hours. If you are on the north side of the Mall, you are not
far from The Pavilion at the Old Post Office and The Shops at National Place, both of which have numerous restaurants and a food
court.

5

CAPITOL HILL

Capitol Hill houses the Congress, the Supreme Court, the massive Library of Congress, Union Station—and one of Washington's most charming residential and commercial neighborhoods. "The Hill" is unique in its contrasts: delicate town houses cozy up to enormous marble government buildings; rows of luxuriously renovated homes neighbor ghettos that have been crumbling for half a century; historic buildings stand next to modern edifices. These contrasts, and the presence of the Congress and the highest court, provide some of the most exciting scenes Washington has to offer.

This bustling community evolved slowly from L'Enfant's idea of locating the "Congress House" on Jenkins Hill. L'Enfant faced the Capitol east, since he expected the new capital city to grow first in that direction, around the deep, commercially-promising Anacostia harbor. While he was wrong in his estimation of where the city would develop, the designer's use of the hill—"a pedestal awaiting a monument"—was exquisite. As you walk throughout the Capitol Hill neighborhood, and on the Mall, you're treated with new vistas of the Capitol with every turn.

When Congress opened in Washington in 1800, the Capitol building was home to both houses of Congress, the Supreme Court and the Library of Congress; Capitol Hill consisted of eight boardinghouses, a washerwoman, a shoemaker, a general store, an oyster house and tobacco farms. The neighborhood slept until after the Civil War, but the real boom didn't occur until the turn of the century. By 1935, the Library of Congress and the Supreme Court had moved into their own imposing homes, Union Station had been moved from the Mall and several thousand homes had taken their places near the Capitol.

The boom continues. Every year beginning in the 1960s several more blocks of renovated homes would claim to be part of "Capitol Hill" in order to reap status and escalated resale values for their houses.

Today the neighborhood is roughly defined as lying between H Street, NE, on the north, Robert F. Kennedy Memorial Stadium on the east, the Southwest Freeway on the south, and the Capitol on the west—but your sightseeing will take place in a much smaller area than this 1.5-mile square. Most of the government buildings and museums lie within several blocks of the Capitol.

Beyond these monumental limits we suggest a stroll along Pennsylvania Avenue, SE, to poke in the many fine restaurants, boutiques, bookstores and miscellaneous shops. Stop in at the Eastern Market and the adjacent shops on 7th Street, SE. On Saturdays and Sundays farmers and craftspeople sell a wonderful selection of wares. Union Station (see site report), which has been impressively renovated, brims with shops, restaurants, a food court and a nine-theater movie complex, as well as a major train station. The Massachusetts Avenue corridor from 2nd to 4th Streets, NE, has spawned a variety of restaurants and small shops.

Some notes. Parking can be difficult on the Hill; it's a mixture of permit-only spaces, two-hour visitor spaces and limited meter parking. Capitol Hill street names can drive you mad. East Capitol Street divides the Northeast quadrant of the city from the southeast; C Street, NE, is six blocks from C Street, SE, so watch the quadrant indicators and proceed carefully.

Crime is a problem on Capitol Hill, so restrict your nighttime travels to well-lighted Pennsylvania and Massachusetts avenues (for restaurants and pubs) or as close as possible to the Folger Theater or Library of Congress if you're attending a play or a concert (the Library of Congress allows parking in its lot for concertgoers). The tone of Hill neighborhoods changes rapidly from block to block, so caution during the day is also advised.

Food choices abound on the Hill; check our recommendations at the end of this chapter.

CAPITOL HILL

1. Capital Children's Museum
2. Folger Shakespeare Library
3. Library of Congress
4. National Postal Museum
5. Navy Yard
6. Sewall-Belmont House
7. Supreme Court of the United States
8. Union Station
9. United States Botanic Garden
10. United States Capitol

A. Cannon House Office Buiilding
B. Longworth House Office Building
C. Rayburn House Office Building
D. Dirksen Senate Office Building
E. Russell Senate Office Building

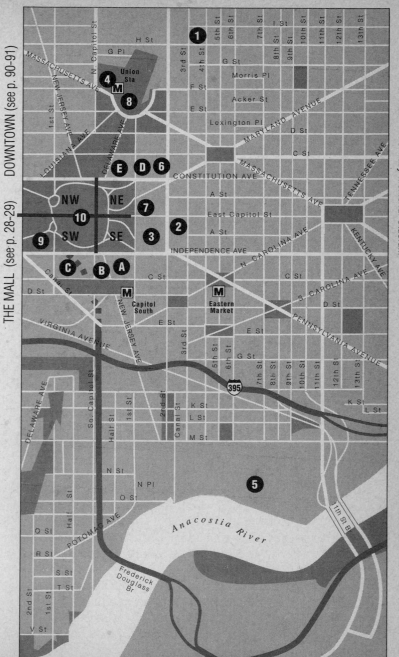

NORTHWEST (see p. 150-151)

DOWNTOWN (see p. 90-91)

THE MALL (see p. 28-29)

to Robert F. Kennedy Memorial Stadium

H St

G Pl

N. Capitol St

MASSACHUSETTS AVE

NEW JERSEY AVE

1st St

LOUISIANA AVE

DELAWARE AVE

Union Sta

M

3rd St

4th St

5th St

6th St

7th St

8th St

9th St

10th St

11th St

12th St

13th St

I St

G St

Morris Pl

Acker St

Lexington Pl

MARYLAND AVENUE

D St

C St

MASSACHUSETTS AVE

F St

E St

TENNESSEE AVE

CONSTITUTION AVE

A St

East Capitol St

A St

INDEPENDENCE AVE

N. CAROLINA AVE

KENTUCKY AVE

NW

NE

SW

SE

Canal St

C St

D St

M

Capitol South

New Jersey Ave

C St

S. CAROLINA AVE

D St

M

Eastern Market

PENNSYLVANIA AVENUE

VIRGINIA AVENUE

E St

E St

3rd St

5th St

6th St

G St

7th St

8th St

9th St

10th St

11th St

12th St

13th St

395

K St

L St

DELAWARE AVE

So. Capitol St

Half St

1st St

2nd St

Canal St

K St

L St

M St

N St

N Pl

O St

11th St B

Half St

Half St

Q St

R St

POTOMAC AVE

Anacostia River

2nd St

1st St

S St

T St

Frederick Douglass Br

V St

CAPITAL CHILDREN'S MUSEUM   (202) 543-8600
800 3rd Street, NE 20002
Hours: 10 A.M.–5 P.M. daily
   Closed Easter, Thanksgiving, Christmas and New Year's
Admission: Ages 2–59—$6

M Union Station stop (red line). Short taxi ride or long walk through transitional neighborhood (H Street overpass from Union Station).
= D2, D4, D6, D8, X2, X4.

3rd Street.

P Metered street parking.

Snack vending machines. An eating room is provided; picnic tables are available on museum grounds.

Highly recommended. Everything here is for kids; however, those under 16 must be accompanied by an adult.

Tours can be arranged for groups of 10 or more by writing or calling (202) 675-4149 three weeks in advance.

Fully accessible.

No special services available, but, since the museum is a "hands-on" place, those with impaired vision can still enjoy the facility.

While an interpreted tour can be arranged, staff feel that the tactile nature of the exhibits will allow those with hearing impairments to enjoy the museum fully without assistance.

T Each exhibit has guides to answer questions and offer assistance.

As its name would suggest, the Capital Children's Museum is a wonderful place for kids; the adults with them will find much of interest, too.

All of the exhibits at the Children's Museum are made to be handled. A City Room, designed to help children learn how to use the city, has workers' uniforms to dress up in, some cars and the front part of a bus to "drive," a kitchen and a working switchboard connected to phones throughout the room. A permanent exhibit on Mexico includes an open-air market where kids can put on ponchos and straw hats and take a stroll to see what the market has to offer. In the

Communications Room, visitors can learn how a printing press works by actually printing a poster.

An exciting new interactive animation exhibit, "Chuck Jones—An Animated Life," covers parts of three floors of the museum. Visitors can create their own animated films or view original film cels, cartoon drawings, and rare animated films of Bugs Bunny, Road Runner, and Daffy Duck, from the library of animation artist Chuck Jones.

Activities such as puppet shows, arts and crafts demonstrations and performances are offered on weekends; call (202) 543-8600 for details.

FOLGER SHAKESPEARE LIBRARY (202) 544-7077

201 East Capitol Street, SE 20003
Hours: 10 A.M.–4 P.M. Monday–Saturday
Closed holidays
Free Admission

M Union Station stop (red line—seven blocks); Capitol South stop (blue and orange lines).

East Capitol Street or 1st Street.

P Limited two-hour street parking.

Not recommended for young children. Group tours for older children can be arranged in advance by calling (202) 544-7077. A Shakespeare Festival for elementary and secondary school-age kids is held in the spring. School groups should reserve at least a month in advance for a tour, which includes dress-up in Elizabethan and Renaissance costumes.

Call (202) 544-7077 or write to arrange for a group tour. For discounted group theater tickets, call (202) 544-7077.

Fully accessible.

A For special tours write or call (202) 544-7077 at least a month in advance.

T Volunteer docents are available to answer questions on a walk-in basis, 11 A.M.–1 P.M., Monday–Saturday.

If you have a special interest in Shakespeare and his times, the Folger Shakespeare Library is a worthwhile stop while you're touring Capitol

Hill. At the behest of Henry Clay Folger and his wife, Emily Jordan, architect Paul Philippe Cret designed the Folger as a research center as well as a permanent home of the couple's superb collection of Shakespeare's works and related manuscripts and objects. The white marble facade of the Art Deco/Greek Revival building is decorated with nine bas-relief panels representing scenes from Shakespeare's plays. A statue of Puck enlivens the 2nd Street side.

The Great Hall, oak-paneled, barrel-vaulted, and decorated to reflect Elizabethan taste, houses the museum exhibits on Renaissance culture and life. Exhibits from the permanent collection include first editions of some of Shakespeare's plays as well as scripts marked by famous actors of the British and American stage who have played Shakespearean roles.

The Shakespeare Library itself, which is administered by the trustees of Amherst College, houses the world's largest collection of Shakespeareana and is a superb source of information on European life in the sixteenth and seventeenth centuries. The library is open only to researchers who have obtained appropriate credentials in advance.

A theater, modeled after an Elizabethan innyard theater, is home to the Folger Consort, an internationally acclaimed ensemble that performs medieval and Renaissance music. It is also the site of a rich offering of lectures, readings of poetry and fiction, and occasional theatrical performances. The former resident theater troupe moved to a new home in downtown Washington to accommodate their growing audience (see "Entertainment" chapter for details).

LIBRARY OF CONGRESS (202) 707-5000
Thomas Jefferson Building: 1st and East Capitol Streets, SE
James Madison Memorial Building: 101 Independence Avenue, SE
John Adams Building: 2nd Street and Independence Avenue, SE
Hours: 8:30 A.M.–9:30 P.M. Monday–Friday
8:30 A.M.–6 P.M. Saturday
12–6 P.M. Sunday
Closed Christmas and New Year's
Free Admission

 Capitol South stop (blue and orange lines).

 1st Street or Independence Avenue.

Competitive street parking. The library has a small parking lot available for those attending events in the evening.

 On premises. The staff cafeteria, located on the sixth floor of the James Madison Memorial Building, and snack bar, located on the ground floor, are open to the public from 9 to 10:30 A.M. and 12:30 to 3 P.M. Monday–Friday.

 Not recommended for young children, although an occasional exhibit may appeal to them.

 To arrange for a tour for 10 or more people, write to the Library of Congress, Visitor Services, or call (202) 287-5458 at least four weeks in advance.

 Fully accessible.

 No special services available, although books are available in Braille and on tape (see text).

 Signed tours are offered after the introductory film on Tuesday at 10 A.M. and Thursday at 1 P.M.

 A 22-minute orientation film is shown in the Visitors Orientation Theater in the James Madison Building every half-hour from 9 A.M. to 9 P.M. Monday–Friday, 9 A.M. to 5:30 P.M. Saturday, and 12 to 5:30 P.M. Sunday. Guided tours are given following the showings at 10 A.M. and 1 and 3 P.M. Monday–Friday.

In 1800, Congress, looking for examples on which to base their fledgling legislation, appropriated $5,000 for European lawbooks to be housed in one room of the Capitol as the Library of Congress. This original collection was burned by the British in 1814, and Thomas Jefferson offered his personal library—for $24,000—to serve as a more well-rounded replacement. Congress accepted his offer, and the collection slowly began to grow.

In 1870, the copyright law was rewritten, requiring two copies of every published manuscript, musical score and map to be sent to the Library of Congress, and its exponential growth began. Today, the library is a massive complex, housing more than 90 million items, including books, periodicals, maps, films, photographs and recordings stored on over 535 miles of shelving. Included are priceless Stradivarius stringed instruments as well as the most valuable book in the world—one of the three remaining Gutenberg bibles, the first books to be printed with movable metal type. The collection grows at the rate of more than 7,000 items each day and has spread from the original building—the Thomas Jefferson Building—into two major adjacent buildings: the John Adams Building, opened in 1939, and the James Madison Memorial Building, completed in 1980.

The Thomas Jefferson Building, which opened in 1897, is a charming, yet grand, American version of the ornate style of the Italian Renaissance. It is still the heart of the library. Undergoing renovation through 1995, the Thomas Jefferson Building is closed to the general public and can only be seen on tour (see key). The Great Hall is a beauty, with its enormous dome, towering columns, statues, carved balustrades and murals, which represent various aspects of civilized life. The Main Reading Room is equally impressive. The 160-foot-high rosetted dome and assorted statues look down on 44,000 reference books and 212 desks—newly wired for fiber-optics.

As much a museum as a library, the Library of Congress offers many varying exhibits of great appeal; all are on display in the Madison Building while the Jefferson Building is undergoing renovation. Call (202) 707-8000 for a recording of what's being shown while you're in town.

The Library of Congress is also the world's largest library and houses several special collections of interest to visitors. Each of the 22 reading rooms has a focus. The Asian Division has the largest collection of Chinese and Japanese books outside their homelands; the European Room boasts the largest assemblage of Russian books in the West; the Music Division contains over 7 million items; and the Rare Book and Special Collections Division possesses such gems as the remains of the private libraries of Thomas Jefferson, Woodrow Wilson and Adolf Hitler.

Since this is the national library of the people of the United States, all adults are welcome to use the facilities for research, although books can't normally be borrowed. The library is heavily used, so the wait for books can be long, but it's fun to be part of this quiet hustle-bustle. A librarian is always available to explain how materials can be requested.

Through its Congressional Research Service, the Library of Congress fulfills its major task as the reference and research arm of Congress. A large staff compiles reports and sends materials to congressional representatives and their staffs.

The library offers several other services of note. An interlibrary loan program extends the use of books and other materials to researchers using public and academic libraries throughout the country.

Through National Library Services for the Blind and Physically Handicapped, the library supplies books and magazines recorded on disc or tape, as well as conventional Braille materials to local libraries.

The Library of Congress sponsors a concert series and a series of literary performances each year. The concert series, usually from October to April, is often of chamber music using the library's collection of fine antique instruments. For concert schedule information call (202) 287-5502. The literary performances run from October to June and feature poets and authors of national renown.

The Mary Pickford Theater is dedicated to showing the library's collection of motion picture and television programming (the largest such collection in the U.S.). These unusual archival films are shown four nights a week, usually weeknights, and are free to the public, but reservations are required. Call (202) 707-5677 for information or to make a reservation. Quarterly schedules are available by writing to the Mary Pickford Theater, Motion Picture, Broadcasting and Recorded Sound Division at the Library of Congress.

The library's monthly calendar of events will provide you with information on concerts, readings and current exhibits. You can pick up a copy at the information desk when you get to the library or write ahead for one.

The shop on the first floor of the Madison Building has publications, postcards, recordings (including those of the American Folklife Center) and posters, as well as reasonably priced crafts. Two informative guides to the Library of Congress are for sale in the shop.

NATIONAL POSTAL MUSEUM (202) 357-2700

2 Massachusetts Avenue, NE 20560
Hours: 10 A.M.–5:30 P.M. daily
        Closed Christmas
Free Admission

 Union Station stop (red line).

 Union Station.

 1,400-space parking garage in Union Station.

 Highly recommended. Computer games, interactive postcard-producing kiosks, videos, and fabulously expensive stamps will entertain kids of all ages. The Discovery Center, designed specifically to combat "museum fatigue," offers hands-on family activities for a change of pace. Call the Education Office at (202) 633-9380 to arrange group tours for kids.

Call (202) 357-2991 to arrange group tours.

Fully accessible. A ramped entrance is at Massachusetts Avenue and First Street, NE.

To schedule a signed tour, call (202) 786-2942 or TTY (202) 786-2414 at least two weeks in advance. For general information, call TTY (202) 357-1729.

T Highlight tours are offered at 11 A.M. and 1:30 P.M. daily.

This newest Smithsonian family member, developed and operated in conjunction with the U.S. Postal Service, is a peach that everyone will find appealing. Housed in the beautifully gussied-up City Post Office Building, the museum is stocked with state-of-the-art interactive devices, videos, and exhibit spaces, all with the mission of displaying the national philatelic and postal history collection. Dry as this may sound, it's quite exciting to see stamps worth millions of dollars, interesting to learn the rationale behind the design of stamps and postal vehicles, and fun to play "Rail, Sail or Overland Mail," a computer game about mail delivery. The five major galleries are devoted to "Moving the Mail," "Binding the Nation," "Customers and Communities," "The Art of Cards and Letters," and "Stamps and Stories."

Designed in the Beaux Arts style by Daniel Burnham, who also designed Union Station next door, the City Post Office Building opened in 1914. The grand granite exterior and lushly restored interior lobby usher visitors to the new museum, which is housed on the lower level; the rest of the building is occupied by a full-service U.S. post office and several federal agencies. Natural light floods through skylights atop the ninety-foot-high atrium, where three airmail planes dangle over exhibits spaced across the intricate stamp and envelope design of the floor.

The museum has two shops: the larger store sells all types of paraphernalia associated with the postal service and stamps, from bookmarks to T-shirts, books and posters; the second store sells stamps, from the rare to the ordinary. A library and research center are available for use by philatelic researchers and scholars from 10 A.M. to 4 P.M., Monday through Friday; call (202) 633-9370 to schedule an appointment. The museum plans to offer a series of educational outreach activities, ranging from lectures on the art of stamps to letter writing.

NAVY YARD
Navy Museum   **(202) 433-4882**
Marine Corps Museum   **(202) 433-3840**
Museum Annex
9th and M streets, SE
Hours: Navy Museum: 9 A.M.–4 P.M. weekdays
                        (through 5 P.M. in summer)
                        10 A.M.–5 P.M. weekends and holidays
        Marine Corps Museum: 10 A.M.–4 P.M. Monday–Saturday
                        (through 5 P.M. in summer)
                        12 P.M. to 5 P.M. Sunday and holidays
Free Admission

Ⓜ Eastern Market stop (blue and orange lines). Walk east on Pennsylvania Avenue to 8th Street, then south to M Street. Gate at 9th and M Streets. It's a long walk through a marginal neighborhood.

🚌 50, 52, 54, 91, 92, 94, A1, A2, A4, A6, A8.

🚕 M Street.

🅿 Free parking at site; enter at 9th and M streets.

🍽 McDonald's is in the Navy Yard.

👪 Highly recommended. This is a great place for kids! Literature for kids is available.

👨‍👩‍👧 Special tours available by appointment. Call (202) 433-4882 for Navy Museum and (202) 433-3840 for Marine Corps Museum.

♿ Fully accessible.

👁 Special tours can be arranged for the Navy Museum by calling (202) 433-4882.

Special tours can be arranged for the Navy Museum by calling (202) 433-4882.

Reservations must be made to attend the Navy's Wednesday night performance by calling (202) 433-2678. Reservations must be made three weeks in advance to attend the Marine Corps' Friday night ceremony by calling (202) 433-6060.

The Navy Yard is a great place to take kids since they can run and climb on the exhibits; the yard and museums are also entertaining for adults who have an interest in military history. Opened by the government in 1799, the Washington Navy Yard is the oldest naval facility in the United States. For a large part of its history it was known as the Naval Gun Factory and was the primary manufacturing site for naval weapons. The Navy Museum, housed in one of the old factory buildings, portrays 200 years of naval history in exhibits of warships, weapons and aircraft. Visitors can play on the movable gun mounts taken from fighting ships and explore the submarine room.

The Museum Annex, opened in 1987, houses two World War II-vintage midget submarines from Axis countries, a submarine-launched Poseidon missile, a Civil War-era submarine and various other exhibits. You can also tour a 1950s Navy destroyer at the pier.

The Marine Corps Museum is a "time tunnel" of Marine history, displaying Marine weapons, clothing and battles presented in chronological order from 1775 to the present.

From June to August, both the Navy and Marine Corps offer evening presentations that are great fun for everyone. On Wednesdays beginning at 8:45 P.M., the Navy gives a historical presentation accompanied by a film and a Navy band. On Friday nights at 8:20 at the Marine Corps Barracks, 8th and I Streets, SE, the Marines put on a 2½-hour parade complete with drill team, drum and bugle corps and a marching band. It's a thrill to see, but reservations must be made for both three weeks in advance.

SUPREME COURT OF THE UNITED STATES (202) 479-3000
1st Street, NE 20543
(corner of 1st and East Capitol streets)

Hours: 9 A.M.–4:30 P.M. weekdays
  Closed holidays
Free Admission

M Capitol South stop (blue and orange lines) or Union Station stop (red line). Each is about six blocks away.

🚗 1st Street.

P Competitive two-hour parking in the neighborhood.

⚪ On premises. A good cafeteria in the building is open from 7:30 to 10:30 A.M. and from 11:30 A.M.–2 P.M. (from noon to 12:15 and 1 to 1:15 P.M.. Court employees have exclusive access). A grill is open from 10:30 A.M. to 3:30 P.M., with the same staff priority.

👪 Not recommended for small children.

👥 For information on group tours call (202) 479-3298 several weeks in advance.

♿ Fully accessible; ramp is on the Maryland Avenue side of building.

👂 Call (202) 479-3298 to arrange for a special tour.

T When the Court is not in session, 20-minute lectures on the history and work of the Court are given every hour on the half hour, 9:30 A.M.–3:30 P.M. weekdays, on a walk-in basis.

One of the most exciting shows in town can be seen from the packed visitors' gallery of the Supreme Court. In these Court chambers, the laws of our land receive their ultimate interpretation with results that can touch, and have affected, us all. Alexis de Tocqueville, the nineteenth-century French political philosopher, observed of the U.S. Supreme Court: "A more imposing judicial power was never constituted by any people." Our highest court is unique in the history of justice; as noted in the Supreme Court's guidebook, few other courts in the world have the same authority of constitutional interpretation and none have exercised it for as long or with as much influence.

Today, the Supreme Court is an institution steeped in power and tradition. This is in sharp contrast to the Court in 1795, when John Jay, its first Chief Justice, resigned to become governor of New York, feeling the Court would never become the respected institution, shielded from day-to-day politics, that it needed to be to review the law effectively. At that time the Court was meeting in a cramped section of City Hall in Philadelphia.

The young Court floundered for its identity, incorporating some British legal traditions and forging some of its own. The justices decided to abandon the British practice of wearing wigs after being hooted at in the streets and in response to Thomas Jefferson's warning to "discard the monstrous wig which makes the English judges look like rats peeping through bunches of oakum."

It was John Marshall, the fourth Chief Justice, who used his powerful leadership abilities to strengthen the Court's self-concept and its doctrine of judicial review, thereby forcing the Court into a central role in the governing process alongside the Executive branch and the Congress. Through setting and observing precedents, the Court interprets the law. It has the final word on what an existing law means in practice, and its power rests in its respect for the law.

This respect for tradition is reflected in the design of the Supreme Court building. The Court has only been at its present location since 1935. Until that time it was a wandering branch of the federal government, spending the years from 1800 to 1935 in seven different locations within the capital. In 1932, Congress finally authorized architect Cass Gilbert to design for the Court ". . . a building of dignity and importance suitable for its use."

The massive classical structure that houses the Court today pays homage to ancient Greece, the birthplace of democracy. Sixteen columns of Vermont marble support the main entrance, which is flanked by two enormous seated statues representing "The Contemplation of Justice" and "The Guardian, or Authority, of Law." The enormous bronze doors, each weighing more than six tons, depict famous scenes in the development of the law as sculpted by John Donnelly, Jr.

One enters the Great Hall, lined with more massive columns and busts of former Chief Justices. Straight ahead is the imposing Court Chamber, with columns, walls and floors of Italian, Spanish and African marble. The furniture is rich mahogany, and the drapery dark red velvet.

On the first Monday in October, the Supreme Court begins its yearly schedule, hearing oral arguments through the end of April. During this period, court is in session for two weeks and in adjournment for the following two weeks while the Justices deliberate the cases they've heard. When in session, the Court meets from Monday to Wednesday, hearing cases from 10 A.M. until 3 P.M., with a break from noon until 1 P.M. Beginning in May, the Court sits only on Mondays, when it hands down orders and opinions at 10 A.M. This schedule continues until the Court adjourns sometime in early July, depending on its workload.

The Court never announces in advance which opinions it plans to release on a given day, but its argument calendar is set a month in advance and printed in the newspaper daily. Since the gallery's limited seating is granted on a first-come, first-served basis, you'd do well to arrive no later than 9:30 A.M. If a very important case is before the Court or a historic decision is to be handed down, you may have to arrive even earlier. Call ahead or check the newspapers to be certain of the Court's schedule.

When the Court is not meeting, courtroom lectures are given every hour on the half hour from 9:30 A.M. to 3:30 P.M. These 15-minute talks provide a good introduction to the history of the Court and the building that houses it. When the Court is in session, these lectures are not given.

On the ground floor of the building are public exhibits and a continuous 20-minute film about the Supreme Court. A small gift shop sells Court-related items.

UNION STATION   (202) 371-9441
50 Massachusetts Avenue, NE
Hours: Building is open 24 hours
        Store hours: 10 A.M.–9 P.M. Monday–Saturday
                Noon–6 P.M. Sunday
Free Admission

 Union Station stop (red line).

 Building entrance.

 1,400-space parking garage in rear; very limited metered parking on street.

 Extensive food court; cafés; fancy restaurants.

 Some retail stores that kids will love.

Call (202) 289-1908 to arrange for a group tour; the cost is $2 per person. The building manager will make arrangements for group dining according to your tastes and budgets; call (202) 289-1908 at least two weeks in advance.

 Fully accessible.

After decades of rack and ruin, accented by political squabbles, Union Station has been, at last, beautifully and painstakingly restored to its original magnificent state.

Washington's first train station was located on the center of the Mall, but was moved to its present site in the early part of this century in order to restore the Mall to L'Enfant's original vision. Union Station was designed as a monumental public entrance to the nation's capital at a time when rail travel was supreme. The architect, Daniel Burnham of Chicago, designed an enormous and grand edifice in Beaux Arts style, complete with linked barrel-vaulted ceilings, statues, friezes, columns and gold leaf galore. When it was built, Union Station was the largest train station in the world—just ahead of Grand Central Station in New York. After years of neglect and decay, the station has been meticulously researched and restored under a partnership including the congressionally created Union Station Redevelopment Corporation, Amtrak, the federal government, Union Stations Venture Ltd., D.C.'s Historic Preservation Board and several architectural and restoration firms.

Union Station still serves its original purpose as a train station, but that seems almost secondary in its new incarnation as an urban center. Over 100 upscale shops fill the concourse and main hall, including Benetton, Ann Taylor, Pendleton, Nature Company, Brookstone, The Limited, Great Train Store and many other bright and interesting retail outlets. AMC offers nine movie screens in what had been the station's turkish baths. A food court entices with possibilities to satisfy every member of your entourage. If your appetites are heartier or attracted to the more refined, the full-service restaurants are sure to please: America, serving over 100 American regional dishes; the Center Cafe; and Sfuzzi, a postmodern Italian restaurant.

The station's spectacular interior is matched by its exterior setting. The center of Union Station Plaza is the lovely Columbus Memorial Fountain, designed by Lorado Taft in 1912.

UNITED STATES CAPITOL   (202) 224-3121
East end of the Mall on Capitol Hill
Hours: 9 A.M.–4:30 P.M. daily
>(in summer, the rotunda and statuary hall are open until 8 P.M.)
>Closed Thanksgiving, Christmas and New Year's

Free Admission

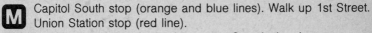 Capitol South stop (orange and blue lines). Walk up 1st Street.
Union Station stop (red line).

1st Street, Independence Avenue or Constitution Avenue.

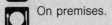 Competitive two-hour parking in neighborhood.

On premises.

Recommended. Kids will especially like the congressional
subway ride. (Kids under 12 must be accompanied by an adult.)

Fully accessible. Handicapped visitors can request special
parking from the parking guards; ramps are at the north and
south entrances. There are special areas for the handicapped in
the visitors' gallery for both the Senate and the House.

Special tours can be arranged for groups of people with visual
impairments by calling (202) 224-4048 in advance.

Special tours can be arranged for groups of people with hearing
impairments by calling (202) 224-4048 in advance. Make
arrangements well in advance to schedule with a guide who
signs. Call TDD (202) 224-4049.

A member of Congress or a senator can arrange for a special
tour if you write in advance (see text).

Free walk-in tours are conducted daily between 9 A.M. and 3:45
P.M. Write or call your congressperson's office well in advance to
make arrangements for a special VIP tour at 8 A.M. These tours
are limited to families, and tickets go quickly. You can also walk
many of the Capitol's impressive corridors on your own.

Pierre L'Enfant's plans for the capital city called for the "Congress
House" to be built on the crest of what was then called Jenkins Hill.
In 1792, a physician named William Thornton won $500 and a city
lot for his design for the Capitol building. Because of difficulty in
recruiting workmen in the new city, basic construction of the Capitol was accomplished in part by slaves and the finishing work done
by imported craftsmen. When Congress convened in November

1800, it met in a building that was but a small section of the structure that stands today. This small building housed not only the House and the Senate, but the Supreme Court and the Library of Congress as well.

During the War of 1812, the British entered the city, and on August 24, 1814, set fire to the Capitol. Had there not been a heavy rainstorm, the building would have been destroyed. In 1815, a group of Washington's leading citizens had a brick hall built nearly on the site of the present Supreme Court Building in order to house Congress in reasonable comfort until the official Capitol could be rebuilt. This "Brick Capitol" was built, it is suspected, to ensure that the government would not move from Washington, wiping out the investments the leading citizens had made in their new city.

The Capitol was ready for reoccupation in 1819. Additions have been made throughout the years, with the greatest enlargements coming in the 1850s and 1860s; these additions gave the Capitol the silhouette so recognizable today. The most recent structural change came in 1962 when the East Front was extended.

During the early months of the Civil War, the Capitol was used as a barracks for Northern troops. For about three months Union soldiers camped out in the hallways, parlors and legislative chambers. Eventually, some rooms were converted into bakeries to feed the men, and the Capitol was transformed into an emergency hospital to care for the wounded returning from Southern battlefields. Despite the troubles of the war, during 1863 the Capitol's 9-million-pound cast-iron dome was completed and the statue of Freedom raised to its top. Lincoln felt the completion of the dome to be an important symbol of faith in the endurance of the nation.

Start your tour of the Capitol by passing through Randolph Rogers' 10-ton bronze doors on the east side of the building. You are now in the Rotunda, the central portion of the Capitol that lies directly beneath the great iron dome. Many of our nation's fallen leaders have lain in state here, including Lincoln and Kennedy. On the walls of the Rotunda are eight historical oil paintings depicting the struggle for independence. John Trumbull, a member of George Washington's war staff, did the four paintings of the Revolutionary War.

Looking up into the dome, you can see Constantino Brumidi's fresco "The Apotheosis of Washington," an allegorical portrayal of an event in the nation's history where the founding fathers mingle with gods and goddesses. Brumidi devoted 25 years to working on the Capitol's interior.

Passing through the Rotunda, you enter Statuary Hall, which served as the House of Representatives' chamber until 1857. Each state has contributed statues of its two most famous citizens; the inhabitants of the room and hall are statues ranging from Robert E. Lee and Will Rogers to Dr. John Gorey, inventor of the ice machine.

Other historic sights in the Capitol are the restored old Senate and the Supreme Court chambers, both located in the north wing of the building, or the Senate side; Senate chambers and committee rooms are here. The southern wing of the Capitol is the House side. Within both chambers, Democrats sit to the right and Republicans to the left of the presiding officers—certainly an ideological switch!

The chambers, committee rooms and corridors and elevators in between can all be a hustle-bustle. When votes are about to proceed, bells are sounded, summoning members of Congress to the chambers for the calling of the roll. You'll be asked to clear the elevators and step to the side of corridors and stairways to facilitate their passage.

To observe a vote or debate from the chamber galleries, you must have a gallery pass. These passes can be obtained easily at your senators' and representatives' offices, and are good for the entire congressional session. For the House, foreign visitors can enter the galleries by showing their passports and obtaining passes from the doorkeeper's office. For the Senate, foreign visitors must stop at the visitors' desk on the first floor of the Senate side. Space is reserved for the physically impaired in both galleries.

Whether or not you want a gallery pass, you can pay your representatives a visit. Staff members are always glad to see constituents, and can provide lots of information to help you enjoy your Washington visit. If you contact their offices well in advance of your trip, the staff can arrange special tours of the Capitol, the White House, the FBI building and other government agencies.

Members of Congress are located in the congressional office buildings adjacent to the Capitol. They consist of the Russell Senate Office Building (Delaware and Constitution avenues, NE), the Dirksen Senate Office Building (1st Street and Constitution Avenue, NE), the Hart Senate Office Building (2nd Street and Constitution Avenue, NE), the Cannon House Office Building (New Jersey and Independence avenues, SE), the Longworth House Office Building (Indiana and New Jersey avenues, SE), and the Rayburn House Office Building (Independence Avenue and South Capitol Street, SW). If you don't know who your representatives or senators are, call the Capitol switchboard at (202) 224-3121. A free miniature subway connects the Capitol to the three Senate office buildings and the Rayburn House Office Building; on this free ride you can rub elbows with politicians, lobbyists and media folks, as well as other tourists.

Be sure to plan to visit Congress while it's in session. It convenes the first Monday in January and adjourns in December, but has frequent recesses, varying with elections and other factors. To be sure of the schedule, call (202) 224-3121, check the *Washington Post*'s daily "Activities in Congress" column, section A, or look for an American flag flying over the chamber you're interested in. A quaint method of telling when your members of Congress are working at night is to see if the lantern in the Capitol dome is lighted; if it is, one of the chambers is in session. To hear cloakroom tapes, which give daily accounts of the proceedings on the House and Senate floors, call (202) 225-7400 (House, Democratic), (202) 225-7430 (House, Republican), (202) 224-8541 (Senate, Democratic) and (202) 224-8601 (Senate, Republican).

Unlike other sights in Washington, the Capitol is at its liveliest in December as the legislators try to cram through legislation to clean their desks and adjourn for the holidays. The lantern in the dome is often beaming well into the night; you can attend these busy nocturnal sessions with your gallery pass.

It's great fun to eat in the cafeterias at the Capitol, Dirksen Senate Office Building (with its gilt and marble surroundings) and Rayburn and Longworth House office buildings. You can surreptitiously peep at the lunchtime fare of congressional and TV news celebrities. Also be sure to enjoy the lovely 68-acre Capitol grounds designed by Frederick Law Olmsted.

During the summer, free evening concerts are given on the west terrace of the Capitol. (We advise you to check for details, for even traditions can change.) The National Symphony Orchestra gives 8 P.M. concerts on Memorial Day, July 4 and Labor Day. The U.S. Navy Concert Band performs each Monday, components of the U.S. Air Force Band entertain on Tuesday, the U.S. Marine Band performs on Wednesday and the U.S. Army Band plays on Friday; all concerts begin at 8 P.M.

WORTH NOTING

The hours of these sites vary; call ahead.

Sewall-Belmont House, 144 Constitution Avenue, NE 20002, (202) 546-1210. Headquarters of the National Woman's Party, the Sewall-Belmont House is a museum of the women's rights movement. Both a National Historic Landmark and a National Historic Site, the house has a portion that dates back to 1680; it is thought to be the oldest house on Capitol Hill.

United States Botanic Garden, 1st Street and Maryland Avenue, SW 20024, (202) 225-8333. The glass conservatory at the foot of Capitol Hill houses both exotic and familiar plants and offers seasonal botanic displays. Across Constitution Avenue, the Frederic Auguste Bartholdi Park beautifully incorporates bulbs, annuals, perennials, and woody plants into an assortment of small gardens.

FOOD ON CAPITOL HILL

Capitol Hill offers a variety of places to eat, many of which we recommend if only for the people-watching. Try the House of Representatives, Senate, Supreme Court or Library of Congress cafeterias and dining rooms. Food is generally more than adequate and prices reasonable. Public access to each facility sometimes changes abruptly—during congressional recesses, for instance—so double-check their hours before proceeding.

Capitol Hill's commercial restaurants are located along several main corridors:

- Pennsylvania Avenue, SE, between 2nd and 4th streets, and then farther up the avenue between 6th and 7th streets, which is a several-block walk from the House side of the Capitol
- 8th Street, SE, between Pennsylvania Avenue and G Street
- Massachusetts Avenue, SE, between 2nd and 3rd streets, which is a several-block walk from the Senate side of the Capitol to Union Station.

The newly renovated Union Station offers a full range of eating opportunities, from an à la carte food court with almost limitless choices to several very fancy establishments.

If the budget is tight, *Hardees* and *McDonald's* are on the Pennsylvania Avenue corridor. Street vendors sell inexpensive food in warm weather, and there are many restaurants and cafés.

Egg Roll King, 653 Pennsylvania Avenue, SE, is a fine source of remarkably inexpensive Chinese/Hunan food. Try not to be put off by the name and the glaring fast-food atmosphere: the food is a real find; we heartily recommend it, especially if you're looking to take out.

6

DOWNTOWN

The Downtown section of Washington is perhaps the city's most disparate area, with its vital mix of federal and local government, international organizations, art museums, the Convention Center, major department stores and smaller retail operations, nonprofit organizations and associations, historic sites, parks, hotels, theaters, offices galore, every type of restaurant and bar imaginable—in fact, the only element Downtown lacks in quantity is residents, and that may change to an extent if the Pennsylvania Avenue Development Corporation's plans are fully implemented. This is Washington at work, with its shirtsleeves rolled up—or three-piece suit buttoned down.

The area is large; we define the borders as Capitol Hill (N. Capitol Street) to the east, the Mall (Constitution Avenue) to the south, Foggy Bottom (18th Street) on the west and M Street to the north. The best modes of conveyance are Metro, buses and taxis; it's best to leave your car outside the city or in a parking lot, since street parking is difficult and driving is most challenging here (see Chapter 2, "Getting To and Around Town," for details).

The Washington Convention Center, between 9th and 11th streets, NW, and M Street and New York Avenue, hosts a variety of trade shows and conventions as well as occasional antique, home and auto shows open to the public.

Although several points of interest in Downtown aren't specific sites, we've included descriptions of them because they're part of Washington's essence: the Lafayette Square area, Pennsylvania Avenue, F Street, Chinatown and the Ellipse.

DOWNTOWN

1. American Red Cross
2. Art Museum of the Americas
3. Bethune Museum and Archives
4. Corcoran Gallery of Art
5. DAR Museum
6. Decatur House
7. The Ellipse
8. FBI Building
9. Federal Reserve Board Gallery
10. Ford's Theater and the House Where Lincoln Died
11. Lafayette Square
12. National Aquarium
13. National Geographic Society
14. National Building Museum

NORTHWEST (see p. 150-151)

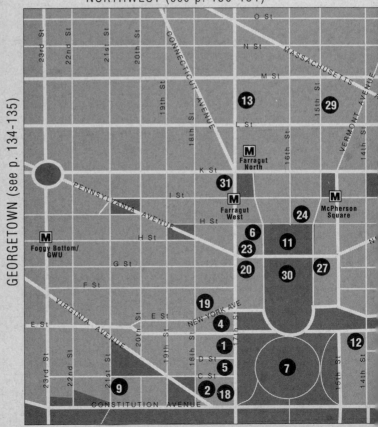

GEORGETOWN (see p. 134-135)

15. National Museum of American Art
16. National Museum of Women in the Arts
17. National Portrait Gallery
18. OAS Building
19. The Octagon
20. Old Executive Office Building
21. Paul VI Institute for Arts
22. The Pavilion at the Old Post Office
23. Renwick Gallery
24. St. John's Church
25. Lillian & Albert Small Jewish Museum
26. Tech 2000
27. Treasury Building
28. U.S. Navy Memorial
29. Washington Post Company
30. White House
31. The Wilderness Society–Ansel Adams Collection

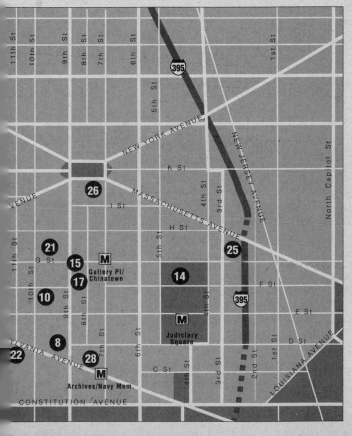

CAPITOL HILL (see p. 68-69)

e p. 28-29)

ART MUSEUM OF THE AMERICAS (OAS)   (202) 458-6016
201 18th Street, NW 20006
Hours: 10 A.M.–5 P.M. Tuesday–Saturday
Closed Mondays and holidays
Free Admission

M Farragut West stop (blue and orange lines); a *long* walk south on 17th Street.

🚌 13's, 80, 81, D1, D3, H1, L5, N1, N3, P1, P9, S1.

🚕 Constitution Avenue.

P Competitive street parking.

👫 Not recommended, unless child is particularly interested in art.

👥 Make arrangements at least two weeks in advance by calling (202) 458-6301.

♿ Inaccessible.

The world's first museum of the modern art of Latin America, this gallery exhibits over 200 paintings, sculptures and other works of art in changing exhibitions by artists from South and Central America, Mexico and the Caribbean. In addition, the museum sponsors lectures, gallery talks, films and a monthly guided tour. Call (202) 458-6016 for information about exhibitions, programs and tours, or for a copy of the museum calendar.

Run by the Organization of American States (OAS), the museum is in the former residence of the secretary general of that organization. The museum shares its backyard, the Aztec Garden, with the OAS Building on 17th Street; it's a peaceful place for a brown bag lunch.

CORCORAN GALLERY OF ART   (202) 638-3211
17th Street and New York Avenue, NW 20006
Hours: 10 A.M.–5 P.M. Friday–Monday, Wednesday
10 A.M.–9 P.M. Thursday
Closed Thanksgiving, Christmas and New Year's
Free Admission.   Suggested Contributions: Adults—$3   Students and Senior Citizens—$1   Families—$5

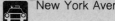 Farragut West stop (blue and orange lines); use 17th and I streets exit. Farragut North stop (red line); use Farragut Square exit. In both cases, walk south on 17th Street.

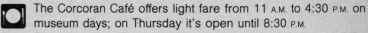 New York Avenue.

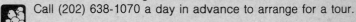 Metered parking on 17th Street and New York Avenue; commercial garages; on-street parking farther down 17th Street on side streets.

The Corcoran Café offers light fare from 11 A.M. to 4:30 P.M. on museum days; on Thursday it's open until 8:30 P.M.

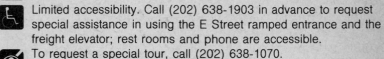 Recommended. The gallery is small enough to keep a child's interest. The Corcoran offers special hands-on events for kids; call the Education Office at (202) 638-3211, ext. 321, for a schedule or to arrange a kids-oriented tour.

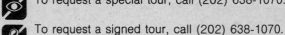 Call (202) 638-1070 a day in advance to arrange for a tour.

Limited accessibility. Call (202) 638-1903 in advance to request special assistance in using the E Street ramped entrance and the freight elevator; rest rooms and phone are accessible.

To request a special tour, call (202) 638-1070.

To request a signed tour, call (202) 638-1070.

Walk-in guided tours are given at 12:30 P.M. Wednesday–Sunday; an additional tour is given at 7:30 P.M. Thursday.

The Corcoran Gallery of Art is the oldest and largest private art museum in Washington. Founded in 1869 by William Wilson Corcoran, a successful Washington banker turned philanthropist, the collection was originally housed in the building that is now the Smithsonian's Renwick Gallery, around the corner on Pennsylvania Avenue. When Corcoran's growing collection demanded more space, the banker commissioned the existing gallery. Completed in 1897, the building is considered by architectural historians to be one of the finest Beaux Arts structures in the city.

Today the Corcoran Gallery houses a collection of American and European paintings, sculpture, prints, drawings and examples of the decorative arts. In fact, the American collection is among the country's best. Gilbert Stuart, John Singer Sargent, Mary Cassatt, Josef Albers and George Bellows are all represented as well as a more contemporary sampling. A European collection bequeathed to the gallery by Senator William Clark Andrews and the Walker Collection of French Impressionists have both enhanced the Corcoran's holdings. As one of the first museums to recognize photography as art, the gallery also has a fine collection of photographic prints, which is displayed in frequently changing exhibits.

The Corcoran is a local museum as well as one of national prominence. The gallery counts among its major purposes the display of works of artists from the Washington metropolitan area, and tries to fulfill that purpose with numerous exhibits and special events.

With the help of the museum's free map/brochure, available at the entrance, you can wander through the exhibits with knowledge and confidence. Be sure not to miss Samuel F. B. Morse's (yes, the inventor of the telegraph) famous painting "The Old House of Representatives" and Hiram Powers' sculpture "The Greek Slave," which was considered quite scandalous in the nineteenth century.

The Corcoran's impressive rotunda is the scene of frequent special events; check the newspapers, call the gallery or pick up the Corcoran's calendar of events while at the gallery to see if anything is scheduled during your visit.

Don't miss the Corcoran Gallery gift shop. One of the best in town, it sells fine crafts, unusually nice toys, jewelry and an excellent selection of cards and books.

THE DAR MUSEUM   (202) 879-3241
(Daughters of the American Revolution)
1776 D Street, NW 20006
Hours: 8:30 A.M.–4 P.M. weekdays
      1–5 P.M. Sunday
Free Admission

 Farragut West stop (blue and orange lines—use 17th Street exit) or Farragut North stop (red line—use K Street exit); walk south on 17th Street five blocks.

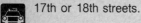 17th or 18th streets.

 Competitive parking along 17th and 18th Streets.

 The "Touch of Independence" tour, held during regular tour hours, is designed for kids 4–11 to let them physically explore replicas of objects from the seventeenth through the late nineteenth centuries. "Colonial Adventure," a program for five- to seven-year-olds, is a one-hour program held the first and third Sundays of most months. Reservations are necessary. "Colonial Child" is a program for elementary-aged children held weekdays for school groups. To arrange for these programs, call (202) 879-3239.

 Arrange for group tours three weeks in advance by calling (202) 879-3254.

 Accessible.

 Quilt and costume programs and American textile identification clinics are available on selected dates each month for a small fee. Reservations are required; call (202) 879-3241 for further information.

 Walk-in tours of period rooms are given continually from 10 A.M. to 2:30 P.M.

In addition to their enormous genealogical library, the Daughters of the American Revolution maintain a decorative and fine arts collection of approximately 30,000 objects at their national headquarters. Memorial Continental Hall, the building housing both the 33 period rooms and the genealogical library, was designed by Edward Pearce Casey in the Beaux Arts style, and completed in 1910. The period rooms are each furnished in the style of a particular period or region of colonial and early America. Together they trace the changing lifestyles of the United States from the seventeenth through the nineteenth centuries. Highlights include a late seventeenth-century New England home, an eighteenth-century tavern and a mid-nineteenth-century kitchen. Perhaps the most charming of the period rooms is the New Hampshire Attic, stocked with a melange of dolls, games and toys that delighted children of other eras. For the most part, furnishings predate the Industrial Revolution, although one wonderful Victorian parlor displays Belter-style sofas and chairs.

Before your tour begins, roam through the Museum Gallery on the first floor of the administration building. Visit one of the changing exhibitions in which diverse themes in American social history are explored, illustrated by the many notable objects in the collection. View the permanent displays of an excellent collection of ceramics (including an unusually fine selection of Chinese export porcelain), silver and glass. A small museum shop has books, needlework kits, postcards, jewelry and decorative items.

The DAR Genealogical Library is open to the public 8:45 A.M.–4 P.M. Monday–Friday and 1–5 P.M. Sunday. Nonmembers must pay a $5 user fee on weekdays, $3 on Sunday. For further library information, call (202) 879-3228.

DECATUR HOUSE   (202) 673-4030
748 Jackson Place, NW 20006
Hours: 10 A.M.–3 P.M. Tuesday–Friday
    Noon–4 P.M. Saturday–Sunday
    Closed Thanksgiving, Christmas and New Year's
Admission: Adults—$3   Children and Senior Citizens—$1.50

M Farragut West stop (blue and orange lines)—walk east on I Street for two blocks and south on Connecticut Avenue for one; Farragut North stop (red line, K Street exit)—walk south across Farragut Square, then one block south on Connecticut Avenue.

🚗 H Street or Pennsylvania Avenue.

P Very difficult street parking; commercial lots in neighborhood.

👪 Not recommended unless a child is particularly interested in American history.

 Group tours can be arranged by calling (202) 842-0920.

♿ Fully accessible, but call ahead to notify staff of your arrival.

T Walk-in guided tours are given on the hour and half-hour.

In 1819, Commodore Stephen Decatur, popular hero of United States sea battles against the Barbary pirates and in the War of 1812, moved into his imposing brick town house near the White House. Decatur House, the first private residence constructed on Lafayette Square, was designed by Benjamin Henry Latrobe, possibly the most prominent architect practicing in America at that time. It is an excellent example of the Federal style, with its very formal, simple facade and its square and sturdy but elegant shape. Unfortunately, neither architect nor owner long survived the construction of the house. A year after moving in, Decatur was killed in a duel with a fellow officer. In the same year, Latrobe succumbed to yellow fever without ever having seen the finished house. Immediately after Decatur's death, his widow left the house and never returned.

Decatur House became the residence of a succession of foreign diplomats and American politicians and statesmen, including Henry Clay, Martin Van Buren and Judah Benjamin (later to become secretary of state for the Confederacy). During the Civil War, Decatur House, like many other homes around Lafayette Square, was seized by the government for use as offices and storage. It was bought in the 1870s by General Edward Fitzgerald Beale, a colorful figure best known for his role in the settlement of the American West. In the 1940s, his daughter-in-law, socialite Marie Beale, restored the exterior of Decatur House to its 1820s appearance. She bequeathed Decatur House to the National Trust for Historic Preservation, and it served for many years as national headquarters of the trust. (The new headquarters is in a beautiful and architecturally significant restored Beaux Arts-style building at 1785 Massachusetts Avenue, NW.)

More than any other Washington building except, perhaps, the White House, Decatur House tells the tale of influence, ambition, statesmanship and diplomacy, of the great men who came to the capital city and how they lived.

A nineteenth-century crafts fair is held annually at Decatur House in November during Historic Preservation Week. The National Trust for Historic Preservation Shop is around the corner at 1600 H Street; it's full of books, reproductions, classy T-shirts and wonderful gifts galore.

FBI   **(202) 324-3447**
(J. Edgar Hoover Building)
10th Street and Pennsylvania Avenue, NW 20535
(entrance on E Street)
Hours: 8:45 A.M.–4:15 P.M. weekdays
          Closed holidays
Free Admission

 Federal Triangle stop (blue and orange lines); Gallery Place stop (red, green and yellow lines); walk down 9th Street toward Pennsylvania Avenue.

Pennsylvania Avenue.

 Commercial parking available along 9th Street.

 Recommended, although fast pace of tour may cause kids to miss some information. The wait for the tour can be as long as three hours.

 Tours available for groups of 20 or more. To make a reservation write on your group's letterhead one year in advance.

 Fully accessible. When you arrive, check at the VIP entrance at the top of the ramp at 9th and E streets; if sufficient tour staff are available, you will be admitted immediately.

 Tours can be arranged if your group brings its own interpreter. Call TDD (202) 324-1016 four weeks in advance to make arrangements.

 Contact your members of Congress well in advance of your trip to arrange for a VIP tour with no wait.

 Walk-in one-hour tours are given continually; the wait in line can be long (up to three hours from April through September). No admittance to the building except on the tours.

In one of the least attractive government buildings in town, the FBI presents a lively, fast-paced tour of its working space that has become one of Washington's most popular tourist attractions. A sure hit with children over kindergarten age, the tour (which is rigidly supervised by cheerful but firm FBI employees) takes visitors quickly past exhibits that feature gangster paraphernalia and relics of some of the more prominent bad guys done in by federal agents, weapon displays, fingerprint and serology labs, a tape recording of an actual kidnap ransom demand and J. Edgar Hoover's office desk and chair. The tour ends with a rousing marksmanship demonstration using a standard FBI Smith and Wesson revolver and a Thompson submachine gun.

FORD'S THEATRE   **(202) 426-6924**
511 10th Street, NW 20004
THE HOUSE WHERE LINCOLN DIED
(Petersen House)
516 10th Street, NW 20004

Hours: 9 A.M.–5 P.M. daily
Closed Christmas
Closed during matinees and rehearsals (call ahead to check)
Free Admission

 Metro Center stop (red, blue and orange lines—use the 11th Street exit); Gallery Place-Chinatown stop (red, green and yellow lines); walk down 10th Street.

F Street.

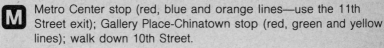 Street parking is practically impossible. Commercial lots are in the neighborhood.

Recommended; kids love the museum and presentations.

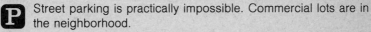 First floor of theater is accessible; ask a ranger for assistance. National Park Service is working on ensuring accessibility to the museum; call ahead to see if the system is working. The second floor of the theater and the House Where Lincoln Died are inaccessible.

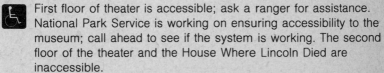 Visitors with visual impairments can enter the box where Lincoln was shot. Call (202) 426-6924 in advance to make arrangements.

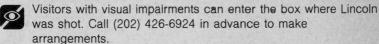 A signed tour is available; call (202) 426-6924 or TDD (202) 426-1749 two weeks in advance to make arrangements.

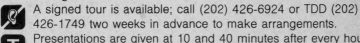 Presentations are given at 10 and 40 minutes after every hour except when a play is in rehearsal.

At Ford's Theatre, where President Lincoln was shot in 1865, the National Park Service effectively interprets the event, both in performance and displays of artifacts. The building, restored in 1968, is once again functioning as a professional theater; it's one of the busiest tourist sites in Washington. But don't despair; the theater seating is generous and there's rarely much of a wait for the tour. In the theater's basement, the Lincoln Museum houses glass cases displaying objects relating to Lincoln's time in Washington and his assassination. An exhibit contains the diary John Wilkes Booth wrote after the killing, as well as other treasures. Books, postcards and posters are sold at the bookstore.

Upstairs in the restored auditorium, park rangers give a 15-minute presentation twice hourly on the events leading up to Lincoln's assassination. (These talks are canceled if a play is being rehearsed or if staff is limited.) If you miss the talk, a well-written free brochure (available in six languages) can provide you with the background information that will make your visit to the theater more meaningful. Visitors are invited to walk around the balcony and peer into the Presidential box from which Lincoln was watching *Our American Cousin* the night he was shot.

You'll probably want to follow your visit to Ford's Theatre with a trip across the street to the Petersen House, where Lincoln was taken after the shooting. This house has been restored and furnished to re-create the way it was on April 15, 1865, the morning Lincoln died there.

See Chapter 13, "Entertainment," for ticket information for Ford's Theatre's stage performances.

NATIONAL AQUARIUM   (202) 482-2825 (recorded information)
14th Street, between Pennsylvania and Constitution avenues, NW 20230
Commerce Department basement
Hours: 9 A.M.–5 P.M. daily
          Closed Christmas
Admission: Adults—$2   Children and Senior Citizens—75¢

M Federal Triangle stop (blue and orange lines).

14th Street or Pennsylvania Avenue.

P Commercial parking north of Pennsylvania Avenue.

On premises. A cafeteria is open from 9 A.M. to 2 P.M. on weekdays.

Highly recommended.

Fully accessible.

The National Aquarium, founded in 1873, is the oldest aquarium in the country. The constant activity of more than 1,200 marine and freshwater animals, viewed through the bottle-green light of the tanks in Commerce's basement, seems to keep visitors of all ages happy. A tiny hands-on tidal pool should delight your small fry; adolescents love shark and piranha feeding times. (Sharks are fed Monday, Wednesday and Saturday at 2 P.M.; piranhas get lunch Tuesday, Thursday and Sunday at 2 P.M.) The Commerce Department's cafeteria provides no-nonsense food at reasonable prices when the lure of the deep wears off. You can replenish your film at the aquarium's small bookstore.

While in the building, pop upstairs to see the census clock in the lobby of the Commerce Department. The clock's face shows the constant changes in our population, as we are born, die, immigrate and emigrate.

NATIONAL BUILDING MUSEUM   **(202) 272-2448**
F Street, Between 4th and 5th Streets, NW 20001
Hours: 10 A.M.–4 P.M. Monday–Saturday
       Noon–4 P.M. Sunday and Holidays
       Closed Thanksgiving, Christmas, and New Year's
Free Admission

M Judiciary Square stop (red line); F Street exit.

Judiciary Square area.

P Competitive street parking; some commercial lots.

Recommended for children. Occasional workshops offered for families and school groups; call (202) 272-2448 for a schedule and reservations or to arrange a child-oriented tour.

Call (202) 272-2448 to arrange for a group tour.

Fully accessible.

A special permanent exhibit, "Washington: Symbol and City," was planned in conjunction with the American Foundation for the Blind. Tactile models, a rail guide and audio tapes are all available.

T Walk-in tours are given at 12:30 P.M. Monday–Friday and 12:30 and 1:30 P.M. Saturday–Sunday and holidays.

The National Building Museum celebrates America's building heritage in grand fashion. Not only does it serve as a monument to the building arts, but it is housed in one of Washington's greatest works of public architecture, the U.S. Pension Building. This massive structure, under construction from 1881 to 1887, is 400 feet long and 200 feet wide and is built of 15.5 million bricks; it's encircled by a 1,200-foot-long terra-cotta frieze representing a continuous procession of Civil War soldiers and sailors.

In an effort to promote a healthy work environment for the 1,500 clerks processing pensions, Montgomery C. Meigs, the architect, designed a single huge hall with plenty of light and air, and for added ventilation, he omitted three bricks below every window. Clearly, Mr. Meigs was ahead of his time with his concern for a healthy and productive workplace.

The Pension Building's Great Hall is a spectacular space, the size of a football field, soaring to 159 feet at its highest point—the height of a 15-story building. It has served as the elegant site for inaugural balls, including that of Bill Clinton.

Permanent exhibits at the Building Museum include "Washington, DC: Symbol and City," an interactive display that traces the building of Washington over the past 200 years; it serves as an excellent orientation to the city. "To Build a Bridge" uses seven large-scale models, photographs, drawings and text to illustrate the stages by which a suspension bridge is built—in this case, the Brooklyn Bridge. "The Pension Building" explores the architectural inspirations and engineering innovations of the Building Museum's grand home.

Each spring and fall, the museum sponsors Construction Watch, a tour of various building sites around town. Call (202) 272-2448 for reservations and specific dates. Free walking tours are given of 7th Street/Judiciary Square and 7th Street/Chinatown on Wednesday at 10:30 A.M. and Saturday and Sunday at 2 P.M. Call (202) 272-2448 for reservations. Every month the museum sponsors classical music concerts in the Great Hall at noon. Call (202) 272-2448 for a schedule. In May, a daylong Festival of the Building Arts is held with hands-on demonstrations of the building arts.

The museum shop offers a fine selection of books on architects and architecture, classy T-shirts and ties, and numerous objects of interesting and fine design.

NATIONAL GEOGRAPHIC SOCIETY HEADQUARTERS

(202) 857-7000

Exhibit Information: (202) 857-7588 (tape)

17th and M Streets, NW 20036

Hours: 9 A.M.–5 P.M. Monday–Saturday and holidays
10 A.M.–5 P.M. Sunday
Closed Christmas

Free Admission

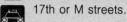 Farragut North (L Street exit); walk one block east to 17th Street, then one block north.

17th or M streets.

P Difficult metered street parking; many commercial lots in area. On weekends and for weeknight programs, limited free parking is available in the building for scheduled programs.

Highly recommended. Lots of interesting interactive exhibits. Call (202) 857-7689 to arrange for special school tours. Children and Society members receive discounts for all ticketed events.

To arrange a tour for 10 or more people, call (202) 857-7689 and ask for the coordinator of Education and Special Tours.

Accessible. There is a ramp on the 17th Street side of the building. Rest room is accessible but the phone is not.

Special tours can be arranged by contacting the coordinator of Education and Special Tours at (202) 857-7689.

Special tours can be arranged by contacting the coordinator of Education and Special Tours at (202) 857-7689. The auditorium is electronically equipped to assist people with hearing disabilities. In addition you can request a signed interpretation for any performance by calling (202) 857-7700 or TDD (202) 857-7198 at least two weeks in advance.

The Explorers Hall exhibit area in the National Geographic Society's headquarters is an extension of the society's glossy, colorful magazine. Dramatic displays, often with audio and interactive graphic accompaniment, inform visitors about some of the exciting exploratory missions of the Society. Permanent exhibits include a freestanding globe—the world's largest, 11 feet from pole to pole; "Geographica," a collection of interactive exhibits that explore research on early man, astronomy, weather and botany, among other topics; and Earth Station One, an interactive theater that simulates an orbital flight above the Earth and quizzes the audience on world geography.

In addition, temporary exhibits are mounted annually; call (202) 857-7588 to find out what's on while you're in town. The Explorers Hall gift shop is the only place where Society publications may be purchased over the counter. Maps, globes and videos are also for sale. The National Geographic Society also houses a reference library that is open to the public from 8:30 A.M. to 5 P.M. weekdays.

The Society sponsors a series of performances, films, and illustrated lectures on weeknights and weekends. Ticket prices vary. Call (202) 857-7700 for information and reservations. Free film and multi-image presentations are offered most Tuesdays in the spring and fall at noon. All performances are held in the Gilbert H. Grosvenor Auditorium, 1600 M Street.

NATIONAL MUSEUM OF AMERICAN ART   (202) 357-2700

8th and G streets, NW 20560
Hours: 10 A.M.–5:30 P.M. daily
　　　Closed Christmas
Free Admission

M Gallery Place stop (red, green and yellow lines); use 9th Street exit.

7th or 9th streets.

P Limited metered street parking; commercial lots on 9th Street between E and I streets.

On premises. Patent Pending, a small but notable cafeteria, offers soups, breads, sandwiches, and hot entrées. In mild weather, you can eat at tables in the museum's courtyard. Cafeteria hours are 11 A.M.–3 P.M. daily.

Recommended for older children.

Arrangements for group tours must be made at least two weeks in advance by contacting the Education Office at (202) 357-3111.

Fully accessible. Wheelchairs are available. A ramped entrance is at 9th and G streets.

Special tours can be arranged by calling (202) 357-3111 at least 48 hours in advance.

Special tours can be arranged by calling (202) 357-3111 or TDD (202) 357-4522 48 hours in advance.

T Noon on weekdays; 2 P.M. on Saturdays and Sundays (one hour) Call (202) 357-3111 for special exhibition tours.

The National Museum of American Art shares elegant quarters with the National Portrait Gallery in the Old Patent Office Building, one of the great neoclassical buildings in the country. While the museum is part of the Smithsonian, the American Art collection predates the Institution's existence by 30 years—it's the oldest Federal art collection in the United States. The original collection was displayed in the Patent Office in the 1840s along with shrunken heads, the original Declaration of Independence, stuffed birds and Benjamin Franklin's printing press. The collection shifted locations throughout the years until it returned permanently to the Patent Office Building in 1968.

The museum holds over 34,000 works, primarily American paintings, graphics, photographs, folk art and sculpture dating from the eighteenth century to the present. (The museum's collections of crafts and design are shown at the Renwick Gallery.) Among modern artists represented are Alexander Calder, Stuart Davis, Edward Hopper, Isamu Noguchi, Franz Kline, Robert Rauschenberg and Helen Frankenthaler. Early American masters like Gilbert Stuart and Benjamin West vie for attention with a large collection of George Catlin's Indian paintings, Hiram Powers' plasters (models for his finished sculptures) and paintings by Winslow Homer and Albert Pinkham Ryder.

The third-floor Lincoln Gallery—called by many "the greatest room in Washington"—houses post-World War II paintings and sculptures. The Hampton Throne, the impressive and eccentric visionary work of Washingtonian James Hampton, is on view on the first-floor. Major exhibitions planned for 1994–1995 include "Thomas Cole" and "Roy DeCarava: Four Decades of Photography."

The Old Patent Office Building is worth a visit just for itself. Designed in the 1830s by William Parker Elliott and Robert Mills (who later designed the Washington Monument and the Treasury Building), the structure is an outstanding example of Greek Revival architecture. When Washington was still swampland with livestock roaming through the streets, the massive building must have been impressive indeed.

During the Civil War, the edifice was used as barracks, hospital and morgue for Union forces. Clara Barton—then a Patent Office clerk and later founder of the Red Cross—tended the wounded, who were visited by President Lincoln and Walt Whitman. In 1865, Lincoln's second inaugural reception was held on the third floor—now the Lincoln Gallery.

Various government agencies used the building until the 1950s, when it was slated to be razed for a new parking lot. Strong opposition convinced Congress to turn the historic site over to the Smithsonian for restoration and use as the home of the National Collection of Fine Arts—now the National Museum of American Art.

Postcards, posters, jewelry, catalogs and books are available in the museum shop, and the cafeteria (shared with the National Portrait Gallery) is a pleasant place to sort your thoughts and decide which gallery to visit next.

Occasional concerts and lectures are given at the museum. Check their calendar of events, which is available at the information desk, or call (202) 357-2700 to see what's on while you're in town. You can make an appointment to see some of the museum's 24,000 paintings, sculptures, prints and drawings not on exhibit. Call (202) 357-2593.

The Archives of American Art, containing 60,000 volumes of American art, history and biography, is open to scholars; for further information, inquire at the information desk or call (202) 357-2781. Slides and photos of the permanent collection are available for loan; for information, call (202) 357-1381.

NATIONAL MUSEUM OF WOMEN IN THE ARTS

(202) 783-5000

13th Street and New York Avenue, NW 20005
Hours: 10 A.M.–5 P.M. Monday–Saturday
　　　 Noon–5 P.M. Sunday
Free Admission

M Metro Center stop (red, blue and orange lines); McPherson Square stop (blue and orange lines). Walk a couple of blocks from either stop.

🚌 30's along Pennsylvania; walk north on 13th Street for three blocks. P2.

🚕 New York Avenue.

P Commercial lots nearby.

🍽 The Mezzanine Café is open 11:30 A.M. to 2:30 P.M., Monday to Saturday. Sandwiches, salads and other light fare are served.

👪 Recommended. Tours are offered for grades 1–12; call the Education Department ((202) 783-7370) at least three weeks in advance. Occasional weekend programs are offered for children; call the Education Department for a schedule.

 Call or write the Education Department ((202) 783-7370) two weeks in advance for information on tours.

 Fully accessible. Ramp and elevator at New York Avenue entrance.

 Special tours can be arranged by calling three weeks in advance.

 Special tours can be arranged by calling three weeks in advance.

 Call two days in advance to request a highlight tour of the museum.

The National Museum of Women in the Arts is the first of its kind in the world. Opened in 1987, this young museum celebrates the contributions of women to the history of art, a long-overlooked segment of the creative world.

From the Renaissance to the present, European to Native American, the permanent collection includes paintings, drawings, sculpture, pottery, prints, books and photography. The earliest work is by Lavina Fontana, a leading artist in Bologna during the 1500s, a court artist to the Pope, painter of altarpieces and mother and supporter of 11 children. More modern works include those of Georgia O'Keeffe and Helen Frankenthaler.

NMWA's exhibitions present women's artistic accomplishments. Historical exhibitions survey the art of centuries past; individual and group shows highlight modern and contemporary art. Major shows in 1994–1995 will include "Traditions in Transition: Artists of the Arab World" and "The Problematic of 'Identity' in Art by Northern California Women."

The museum is housed in a beautiful and elegant Renaissance Revival building designed by Waddy Butler Wood in 1907. Originally a Masonic temple, the edifice hosted an adult movie theater before the award-winning renovation converted it to the National Museum of Women in the Arts.

The Library and Research Center is the world's most extensive collection of information on women artists. Scholars and students may consult the books, periodicals, slides and photographs by appointment. Lectures, film and art seminars and musical, dance and theatrical performances are held in the auditorium (ask for a schedule); in addition, conferences and workshops are held regularly at the museum. Don't miss the notecards, posters, scarves and other gifts available in the shop.

NATIONAL PORTRAIT GALLERY   **(202) 357-2700**
8th and F streets, NW 20560
Hours: 10 A.M.–5:30 P.M. daily
      Closed Christmas
Free Admission

M Gallery Place stop (red, green and yellow lines); use 9th Street exit.

7th or 9th streets.

P Limited metered street parking; commercial lots on 9th Street between F and H streets.

On premises. Patent Pending, a small but notable cafeteria, offers soups, breads, sandwiches, and hot entrées. In mild weather, you can eat at tables in the museum's courtyard. Cafeteria hours are 11 A.M. to 3 P.M. daily.

Recommended—especially the Hall of Presidents. Special programs are available for school-aged children. Call (202) 357-2920 for a brochure or to make arrangements.

Group tours available. Make arrangements at least two weeks in advance by calling the Education Department at (202) 357-2920.

Fully accessible. Ramped entrance is at 9th and G streets.

Special tours can be arranged by calling (202) 786-2942 at least three days in advance.

Special tours can be arranged by calling TDD (202) 357-1696 at least three days in advance.

T Walk-in guided tours are available from 10 A.M. to 3 P.M. on weekdays and 11 A.M. to 1:30 P.M. on weekends and holidays.

The National Portrait Gallery is the nation's official picture album. The best-known faces in American history—and some little-known ones as well—are represented here in paintings, sculpture, drawings, prints, silhouettes and photographs. The Hall of Presidents and the

Gallery of Notable Americans are permanent exhibits. Temporary exhibits abound, offering frequent changes of pace and subject; call (202) 357-2866 to request a calendar of events. Exhibits planned for 1994–1995 include: "Reporting the War: Journalistic Coverage of World War II," which commemorates the fiftieth anniversary of the war; "Pictorialist Portraits from the National Portrait Gallery Collection," a collection of stunning photos; "Photographs of Gertrude Kasebier," an early woman photographer—this show has been organized by the Museum of Modern Art; and a blockbuster, "Striving for the Ideal: Cecilia Beaux and the Portrait Tradition," which is the first retrospective of this gifted contemporary of John Singer Sargent.

Slide and lecture programs are given throughout the year; call (202) 357-2920 for information and scheduling.

The Portrait Gallery shares the building, cafeteria and gift shop with the National Museum of American Art. See that site report for the building's interesting history.

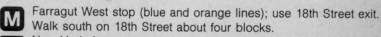

THE OCTAGON   **(202) 638-3105**
1799 New York Avenue, NW (at 18th Street) 20006
Hours: 10 A.M.–4 P.M. Tuesday–Friday
          Noon–4 P.M. weekends
          Closed Thanksgiving, Christmas and New Year's
Donations Requested (Adults—$1   Senior Citizens and Children—50¢; half-price during renovation)

M Farragut West stop (blue and orange lines); use 18th Street exit. Walk south on 18th Street about four blocks.

New York Avenue.

P Competitive street parking on side streets in area; commercial lots on New York Avenue.

Not recommended for kids under 12.

Tours available. Reservations must be made at least two weeks in advance for groups of 10 or more. Fee charged for groups: $3 for adults, 50¢ for senior citizens and kids.

Limited accessibility. Only the first floor is accessible to people in wheelchairs; enter through the garden. The rest room is not accessible; there is no phone. A video showing the entire house is available for viewing on the first floor.

Call TDD (202) 638-1558 one month in advance to arrange a tour.

Walk-in tours are given continually.

The Octagon, built from 1799 to 1801, is one of the few central Washington buildings that survived the British entry into the capital during the War of 1812. A fine example of Federal-style architecture, the Octagon was built as the city home of the John Tayloe family. Tayloe, a Virginia plantation owner, was persuaded by his friend, George Washington, to build his winter home in the new capital rather than in Philadelphia. The house was designed by William Thornton, who served as the first architect of the Capitol.

When the British burned The White House and the Capitol, the Octagon was spared—perhaps because the French minister who was residing there prominently flew his nation's flag from the house. When President James Madison and his wife, Dolley, returned to the city to find their house in ruins, they stayed at the Octagon. It was here, in the second-floor parlor, that Madison signed the Treaty of Ghent that ended the War of 1812. The table on which the document was signed is on display, along with other Federal-period furnishings.

Today, the Octagon is operated as a historic house museum by the American Architectural Foundation; not only can visitors tour the house, but they can also see changing architectural and historical exhibitions in the second-floor exhibit area. The Octagon is undergoing extensive renovations, so not all rooms may be open for viewing during your visit.

The Octagon is reported to harbor a number of Tayloe family ghosts, but this is a topic not stressed in the architecturally oriented tours. Visitors are treated very graciously. A small sales area in the entrance hall offers books and pamphlets of architectural interest.

The American Institute of Architects headquarters building is located behind the Octagon; occasional exhibits are presented in the first- and second-floor lobbies of that building.

THE PAVILION AT THE OLD POST OFFICE (202) 289-4224
THE NANCY HANKS CENTER
National Park Service Tour: (202) 606-8691

Pennsylvania Avenue at 12th Street, NW 20004
Hours: Retail: 10 A.M.–8 P.M. Monday–Saturday
        Noon–6 P.M. Sunday
     Cookery: 10 A.M.–9 P.M. Monday–Saturday
        (check for winter hours)
        Noon–8 P.M. Sunday
     Tour: April–September 8 A.M.–11 P.M.
        October–March 10 A.M.–6 P.M.
Free Admission

M Federal Triangle (orange and blue lines).

Pennsylvania Avenue.

P Commercial garages north of Pennsylvania Avenue.

A wide assortment of restaurants and food kiosks on premises.

Recommended.

Coupons are available to groups for meal deals and discounts at the retail outlets.

Accessible.

An interpreter is available to accompany tours; call in advance to make arrangements.

T Walk-in guided tours of the tower are given every 20 minutes.

The Pavilion at the Old Post Office/Nancy Hanks Center offers lunch, dinner, snacks, entertainment, shopping, a workplace for federal employees and the second best view of Washington you can find (the Washington Monument is still the best, but the waiting time at the Post Office is a fraction of the monument's line time). Although today the building exemplifies the best in cooperative use of public space, it's a wonder that it stands at all.

In 1899, the *New York Times* labeled the newly completed U.S. Post Office Department building "a cross between a cathedral and a cotton mill." Designed by Willoughby J. Edbrooke in the Richard-sonian Romanesque style (identified by some as the first truly American architectural style), the building attracted a bevy of critics who called for its demise, particularly after the postmaster general moved to new quarters in 1934. A demolition permit was issued in 1971, but a coalition of preservationists and Nancy Hanks, then head of the National Endowment for the Arts, saved the structure. The Old Post Office became the first building to be renovated under the Public Building Cooperative Use Act, changing government space into a shared public space. Congress named the Old Post Office and its adjacent plazas The Nancy Hanks Center in honor of Ms. Hanks' preservationist efforts. A 15-minute video, *All But Condemned . . . ,* details the history of the Old Post Office Building (shown continually 8 A.M.–11 P.M. April–September, 10 A.M.–6 P.M. October–March.

The Pavilion, as the retail/restaurant/eatery section is called, is a cheerful, bustling place. A variety of ethnic and American food kiosks and restaurants will give even the most exhausted tourist new energy to shop for souvenirs, bubble bath, toys, sunglasses and so forth. Entertainment is offered daily at noon and 5 P.M. on the central stage.

The National Park Service conducts a 15-minute tour of the clock tower, its 270-foot observation deck and the Congress Bells, a 1976 gift to Congress from the Ditchley Foundation of Great Britain to commemorate the 200th anniversary of the end of the American Revolution. The bells are played on national holidays, the opening and closing sessions of Congress and every Thursday evening from 7 to 9 P.M. (the tower is closed when the bells are rung).

Every New Year's Eve at midnight, a large replica of a postage stamp is lowered from the tower.

RENWICK GALLERY   (202) 357-2700
17th Street and Pennsylvania Avenue, NW 20560
Hours: 10 A.M.–5:30 P.M. daily
      Closed Christmas
Free Admission

 Farragut West stop (blue and orange lines) or Farragut North stop (red line); walk south on 17th Street.
 Pennsylvania Avenue.

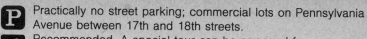

P Practically no street parking; commercial lots on Pennsylvania Avenue between 17th and 18th streets.

Recommended. A special tour can be arranged for elementary-school children by calling (202) 357-2531 two–three weeks in advance.

Call (202) 357-2531 three weeks in advance to make arrangements for group tours.

Limited accessibility. People in wheelchairs will need to use the ramp at the corner of Pennsylvania Avenue and 17th Street. Wheelchairs are available at the gallery.

Tours for visually impaired people can be arranged by calling (202) 357-2531 two or three weeks in advance.

Tours for hearing-impaired people can be arranged by calling (202) 357-2531 two or three weeks in advance.

A All tours are given by appointment only. Call (202) 357-2531 for an appointment.

If you enjoy crafts, the Renwick Gallery will be a most exciting place to visit. The Renwick is the National Museum of American Art's department of American crafts, decorative arts and design. Since opening in 1972, the gallery's exhibits have ranged from stark Shaker household goods to architectonic furniture and stained glass by Frank Lloyd Wright to the masterworks of Louis Comfort Tiffany.

Constructed in 1859, the Renwick was originally designed to hold the art collection of William Wilson Corcoran. Look for his monogram and his portrait in stone on the building's front facade. Its architect and namesake was James Renwick, who pulled out all the stops to create one of Washington's highest expressions of surpassingly high-style French Second Empire architecture. Renwick also designed the Smithsonian Castle building on the Mall.

During the Civil War, the building was used by the U.S. Army's Quartermaster Corps and, in 1871, was the site of a gala ball attended by President and Mrs. Grant to raise funds for completion of the Washington Monument. The building was restored to Corcoran in 1874. Taking a cue from the octagonal gallery designed to show off the "Venus de Milo" at the Louvre, Corcoran raised Victorian eyebrows by building his own Octagon Room to display Hiram Powers' graceful nude sculpture, "The Greek Slave."

By 1897, Corcoran's collection had grown too large for the Renwick and was moved to its present quarters, the great Beaux Arts structure on 17th Street that bears Corcoran's name (see site report). The U.S. Court of Claims took possession of the Renwick and used it for the next 65 years.

When its demolition was contemplated in the 1960s, the Smithsonian rescued the building and meticulously restored it to a purpose more compatible with its origins. Corcoran's times, if not his collection, are evoked in the Renwick's plush second-floor Grand Salon and Octagon Room, hung with nineteenth-century American paintings and dotted with sculpture of the same period. The rest of the exhibit space is devoted to changing displays of American crafts as well as a selection of twentieth-century objects from its permanent collection. Exhibitions planned for 1994–1995 include "Contemporary Navajo Weaving: The Gloria F. Ross Collection of the Denver Art Museum" and "From Hand to Hand: The Saxe Contemporary Crafts Collection."

The gift shop is terrific, offering crafts and an excellent selection of books and publications devoted to crafts.

The gallery also hosts occasional concerts, films, lectures and crafts demonstrations. Call the gallery to see what's scheduled during your visit, or request the monthly calendar of events for the National Museum of American Art, of which the Renwick is a part. Send your name and address to Office of Public Affairs, Room 182, National Museum of American Art, Smithsonian Institution, Washington, D.C. 20560.

———————————

TECH 2000   **(202) 408-8037**
Techworld Plaza—8th and K streets, NW 20001
(one block east of Washington Convention Center)
Hours: Noon–8 P.M. Monday
          11 A.M.–5 P.M. Tuesday–Sunday
          Closed Thanksgiving, Christmas and New Year's
Admission: Adults—$5   Students—$4   Children under 12 and Senior Citizens—$3

Gallery Place-Chinatown stop (red line), Chinatown exit; walk north two blocks to Mount Vernon Square, then one block west. Mount Vernon Square stop (yellow and green lines).

K Street, Massachusetts Avenue or New York Avenue.

Garage entrances at 7th and K streets, NW, or 9th and I streets, NW.

 Restaurants, food court and outdoor cafe in Techworld Plaza.

 Highly recommended, especially upstairs games.

 An hour-long guided tour is available for $25 for the group, plus admission. Contact Visitor Services Director.

Fully accessible.

 No special services available. Gallery includes a special application.

 No special services available. Gallery includes a special application.

Tech 2000 is the world's first hands-on gallery of interactive multimedia. More than 70 exhibits demonstrate how the marriage of computer and video technology is changing the ways we learn, work, entertain, acquire information and communicate.

This is a dazzling and fun tour, whether for the electronics whiz or the computer-shy. Orientation starts with a two-minute video explanation of visual information, where film, video, text, audio and computer software all combine to create interactive media programs. Then you'll see—and get to play with—a variety of exciting exhibits.

In the Arts and Culture Area, embark upon a variety of art tours: see much of the collection of the National Gallery of Art, selecting paintings by artist, style or subject; see any of Van Gogh's paintings by accessing just a key word, for instance; or learn about the history of illuminated manuscripts and see some of the world's finest examples, among other things.

An exhibit in the Town Square is on drug and alcohol education where the viewer watches a video of a high school party and selects which partygoer to follow and interact with in a series of questions. In the Working Area, exhibits demonstrate interactive video applications including sales training, aircraft maintenance and simulations for fire fighters.

The Education and Learning Center contains American Memory, a captivating encyclopedia of twentieth-century events on laser disc. Here, you can call up actual news footage in a variety of categories, even your favorite President on the golf course.

An exhibit called "ConFINGERation" teaches sign language; when you type in a letter, its image appears on the video monitor almost instantaneously. Screen Reader, an educational tool for visually impaired people, provides users with voice output of information on a screen, for popular software programs.

American Nature is a video wall presentation; on 16 screens you'll be treated to a spectacular half-hour tour—one laser disc runs the show and a computer splits the images.

Upstairs in the Home area, you'll discover Home Theater Jukebox, which serves up popular movies at the touch of a button (72 laser discs store a couple of dozen feature films). Young kids especially will enjoy video-painting, part of early learning on a personal computer. Kids of all ages will have great fun with the simulations, whether playing golf or maneuvering an ice run; don't miss the opportunity to see a simulation of yourself performing in a band.

The center was developed jointly by the 170-member organizations of the Interactive Video Industry Association and Techworld Plaza, Washington's largest mixed-use center.

Take a break from your more serious Washington touring and go marvel and play at Tech 2000!

THE WHITE HOUSE   **(202) 456-7041 (recorded information)**
1600 Pennsylvania Avenue, NW 20500
Hours: 10 A.M.–noon Tuesday–Saturday
        Closed Christmas and New Year's
Free Admission

Farragut West stop (blue and orange lines); 18th Street exit. Walk south on 18th Street two blocks; go east on Pennsylvania Avenue two more blocks.

Pennsylvania Avenue.

Commercial lots at 17th and H streets, along Pennsylvania Avenue between 17th and 18th streets.

Recommended, although the wait can be long.

Reserve Group Tours can be arranged for a maximum of 50 on a very limited basis through members of Congress. These guided tours view the same areas shown on the public tour.

Fully accessible. People with disabilities need not wait in line for the White House tour; go directly to the Northeast Gate on Pennsylvania Avenue for immediate admittance.

 People with disabilities need not wait in line for the White House tour; go directly to the Northeast Gate on Pennsylvania Avenue for immediate admittance.

 Special group tours given in sign language can be arranged by calling (202) 456-2202 or TDD (202) 456-2216.

 Visitors who plan ahead may be able to arrange for special tours through their members of Congress. Six months is not too far in advance, since congressional offices are deluged with requests for tickets virtually year-round. Bear in mind that senators and representatives receive a limited number of passes per day, so they are not equipped to handle large groups or last-minute requests. Foreign visitors may be able to pick up tickets at their embassies.

 Tours are given Tuesday to Saturday between 10 A.M. and noon. Because of the number of visitors who pass through the White House during this tight schedule, sightseers who want a tour of the executive mansion should be prepared for long lines and, at times, long waits. In the summer, admission is by ticket only, and tickets must be picked up in person; they are good only on the day issued and at the time specified. The tickets indicate the approximate time of your tour. They are distributed on a first-come, first-served basis beginning at 8 A.M. (often all tickets have been distributed by 9 A.M.) on the Ellipse (the park south of the White House); from Labor Day through Memorial Day, tickets are not necessary; line up at the East Gate by 10 A.M. If you are in line by noon, you are usually assured a tour. While tours aren't available in foreign languages, free brochures are printed in Spanish, French, Italian, Russian, Chinese and Japanese. Tours are not conducted during official Presidential events, so call ahead for updated tour information.

Each year more than a million and a half visitors pay their respects to the White House, home to every President and his family since 1800. When you catch sight of the lines waiting to see the White House in July and August, you may think a good portion of them have chosen the same day as you to view the "President's Palace"—so named by the city's first planner, Pierre L'Enfant. Since your visit in the White House may be as short as 10 minutes during peak tourist time, and since the tours aren't guided, it's wise to study what you'll be seeing before you arrive. For a detailed description, try an excellent guidebook to the White House and grounds, the White House Historical Association's *The White House: An Historic Guide,* available at the beginning of the tour or in many of Washington's bookstores.

In 1792, Thomas Jefferson announced a national design competition for the Presidential residence. Jefferson himself submitted a design—anonymously—and lost. The winner, James Hoban, was an Irish architect practicing in Charleston, South Carolina, who proposed a building similar to Leinster Hall in Dublin.

John Adams found the house habitable, but not comfortable, when he became its first resident in 1800. Mrs. Adams hung her laundry to dry in the drafty and unfinished East Room—Theodore Roosevelt's children later roller-skated here. And Jefferson, who had grumbled at Hoban's Anglo-Palladian design as too grand for the chief executive of a new republic ("Big enough for two emperors, one Pope and the grand Lama," he sniffed), nevertheless became the first in the long succession of Presidents who have altered, added to, repaired or redecorated the mansion when he took up residence in 1801. He added the low service wings on either side of the main block of the house.

The executive mansion was nearly burned to the ground by British troops in August 1814. In 1902, Theodore Roosevelt found the mansion in such sad disrepair that he moved to a house on Jackson Place across Lafayette Square while the White House was repaired. Harry Truman also found it necessary to leave his home in the White House when, in 1948, he found the structure so unsound—"standing up purely from habit"—that it had to be virtually rebuilt around a new steel frame. During the renovation, the Truman family lived across the street at Blair House, where visiting dignitaries now stay.

On your tour, you'll see only a few of the mansion's 132 rooms, but they're among the most historic. Visitors enter through the East Wing Lobby; through the windows you can see the Jacqueline Kennedy Rose Garden. Portraits of Presidents and their First Ladies hang in the hallway. As you pass through the Colonnade, enclosed with handmade antique glass, to the East Room, you can admire the changing exhibits on White House history.

You'll undoubtedly recognize the East Room as the site of Presidential press conferences. The portrait of George Washington that hangs here is the oldest original White House object; Dolley Madison saved it as she and President Madison fled from the advancing British fires. The East Room has been the site of great moments in history: four First Family weddings (Nellie Grant, Alice Roosevelt, Jessie Wilson and Lynda Bird Johnson), the funerals of six Presidents (Harrison, Taylor, Lincoln, Harding, Franklin Roosevelt and Kennedy), as well as Richard Nixon's farewell address to his staff. The East Room today looks much as it did after the 1902 renovation, and is used to present plays, concerts and receptions.

The Green Room is a parlor that has been bedecked with some shade of green since James Monroe refurnished the White House after the 1814 fire. Of note are: a French cut-glass chandelier, 1790; furniture pieces by Duncan Phyfe, particularly the window benches, desk and sofa, 1800–15; and the Italian marble mantel, purchased by President Monroe after the 1814 fire.

The most formal of the parlors is the Blue Room, Hoban's "elliptical salon," which now sports French Empire furnishings that date from—or are facsimiles of the furnishings of—Monroe's postconflagration decorating. The "blue" tradition of the room began in 1837 with President Van Buren. It was here that President Grover Cleveland married Frances Folsom in 1886. In this room, the President and First Lady officially receive their guests for receptions.

The final parlor, the Red Room, is furnished in the American Empire style, popular between 1810 and 1830. Perhaps the best example of this style is the small, round, inlaid mahogany and fruitwood table opposite the fireplace.

The elegant gold and white State Dining Room, where 140 dinner guests can be seated, is next on the tour. George Healy's portrait of Abraham Lincoln hangs above the marble mantel, which is inscribed with President John Adams' prayer: "I pray Heaven to Bestow the Best of Blessings on THIS HOUSE and on ALL That shall hereafter Inhabit It."

The tour concludes in the Cross Hall and North Entrance Halls, passing the main stairway to the Presidential living quarters.

For relatively uncrowded, unhassled viewing, the best visiting time is from September through February, excluding December. The spring is usually heavy with school groups, summer with vacationing families and December with those who want to see the White House Christmas decorations.

Several special tours are held each year. In December an evening candlelight tour of the seasonally decorated White House is given.

The famous White House Easter Egg Roll takes place Easter Monday for kids under 8 and their parents. In spring and fall an afternoon garden tour is conducted. The schedules for these tours are determined anew each year, so call (202) 456-7041 to check if one is planned during your visit.

WORTH NOTING

The hours of these sites vary widely, and some are only accessible by appointment. Call ahead.

American Red Cross, 431 17th Street, NW 20006, (202) 737-8300. The "Marble Palace," constructed in 1917, is the national headquarters for the American Red Cross. Of note are stained-glass windows by Louis Tiffany in the second-floor assembly hall and a garden containing sculptures honoring Red Cross workers and nurses.

Bethune Museum-Archives, 1318 Vermont Avenue, NW 20005, (202) 332-1233. Mary McLeod Bethune, one of 17 children born to ex-slaves in South Carolina, founded Bethune-Cookman College and the National Council of Negro Women, and served as an adviser to President Franklin D. Roosevelt; this museum celebrates her accomplishments. Also housed here are the National Archives for Black Women's History, documents from the National Committee on Household Employees and records from the National Council of Negro Women.

Federal Reserve Board Gallery, C Street between 20th and 21st Street, NW 20006, (202) 452-3686. Small but excellent exhibits of nineteenth- and twentieth-century American art.

Lillian and Albert Small Jewish Museum, 701 3rd Street, NW 20001, (202) 789-0900. This building served as the original home of the Adas Israel Synagogue and is a good example of nineteenth-century religious architecture—simple, unadorned, functional. The modest displays offer a glimpse of Jewish life in the Washington community over the last 100 years, including old photographs, ritual objects, letters and congregational records.

OAS Building, 17th Street and Constitution Avenue, NW 20006, (202) 458-3000. Founded in 1890, the Organization of American States is the world's oldest international organization of nations; its members include 33 nations from North, South and Central America and the Caribbean. The building was designed by Albert Kelsey and Paul Philippe Cret and constructed in 1910; the ground floor, which includes a small gallery exhibiting artworks from member nations, is open to the public.

Old Executive Office Building, Pennsylvania Avenue and 17th Street, NW 20006, (202) 395-5895. President Ulysses S. Grant declared that no general should have to function in the cramped space then available for the Army Department; he ordered the construction of the mammoth State, War and Navy Building (now the Old Executive Office Building) in 1871. Designed by A. B. Mullet in the Second Empire style, the building was completed in 1888. It satisfied Grant's requirement of spaciousness—the building was then the largest office building in the world (the Pentagon now holds that record). Tours are given every Saturday morning to view rooms restored to their appearance of 100 years ago.

Paul VI Institute for the Arts, 924 G Street, NW 20001, (202) 347-1450. This small art museum operated by the Archdiocese of Washington mounts exhibits celebrating artistic expressions of spiritual truths.

St. John's Church,16th and H Streets, NW, 20006, (202) 347-8766. Often called the Church of the Presidents, since every President since James Madison has worshiped there on some occasion, St. John's Church was originally designed in 1816 by Benjamin Henry Latrobe in an elegant Greek Revival style. Subsequent additions have obscured some of the original, but the building is still full of historical anecdotes and charm.

The Washington Post Company, 1150 15th Street, NW 20005, (202) 334-7969. On an informative one-hour tour, you can see how *The Washington Post* gets put together each day; you'll see the newsroom and printing plant and learn of the newspaper's history since it first published in 1877.

The Wilderness Society's Ansel Adams Collection, 900 17th Street, NW, 2nd floor, 20006, (202) 833-2300. Seventy-five of Ansel Adams' most important landscape photographs are on permanent display in the Wilderness Society's gallery. A gift from the artist, the photographs have played a critical role in the evolution of American attitudes toward nature and conservation.

Treasury Building, 15th Street and Pennsylvania Avenue, NW 20220, (202) 622-0896. Weekend tours are given of this National Historic Landmark, highlighting its architecture, history and recent restoration projects.

U.S. Navy Memorial, 7th Street and Pennsylvania Avenue, NW 20004 (202) 737-2300. A circular plaza with waterfalls and Stanley Bleifeld's sculpture "Lone Sailor" commemorate sailors through the U.S. Navy's long history. The visitors' center continuously displays "At Sea," a film that despicts this illustrious history. Military bands perform many summer evenings; call for a schedule of performances.

A STROLL DOWN THE MAIN STREET
OF THE NATION—PENNSYLVANIA AVENUE

Pennsylvania Avenue is undergoing a major revitalization campaign intended to complete, once and for all, L'Enfant's conception of a grand boulevard extending from the White House to the Capitol. While the Mall blossomed into L'Enfant's original vision, Pennsylvania Avenue deteriorated, becoming the home of Washington's red-light district. (During the Civil War, General Hooker attempted to control the ever-increasing number of ladies of the night who were attracted to Washington by the permanent presence of thousands of soldiers. He created a red-light district south of Pennsylvania Avenue from 7th to 14th streets. The ladies became known as "Hooker's Division"—later shortened to "hookers.") On his inaugural ride from the Capitol to the White House in 1961, President Kennedy viewed Pennsylvania Avenue's plight—tired retail shops, abandoned lots and buildings, dreary federal offices—as a national disgrace, planting the seed of its renaissance.

The Pennsylvania Avenue Development Corporation (PADC) has drawn a master plan for the avenue that, when completed, will provide the area with 1,200–1,500 hotel rooms, over 1,700 residential units, a slew of retail spaces, acres of offices, 700 willow oak trees, various street furniture and seven parks and plazas. Many of the architectural gems that remained on the avenue have been renovated for modern use. Concentrated on the north side of the avenue, the plan fills in the gaps left by two centuries of sporadic and unplanned development. Construction is under way—there's no telling what you'll encounter on your visit.

From the White House, follow the avenue east one block to the Treasury Building, considered to be one of the finest Greek Revival civic structures in the United States. The entire building, which covers five acres, is now faced with granite, but original wings were constructed of aquia sandstone, like the White House. The existing edifice is the third Treasury Building on this site. The first one suffered two disastrous fires, one accidentally in 1801, the other in 1814 at the hands of British troops. The second building also burned, in 1833. The present structure was designed by Robert Mills, Thomas U. Walter, Ammi B. Young, Isaiah Rogers and Alfred Bult Mullet (yes, *all* of them—but not all at once) and took 31 years to complete. Congress mandated that *this* building be fireproof. The east and center wings were constructed between 1838 and 1842, the south wing in 1860, the west wing in 1863, and the north wing in 1869—this addition required the demolition of the State Department Building and blocked forever the unobstructed vista from the White House to the Capitol.

The statue to the north of the building is of Albert Gallatin, the fourth secretary of the treasury, who served in that office longer than anyone else (1801–14); the one to the south is of Alexander Hamilton, the first secretary of the treasury (1789–95). The park directly south is Sherman Park, an imposing memorial to the Civil War general.

Along the way around the Treasury, you'll see Washington's financial district, which sprang up in the late nineteenth century. American Security and Trust Co. and Riggs National Bank—both in the Greek Revival style—are testimony to the fact that, at the turn of the century when banks often failed, investors wanted their bank to look solid. The red-brick National Savings and Trust Company Building, designed in the 1880s, is a bit less imposing than its neighbors—indeed, even quirky in its ornamentation.

The 15th Street leg connecting the two diagonals of Pennsylvania Avenue has undergone a massive face-lift: Metropolitan Square houses the new Old Ebbitt Grill in cosmopolitan flair; the Hotel

Washington has had its elegant sgraffito (etching on stucco) ornamentation restored by artisans from Italy and throughout the United States.

At the northwest corner of 14th Street and Pennsylvania Avenue, take a look at the Willard Hotel, an impressive Beaux Arts structure built in 1901. Designed by Henry Hardenbergh, noted also for the Plaza Hotel in New York, the Willard was often called the Hotel of Presidents because many stayed here at one time or another. In an earlier hotel on this site, Julia Ward Howe wrote "The Battle Hymn of the Republic." The Willard has been lushly and faithfully restored to its turn-of-the-century opulence. The Washington Visitor Information Center can be found in the Willard-Intercontinental's courtyard; you can pick up free maps and brochures of sites, tours and hotels here (open 9 A.M. to 5 P.M. Monday to Saturday).

Pershing Park, in the middle of the avenue between 14th and 15th streets, is an enticing spot for lunch on a sunny day (there's a food kiosk and shaded tables by a waterfall and pool) or for ice skating on a winter afternoon. The park serves as a peaceful memorial to John J. Pershing, General of the Armies.

Don't overlook what you're walking on as you traverse Freedom Plaza between 14th and 13th streets; it's a granite replica of L'Enfant's plan for Washington, surrounded by quotes about the city by political and cultural figures. A time capsule containing memorabilia from the life of Dr. Martin Luther King, Jr., was embedded in Freedom Plaza in 1988 beneath an inscription from his "I Have a Dream" speech, which he completed at the Willard. Concerts and other events are held on the Plaza throughout the year.

To the north of Freedom Plaza is National Place, which contains the restored National Theater (Washington's oldest playhouse), the sparkling flagship of the Marriott hotel chain and The Shops at National Place, a lively and elegant urban shopping galleria with 85 stores, restaurants and cafes. The beautifully renovated National Press Building, home of the National Press Club, completes the block, which backs on F Street, Washington's downtown shopping mall.

To the south of the avenue between 14th and 6th streets lies the Federal Triangle, the bureaucratic center of the nation. With the exception of the Old Post Office Building and the District Building, which early twentieth-century planners expected to demolish, all the buildings in the Triangle were designed in the neoclassical style and were constructed between 1928 and 1938. Their facades are more coherent but no less intimidating along the southern edge of the Triangle, Constitution Avenue.

Facing 14th Street from the west is the Department of Commerce Building (which houses the National Aquarium in its basement—see site report). When built, it was the largest office building in the world.

On the eastern side of 14th Street is the Beaux Arts-style District Building, Washington's city hall. Wrapping around the District Building is a construction site that will become Washington's biggest government building with 3-million square feet of shops, restaurants, exhibit and performing arts space, a conference facility and private and federal offices. Originally intended to become the Great Plaza, a landscaped crown for the western head of the Triangle, this space, when filled, will complete the Federal Triangle. The one remaining outdoor vestige, a fountain commemorating Oscar Straus, first secretary of the Department of Commerce and Labor, will be incorporated into the building's entrance.

At 12th Street, the Old Post Office, with its 315-foot clock tower, survives as one of Washington's few major examples of the Richardsonian Romanesque style popular in the 1890s. The Old Post Office, despite periodic schemes to tear it down and complete the Pennsylvania Avenue facade in a more compatible Greek or Roman style, has been restored and renovated as The Pavilion at the Old Post Office, a collection of shops, restaurants and food carts, with federal offices above (see site report). The National Park Service offers tours of the tower, which is the second-highest building in Washington. The view is splendid, with less of a wait than at the city's tallest structure, the Washington Monument.

On the north side of the avenue between 9th and 10th streets lurks the massive, unwelcoming J. Edgar Hoover (FBI) Building. Despite PADC's attempts to humanize the building with the addition of eight historical panels depicting scenes from the lives and times of eight U.S. Presidents, the building still seems massive and inhospitable.

The space between 7th and 9th streets, in contrast, is far more welcoming to pedestrians. Twin 13-story buildings (office, retail and residential) frame the Market Square Park/Navy Memorial. A bronze statue named "Lone Sailor," by sculptor Stanley Bleifeld, overlooks the plaza, which features a 100-foot-wide stonework map of the world. Fountains inscribed with maritime quotations surround the space, where military bands play during the summer. Two sculpture walls on the south side of the map will eventually display 22 bronze bas-relief panels depicting events in Navy history. A visitor center is housed in the eastern Market Square building; interactive videos and a large-screen motion picture theater will portray the adventure of going to sea.

Across the avenue from Market Square is the National Archives, repository of such venerable documents as the Declaration of Independence, the Bill of Rights and the Constitution (see site report). Farther along the south side of the avenue is a simple block of marble—the only public monument in Washington to Franklin D. Roosevelt, perhaps the most influential President of this century. FDR specifically requested that no fancy monument to him be constructed.

The Triangle tapers to a close at the Andrew Mellon Memorial Fountain (the largest bronze fountain basin ever cast), at the intersection of Pennsylvania and Constitution, across 6th Street from the rounded facade of the Federal Trade Commission Building. The Canadian embassy, designed by AIA gold medal recipient Arthur Erickson, is across the street at 6th Street and Pennsylvania Avenue.

A WALK AROUND LAFAYETTE SQUARE

Lafayette Square, directly across Pennsylvania Avenue from the north entrance of the White House, began its official life in 1790 as part of the President's front yard in L'Enfant's plan for the federal city. Thomas Jefferson found the seven-acre plot too imposing for the use of a republican Chief of State; he declared the area a public park, and Pennsylvania Avenue was cut through to separate it from the presidential grounds. The park came to be called Lafayette Square after an enormous public reception was held there in honor of the Marquis de Lafayette during his final visit to the United States in 1824.

The park in those days was hardly the landscaped gem we see today. An orchard when it was acquired for use by the federal government, it served as the site of brick kilns and laborers' huts during the construction of the White House. In the early nineteenth century, a racetrack ran along its western edge. The park was generally neglected as a young nation tended to its more pressing business.

Things began to look brighter in the 1850s when a planting program was devised by the brilliant young landscape architect Andrew Jackson Downing. In 1853, the dashing statue of Andrew Jackson—

the first equestrian monument produced in America by a hometrained sculptor—was erected in the center of the park. The statue was a rousing public success, and for a time the park was renamed Jackson Square.

In the 1890s and the early twentieth century, other statues commemorating foreign military leaders who aided in the Revolution were added at the corners of the square. Lafayette came first, taking his position at the southeast corner (nearest the Treasury) in 1891. His compatriot, Major General Comte Jean de Rochambeau (the commander of the French Expeditionary Force), followed in 1902 at the southwest corner. Brigadier General Thaddeus Kosciuszko, the gallant Pole who built the fortifications at West Point and Saratoga before returning to fight in his own country's war of independence, occupies the northeast corner, and the Prussian hero who trained America's troops at Valley Forge, Baron von Steuben, stands at the northwest corner.

A less obvious memorial to a twentieth-century noncombatant is located near Jackson's statue—the Bernard Baruch "Seat of Inspiration," a park bench from which the noted philanthropist is said to have contemplated the world and mulled over his advice to his friend in the White House, Franklin D. Roosevelt.

The park still attracts lunchtime philosophers—as well as chess players and sun worshipers—since Lafayette Square is one of the most popular lunch sites for brown-baggers. You may recognize the park as the locale of past demonstrations shown on the nightly news; its proximity to the White House makes it popular with protesters. It has also become a gathering place for "permanent" protesters and the homeless, adding an air of reality to the square's bucolic touch.

Today the buildings around Lafayette Square are occupied almost exclusively by governmental or quasi-governmental agencies. The square's delightful present appearance is the result of a federal decision in the late 1960s to preserve as many of the older residential buildings as possible while still adding the huge amount of office space needed for federal workers.

Start your tour of the square area at the White House or Treasury Building. Then cross Pennsylvania Avenue at the east end of the block onto Madison Place. The Treasury Annex (1921; Cass Gilbert, architect) will give you an idea of how early twentieth-century planners intended the area around the White House to look—plans and tastes changed later. In the middle of the block you'll find the red-brick, modern entrance to the new Court of Claims complex, constructed in the 1970s on a design by California architect John Carl Warnecke and Associates. Look behind you, across the square, and see its twin, the New Executive Office Building. Both buildings are set well back from the street behind low entrance courts to keep them from overpowering the smaller buildings around them. Farther down the street are the 1820s Tayloe House and the Dolley Madison House (properly, the Cutts-Madison House—Dolley lived there after her husband died, but it was built by her brother-in-law). Both are part of the Court of Claims complex, and the Tayloe House has a pleasant and charming government cafeteria—complete with chandeliers and antique-glass windows.

Across H Street, where 16th Street meets the square, is St. John's Church, with its parish house next door. Look up 16th Street and you'll see the carillon tower of a very different church—the Third Church of Christ Scientist—designed by architect I. M. Pei in the 1970s.

Starting at Decatur House (see site report) on the square's northwest corner, walk along Jackson Place (the western boundary of the square) and notice that many of the buildings are "in-fill" architecture—that is, structures designed simply to fill the spaces between existing ones without changing the character of the block. Decatur House, built in 1819, is the oldest residence remaining; it was the first building on the square constructed after the White House. Down the block are Victorian buildings dating from the 1860s to the 1890s. Theodore Roosevelt lived in one of them while the White House was being remodeled in 1902.

Take a right at the corner onto Pennsylvania Avenue. The Blair and Lee houses are in the middle of the block. They are the home-away-from-home for high-ranking foreign dignitaries on official visits to the United States. President Truman lived in Blair House while the White House underwent its massive restoration from 1948 to 1952. A plaque on the fence notes the attempt on his life by Puerto Rican fanatics and commemorates the life of a White House guard who died in that attack.

Next door is the Renwick Gallery, now part of the Smithsonian Institution (see site report). The Renwick is in the elaborate Second Empire style. Across Pennsylvania Avenue, you confront the Old Executive Office Building (formerly State, War and Navy), a mammoth Victorian edifice also in the Second Empire style popular during

President Grant's administration. Grant insisted that no general should have to function in the cramped space then allotted to the Army Department, so he ordered construction in 1871 of what Harry Truman would fondly refer to as "the greatest monstrosity in America."

THE ELLIPSE—BACKYARD TO THE WHITE HOUSE

Immediately south of the White House, the Ellipse—now officially called the President's Park South—is a 54-acre oval of lawn bounded by 15th and 17th streets and Constitution Avenue. In L'Enfant's 1791 plan for the city, the Ellipse was the southernmost portion of the grounds of the President's palace, but like much of the early capital, it remained marshland through most of the nineteenth century. The Ellipse was bounded on the south by the Tiber Canal, the present-day site of Constitution Avenue. Unfortunately, the canal, which was never a great success, had become an open sewer flowing past the White House by the time of the Lincoln administration. At the same time, the Ellipse itself served as a military campground and a corral for mules, horses and cattle; to avoid the stench, Lincoln spent many summer nights at the Old Soldiers' Home. After the completion of the Washington Monument (originally planned for the Ellipse but moved because of the unstable soil conditions), the Army Corps of Engineers filled and graded the land; with plantings designed by the great landscape architect Andrew Jackson Downing, the Ellipse took its present form in 1880. During the summer, on Wednesdays at 7 P.M. components of the U.S. Army Band perform on the Ellipse.

VISITING F STREET—A SMALL PIECE OF HISTORY

A visit to Ford's Theatre, the National Portrait Gallery or the National Museum of American Art (see site reports) affords an opportunity to look in on Washington's downtown shopping district. It's easily accessible by Metrorail, via the Metro Center or Gallery Place stops. Many of the buildings between 7th and 11th streets on F Street date from the nineteenth century, including the fine classical revival structures of the Old Patent Office (between 7th and 9th streets—now the home of the aforementioned art galleries) and the LeDroit Building, a pre-Civil War office building at 8th Street, which will be renovated under the auspices of PADC.

Architecture buffs will want to see the only Mies van der Rohe building in Washington—the Martin Luther King, Jr., Memorial Library at 901 G Street, with yet another pedestrian mall fronting it.

CHINATOWN

Washington's tiny Chinatown was established at its present location (G Street to the south, I Street to the north, 5th Street to the east, 7th Street to the west) in the early 1930s, after being moved off the eastern end of Pennsylvania Avenue to make way for construction of the city's municipal center. The Chinese Friendship Archway marks the entrance to Chinatown at 7th and H streets, NW; this colorful entry was built by the District government in coordination with the Municipality of Beijing as part of a sister city exchange program.

Primarily a commercial center, Chinatown offers a rich variety of decorative arts, handicrafts, clothing and foodstuffs from China, as well as numerous excellent restaurants serving many regional cuisines (see recommendations in Chapter 21, "Dining"). Since part of Chinatown is in the Downtown Historic Preservation District, an interesting blend of preserved Victorian and renovated-in-Chinese-style architecture prevails.

One block west of Chinatown at 9th and H streets is the Washington Convention Center, which hosts more than a million persons a year at conventions, trade shows and local events. At 9th and I streets is Techworld Plaza, which includes a hotel, office and showroom space, retail outlets, Chinese gardens and streetscapes, and Tech 2000, a gallery of video technologies (see site report).

SAMPLING DOWNTOWN DINING

Downtown now has so many restaurants that to make sense of the possibilities, from the fancy Continental through a bazaar of ethnic foods to the countless carry-outs and fast-food vendors, we've divided the area into a number of logical eating areas: Old Downtown (closest to the Mall attractions), Chinatown, the White House area, New Downtown (north and west of the White House), and the West End (a newly developed area west of Washington Circle on Pennsylvania Avenue stretching to Georgetown).

Old Downtown—The Capitol to the White House

As Pennsylvania Avenue has been renewed and new office buildings have brought many more thousands of eaters to the area, restaurants have appeared. The best bets are located in the Old Post Office Pavillion, at 15th Street and Pennsylvania Avenue, NW, and The Shops at National Place, 13th Street and F Street, NW. Both feature sit-down restaurants and food halls. The Pavilion has three major restaurants: *Hunan* (Chinese), *Enrico's Trattoria* (Italian) and *Blossoms* (salads, burgers, light fare). National Place has the *American Café* (soups, sandwiches, new American cuisine) and *Boston Seafood* (seafood and more). Both malls have an assortment of fast-food establishments serving just about everything—hot dogs, hamburgers, pizza, deli, barbecue, fresh fruit salads, you name it. Of special note in the Old Post Office pavilion is the Indian food stand; at National Place you can even get sushi to go!

Worth mentioning is the carry-out in Pershing Park, at 14th Street and Pennsylvania Avenue. It has a very limited menu of hot dogs, burritos and the like, but the park is lovely, an oasis of trees and water. Moreover, the park has nice public facilities and is accessible to those in wheelchairs.

Chinatown

Among the many impacts of the Convention Center is the revitalization of Washington's small Chinatown. Its borders are expanding, and its restaurants multiplying. Our old favorite, the *Ruby,* 609 H Street, has been joined by several restaurants of note. *Hunan Chinatown,* 624 H Street and *The China Inn,* 631 H Street, have a wide variety of all styles of Chinese cuisine. *Ms. Tao,* 817 7th Street, offers excellent seafood.

As is true with most Chinese restaurants, you will usually find good, inexpensive food wherever you go in Chinatown. For conventioneers, Chinatown is a good bet.

The White House Area—16th to 22nd Streets, Pennsylvania Avenue

Among the inexpensive eateries, a good bet is *Metro Market,* 19th and I streets, with more than 20 varied fast-food stands—Italian, Greek,

Chinese, bagels, barbecue, fish, chicken, etc. The *Paramount Coffee Shop*, 18th and I streets, has a wide variety of sandwiches, salads, Greek specialties and daily specials at reasonable prices. *The Lunch Box* carry-outs can be found throughout downtown, including 825 20th Street and 1622 I Street. *Yummy Yogurt*, also in various downtown locations, including 1825 I Street, 1724 M Street and 1010 17th Street, has salads, pita bread sandwiches and yogurts. *La Prima* has an excellent selection of hot and cold sandwiches at several locations, including 1850 K Street, NW, and 1050 Connecticut Avenue, NW.

The Esplanade Mall, 20th and I streets, has a variety of restaurants, plain to fancy: pizza, Chinese, and *Sholl's Colonial Cafeteria*, a Washington landmark for solid, inexpensive food. *Vie de France*, a French cafe, has an outlet in Esplanade at 1615 M Street and at 1723 K Street, too.

New Downtown

Where to start? The area north and northwest of the White House up to M Street has almost too many choices. Along the K Street corridor as well as the numbered streets (18th, 19th and 20th) and Connecticut Avenue, you will find an assortment of food to suit any taste. Carry-outs, fast food and simple fare abound. *Connecticut Connection* is an underground food court at the Farragut North Metro stop at L Street and Connecticut Avenue; it's one stop sure to satisfy everyone in your group.

7

GEORGETOWN/ FOGGY BOTTOM/ THE WEST END

GEORGETOWN—AN INTRODUCTION

Georgetown is history, trendy boutiques, crowded cobblestoned streets, peaceful and staid grand estates, a watering hole for the "in crowd," canal walkers/joggers, galleries, music, fine and frilly food—and much, much more. It's a hustle, steeped in times gone by, and the contrasts lead to delight and entertainment at every turn. If there's one place in Washington where folks just go to walk around, day or night, it's Georgetown.

Georgetown began as an Indian trading center. The earliest recorded description of the confluence of the Potomac River and Rock Creek was written by Captain John Smith, who sailed up the Potomac in 1608, noting several tribes of farming Indians. In 1703, Lord Baltimore ceded most of the Georgetown area to Ninion Beall, who established a plantation, and George Gordon, a merchant who made a fortune by founding a tobacco-inspection station. In 1751, the State of Maryland recognized the town of George as a major tobacco port; the Potomac was wide and deep enough to be navigable by ships, and the town of George was the last port point before the river's Great Falls.

The town boomed and was incorporated in 1789 as "George Town." In the same year Georgetown University was founded as the first Roman Catholic university in the United States. Wealthy merchants and middle-class tradesmen resided in town and sneered at their uncultured country cousins setting up the new city of Washington just down the river. While L'Enfant envisioned the capital grow-

GEORGETOWN

1. Diplomatic Reception Rooms (U.S. Department of State)
2. Dumbarton House
3. Dumbarton Oaks
4. Interior Department Museum

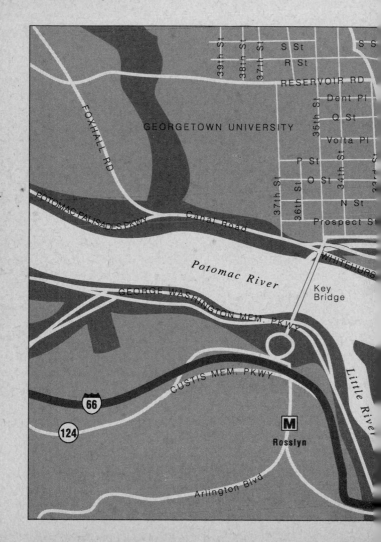

5. International Monetary Fund
6. John F. Kennedy Center for the Performing Arts
7. National Academy of Sciences
8. Old Stone House
9. Tudor Place

NORTHWEST (see p. 150–151)

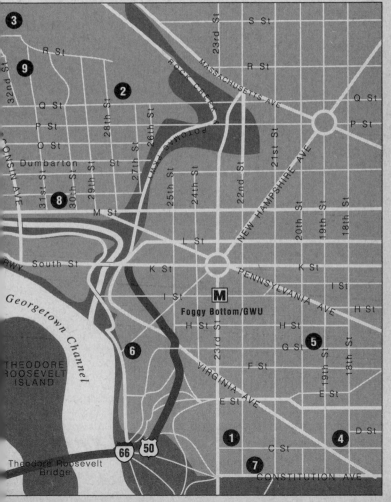

THE MALL (see p. 28-29)

ing eastward, it expanded west—many feel as a result of Georgetown's civilized attractiveness.

The glory days were soon over, however, as the railroads, steam-powered ships and river silt destroyed Georgetown's usefulness as a port. Despite the construction of the Chesapeake and Ohio Canal and the diversification into flour, munitions and paper industries on the waterfront, Georgetown declined, losing its charter in 1871 when it was officially annexed by the capital city.

From 1880 through 1890, a multitude of brownstone Victorian houses were built for the benefit of federal workers. Today, almost half of Georgetown's houses date from that period or before. By the 1920s, more than half of Georgetown's population were poverty-stricken blacks who had few means to repair the deteriorating housing stock—but Georgetown's charm was still visible. Though some restoration began in the 1920s, the New Dealers gentrified the area; today Georgetown is one of the city's most exclusive—and expensive—places to live.

For a glimpse into Georgetown's past, take a look at a small display selected from the thousands of artifacts unearthed during the excavation for the shopping mall, Georgetown Park (3222 M Street, NW). Here, in a tiny storefront called Museum, you'll see fragments of Georgetown life during the past 200 years, some from the site's earliest days as a tobacco warehouse and trading post.

Beyond the sites noted in this chapter (Dumbarton Oaks, a marvelous Georgian estate, and Old Stone House, a humble middle-class residence dating from the 1760s, Tudor Place, one of the great houses of federal Washington and Dumbarton House, a fine house museum temporarily closed for restoration), Georgetown is a delight in itself. Shopping opportunities abound, eating possibilities boggle the mind (see our recommendations at the end of this chapter), nighttime entertainment potentials challenge the hardiest (see Chapter 13, "Entertainment") and the peacefulness of the restored C&O Canal beckons (see the site report in Chapter 11, "Nearby Maryland").

Of course, explore the main drags of Wisconsin Avenue and M Street—but don't stop there. The real charm of Georgetown lies in its shaded, elegant back streets, so stroll about for as long as your feet hold out to savor its flavor. If you're here in April, check the newspapers for the schedules of the annual Georgetown House and Garden Tours for a more intimate view.

Don't overlook a stroll through Georgetown's new waterfront development, Washington Harbor. After many years, this area has finally become an attraction deserving of its capital views. It features a variety of expensive shops and restaurants and offers public access to a river walk with majestic views of the Kennedy Center, Watergate and the Potomac. The fountained plaza has several sculptures by J. Seward Johnson, Jr., amusing and eerily lifelike street scenes. It's also great fun to take a barge trip on the C&O Canal (see Chapter 15, "Outdoor Washington/Sports").

There are no Metro stops in Georgetown (the Citizen Association of Georgetown, an extremely powerful civic group, rejected the idea), but buses run along M Street and Wisconsin Avenue (30, 32, 34 and 36). You can also view M Street on an Old Town Trolley Tour, as part of a 12-stop tour of the city. Riders can get off, explore the area and reboard later (call (202) 269-3020 for details). The excitement of Georgetown has in recent years resulted in an increase in muggings and other occasional violent acts. By all means go and enjoy Georgetown, but do keep your wits about you, especially on warm summer evenings.

Parking in Georgetown is incredibly difficult, especially on weekends, so it's best to leave your car behind (with the possible exception of your trip to Dumbarton Oaks, Tudor Place and Dumbarton House, a healthy uphill distance from Georgetown's commercial center).

DUMBARTON OAKS   **(202) 338-8278 (recorded information)**
(202) 342-3200 (main number)
(202) 342-3212 (guided tours)
1703 32nd Street, NW 20007 (museum entrance)
31st and R streets, NW (garden entrance)
Hours: Gardens: April–October   2–6 P.M. daily
November–March   2–5 P.M. daily
Byzantine and pre-Columbian collections: 2–5 P.M.
Tuesday–Sunday
Closed holidays
Admission: Adults—$2   Children and Senior Citizens—$1   Seniors
free on Wednesdays

D2, D4, D6, D8 on Q Street, G2, M12, even-numbered 30s or any other Wisconsin Avenue bus.
Wisconsin Avenue.

Competitive two-hour parking in neighborhood; especially difficult on weekends.

 Gardens are recommended, though visitors must stay on paths.

 Group tours available for 10 or more people. Tours of the Byzantine collection and the music room, which contains important paintings, can be arranged by calling (202) 342-3212 well in advance.

 Inaccessible to people in wheelchairs without assistance. Steps must be traversed, and the garden has gravel/cobblestone paths that could be difficult. Rest room and phone are not accessible.

 Call recording at (202) 338-8278 to find out when museum tours are being offered, and what's in bloom in the garden.

 Walk-in guided tours are given. House itself not open for tours.

Though it's just around the corner from Georgetown's heavily trafficked Wisconsin Avenue, Dumbarton Oaks feels like a well-mannered country retreat. Ten acres of formal gardens surround a grand home as well as a museum that houses two collections, one of Byzantine art and the other of pre-Columbian artifacts.

The land on which Dumbarton Oaks is built was part of the original 1702 grant by Queen Anne of what was to become the thriving port of Georgetown, then part of Maryland. The original house was built in 1801 by William Dorsey and was the home of a series of prominent owners.

In 1922 Dumbarton Oaks was purchased by Robert and Mildred Bliss, a wealthy couple who for many years served abroad in the diplomatic corps. They had amassed a fine collection of Byzantine art as well as an extensive collection of books on the topics of Byzantine art and landscape gardening. Mrs. Bliss worked with Beatrix Jones Farrand to design each element of the beautifully landscaped grounds. In 1940, the Bliss family gave Dumbarton Oaks, the collections and research libraries to Harvard University, which still owns and oversees the property.

Today, Dumbarton Oaks serves as a research center on Byzantine and pre-Columbian studies and landscape architecture. Philip Johnson designed a pavilion for the display of selections from the collections: the pre-Columbian pieces are arranged according to culture in a generally geographical and chronological sequence; the Byzantine collection includes jewelry, metalwork and textiles. The music room is also open for viewing; it contains various fine works, fourteenth-century paintings and antique furnishings among them. In this room in 1944 the conferences were held that led to the formation of the United Nations. And of course the gardens, just about the finest in the city, are open for meandering.

The research libraries are open only to scholars, although the rare-book room of the garden library is open for viewing on weekends from 2 to 5 P.M.

A sales shop sells a few good replicas of pieces in the museums as well as postcards and scholarly publications on the collections.

OLD STONE HOUSE   **(202) 426-6851 (voice and TDD)**
3051 M Street, NW 20007
Hours: 8 A.M.–4:30 P.M. Wednesday–Sunday
          Closed all Federal holidays
          Garden open 8 A.M.–4:30 P.M. daily
Free Admission

 30, 32, 34, 36, 38, D3, G2, M12.

 M Street.

 Competitive parking; commercial parking lots on M and Jefferson streets.

 Recommended.

 Small group tours can be arranged by calling (202) 426-6851.

 Limited accessibility. The first floor and garden are accessible; a photo album of the second floor, which is inaccessible, is available for viewing. There are no rest rooms or phones.

The oldest house in Washington, this is a charmer. Built in 1765, and added on to by subsequent tenants, Old Stone House was owned by a cabinetmaker; it's quite representative of middle-class dwellings of the late eighteenth and early nineteenth centuries and, as such, provides pleasant contrast to the grand houses of the Washington wealthy that are also open to the public.

The house's five rooms include a small shop where occasional craft demonstrations are given by women garbed in eighteenth-century costume. Those who give the demonstrations are extremely knowledgeable on the house and are quite pleased to answer questions. A small but lovely colonial garden is in back of the house. Together the house and garden provide an appealing respite from one of the busiest streets in the city.

TUDOR PLACE   **(202) 965-0400**
1644 31st Street, NW 20007
Mailing Address: Tudor Place Foundation,
                    1605 32nd Street, NW 20007
Hours: Saturday, 10 and 11:30 A.M., 1 and 2:30 P.M. Tuesday–Friday, by
    appointment only.
Admission: $5 house and grounds (donation), $2.50 grounds only.

D2, D4, D6, D8 on Q Street; G2, M12; even-numbered 30's or any other Wisconsin Avenue bus.

Wisconsin Avenue.

Competitive neighborhood parking.

Of interest to older children.

Call or write to make arrangements.

First floor accessible with assistance. Call ahead to make arrangements. Second floor and gardens are not accessible.

Tours given Tuesday to Saturday at 10 and 11:30 A.M. and 1 and 2:30 P.M. For tours Tuesday–Friday, you must call two weeks in advance to reserve a space. House tour is about 45 minutes, then stroll through the garden on your own. (Closed for part of February.)

Tudor Place is an architectural, historical and cultural gem, one of the finest examples of architecture of the Federal period in Washington. It was designed by William Thornton, who was actually a physician by training; nonetheless, he entered and won the competition for the original design for the United States Capitol, served as the first Architect of the Capitol and, on the side, designed friends' houses for free, including Woodlawn Plantation and Octagon House (see site reports).

A rare phenomenon in American history, the house was lived in by succeeding generations of the same family from 1805 to 1984. The Peter family was closely tied to George Washington, the Marquis de Lafayette, Robert E. Lee and others who shaped America's history. These historical connections are vividly illustrated by the varied contents of the house, including many furnishings from Mount Vernon, such as Washington's folding military stool and the andirons from his bedroom fireplace. The family evidently treated Washington with such reverence that curators recently found a piece of soap that he had used, carefully wrapped and labeled.

The builder of Tudor Place, Thomas Peter, was the son of a successful Scottish tobacco merchant who had become the first mayor of the port of Georgetown. His wife, Martha Custis, was a granddaughter of Martha Washington and, in fact, used George Washington's $8,000 legacy to purchase the Tudor Place property, comprising one city block.

During the 180 years of Peter family ownership, the house assumed that fascinating character which can only come through the continual enrichments of marriage, purchase and inheritance. Furniture, silver, china and glass, sculpture, portraits and photographs, textiles, books and manuscripts not only testify to the continuous thread of family life at Tudor Place but give a rare insight into American cultural history.

The exceptionally lovely gardens feature specimen trees planted in the early nineteenth century, as well as a large collection of period flowers and shrubs.

WORTH NOTING

Dumbarton House, 2715 Q Street, NW 20007, (202) 337-2288. Dumbarton House, a Federal-style brick house built in the last years of the eighteenth century, is a fine example of a well-to-do home from the period. Furnished with period pieces, including Hepplewhites and Sheratons, Dumbarton House includes other fine examples of the work of American cabinetmakers from the New England states to Georgia. In addition to being a museum, the house also serves as headquarters of the National Society of the Colonial Dames.

FOGGY BOTTOM—AN INTRODUCTION

Belying its humorous name, Foggy Bottom is an impressive place these days, the locale of the Kennedy Center for the Performing Arts, George Washington University, international monetary organizations, the Departments of State and Interior and swanky retail/residential complexes. It wasn't always so. When Jacob Funk purchased 130 acres in this area in 1765, much of the land was malarial river marsh. Initially incorporated as Hamburg, and known as Funkstown, this land was included in the planned capital in 1791. The area became Washington's industrial center, with a glass factory, gas works, coal depot and brewery—the foul industrial emissions led to the nickname Foggy Bottom. Irish, Italian and German immigrants lived and worked here, west of 23rd Street; to the east, the middle-class civil servants made their homes. The university, founded in 1821, has been expanding ever since. Federal agencies began their influx to Foggy Bottom after World War II, and redevelopment of the area followed.

The area today is roughly defined by the following borders: 18th Street on the east; Constitution Avenue on the south; the Potomac River and 26th Street on the west; and Pennsylvania Avenue on the north. Street parking, of course, is difficult, but you can appreciate the essence of the area by driving through—although traffic can also be horrendous. The Kennedy Center has ample parking.

DIPLOMATIC RECEPTION ROOMS
(U.S. Department of State)

(202) 647-3241

2201 C Street, NW 20520
Hours: Weekdays, by appointment only.
Free Admission

  Foggy Bottom stop (blue and orange lines); walk south on 23rd Street about five blocks and turn east on C Street.
23rd Street.

 Competitive meter parking. Commercial lot nearby.

 This is a fine arts tour not recommended for kids under 12; no strollers are permitted.

Groups up to 50 people can be accommodated; call or write at least three months in advance.

 Fully accessible.

 Interpreted tours can be arranged when you make your tour reservation. Call (202) 647-3241 or TDD (202) 736-4474.

 Call or write the tour office, Room 1493, at least a month in advance. Your congressional representative's office can also make arrangements for your tour.

 Tours are given weekdays at 9:30 and 10:30 A.M. and 2:45 P.M. (closed Federal holidays). You must make advance reservations for these tours.

The Diplomatic Reception Rooms of the U.S. Department of State represent one of the finest collections of American design and decorative arts from 1740 to 1825. Anyone with an interest in our architectural and decorative heritage will be in heaven here. You'll see specific examples of American craftsmanship at its finest, from the 1753 Boston desk signed three times by its proud cabinetmaker to the Paul Revere silver.

The rooms include several quintessentially American styles: a Virginia River plantation reception hall; a mid-Georgian Philadelphia drawing room; the Thomas Jefferson diplomatic room, which incorporates some of Jefferson's favorite design motifs; and the Benjamin Franklin dining room. As the rooms are actually used to receive our country's diplomatic guests, the day's tours may occasionally be suspended when a special guest is being entertained.

JOHN F. KENNEDY CENTER FOR THE PERFORMING ARTS

(202) 467-4600

New Hampshire Avenue and Rock Creek Parkway 20566
Hours: 10 A.M.–11 P.M. daily
Free Admission

 Foggy Bottom stop (blue and orange lines); walk west on H Street, then south on New Hampshire Avenue.

 Building entrance or Virginia Avenue.

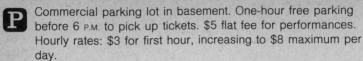

P Commercial parking lot in basement. One-hour free parking before 6 P.M. to pick up tickets. $5 flat fee for performances. Hourly rates: $3 for first hour, increasing to $8 maximum per day.

The Roof Terrace level offers three eating facilities catering to different tastes and budgets, with splendid views of the Potomac River, Georgetown and the Mall. The Hor d'Oeuverie serves appetizers, desserts and beverages from 5 P.M. until a half-hour after the last performance curtain. The Encore Café is a cafeteria offering a wide range of soups, salads, hot entrées and desserts from 11 A.M. to 8 P.M. daily. The Roof Terrace Restaurant serves sophisticated, and more expensive, American regional fare; it's open for lunch 11:30 A.M.–3 P.M. Monday–Friday and for weekend matinees, and for dinner 5:30–9 P.M. Tuesday–Saturday and other performance evenings.

Recommended. The Kennedy Center has some terrific entertainment series for kids. Free programs for children and youth are presented on a dozen Saturdays throughout the year; these wonderful productions include dance, plays, musicals, puppets, music and mime. Check the daily newspapers or call (202) 467-4600 to see what's on while you're in town. A limited number of half-price tickets are available for students on the day of performance or before a run opens; call (202) 467-4600 for more information.

Call (202) 416-8341 to make arrangements for tours for groups of 25 or more.

Fully accessible. For performances, reserve wheelchairs one hour before curtain by calling (202) 416-8340. Contact the usher to be guided to special theater entrances. Half-price tickets are available to most performances; call (202) 467-4600 for information.

Large-print and Braille scripts are available for all tours. In addition, you can make arrangements for a special "touch tour" by calling (202) 416-8303. Half-price tickets are available for most performances; call (202) 467-4600 for information. Call (202) 416-8340 to find out if audio descriptions are available for a particular performance.

Make arrangements for a signed tour by calling (202) 416-8303 two weeks in advance. The Eisenhower Theater, Opera House and Terrace Theater are equipped with a number of receiver headsets and hearing-aid receivers. Half-price tickets are available for most performances; call (202) 467-4600 or TDD (202) 416-8524.

A limited number of half-price tickets for most performances are available for students, senior citizens, low-income patrons, people with disabilities and enlisted military personnel (E1–E4). These tickets are not available by phone; either present proof of eligibility at the box office or at the Friends of the Kennedy Center Volunteer Desk in the Hall of States before purchasing the tickets. Call (202) 416-8340 for further information. Special tours of the Kennedy Center can be arranged by contacting your congressional representative well in advance of your trip. Free one-hour tours are given daily from 10 A.M. to 1 P.M., starting in Motor Lobby A. You'll see much more on these tours than you can on your own, including the exquisite theater lounges that house gifts from various nations. Written tour scripts are available in Chinese, French, German, Hebrew, Italian, Japanese, Spanish, and Portuguese.

Before the Kennedy Center for the Performing Arts opened in 1971, Washington was considered by many to be culturally anemic; with the center's advent, however, the capital has become a national—and, indeed, international—cultural force. The finest opera, dance, music and theater companies in the world perform in the center's four theaters, and classic and contemporary films are shown in the American Film Institute.

The center is far more than a cultural bonanza, however; it is the sole official memorial to President John F. Kennedy in the nation's capital. A seven-foot-high bronze bust of the slain President by Robert Berks stands in the center of the Grand Foyer, and excerpts from his speeches are carved into the center's river facade, clearly visible from the River Terrace. In JFK's memory, many nations gave exquisite gifts that have been incorporated into the building.

The marble structure (the marble was a gift from Italy), designed by Edward Durell Stone, commands a spectacular view of the Potomac River, Georgetown and bits of the Mall. An elegant Entrance Plaza (the bronzes were gifts from West Germany) fronts the building's two entrances, one to the Hall of States wherein flags of America's states and territories are flown, and one to the Hall of Nations, wherein flags of all nations officially recognized by the U.S. are displayed. These halls lead to the 630-foot Grand Foyer, where 18 Orrefors crystal chandeliers sparkle (a gift from Sweden) in front of enormous mirrors (gifts from Belgium). The Grand Foyer opens onto the River Terrace, a lovely and romantic composite of marble, fountains and willow trees.

The three major performance stages are entered from the Grand Foyer: the gold-and-white Concert Hall, which seats 2,750, has fine acoustics—and elegant chandeliers (from Norway); the Opera House, which seats 2,300, is designed for opera, ballet and musical-theater presentations (note the gold silk stage curtain from Japan and starburst chandelier from Austria); the Eisenhower Theater seats 1,200 and is paneled with East Indian laurel (the stage curtain was a gift from Canada). The entrance to the American Film Institute Theater is in the Hall of States.

The Roof Terrace often has notable exhibits. The Terrace Theater, a bicentennial gift to the center from Japan, opened in 1979. This small, 500-seat theater is ideal for chamber music, poetry readings and theater performances. Also on this level is the Theater Lab, offering free performances, often for children. Ticket information for the various stages can be obtained by calling (202) 467-4600. Telephone ticket sales are handled by Instant Charge at (202) 467-4600. For more information about entertainment possibilities at the Kennedy Center, see Chapter 13, "Entertainment."

The Roof Terrace offers a grand view. To the center's north is the Watergate complex, home of exceedingly expensive apartments, a hotel, exclusive shops and offices (you'll recall the Watergate break-in of the Democratic National Committee offices, which eventually led to President Richard Nixon's resignation).

The Performing Arts Library is open to the public from 11 A.M. to 8:30 P.M. Tuesday to Friday, and 10 A.M. to 6 P.M. on Saturday. As well as housing a wealth of information on the performing arts, the library has changing exhibits of manuscripts and visual displays supplied by the Library of Congress. For information, call (202) 416-8780.

Christmas is a particularly exciting time at the center; check the newspapers or call (202) 467-4600 to see what's on—especially the enormous Christmas caroling fest.

The Kennedy Center has a gift counter in the Hall of States on the main level and a large shop on Parking Level A. Souvenirs appropriate to the center and its performances are sold.

WORTH NOTING

The hours of these sites vary; call ahead.

Interior Department Museum, 18th and C streets, NW 20240, (202) 208-8743. The museum is a microcosm of the myriad agencies that come under the Interior Department umbrella—National Park Service, Bureau of Land Management, Bureau of Reclamation, Geological Survey, Bureau of Indian Affairs, and others. The ten exhibit galleries include paintings, dioramas, Native American handicrafts, maps, aerial surveys, scientific models and a wealth of other specimens, artworks and artifacts. Authentic handmade Native American objects are sold in the Indian Crafts Shop.

International Monetary Fund (IMF) Visitors Center, 700 19th Street, NW, (202) 623-6869. The center consists of a bookstore, a reading area, a gallery and an auditorium. The gallery features three permanent exhibits on the purposes and functions of the IMF, as well as its history and structure.

National Academy of Sciences, 2101 Constitution Avenue, NW. The academy's lovely grounds contain a massive bronze and granite monument to Albert Einstein; though oversized, the memorial presents a very human visage of the great man.

THE WEST END—AN INTRODUCTION

The West End is a neighborhood just coming into its own. Situated north of Pennsylvania Avenue and between Washington Circle and Georgetown, the West End, until recently, was something of a neglected stepchild, never really part of Downtown and shunned by nearby Georgetown.

Now it has become a lively neighborhood in its own right. Glitzy new office buildings dot the area, and many restaurants, hotels and cinemas have ushered in new life. Although there are no specific sights of note, you may want to try a restaurant here and then explore the neighborhood starting at 23rd Street.

GEORGETOWN/FOGGY BOTTOM/THE WEST END—
THE EDIBLE FARE

Georgetown is tricky. Every time you look, new restaurants have appeared, and those you thought would last forever are gone. And other areas of the city have blossomed with new restaurants, luring diners away from old Georgetown haunts. But don't get us wrong; you can still eat at a different restaurant every day and not repeat yourself for several seasons of the year. See Chapter 21, "Dining," for suggested fine-to-funky dining options.

But if you're on the run and carry-out or fast food is what you seek, the western end of the city can still oblige. Georgetown Park, the upscale mall at the intersection of M Street and Wisconsin Avenue, sports a new food court. Next door at 3210 M Street is *Burger King;* across the street at 3211 M Street is *Pizzeria Uno;* further down the block is *Georgetown Bagelry,* at 3245 M Street. A block north, at 1226 Wisconsin Avenue, is *Roy Rogers.* Across the street is *American Café.* In Georgetown's northern reaches is the perfect way to conclude your meal—*Bob's Famous* tempts with great ice cream at 2416 Wisconsin Avenue. In Foggy Bottom, head for the campus of George Washington University and follow the lunchtime crowds.

8

NORTHWEST

The Northwest quadrant of Washington is a collection of distinct—
and distinctive—neighborhoods. Because of their unique and concentrated nature, Downtown and Georgetown/Foggy Bottom/The West
End have been discussed as separate chapters; here we cover the rest
of Northwest.

The city grew slowly in this direction; few houses stood along the
dirt roads in Northwest until after the Civil War, and even then this
section of Washington remained a vast picnic grove for most of the
city until well into the twentieth century. With the exception of a few
major commercial arteries (Massachusetts, Connecticut, Georgia and
Wisconsin Avenues, and Columbia Road), the area is predominantly
residential.

A major expansion into Northwest occurred at the turn of the
century when the city's rapidly growing wealthy class built their
ornate homes in the Dupont Circle and Kalorama neighborhoods;
many of the sights you'll want to see in Northwest are in these
restored mansions (Anderson House, the Historical Society of Washington, D.C., the Phillips Collection, the Textile Museum, the Woodrow Wilson House and Embassy Row).

While the remaining points of interest are widely scattered, they
include at least two of Washington's most impressive sites: the National Zoo and the Washington National Cathedral.

Because the attractions are dispersed in the Northwest quadrant,
the best means of transportation is a car, although parking will be
difficult. Buses can also take you to within a few blocks of most of your

NORTHWEST

1. Anderson House
2. Art, Science and Technology Institute and Holography Collection
3. B'nai B'rith Museum
4. Columbia Road/Adams-Morgan
5. Dupont Circle
6. Embassy Row
7. Fonda del Sol Visual Arts Center
8. Hillwood Museum
9. Historical Society of Washington, D.C.
10. INTELSAT
11. Islamic Center
12. Kalorama Area
13. Museum of Health and Medicine of the Armed Forces Institute of Pathology
14. National Firearms Museum
15. National Zoological Park
16. Peirce Mill
17. Phillips Museum
18. Textile Museum
19. United States Naval Observatory
20. Washington National Cathedral
21. Woodrow Wilson House

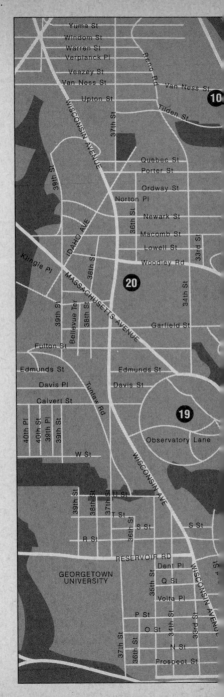

DOWNTOWN (see p. 90-91)

GORGETOWN (see p. 134-135)

destinations. Old Town Trolley Tours (see Chapter 2, "Getting To and Around Town") also provides access to the area.

ANDERSON HOUSE—SOCIETY   **(202) 785-2040**
OF THE CINCINNATI
2118 Massachusetts Avenue, NW 20008
Hours: 1–4 P.M. Tuesday–Saturday
     Closed holidays
Free Admission

 Dupont Circle stop (red line; Dupont Circle exit); walk two blocks west on Massachusetts Avenue.

 Massachusetts Avenue.

 Competitive street parking.

 Not recommended for younger children.

 Tours available for groups of 20 or more. Make reservations in advance by calling (202) 785-2040.

Limited accessibility to ground floor (two front steps). Elevator to upper floors.

 No scheduled tours. A very good free pamphlet is available to facilitate a self-guided tour.

Anderson House is a delight that even many longtime Washingtonians don't know about, although it's right off heavily trafficked Dupont Circle and practically across the street from the well-known Phillips Collection (see site report). The Beaux Arts mansion was built in 1902 for Ambassador and Mrs. Larz Anderson—he was a special envoy to Belgium from 1911 to 1912 and ambassador to Japan from 1912 to 1913, and she was one of the wealthiest young women in the country. Anderson was a member of the Society of the Cincinnati, an organization of male descendants of officers who served in the Continental Army or Navy during the Revolutionary War; the Andersons bequeathed their mansion to the society in 1937.

Today the mansion serves two purposes. The ground floor holds the society's collection of Revolutionary War memorabilia and a reference library of over 30,000 volumes on our war for independence; the library is open to the public by appointment. The second floor is furnished much the way it was when the Andersons lived there, complete with their fine art collection and the treasures they collected while serving abroad. Since the ambassador entertained lavishly, the house portrays life in wealthy Washington society in the early twentieth century. A glance across the street at the exclusive Cosmos Club and at the corner of 20th Street and Massachusetts Avenue to the Evalyn Walsh McLean mansion (now the Indonesian embassy) will give you a further idea of what the neighborhood was like in its heyday. Concerts are held on occasional Saturday and Wednesday afternoons; check for details.

HILLWOOD MUSEUM   (202) 686-5807
4155 Linnean Avenue, NW 20008
Hours: Grounds: 11 A.M.–3 P.M. Tuesday–Saturday
        House: by appointment
Admission: $10 house and grounds $2 grounds only

Significant walk from Connecticut Avenue bus routes L2, L4, L5, L6, L7.

It's best to telephone for a taxi from the mansion.

Free parking; buses may enter the gates.

Light lunch and tea served at the Hillwood Museum Cafe; 11 A.M.–4:30 P.M. Reservations suggested. Call (202) 686-8893.

Children under 12 years old (including infants) are not permitted on house tours but are permitted to visit the grounds and auxiliary buildings.

Arrangements can be made for a group tour by calling (202) 686-5807 or by writing well in advance of your trip; a maximum of 25 people are allowed on each tour.

Limited accessibility. The first floor and rest rooms are accessible; part of the second floor is accessible.

A special "touch tour" can be arranged when you are making your reservations.

Arrangements can be made for a special tour if the group provides its own interpreter. Call (202) 686-5807 well in advance of your trip. Hearing enhancers are available for the tour; the introductory film is captioned.

Tours of Hillwood are given at 9 and 10:30 A.M., noon, 1:30 P.M. and 3 P.M. (2 hours). You must make a reservation to go on the tour; because the tour is popular and limited in size, call at least two months ahead in spring and fall.

For many years the home of Mrs. Marjorie Merriweather Post, cereal heiress and grande dame of Washington society, Hillwood is a grand estate. Built in 1926, this opulent 40-room Georgian mansion houses many of Mrs. Post's fine artworks and furnishings. Hillwood's collection of Russian icons, gold and silver pieces, porcelain and Fabergé eggs has been called the most representative outside Russia. French furniture and Sèvres porcelain are also displayed.

The 25 acres of land bordering Rock Creek Park contain Japanese and formal French gardens, a small dacha or Russian summer house, a Native American building to house Mrs. Post's Indian collection on loan from the Smithsonian and a greenhouse with an impressive collection of orchids. The gardens were designed primarily by Perry Wheeler, who helped establish the White House Rose Garden.

HISTORICAL SOCIETY   (202) 785-2068
OF WASHINGTON, D.C.
(Christian Heurich Memorial Mansion)
1307 New Hampshire Avenue, NW 20036
Hours: 10 A.M.–4 P.M. Wednesday, Friday, Saturday
Admission: House Tour: Adults—$3   Children free   Senior Citizens—$1.50

M Dupont Circle stop (red line); use Dupont Circle exit.

New Hampshire Avenue.

P Competitive street parking; several commercial lots in neighborhood.

Arrangements should be made at least two weeks in advance for groups of 10 or more by calling (202) 785-2068.

Accessible.

T All visitors must go on guided tours, given continually during museum hours (45 minutes).

The Christian Heurich Mansion is the headquarters of the Historical Society of Washington, D.C., but most out-of-town visitors will be interested in the 1894 Romanesque Revival mansion near Dupont Circle as the home of a successful Washington burgher. Christian Heurich, a German immigrant, made his fortune in beer and spent it lavishly on his elaborate, 31-room brown sandstone mansion. The superb, if overpowering, interior woodwork, an airy conservatory, a pretty garden and many of the original furnishings suggest the opulence of turn-of-the-century life among the nation's rising merchant class.

The library, open to the public, houses an excellent collection of prints, photographs, books and other materials about Washington's history.

Visitors should note that most historic houses in Washington keep their doors locked as a security measure. No need to feel put off by the practice—they still want you. Ring the bell, wait patiently and, provided you have arrived during advertised hours, someone will appear.

ISLAMIC CENTER   (202) 332-8343
(The Mosque)
2551 Massachusetts Avenue, NW 20008
Hours: 10 A.M.–5 P.M. daily; closed to groups on Friday 1–2 P.M.
Free Admission

Dupont Circle stop (red line); a very long walk west on Massachusetts Avenue.

N2, N4, N6.

Massachusetts Avenue.

Difficult street parking in neighborhood.

Recommended for older children.

Call (202) 332-8343 to make arrangements for group tours.

Inaccessible.

Tours are offered on a walk-in basis.

The Islamic Center, a Moorish jewel on Embassy Row, transports you from the buzz of Washington streets to the peace of a Muslim house of worship. The mosque, which faces Mecca, has a striking exterior and a lush interior: thick Persian carpets provide a place for the devout to pray (Muslim tradition bars chairs—and shoes, which you must leave at the entrance), and wonderfully ornate Turkish tiles grace the walls. The interior designs are outstanding examples of Islamic craft. A muezzin calls the devout to prayer from the minaret five times a day.

Women are asked to cover their heads before entering the mosque; head coverings are provided. Visitors should not wear shorts or other brief attire.

Religious services are held on Friday from 1 to 2 P.M. During this period groups are not allowed in the mosque; individual visitors, however, are invited. Women must wear head coverings, long skirts or slacks and long-sleeved tops.

Those visitors with a special interest in Islamic religion might want to investigate the library in the center, which is open to the public the same hours as the mosque. The Islamic Center also houses a gift shop that sells prayer rugs, books on Islam, incense and postcards.

NATIONAL   **(202) 673-4800 (recorded information)**
ZOOLOGICAL PARK   **(202) 673-4717**
3001 Connecticut Avenue, NW 20008
Hours: April 15–October 15 Buildings: 9 A.M.–6 P.M.
                                 Grounds: 8 A.M.–8 P.M.
       October 16–April 14 Buildings: 9 A.M.–4:30 P.M.
                                 Grounds: 8 A.M.–6 P.M.
       Closed Christmas
Free Admission

 Woodley Park/Zoo stop (red line); walk up the hill on Connecticut Avenue.
 L2, L4, to Connecticut Avenue entrance.

Connecticut Avenue.

 Limited parking in zoo lots at an hourly rate (free to FONZ members); during peak times, lots are often filled by 10 A.M. Street parking in the area is very difficult. Areas are set aside for bus-passenger discharge, pickup and free parking.

 On the grounds. The Mane is a cafeteria/snack bar open year-round for lunch. The fare is limp burgers, hot dogs and fries. In warm weather, food choices expand to include the Panda Garden, selling pizza, hot dogs and beverages at reasonable prices. In the summer months, several stands throughout the zoo sell soda and ice cream. The zoo is a great place to picnic.

 Highly recommended. The National Zoo is a terrific place for kids, even if they're not interested in animals. There's lots of room to run, hills to roll down, etc. Special tours can be arranged for school groups on weekdays by calling (202) 673-4955. Strollers can be rented; you must leave your driver's license at the rental booth.

 Guided tours can be scheduled one month in advance for groups of 10 or more. In the summer, tours are given only on weekends. Call (202) 673-4955 to make arrangements.

 Fully accessible. Special parking is reserved in Parking Lots B and D; all exhibit space is wheelchair-accessible, as are phones and rest rooms. While the zoo is accessible, it is on a very steep hill.

 Special tours for the visually impaired are not standard but can be arranged one week in advance by calling (202) 673-4954. Beepers have been installed at the Connecticut Avenue traffic light to assist crossing for those who are visually impaired.

 Sign language tours can be arranged by calling (202) 673-4955 at least three weeks in advance.

 Free guided tours can be arranged by calling (202) 673-4955 at least one month in advance.

If you like zoos, you'll love our National Zoo—it's among the finest in the world. The zoo is just about everything it should be: spacious (over 160 acres, originally designed by Frederick Law Olmsted) with an extensive variety of fauna (over 5,000 animals of 500 species) that are comfortably lodged for study, preservation and enjoyment. Well-designed and beautifully marked pathways allow you to meander through the exhibit areas, which mimic the animals' natural habitat wherever possible.

An extensive rebuilding program has been under way for the past 15 years; some of the truly lovely results include the 1.5-acre lion-tiger exhibit, the Great Ape House and the 90-foot-high Great Flight Cage, wherein visitors mingle with birds among waterfalls, foliage and pools. The Small Mammal House is a gem and is bordered by the Heritage Garden, which demonstrates how plants influence our use of food and medicine. The Reptile Discovery Center has recently been totally refurbished, a gibbon environment has been created to allow them plenty of room to swing through the "treetops," and a rainforest has been replicated in Amazonia.

Some of the more popular exhibits have been designated as "limited access"—entry hours may differ from the rest of the zoo, and you may have to wait in lines for entry. These exhibits place heavy emphasis on education; animal keepers are usually available for questions, and it's suggested you budget more time to absorb all there is to offer. Included are Amazonia (10 A.M.–6 P.M. in summer, 10 A.M.–4 P.M. in winter), Reptile Discovery Center (10 A.M.–6 P.M. in summer, 10 A.M.–4:30 P.M. in winter), Invertebrate Exhibit (10 A.M.–6 P.M. Wednesday–Friday, 9 A.M.–6 P.M. Saturday–Sunday), and Zoolab in the Education Building (10 A.M.–1 P.M. Friday, 10 A.M.–2 P.M. Saturday–Sunday).

Exotic treasures abound. Hsing-Hsing, a gift to the nation from the People's Republic of China in 1972, is the only giant panda in the U.S. Millions of visitors have come to see him waddle through his compound, pensively chew bamboo or, most often, lie on his back fast asleep. Many endangered species—orangutans, Komodo dragons, pygmy hippopotami and bald eagles among them—are zoo inhabitants. More common creatures are just as charming: a prairie dog village is always lively and amusing, as are the large pools for seals and sea lions.

If you can arrange it, the best time to see the animals is early morning or late afternoon; at midday the animals tend to snooze. The only scheduled feeding times are for the giant panda, 11 A.M. and 3 P.M. Other animals are fed on a varied schedule. BIRDlab is conducted in the beautifully refurbished Bird House, Friday–Sunday, noon–3 P.M.; visitors learn about birds by participating in lab activities. HERPlab in the Reptile House is open daily 9 A.M.–6 P.M. in the summer and 9 A.M.–5 P.M. in winter.

Two gift shops sell zoo souvenirs—panda mugs and so forth. A gallery and gift shop in the education building offers classier mementos (at higher prices), including books, cards and handcrafted articles with animal motifs. These shops and the food operations are operated by Friends of the National Zoo, and proceeds benefit the zoo's programs.

PHILLIPS COLLECTION   (202) 387-0961
1600–1612 21st Street NW 20009

Hours: 10 A.M.–5 P.M. Monday–Saturday
Noon–7 P.M. Sunday
Closed July 4, Thanksgiving, Christmas and New Year's

Admission: Weekends: Adults—$6.50
Students and Senior Citizens—$3.25
Members and Kids Under 18—Free
Weekdays: Admission by contribution.

Ⓜ Dupont Circle stop (red line); use Q Street exit and walk one block west.

🚕 Massachusetts or Connecticut Avenue.

Ⓟ Limited street parking.

🅘 A small café offers light fare 10:45 A.M.–4:30 P.M.
Monday–Saturday, Noon–6 P.M. Sunday.

Recommended. A booklet entitled "A Child's Adventure into the Artist's World of Color" is available at the museum. School groups are welcome for free general or thematic tours; call the education office at (202) 387-7390 one month in advance to make arrangements.

Arrangements for group tours for 10 or more people should be made at least one month in advance by calling (202) 387-7390. There is a charge of $7 per person.

Fully accessible. A wheelchair is available.

Special tours can be arranged by calling (202) 387-7390 at least one month in advance.

Special tours can be arranged by calling (202) 387-7390 at least one month in advance.

Ⓣ Tours are given at 2 P.M. on Wednesday and Saturday.

The Phillips Collection is one of the true delights of Washington. The collection was gathered by Duncan Phillips and his artist-wife, Marjorie; they opened their home to the public as a museum in 1921. The collection is composed largely of twentieth-century paintings, along with those of earlier artists who influenced their modern counterparts. The house itself is a late-Victorian brownstone, an unexpected setting for what was, in fact, the first museum of modern art in the United States.

The museum's public space was doubled with an addition in 1989 that was designed by Arthur Cotton Moore. This allows the display of pieces from the permanent collection of 2,500 works of art, as well as the mounting of temporary exhibits. The works of the permanent collection are choice, and the opportunity to view them in the intimate surroundings of parlors and sitting rooms furnished with armchairs and couches is a further enticement. Among works on display are Daumier's "The Uprising"; Cézanne's 1877 "Self-Portrait"; Renoir's "Luncheon of the Boating Party"; O'Keeffe's "Red Hills and Sun"; Eakins' "Miss Van Buren"; a whole roomful of small but wonderful Klees; major works by Rothko; an impressive collection of Braques and Bonnards; and paintings by Van Gogh, Degas, Monet and Manet.

For many years the museum has sponsored a series of free concerts from September to May at 5 P.M. Sunday. Gallery talks are given the first and third Thursday of each month; meet in the foyer at 12:30 P.M.

The museum shop sells art books, notecards and art objects as well as children's art books and supplies.

TEXTILE MUSEUM   **(202) 667-0441**
2320 S Street, NW 20008
Hours: 10 A.M. to 5 P.M. Monday–Saturday
              1–5 P.M. Sunday
              Closed holidays
Free Admission, Suggested Donations: Adults—$5   Children—50¢

 Dupont Circle stop (red line); use Q Street exit. Walk up Connecticut Avenue and turn left at S Street (half mile).
 37, D2, D4, D6, D8, L4, L5, N2, N4, N6—walk one block off Massachusetts Avenue on S Street.

Massachusetts or Connecticut Avenue.

 Difficult street parking.

 Not recommended unless the child has a particular interest in design and handicrafts.

 Call (202) 667-0441 to make arrangements for group tours at least two weeks in advance.

 Limited accessibility. Call ahead on the day of your visit for staff assistance in negotiating the one-step entrance and the several steps to one exhibit room.

 A large-print version of the exhibit's labels is available from the receptionist.

 Walk-in tours are given Saturday, Sunday and Wednesday at 2 P.M., September–May. Call (202) 667-0441 to arrange tours at other times.

The Textile Museum, located in a house designed by John Russell Pope, is on a quiet, elegant residential street northwest of Dupont Circle. Founded in 1925 with the collection of George Hewitt Myers, the museum houses over 14,000 woven pieces of both artistic and archaeological significance; only a fraction of the works can be displayed at one time. If you have an interest in Oriental rugs or Navajo blankets or any of the more obscure aspects of fine weaving, you'll want to make a stop here; it is one of only two museums in the world devoted entirely to handwoven rugs and fabric, and has the world's finest collection of Peruvian weavings.

For visitors without a background in textiles, we recommend the museum tour because, although the works are well displayed and labeled, there is very little explanatory text to inform you of the various processes or significance to the exhibits.

The Textile Museum mounts a half-dozen major exhibits a year that are accompanied by a series of lectures and luncheon seminars. Occasional workshops and demonstrations are also given. Saturday morning is rug morning: at 10:30, discussions on scheduled topics are held and visitors bring in pertinent textiles for examination by experts. The first Wednesday each month is a potpourri; folks bring in any textile with which they're having conservation problems for expert advice. Call (202) 667-0441 for a copy of the museum's newsletter.

The Museum Arts Library is divided into sections on fine arts, decorative arts, techniques, costumes and textile processes, all organized by nationality. The library is open to the public 10 A.M.–2 P.M. Wednesday–Saturday. The museum also has a very fine shop with books on every conceivable variety of textile work, as well as yarn, rugs, scarves, beads and handcrafted gift items. Don't miss a stop in the lovely garden.

WASHINGTON NATIONAL CATHEDRAL   (202) 537-6200
(The Cathedral Church of St. Peter and St. Paul)
Wisconsin Avenue at Woodley Road (Mt. St. Alban) 20016
Hours: Main Floor: 10 A.M.–4:30 P.M.
               May 1–Labor Day   10 A.M.–9 P.M.
      Pilgrim Observation Gallery: 10 A.M.–3:15 P.M. daily
                      12:30–3:45 P.M. Sunday
      Services: 7:30 A.M., Noon, 4 P.M. Monday–Saturday
             8, 9, 10 (except July and August), 11 A.M., 4 P.M.
             Sunday
Free Admission, Donations Accepted

 30, 32, 34, 36 (Wisconsin Avenue); N2, N4, N6 (Massachusetts Avenue); Old Town Trolley stop.
 Wisconsin Avenue.

 Free limited parking on cathedral grounds.

 Recommended. Special tours dealing with subjects of interest to kids can be arranged; call (202) 537-6207. Kids like the massive scale, ornate decor and the gardens. The Medieval Workshop is held 11 A.M. to 2 P.M. Saturdays (except August); hands-on family activities include stone carving and stained-glass production. Call (202) 537-2930.
 Call to request group tours at (202) 537-6207.

 Accessible. Wheelchairs are available and can go on tour, though steps may limit unassisted wheelchair access to the main nave area. Phones and rest rooms are accessible. Gift shop is not accessible.
 Tours can be arranged for the visually disabled by calling (202) 537-6207.

Amplification devices are available for services and events; request one from an usher. TDD (202) 537-6211.

A wide variety of special-interest tours are available, as are tours in foreign languages; call (202) 537-6207 or write: Washington National Cathedral, Wisconsin Avenue and Massachusetts Avenue, NW, Washington, D.C. 20016. A special "Tour and Tea" is available Tuesday and Thursday at 1:45 P.M. in one of the Cathedral's towers for a fee of $15. Call well in advance for reservations; they can be made noon–2 P.M. Wednesday and Friday at (202) 537-8993.

Walk-in tours are given from 10:15 A.M. to 12:30 P.M. and 2 to 3:15 P.M., Monday to Saturday (30 minutes). Meet at the west entrance of the Cathedral (Wisconsin Avenue end).

The glorious Washington National Cathedral is a twentieth-century church in fourteenth-century form. This massive Gothic structure, designed by Philip Hubert Frohman and under construction since 1907, was completed in 1990 and dedicated in September of that year. It is the sixth-largest cathedral in the world, and second in size in the U.S. to New York's Cathedral of St. John the Divine. Though under the jurisdiction of the Episcopal Church, the cathedral acts as the national church envisioned by George Washington, hosting many interdenominational services and events.

Even for those not interested in worship, the Washington National Cathedral is a fascinating place to visit. Modeled after the churches of medieval Europe, the cathedral is perhaps one of the last pure gothic buildings to be constructed. No structural steel is used; flying buttresses, adorned with gargoyles and grotesques, balance the outward thrust of the Indiana-limestone walls. Still, it's distinctly modern: imbedded in the Space Window is a piece of moon rock retrieved by our astronauts. Four of the grotesques on the West Tower were designed by kids; one holds an umbrella, another wears braces; the third is a raccoon and the fourth bears the face of Darth Vader. Everything in the Children's Chapel is scaled to a child's dimensions. The Pilgrim Observation Gallery on the seventh floor of the West Tower provides a magnificent panoramic view of Washington from the area's highest point.

The 30-minute tours are very informative, providing the visitor with an understanding of the sources and meaning of Gothic architecture. Specialized tours dealing in more depth with the architecture, stained glass and the cathedral's tower can be arranged. If you prefer to tour by yourself, you can purchase the excellent *The Washington National Cathedral* at the cathedral gift shop. This booklet is available in German, Japanese, Spanish and French, as well as in English.

The grounds of the cathedral, designed by Frederick Law Olmsted, Jr., are lovely. The Bishop's Garden, with its roses, perennials, boxwood, medieval herbs and flowers, is an especially peaceful place; its entrance is a twelfth-century Norman arch. A greenhouse, open Monday to Saturday, 9 A.M. to 5 P.M., and Sunday 10 A.M. to 5 P.M., sells annual, perennial and herb plants; an herb cottage (open 9:30 A.M. to 5 P.M. weekdays, 10 A.M. to 5 P.M. Sundays) sells dried herbs and gift items. A brass-rubbing center is located in the gift shop crypt; visitors can see an exhibit of rubbings and do their own for a nominal fee. The Cathedral Museum Shop sells cards, books, miniature gargoyles and toys, as well as information about the cathedral; it's open from 9:30 A.M. to 5 P.M. in winter, 9:30 A.M. to 7:30 P.M. in summer. A rare-book library is open to the public from noon to 4 P.M. Tuesday to Saturday.

Free organ concerts are given Sunday afternoons at 4:45 P.M.; a carillon concert can be heard on Saturdays (call for hours, since they change seasonally). The Cathedral holds an open house the last Saturday in September; it's a day of performances and is the one time visitors can climb the bell tower. Many other special events occur throughout the year; call (202) 537-6207 to see what's on while you're in town.

WOODROW WILSON HOUSE   (202) 387-4062
2340 S Street, NW 20008
Hours: 10 A.M.–4 P.M. Tuesday–Sunday
       Closed national holidays
Admission: Adults—$4.00   Children, Students and Senior
       Citizens—$2.50   Children 6 and younger—free

 Dupont Circle stop (red line); use Q Street exit. Walk north on Connecticut Avenue and turn left on S Street (half mile).
 37, D2, D4, D6, D8, L4, L5, N2, N4, N6 (exit at 24th Street and Massachusetts Avenue).

Massachusetts Avenue.

 Competitive street parking.

 Recommended for a brief visit: kids who are collectors may enjoy seeing a President's sports and vaudeville collection in his bedroom.

 Make reservations for group tours in advance by calling (202) 387-4062. Discounts are available for groups of 10 or more.

 First floor is accessible; second floor is accessible via an antique elevator that cannot accommodate standard wheelchairs; a smaller wheelchair is available at the site.

 Large-print text available.

 Printed text of tour available.

 Walk-in guided tours (45 minutes) are given as needed. Last tour at 3:30 P.M. Tour text available in Spanish, German, Italian and Japanese.

Of all the American Presidents, only Woodrow Wilson chose to make his retirement home in Washington. Wilson and his second wife, the former Edith Bolling Galt, came directly from the White House to this brick Georgian Revival house (designed by Waddy Wood) in what was, in 1921, a quiet, wooded neighborhood. Wilson lived here for only three years until his death in 1924. Mrs. Wilson continued to live in the house for another 37 years, leaving it at her death to the National Trust for Historic Preservation as a permanent Washington memorial to the former President.

The house is chockablock with the furnishings, gifts and memorabilia not only of Wilson's presidency but also of his earlier career as a college professor, president of Princeton University and governor of New Jersey. (An unexpected aspect of Wilson's personality: his avid interest in sports and vaudeville.)

On display are the President and Mrs. Wilson's bedrooms (and her bathroom), which contain many furnishings dating from the Wilsons' occupancy; the parlor, dominated by an enormous Gobelin tapestry presented as a personal gift to Mrs. Wilson by the French government; the library, from which Wilson made the first radio broadcast from a private house; the dining room and—a real delight—the first-floor kitchen, restored to an early twentieth-century appearance with a combination gas-and-coal stove and a wealth of appropriate kitchen gear.

Gifts, and books on Wilson, the presidency and history are available for purchase at the small shop.

WORTH NOTING

Hours for these sites vary; call ahead.

Art, Science and Technology Institute and Holography Collection, 2018 R Street, NW 20008, (202) 667-6322. This tiny but fascinating exhibit space shows and sells holographic art and applications.

B'nai B'rith Museum, 640 Rhode Island Avenue, NW 20036, (202) 857-6583. The museum has on permanent display over 500 objects relating to Jewish ceremony and daily life dating from earliest times. Temporary exhibits examine specific themes from modern art to archaeological findings.

Fonda del Sol Visual Arts Center, 2112 R Street, NW 20008, (202) 483-2777. This artist-directed community organization presents, promotes and preserves the cultural heritage and arts of the Americas through exhibiting the work of contemporary artists and craftspeople, as well as pre-Columbian art, Santos and folk art. Fonda del Sol sponsors concerts, lectures, poetry readings, performance art programs and educational programs throughout the year, as well as the Caribbean Festival in late summer.

INTELSAT, 3400 International Drive, NW 20008, (202) 944-7500. Make an appointment for a tour of the International Telecommunications Satellite Organization (INTELSAT), ensconced in a futuristic building on Connecticut Avenue. The tour begins with a film about the organization, moves on to the operations center—a fascinating beehive of electronic activity—and proceeds to models of satellites and launch vehicles.

National Firearms Museum, 1600 Rhode Island Avenue, NW 20036, (202) 828-6253. Housed in the national headquarters of the National

Rifle Association, this museum preserves one of the largest firearm collections in the U.S.—more than 1,000 rifles, shotguns, pistols and air guns, some of which are one-of-a-kind.

National Museum of Health and Medicine of the Armed Forces Institute of Pathology, 6825 16th Street, NW 20306, (202) 576-2418. The focus of this museum is the cultural aspects of health and medicine; its goal is public education on current critical health concerns. Through the use of state-of-the-art museum techniques, exhibits probe issues surrounding such topics as AIDS and addictions to tobacco, alcohol and drugs.

Peirce Mill, Tilden Street and Beach Drive in Rock Creek Park, (202) 426-6908. Peirce Mill began grinding grain into flour in the 1820s, harnessing its power from Rock Creek. After an incarnation as a teahouse, the mill has been restored and is back in business, grinding wheat and corn for sale to visitors. The National Park Service staff demonstrate each step of the milling process.

United States Naval Observatory, 34th Street and Massachusetts Avenue, NW 20392, (202) 653-1507. Make an appointment well in advance to go on a fascinating tour of the Naval Observatory—tours are available at night as well as during the day. You'll see the atomic clocks that keep the most accurate time in the U.S. as well as the telescopes used to track the positions of the sun, moon, stars and planets.

DUPONT CIRCLE

Dupont Circle, the largest circle park in the District of Columbia, is also one of the liveliest—and, many think, one of the loveliest. Its centerpiece, a large, graceful fountain designed in 1921 by Daniel Chester French (the sculptor of Lincoln in the Lincoln Memorial), is a tribute to Rear Admiral Samuel Francis Dupont, a naval hero of the Union cause during the Civil War. The figures supporting the fountain represent the Arts of Ocean Navigation—Sea, Wind and Stars. Today, the circle is a favorite gathering ground for brown-bag lunchers, chess players, dog walkers, jugglers and assorted colorful characters. Any day of the week you may find an impromptu concert or a protest demonstration in progress. (Demonstrations often start here and move down Connecticut Avenue to Lafayette Square.) The neighborhood around the circle is home to galleries, nontraditional retail operations and many nonprofit organizations.

The commercial bustle that surrounds the circle today gives little hint of its more elegant nineteenth-century beginnings. From the 1880s until the turn of the century, it was the most western—and the most expensive—residential neighborhood in the city. Architectural holdouts from that period, like the gleaming Patterson House (now the private Washington Club) at the eastern corner of Massachusetts Avenue and the circle (15 Dupont Circle), and the earlier, red-brick Blaine Mansion on the western edge (2000 Massachusetts Avenue) contrast sharply with modern high-rise office buildings (the most impressive of which is the Euram Building at 21 Dupont Circle).

Delightful shops and restaurants radiate generally north and south of the circle, and the enormous Beaux Arts mansions of the traditional embassy section march west along Massachusetts Avenue. Nightlife is particularly active along Connecticut Avenue above and below the circle and south along 18th and 19th Streets. To the northeast lies Columbia Road, a vibrant ethnic mélange that provides some of the best Latin American food and the most spirited street life in Washington.

THE DIPLOMATIC WORLD—EMBASSY ROW

Washington's large, official diplomatic community clusters in Kalorama and along Massachusetts Avenue, from Scott Circle to Wisconsin Avenue, giving the avenue its nickname—Embassy Row. The lower part of Embassy Row around Scott, Dupont and Sheridan circles remained virtual countryside until the turn of the century; the upper part remained bucolic even longer. A few country estates were scattered through the area, but most Washingtonians viewed this as space for picnicking in the wilds for the adventuresome.

From 1900 until World War I, Massachusetts Avenue, as the southern border of Kalorama, became the residential neighborhood of the very wealthy. In contrast to much of the housing elsewhere in Washington, the houses here were large, detached and designed by architects—a great many in the Beaux Arts–revival styles of the period. Society was high, and entertaining was lavish in these palatial homes. As fortunes began to fade in the Depression and as the wealthy sought greater privacy elsewhere, some of the houses were demolished to make room for hotels and apartments, but many were sold to foreign legations to serve as their embassies and chanceries; others are now used and maintained by private organizations and clubs. New embassies have been built alongside the old residences, and the charm of Embassy Row is undiminished.

Most of the embassies are well marked with identifying plaques and national flags. Among those most easily recognizable are the chancery of India (2107 Massachusetts Avenue) with elephants flanking its entrance; the Japanese chancery (at 2520); the closed Iranian embassy, decorated with blue and white ceramic tile (at 3005); the modernistic Brazilian embassy (at 3006); and the British embassy (at 3100), recognized for its stately Queen Anne architecture and its statue of a striding Winston Churchill. Also along the route are the Phillips Gallery (see site report), the Islamic Center (see site report), the U.S. Naval Observatory, Saint Sophia Greek Orthodox Cathedral and the Washington National Cathedral (see site report).

Each spring, usually in early April, a half dozen of these elegant buildings are opened for tours to benefit area charities.

ELEGANCE PAST AND PRESENT IN KALORAMA

When you walk through the stately streets of Kalorama today, it's difficult to imagine that virtually no development had taken place in this neighborhood at the turn of the century. The neighborhood, bounded by Massachusetts Avenue, Rock Creek Park, Connecticut Avenue and Florida Avenue, didn't become part of the city of Washington until 1890; before then, all land beyond Florida Avenue (then called Boundary Street) was part of Washington County, true wilderness to most of those who lived in the civilized city.

Kalorama was the name of the area's first estate, part of a colonial patent granted by Lord Baltimore to John Langworth in 1664. Joel Barlow, a diplomat, built his large country house in 1807, coining its name from the Greek word for "beautiful view," since the site looked out across the capital and Potomac River to northern Virginia. Until the 1890s, fewer than a dozen other residences were built—and by that time, the original Kalorama manor house had been demolished.

By 1890, Washington was beginning to boom with post–Civil War fervor. The population expanded—particularly the wealthy class—pushing the physical bounds of the city westward. Massachusetts and Connecticut Avenues were extended beyond Florida Avenue, Rock Creek Valley was preserved as a park for all to enjoy, bridges were constructed across Rock Creek, and the very rich moved beyond Dupont Circle. During the next 20 years, the houses built in Kalorama were palatial, custom designed in the Beaux Arts manner for elegant entertaining. Presidents, members of Congress, Supreme Court Justices and the very wealthy lived in this neighborhood. Fortunately, a good sampling of these sumptuous houses survives, though many are no longer private homes. Many of the grand estates now serve as embassies, chanceries, museums and private clubs.

Seven cultural institutions, each in a building originally designed as a home, have banded together to form the Dupont-Kalorama Museums Consortium (Phillips Collection; Textile Museum; Woodrow Wilson House; Anderson House; Historical Society of Washington, D.C.; and Fonda del Sol). Together they sponsor Dupont-Kalorama Museum Walk Day—free music, special exhibitions and tours, hands-on activities and free admission to all the museums—on the first Saturday in June. By touring them all, one savors the full flavor of this elegant neighborhood.

The best representation of Kalorama at its most prosperous is Sheridan Circle; if you can block out today's hustle, it's easy to imagine the heyday. Much of the Kalorama area has been designated part of the Sheridan-Kalorama D.C. Historic District.

COLUMBIA ROAD—A TOUCH OF SALSA

The Columbia Road/Kalorama Triangle/Adams-Morgan neighborhood forms the most diverse residential area of the city—economically, racially and ethnically. Columbia Road itself is one of the oldest thoroughfares in Washington, and has long been a commercial center for small businesses and trades. Today, it has a particularly Latin flavor, since Columbia Road is the heart of Washington's Latin American community. Restaurants and carry-outs abound, offering paella, chorizo, sangria, black beans and other Spanish/Latino delicacies. Latino groceries share Columbia Road and 18th Street with community art galleries, dance and art studios, discount clothing stores, antique shops, a farmers' market and the city's best collection of African restaurants—it's a thriving, vital spot.

The joys of urban life are shadowed by its sorrows here; the area was "rediscovered" in the 1960s, attracting many young, white professionals who have restored houses to their original charm but have displaced residents from their lifelong homes. As a result, the neighborhood is politically concerned, active and vocal—and one of Washington's more vibrant places.

In recent years, what was a local celebration of the area's diversity has become "the biggest block party in the world," according to the organizers of Adams-Morgan Day. Held in mid-September, this vivid street fair draws many visitors. Music fills the air from multiple stages around the neighborhood, and hundreds of vendors sell food and merchandise.

NOSHING IN NORTHWEST

Northwest is a large area, but there are some concentrations of quick and tasty food operations to revive you while you're touring. Check out Connecticut Avenue just north of Dupont Circle, north of Calvert Street and again at Tenley Circle. In Adams-Morgan, you'll have your choice of ethnic fare around the intersection of 18th Street and Columbia Road. Neighborhood and fast-food restaurants abound along Wisconsin Avenue from Van Ness Street north to Friendship Heights at Western Avenue (the Maryland line).

9

OTHER
D.C. AREAS

This chapter is a catchall for points of interest that fall outside the usual tourist areas in the capital city. While these sites aren't among the most spectacular of Washington's offerings by any means, each provides an interesting change of pace that might be welcome in an otherwise hectic trip.

Since these sites are scattered throughout Northeast and Southeast Washington, driving is the best way to get to them; parking won't be a problem, because these areas are well off the usual tourist circuit. While the National Shrine of the Immaculate Conception has a cafeteria, none of the other sites has eating facilities, and restaurants are few and far between. Accordingly, spend your mealtimes in other parts of the city.

FREDERICK DOUGLASS NATIONAL HISTORIC SITE
(Cedar Hill)

House: (202) 426-5961
Visitor Center: (202) 426-5960

1411 W Street, SE 20020
Hours: October–April 9 A.M.–4 P.M.
May–September 9 A.M.–5 P.M. daily
Closed Thanksgiving, Christmas and New Year's
Free Admission

 94, A2, A4, A6, B2, B5.

Martin Luther King, Jr., Avenue, though it's best to telephone for a cab.

 Street parking available.

 Recommended if related to schoolwork.

 Groups of five or more are asked to schedule their visit in advance. Call (202) 426-5961.

 Limited accessibility. Only the first floor is accessible; rest room in visitor center is accessible. A photo album of the second floor is available.

 Walk-in tours given on the half hour; a film of Douglass' life is shown on the hour.

The fiery black abolitionist Frederick Douglass lived in this house from 1877, when he was 60 years old, until his death in 1895. Douglass was an escaped slave who became one of the country's most eloquent spokesmen for the abolition of slavery. By the time Douglass moved to this house, he was a prosperous man who had held high positions in the government.

Cedar Hill is a comfortable house that overlooks the city from the far side of the Anacostia River. The house has been restored by the National Park Service to appear much as it did when Douglass lived here, and it contains many of his personal effects as well as his large library.

NATIONAL ARBORETUM   **(202) 475-4815**
24th and R streets, NE 20002
Hours: 8 A.M.–5 P.M. weekdays
          10 A.M.–5 P.M. weekends and holidays
          Bonsai collection: 10 A.M.–3:30 P.M. daily
          Closed Christmas
Free Admission

 B2, B4, B5.

 In front of administration building, but it's best to telephone for a cab.

Plenty of parking except when the azaleas are blooming; driving is best for this site.

 Recommended. There are lots of wide open spaces to run in.

 A guided tour will be provided for groups of 10 or more. Set up an appointment at least three weeks in advance by calling (202) 475-4815.

 Roads wind throughout the Arboretum, and much can be viewed from your car; the footpaths are difficult to navigate. The National Bonsai and Penjing Museum, the Friendship Garden and the Herb Garden are all accessible with gravel walks. The Administration Center and gift shop are fully accessible.

No matter what season you visit Washington, try the National Arboretum for a breath of fresh air. The facility's 444 hilly acres abound with herbaceous plants, shrubs and trees that you can enjoy as you drive along the 9.5 miles of roadway or stroll on one of the many pleasant footpaths. Since the arboretum includes the second highest point in the city, the hillsides offer dramatic views of the Capitol, Washington Monument and Anacostia River, as well as changing vistas of flowers and foliage.

The arboretum is most famous for its collection of 70,000 azaleas that usually bloom from the end of April until mid-May. When the azaleas are at their peak, as many as 20,000 people may visit the arboretum in a single day. This may be the arboretum's flashiest hour, but each month has its special offerings. The conifers and hollies dominate the winter; one of the most significant collections is over 1,500 dwarf and slow-growing conifers assembled on a five-acre hillside. Winter's conclusion is marked by the jasmine and camellia blossoms. Spring presents bulbs, the azaleas, wildflowers, ornamental cherries, crabapple and an extensive array of dogwood. Fern Valley and the National Herb Garden are delightful summer spots, as are the collections of peonies, daylilies and crepe myrtle. The autumn foliage is spectacular.

A year-round treat is the National Bonsai Collection and Japanese Garden, a stunning bicentennial gift to our country from the Nippon Bonsai Association of Japan. The pavilion garden is a work of art; some of the treasured specimens are over 350 years old. This garden's cultivated compactness contrasts beautifully with the arboretum's hills and dales, and is worth a trip on its own. The Friendship Garden, a twenty-first-century succession garden, provides visual treats throughout the year.

The Carl Buchheister National Bird Garden is currently under construction. Buchheister was a pioneering environmental educator and president of the National Audubon Society in the 1960s. The garden will be "a kind of living bird feeder," according to its designer, providing a sanctuary and focusing the attention of visitors on how birds use the garden and can be a part of a human habitat.

The arboretum, in its role as a major research and education facility, offers special demonstrations, lectures, films and flower shows in the Administration Center throughout the year. Call (202) 475-4815 to find out what's offered—and what's blooming—while you're in town.

A car is just about essential to enjoy the arboretum thoroughly.

NATIONAL SHRINE OF THE IMMACULATE CONCEPTION

(202) 526-8300

4th Street and Michigan Avenue, NE 20017
Hours: November 1–April 1   7 A.M.–6 P.M. daily
April 2–October 31   7 A.M.–7 P.M. daily
Free Admission

 Brookland-CUA stop (red line).

 Michigan Avenue.

 Ample free parking.

 On premises. A cafeteria-style dining room is open from 8 A.M. to 2 P.M. year-round.

 Groups of 30 or more should notify the shrine at least a week in advance of their visit; call (202) 526-8300.

 Limited accessibility. Wheelchairs are available.

Walk-in tours given every half-hour from 9 to 11 A.M. and 1 to 3 P.M. (40 minutes); Sunday tour schedule varies, so call ahead.

The National Shrine of the Immaculate Conception is the largest Roman Catholic church in the United States and the eighth largest religious building in the world. The shrine seats over 3,000 people and has 59 chapels. Located right off the campus of Catholic University, the shrine's architecture is a blend of contemporary, Byzantine and Romanesque styles. Work on the building, which is shaped like a Latin cross, began in 1920; while it is structurally complete today, decorative work continues. The structure is noted for its statuary, stained-glass windows and beautiful mosaics. A gift shop is on the lower level.

The National Shrine Music Guild gives frequent musical performances; call (202) 526-8300 for their schedule.

WORTH NOTING

The hours of these sites vary; call ahead.

Anacostia Museum, 1901 Fort Place, SE 20560, (202) 287-3369. The Anacostia Museum, a branch of the Smithsonian Institution, serves the educational and cultural needs of Washington's African-American community. Exhibits deal largely with black history, urban problems, and arts and crafts, and have included displays on achievements of black women, Harlem photography, Frederick Douglass and Anacostia.

Franciscan Monastery, 1400 Quincy Street, NE 20017, (202) 526-6800. The Franciscan Monastery is also the official "Commissariat of the Holy Land for the United States"; its function is to preserve and maintain shrines in the Holy Land by raising funds in the U.S. The Byzantine-style church and beautifully maintained grounds are studded with reproductions of the Holy Land shrines that the monastery strives to support.

Kenilworth Aquatic Gardens, Kenilworth Avenue and Douglas Street, NE 20019, (202) 426-6905. Over 100,000 water lily, lotus, water hyacinth, bamboo and other water plants grow here in ponds formed by diking the Anacostia River's marshland along this stretch of its shoreline. The federal government purchased the gardens in 1938 from W. B. Shaw, a Civil War veteran and government clerk who was also a self-taught authority on water plants. The flowers are in bloom from June through August, especially in the early morning before the heat of the day hits.

10

SUBURBAN

VIRGINIA

The sites in suburban Virginia are primarily historic and/or military in nature, and many are associated with the activities of the Washington and Lee families. In Old Alexandria, the many noteworthy historic homes and commercial buildings include Robert E. Lee's boyhood home, the Lee-Fendall House, Carlyle House, Gadsby's Tavern and the Stabler-Leadbeater Apothecary, as well as Christ Church. Within 15 miles are Mount Vernon, Woodlawn Plantation and George Washington's Grist Mill, with their rich details of eighteenth-century life. Arlington National Cemetery, the Iwo Jima Memorial and the Pentagon, all of which are in Arlington, appeal to many beyond the military buffs among us.

If your sightseeing exhausts you, retreat with a picnic to one of the several parks in the area, including Great Falls Park or Theodore Roosevelt Island. If your food tastes run more to restaurant fare, check our recommendations in Chapter 21, "Dining."

ARLINGTON HOUSE   **(703) 557-0613**
(Robert E. Lee's Home)
On the grounds of the Arlington National Cemetery
Mailing Address: Arlington House
                George Washington Memorial Parkway
                McLean, VA 22101
Hours: April–September   9:30 A.M.–6 P.M.
         October–March   9:30 A.M.–4:30 P.M.
Free Admission

Arlington Cemetery stop (blue line); the stop is 1½ blocks from the visitor center, which is a long trek from Arlington House.
 The Tourmobile will take you right up to the house.

 Arlington National Cemetery visitor center.

 Pay parking is available near the National Cemetery visitor center, which is a long hike from the house.

 Educational programs for school groups, geared toward the fourth-grade level and above, are offered October–May. Call (703) 557-0613 or write several months in advance to make arrangements for a tour for children.

 Groups can make advance arrangements for the standard tour by calling (703) 557-0613.

 Accessible to first floor. No rest room, phone or fountain.

 The staff will try to arrange a special tour if called at least one week in advance at (703) 557-0613.

 The staff will try to arrange a special tour if called at least one week in advance at (703) 557-0613.

T Walk-in tours are given during slow months (i.e., nonsummer, nonholiday). Self-guided tour brochures are always available. National Park Service personnel are available to answer questions.

Arlington House is located on the grounds of Arlington Cemetery, overlooking the Potomac River. The history of the mansion centers on the two most powerful families in Virginia—the Washingtons and the Lees—and the roles they played in the history of their country.

The original enormous tract of land was purchased in 1778 by George Washington's stepson, John Parke Custis, as the site where he intended to build his estate. But before he could build his home, Custis died at Yorktown during the Revolutionary War. In 1802, Custis' son, George Washington Parke Custis (who had been raised by his grandparents, George and Martha Washington), actually began construction on the Greek Revival mansion that we see today. When Custis finally completed the mansion in 1818, he filled it with Washington family heirlooms and made it famous for gracious Washington-style hospitality.

George Washington Parke Custis' only surviving child, Mary Ann, married the dashing Lt. Robert E. Lee in 1831. The Lees considered it home for 30 years, until the Civil War. In his chamber in Arlington House on April 20, 1861, Lee wrote the letter resigning his commission from the United States Army upon the secession of Virginia from the Union. The next day Lee left the house to assume command of the forces of Virginia in Richmond; he never returned to Arlington House. Mrs. Lee departed the mansion a few weeks after her husband.

The Union Army found Arlington House to be of prime importance because of its strategic position overlooking the Potomac River; during the Civil War the mansion and its grounds became an armed Union camp. Many of the Washington heirlooms remaining in the house were moved to the Patent Office for safekeeping and were not returned to the Lee family until 1901.

In 1864, when Mrs. Lee failed to appear in person to pay her property taxes, the house and land were confiscated by the federal government for back taxes, and 200 acres were set aside to serve as a national cemetery. The Supreme Court restored the property's title to the Lee family in December 1882, and in early 1883 the Lees sold it back to the government for $150,000.

In 1925, the house was dedicated as a national memorial to Lee, and Congress appropriated funds for its restoration to its 1861 appearance.

ARLINGTON NATIONAL CEMETERY　　　　**(703) 692-0931**
Arlington, VA 22211
Hours: April–September　8 A.M.–7 P.M.
　　　　October–March　8 A.M.–5 P.M.
Free Admission

 Arlington Cemetery stop (blue line); visitor center is a 1½-block walk.

 Tourmobile; Old Town Trolley.

 Visitor center.

 Pay parking is available in lots near the visitor center directly across Memorial Bridge from Washington. The visitor center will issue a special car pass to any visitor who wants to visit a particular gravesite.

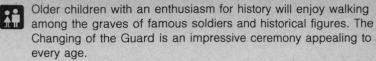 Older children with an enthusiasm for history will enjoy walking among the graves of famous soldiers and historical figures. The Changing of the Guard is an impressive ceremony appealing to every age.

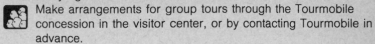 Make arrangements for group tours through the Tourmobile concession in the visitor center, or by contacting Tourmobile in advance.

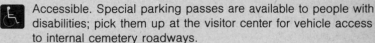 Accessible. Special parking passes are available to people with disabilities; pick them up at the visitor center for vehicle access to internal cemetery roadways.

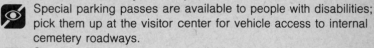 Special parking passes are available to people with disabilities; pick them up at the visitor center for vehicle access to internal cemetery roadways.

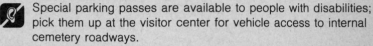 Special parking passes are available to people with disabilities; pick them up at the visitor center for vehicle access to internal cemetery roadways.

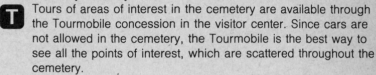 Tours of areas of interest in the cemetery are available through the Tourmobile concession in the visitor center. Since cars are not allowed in the cemetery, the Tourmobile is the best way to see all the points of interest, which are scattered throughout the cemetery.

Arlington National Cemetery is located on 620 acres of land, about half of which was once part of the estate of Mrs. Robert E. Lee. The land was acquired by the federal government during the Civil War for use as a burial ground for Union dead. The first man buried here, however, was not a Union soldier, but a Confederate prisoner of war who had died in a local hospital.

Among the 215,000 buried here are more than 60,000 American war dead including those who served in the Revolutionary War, the War of 1812, the Civil War, the Spanish-American War, World Wars I and II, the Korean and Vietnam conflicts, as well as casualties of the Lebanese terrorist bombing, the *Challenger* disaster, and the action in Panama. Burial in the cemetery is reserved for those who have served in the military, Medal of Honor recipients, high-level government officials and their dependents.

Pierre L'Enfant, Washington's first planner, is buried south of Arlington House on a slope overlooking the city that he designed. Mary and George Washington Park Custis, the builders of the mansion, are also buried here.

On a slope below the mansion is the grave of President John F. Kennedy, marked by a slate headstone, covered with Cape Cod fieldstone and surrounded by marble inscribed with quotations from Kennedy's Inaugural Address. Nearby, in a grass plot, is the grave of Senator Robert F. Kennedy.

The simple marble Tomb of the Unknowns is inscribed, "Here rests in honored glory an American soldier known but to God." In the tomb are the remains of an unidentified soldier slain in World War I; crypts at the head of one tomb contain the remains of unknown military personnel who died in World War II, the Korean conflict and the Vietnam conflict. The tomb is guarded by a single soldier from the 3rd U.S. Infantry; the watch is changed in a simple yet impressive ceremony every hour on the hour from October to March and every half hour from April to September.

If you're visiting the cemetery on a Saturday or holiday afternoon from April to September, you should stop at the nearby Netherlands Carillon. Carillon concerts are given at 2 and 4 P.M., sponsored by the National Park Service. Also visit the Marine Corps Memorial (see site report).

CLAUDE MOORE COLONIAL FARM   **(703) 442-7557**
AT TURKEY RUN
6310 Old Georgetown Pike, McLean, VA 22101
Hours: 10 A.M.–4:30 P.M. Wednesday–Sunday
       Open from April 1 to pre-Christmas
       Closed Thanksgiving and in inclement weather
Admission: Adults—$2   ($3 for special events)
            Children (3–12) and Senior Citizens—$1   ($1.50 for special events)

P   Free lot. Take Capital Beltway (I-495) to Exit 13. Turn south on Rt. 193 and go 2.3 miles to Claude Moore Colonial Farm sign. Go left and follow signs to lot. Take care not to confuse the Farm with Turkey Run Park.

Highly recommended. Schoolchildren from preschool on up can participate in Colonial Experiences for a modest fee. They can dip candles, spin yarn and make toys. Call three months in advance.

Groups should call in advance at (703) 442-7557 to reserve space and time.

Limited accessibility. The path to the farm is hilly and hard to pass with a wheelchair. With a day's advance notice, the farm staff will allow people to enter a special gate near the cabin. Call (703) 442-7557. Rest rooms are inaccessible.

No walk-in tours are given, but the costumed "family" is always on hand and very willing to answer questions.

The Claude Moore Colonial Farm at Turkey Run is a 12-acre working farm operated by a private foundation. A "family" of volunteers re-creates the life of a low-income, rural family in the 1770s. You may find this especially interesting after visiting some of the larger, more prosperous historical plantations in Virginia and Maryland.

The family grows tobacco, corn and wheat and works in two kitchen gardens and an apple orchard. The daily routines of the farm vary seasonally, and include cooking lunch over a log fire, washing dishes in a wooden tub, planting, cultivating, harvesting and preparing corn and wheat and weeding the gardens. Such domesticated animals as quarter horses, red Devon milking cows, chickens, turkeys and razorback hogs roam the farm. And if you keep a sharp eye out, you are likely to see white-tailed deer, opossums, skunks and migratory geese and ducks nearby.

Special programs, featuring music and crafts, are conducted on the third weekend of each month from May to December. Market fairs are held three times each year. Call (703) 442-7557 to find out what's on while you're in town.

FRANK LLOYD WRIGHT'S   **(202) 780-4000**
POPE-LEIGHEY HOUSE
9000 Richmond Highway (Route 1)
Hours: 9:30 A.M.–4 P.M. daily March–December
       Closed Thanksgiving and Christmas
Admission: Adults—$4 Children—$3
          Senior Citizens and Students—$2.75
          Ticket rate reduced if purchased jointly with Woodlawn
          Plantation ticket.

Free parking. Take 14th Street Bridge to the George Washington Memorial Parkway south. At the Mount Vernon traffic circle take

Rt. 235 south for 3 miles. Woodlawn is at the intersection of Rt. 235 and Rt. 1.

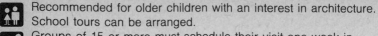 Recommended for older children with an interest in architecture. School tours can be arranged.

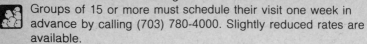 Groups of 15 or more must schedule their visit one week in advance by calling (703) 780-4000. Slightly reduced rates are available.

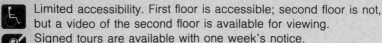 Limited accessibility. First floor is accessible; second floor is not, but a video of the second floor is available for viewing.

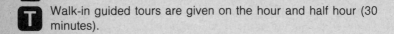 Signed tours are available with one week's notice.

T Walk-in guided tours are given on the hour and half hour (30 minutes).

The Pope-Leighey House, designed by Frank Lloyd Wright in 1940, reflects the architect's belief that living in well-designed space should not be a privilege reserved for the wealthy. This house is one of five built by Wright on the East Coast in what he called the Usonian style, which involved the use of available industrial technology to create modest homes.

Built for the Loren Pope family, the house contains many architectural features that, although commonplace today, were revolutionary in 1940. For instance, Wright designed a carport instead of an enclosed garage, a flat roof rather than a sloped one, and built-in furniture; he also placed heating coils in the floors.

In 1964, when the construction of a highway threatened the house's existence, the National Trust for Historic Preservation dismantled the Pope-Leighey House and reassembled it here on the grounds of the Woodlawn Plantation (see site report).

GADSBY'S TAVERN MUSEUM   **(703) 838-4242**
134 N. Royal Street, Alexandria, VA 22313
Hours: 10 A.M.–5 P.M. Tuesday–Saturday
1–5 P.M. Sunday
Closed Thanksgiving, Christmas and New Year's
Admission: Adults—$3   Children 11–17—$1   Under 11—Free
Group Rates: Ten or more adults—$2

M King Street stop (yellow line); DASH to Old Town.

DASH to Old Town; 65¢, exact fare required. 10's, 11's, 28's, 29's.

 Expensive from Washington. Take Metro to National Airport and catch a cab there.

 On-street parking and nearby commercial lots. From D.C. take 14th Street Bridge; take second right, George Washington Memorial Parkway south to Alexandria. The parkway becomes Washington Street once you are in Alexandria. Turn left onto Cameron Street; go three blocks, and turn right onto Royal Street.

 Gadsby's Tavern Restaurant, (703) 548-1288, is open from 11:30 A.M. to 3 P.M. and 5:30 to 10 P.M.; waiters wear period costumes.

 See special rates above. Make arrangements two weeks in advance. For groups of more than 20 people, after-hours museum tours can be arranged, often in conjunction with dinner at the Tavern.

 Limited accessibility. First floor of the City Tavern Museum is accessible. The rest room is inaccessible.

 The tour text is available in Braille.

Tours start 15 minutes before and after the hour to coordinate with other nearby Alexandria attractions.

Gadsby's Tavern Museum, operated by the city of Alexandria, combines the two-story pre-Revolutionary City Tavern, built circa 1770, with the larger City Hotel, added in 1792. The tavern was described by many as the finest public house in America. Both buildings were well known to George Washington, who came here often; he used the City Tavern as his headquarters several times during the French and Indian War. He and Mrs. Washington often danced in the ballroom of the hotel. Other well-known visitors to the tavern included John Paul Jones, Aaron Burr, George Mason, Francis Scott Key, Henry Clay and the Marquis de Lafayette.

In the City Tavern, a guest could enjoy a meal and a drink in the taproom, or visit the gaming room across the hall. Upstairs in the assembly room one could take dancing lessons or attend lectures or club meetings. Above, under the gabled roof, one might find lodgings. The addition of the hotel provided more commodious sleeping arrangements plus a lovely ballroom. After the Civil War, the buildings fell into decay and the hotel closed by 1900.

The beautiful woodwork that you see in the ballroom is a reproduction; the original is in the American Wing of the Metropolitan Museum of Art in New York. While you are in the ballroom, note the musicians' gallery.

At Christmas, the staff gives a lovely candlelight tour of the tavern. Call (703) 838-4200 for the time and date of this event.

GREAT FALLS PARK   **(703) 285-2966**
9200 Old Dominion Drive, Great Falls, VA 22066
Hours: 7 A.M.–½ hour after dusk
          Visitor Center 10 A.M.–6 P.M. daily
          Closed Christmas
Free Admission

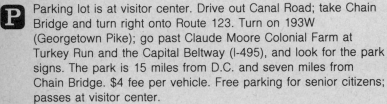

P Parking lot is at visitor center. Drive out Canal Road; take Chain Bridge and turn right onto Route 123. Turn on 193W (Georgetown Pike); go past Claude Moore Colonial Farm at Turkey Run and the Capital Beltway (I-495), and look for the park signs. The park is 15 miles from D.C. and seven miles from Chain Bridge. $4 fee per vehicle. Free parking for senior citizens; passes at visitor center.

Snack bar at the visitor center is open daily from Memorial Day to Labor Day. Picnicking is allowed.

Recommended, in the presence of attentive adults.

The park staff will arrange guided tours of the park with a week's notice. Call (703) 285-2966 (TTY/TDD/V).

Limited accessibility. The visitor center has long ramps and accessible phones and rest rooms. Some trails are accessible with assistance. Overlook #2 is accessible.

Park interpretive brochures are available in Braille.

With two weeks' notice, a signed tour can usually be arranged. Call (703) 285-2966.

A With two days' advance notice, tours can be arranged on the topics of geology, culture, or plant and animal life of the Great Falls area.

T A Potomac Canal tour is given at 1 P.M. daily.

Great Falls Park is aptly named, for it is here that the Potomac River plunges 76 feet over a series of huge boulders through the mile-long Stephen Mather Gorge. The river is a quarter-mile wide in this gorge and, at places, up to 50 feet deep.

The wooded park lends itself to hiking, picnicking and bird watching. In addition, it is possible to see a great deal of wildlife, including beaver, skunks, opossum, red fox, white-tailed deer and cottontail rabbits.

The park encompasses the relics of George Washington's ill-fated dream of operating a canal on the Virginia side of the river to bypass the unnavigable sections of the Potomac. Washington founded the Potowmack Canal Company (an Indian word meaning "trading place") in 1785 and the canal was completed in 1802. Light-Horse Harry Lee, the father of Robert E. Lee, founded a town nearby named Matildaville. Within 26 years, however, trade declined, the canal company folded and the town fell into ruins. The remains of Matildaville are in the park. Self-guided tour brochures can be found at the visitor center. You will find two of the five canal locks still standing. Note the beaten marks of the proud stonemen's "signatures." Only a few vine-covered foundations and the chimney of Dickey's Tavern remain to mark the town of Matildaville.

One final word of warning about visiting Great Falls Park: because of the danger of drowning, it is illegal to climb on the rocks near the water's edge or swim or wade near the falls. Alcohol is strictly forbidden on park land.

GUNSTON HALL PLANTATION (703) 550-9220
Route 242 (4 miles east of Route 1), Lorton, VA 22079
Hours: 9:30 A.M.–5 P.M. daily
    Closed Thanksgiving, Christmas and New Year's Day
Admission: Adults—$5   Students—$1.50   Senior Citizens—$4

 Parking at visitor center. Take US-1 South to Virginia Route 242; go left on Route 242 to Gunston Hall. The plantation is 20 miles southwest of Washington.

 A special "Touch Museum" is open to school groups only with advance notice; call (703) 550-9220. Kids will also enjoy the nature trail where they may see deer, bald eagles and other wildlife (two miles round-trip to river and back).

Discount rate ($4 adult) and special tours are available to 12 or more; call (703) 550-9220 to make arrangements or stop at desk.

 Limited accessibility. Visitor center and grounds are fully accessible. No ramps to house; eight steps; upper floors inaccessible.

 Walk-in guided tours are given every half hour. The guides are well versed in the historical and domestic details of the house. French, Spanish, Portuguese, Russian, Japanese and Italian language brochures are available.

Gunston Hall was the home of George Mason, whom Thomas Jefferson called one of the wisest men of his generation. Mason is best known as the father of the Bill of Rights of the United States Constitution. A visit to Gunston Hall (a Commonwealth of Virginia property now administered by the National Society of Colonial Dames of America) and its 550 acres of gardens and woodlands will reward you with an unparalleled view into the life, architecture and horticulture of the era when Mason lived.

Construction began on the mansion in 1755. Fine craftsmen—both freemen and indentured servants—worked on the house, as is particularly evidenced by the carved woodwork throughout.

The formal gardens, which are comparable to those at the Governor's Palace in Williamsburg, are divided by boxwood planted by Mason more than 200 years ago. All the plants and shrubs in the garden are varieties found in colonial times. A two-mile (round-trip) nature trail leads down to the Potomac River.

In addition to the house and the grounds, take time to visit the restored kitchen, smokehouse, dairy, washhouse and schoolhouse, for they provide an excellent view of everyday plantation life.

Gunston Hall Plantation is 20 miles southwest of Washington.

LEE'S BOYHOOD HOME   **(703) 548-8454**
607 Oronoco Street, Alexandria, VA
Hours: 10 A.M.–4 P.M. Monday–Saturday
          1–4 P.M. Sunday
          Closed December 15 through January 31, except by
          appointment and for the Sunday closest to Lee's birthday
Admission: Adults—$3   Children—$1

King Street stop (yellow line), DASH to Old Town.

 DASH to Old Town; 65¢, exact fare required. 9's, 10's, 11's, 29's.

 Very expensive from D.C.; take Metro to National Airport stop and a taxi from there.

 On-street parking. From D.C. take the 14th Street Bridge; take the second right onto the George Washington Parkway south. This becomes Washington Street in Alexandria. Take a left onto Oronoco.

 Recommended for older children.

 Admission is lowered to $2 for groups of 10 or more. The staff requests several days' notice for groups of 10 or more so they can arrange for extra guides; call (703) 548-8454 to notify staff of your plans.

 Limited accessibility; first floor can be accessed through the garden.

 Walk-in guided tours are given continually (30 minutes).

The Revolutionary War hero, Light-Horse Harry Lee, leased this early-Federal–style house in 1812. When Lee died in 1818, Mrs. Lee kept the house and raised her five children here until 1825. The young Robert E. Lee attended the Quaker School next door; he left in 1825 to attend West Point and begin his military career.

The house is full of charming Lee memorabilia and rare antiques. You will see that the table in the morning room is laid out for a game of cards.

Several special events take place during the year: in January the birthdays of Light-Horse Harry Lee and Robert E. Lee are celebrated; in July, the wedding celebration of Molly Fitzhugh and G. W. P. Custis (Martha Washington's only grandson), who were the parents of Mary, wife of Robert E. Lee, takes place; in October, a celebration honors the visit of General Lafayette to Mrs. Lee in 1824; and in December, candlelight tours of the house are conducted. Call (703) 548-8454 to find out the precise times of these events; the dates change each year.

MARINE CORPS WAR MEMORIAL   (703) 285-2600
(Iwo Jima Memorial)
Adjacent to the Arlington National Cemetery
Mailing Address: George Washington Memorial Parkway
         Turkey Run Park, McLean, VA 22101
Hours: 7 A.M.–dark
     (Night visits are not advised)
Free Admission

Rosslyn stop (blue and orange lines); it's a long walk to the memorial via Fort Myer Drive.
Take the Metro to Rosslyn and catch a cab from there.

Free lot. Take the Roosevelt Bridge from D.C. to Virginia. Follow the signs for Route 50 (you will see the memorial to your left once you are on 50). Take the first exit off 50 to the right—it's marked "Rosslyn/Key Bridge," and a second smaller sign says "Fort Myer." Take a left at the top of the ramp onto Meade Street. Continue on past the memorial, which you will pass again on your left, and take the first left onto Jackson Avenue. Take the first left after the Netherlands Carillon and follow the drive to the parking lot.

Recommended for a quick visit.

Accessible. No rest rooms or phones.

TDD number is (703) 285-2620.

Better known as the Iwo Jima Memorial, the Marine Corps War Memorial commemorates all the marines who have died in the defense of the United States since the Corps was founded in 1775. Designer Horace W. Peaslee based the statue on Joseph Rosenthal's photograph of five marines and one sailor raising the U.S. flag on Mount Suribachi after a bloody World War II battle in the Pacific. Sculptor Felix W. de Weldon created this 78-foot-high piece, the largest bronze statue ever cast. The flag incorporated into the monument is a real flag, which flies day and night by Executive Order. The Marine Sunset Parade occurs Tuesdays, June to August, at 7 P.M.

     Try to plan your visit to the memorial to coincide with the concert given adjacent to the memorial at the Netherlands Carillon, a 127-foot bell tower complete with 49 bells, which was presented to the United States by the people of the Netherlands after World War II. The free concerts are given on the carillon from Easter Sunday through September on Saturdays and national holidays, 2 to 4 P.M. and 6:30 evenings during the summer. It is possible during concerts to climb the carillon tower, from which the view of the Washington skyline is breathtaking.

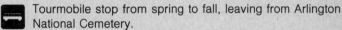

MOUNT VERNON PLANTATION   (703) 780-2000
Southern terminus of the George Washington Memorial Parkway
Mailing Address: Ladies Association
                Mount Vernon, VA 22121
Hours: April–August   8 A.M.–5 P.M. daily
        March, September, October   9 A.M.–5 P.M. daily
        November–February   9 A.M.–4 P.M. daily
Admission: Adults—$7
            Senior Citizens—$6
            Children (6–11)—$3
            Annual pass—$10
            Free on federal holiday of George Washington's Birthday

Tourmobile stop from spring to fall, leaving from Arlington National Cemetery.

Free. The walk from the lot to the house is long. Mount Vernon is eight miles south of Washington on the George Washington Memorial Parkway.

None allowed on premises. The Mount Vernon Inn, just outside the gates, offers both restaurant and snack-bar fare, with picnic tables available outside the snack bar.

Recommended. "Colonial Days" special programs are held for school groups in spring and fall. Call for details.

Reduced admission is available for groups of 20 or more.

Limited accessibility in house. First floor and museum are accessible; higher floors are not, but photo album of those areas is available. Rest rooms are accessible. A limited number of wheelchairs are available at the main entrance on a first-come, first-served basis. Electric wheelchairs may be rented at that location.

Services under development. Call ahead to see if a special tour can be arranged.

Services under development. Call ahead to see if a special tour can be arranged.

From April through August, landscape and garden tours are offered every half hour from 9 A.M. to 4 P.M. Self-guided tours of the mansion, although docents are stationed throughout to answer questions. An excellent inexpensive guide, *Mount Vernon, An Illustrated Handbook,* can be purchased at the gift shop.

The 2,500 acres of land that originally composed the Mount Vernon estate were granted to George Washington's great-grandfather, John Washington, in 1674. George Washington lived here from 1754 until his death in 1799. Washington had to spend many of those years away from his beloved estate, however, to serve as commander-in-chief of the Continental Army, delegate to the Constitutional Convention and first President of the United States. Despite his long absences from Mount Vernon, Washington directed the enlargement of the house from 1½ to 2½ stories and increased the estate's size to 8,000 acres. Of the five independently operating farms that thrived on the estate during the years of Washington's management, only the mansion house farm remains intact today.

As you walk up the path to the mid-Georgian-style mansion, you pass nine outbuildings, all of which are original, with the exception of the coach house and the greenhouse/slave quarters. Once inside, you can view 14 rooms of the house. Some of the main points of interest in the mansion are the Palladian window in the large dining room, the decorated ceiling and Washington family coat-of-arms above the mantel in the west parlor, and Washington's study where the President wrote in his diary, kept the farm's records and carried on his tireless correspondence. Upstairs are five bedrooms. As you exit the mansion, stop to enjoy the unspoiled view of the Potomac River from the porch; the view is very much as it was when Washington gazed out over the same fields.

Stroll around the 30-acre grounds; visit Washington's tomb as well as the cemetery memorial to the slaves whose labor made Mount Vernon such a successful farm, the lovely gardens, the museum and outbuildings. In addition, stop by a new attraction by the wharf called "George Washington: Pioneer Farmer," which through exhibits and demonstrations shows some of the innovative farming techniques that

Washington developed. A small gift shop is located on the grounds; a larger shop is outside the entrance gate.

Several special events are held at Mount Vernon throughout the year. "Gardening Days at Mount Vernon" takes place in April or May and includes demonstrations, exhibits and plant sales of cuttings taken from the floral descendants of George Washington's garden. The third Monday in February celebrates Washington's birthday; admission to the estate is free, and a fife and drum corps performs for the 10,000 or more visitors. "Holidays at Mount Vernon" are celebrated from December 1 to January 6; special tours and exhibits display how the Washingtons entertained during the holiday season.

A lovely way to see the mansion and grounds is to take the four-hour round-trip cruise from Pier 4 in Washington. See Chapter 15, "Outdoor Washington/Sports," for details.

PENTAGON (703) 695-1776
Right off I-395
Mailing Address: Pentagon, Washington, D.C. 20301
Hours: 9:30 A.M.–3:30 P.M. Monday–Friday
　　　Closed holidays
Free Admission

M Pentagon stop (blue line). The stop is inside the Pentagon. Follow the arrows at the top of the escalator to the tours.

Telephone for a cab to pick you up at the south parking entrance.

P Pay lot. From D.C. take the 14th Street Bridge, which will lead you to I-395. Follow the signs to the Pentagon.

Not recommended. The tour is fast and there is little except pictures to see.

Groups of 20 or more are requested to give one week's notice by phone ([703] 695-1776), or write to Pentagon Tour Director's Office, 20301.

Accessible.

T Tours are given 9:30 A.M. to 3:30 P.M. every half hour. The tours are confined to certain corridors and the guide walks backward to make sure that you do not stray into secured areas. Among the points of interest on the tour are the cases of models of past and present aircraft and the corridor of Time-Life World War II paintings.

The Pentagon, one of the world's largest office buildings, is the head-quarters of the Defense Department. It took only 16 months to build and was finished in January 1943. Most people are familiar with its five-sided exterior shape. Within those five walls are five concentric inner-to-outer rings connected by 10 spokelike corridors. Although there are 17.5 miles of corridors, no office is any farther than a seven-minute walk from any other office.

The Pentagon houses the secretaries of defense, Army, Navy, Air Force and Coast Guard, as well as the Joint Chiefs of Staff. The military and civilian employees who work here are concerned both with making policy decisions and with housing, training, feeding, equipping and caring for the members of the armed services.

SULLY HISTORIC SITE

1-(703) 437-1794
(this is a long-distance number)

Route 28, between U.S. 50 and the Dulles Toll Road, Chantilly, VA
(4 miles from Dulles Airport)
Mailing Address: Fairfax County Park Authority
4040 Hummer Road, Annandale, VA 22003
Hours: March–December   11 A.M.–4 P.M. Wednesday–Monday
January   11 A.M.–4 P.M. weekends only
Admission: Adults—$3   Children—$1   Seniors—$1.50

P Free parking lot. Take Route 66 west to Route 50 (Exit 15). West on Route 50 to Route 28. North on 28 to site.

◖◗ Picnicking is allowed.

👫 There are lots of special events for kids. Sunday afternoon family activities include open-hearth cooking, craft demonstrations and music (included in the price of admission). During the summer, there is an eighteenth-century-type round-robin of activities for kids. School groups and scout troops can arrange for special tours.

🏛 Call or write several weeks in advance to set up a tour.

♿ Limited accessibility. Grounds are accessible using the brick walkway. There are eight steps leading to the house.

👁 Braille brochure is available.

T Entry to house is by tour only; tours are given every half hour.

An excursion to the Sully Historic Site is an enjoyable escape from the city. This Federal-period plantation house was built in 1794, and is authentically furnished. It stands as an intriguing example of Federal architecture, handsome and pleasing to look at yet lacking the symmetry so characteristic of its period.

Richard Bland Lee, a member of the first U.S. Congress, a judge of the District of Columbia Orphans Court and brother of Revolutionary War hero Light-Horse Harry Lee, once lived here. The house was continuously lived in until the government bought the land for Dulles Airport in 1958.

You may be interested in the program of special events (call or write for a schedule), which includes a Civil War life event in May, an antique auto show in June, a September quilt show, an October Harvest Festival and a Christmas celebration.

THEODORE ROOSEVELT ISLAND   (703) 285-2600

In the Potomac River between Roosevelt and Key bridges
Mailing Address: George Washington Memorial Parkway
                          McLean, VA 22101
Hours: 7 A.M.–dark
Free Admission

 Rosslyn stop (blue and orange lines); pedestrian overpass connects to island (10-minute walk).

 Free lot on the Virginia shore. Access to the park is from the northbound lane only of the George Washington Memorial Parkway.

 None on premises. Picnicking is permitted but no tables are provided and no fires allowed. Rest room and water fountain on island.

 Recommended. There are lots of trails and different sorts of ecosystems.

 The park rangers will give a combined nature and historical walk for groups of 10 or more with seven days' advance notice; call (703) 285-2598 to make arrangements.

 Limited accessibility. The island is accessible by wheelchair, but the trails are not paved. The rest room is inaccessible and there is no phone.

TDD number is (703) 285-2620.

Theodore Roosevelt Island is an appropriate memorial for the nature-loving President who created the national park system. Although the island is within sight and sound of D.C., it is a home to wildlife and a tranquil haven for humans as well. No cars are allowed on the island, which is accessible only by a footbridge from the parking lot.

In the center of the island is a bronze memorial, designed by Paul Manship, consisting of a 17-foot statue of the President in a familiar speaking pose and four 21-foot granite tablets inscribed with Roosevelt's philosophy on citizenship.

If you're feeling energetic, take the time to hike the 2.5 miles of nature trail. The island provides examples of marsh, swamp, upland wood and rocky shore ecosystems. You may even spy some of the wildlife that lives on the island, including pileated woodpeckers, wood ducks, beaver, kingfishers and marsh wrens.

WOODLAWN PLANTATION   **(703) 780-4000**
9000 Richmond Highway (Route 1), Mount Vernon, VA
Mailing Address: P.O. Box 37, Mount Vernon, VA 22121
Hours: 9:30 A.M.–4:30 P.M. daily; closed weekdays in January
          Closed Thanksgiving, Christmas and New Year's
Admission: Adults—$5   Senior Citizens—$3.50   Students (through high school)—$3.50   *Joint tickets with the Pope-Leighey House are less expensive*

P Plenty of free parking. Take 14th Street Bridge to the George Washington Memorial Parkway south. At the Mount Vernon traffic circle take Rt. 235 south for 3 miles. Woodlawn is at the intersection of Rt. 235 and Rt. 1.

Recommended for the Audubon nature trail. School tours should be arranged in advance by calling (703) 780-4000.

Groups of 15 or more must schedule a visit in advance and will receive slightly reduced entrance rates; call (703) 780-4000 or write to make arrangements.

Limited accessibility. Ramps. No rest room. A video is available of the second floor, which is inaccessible.

Signed tours available with one week's notice.

T Guided tours on the hour and half hour.

Woodlawn Plantation provides an excellent picture of the life of the Virginia gentry in the early nineteenth century. Woodlawn's 2,000 acres of land were once a part of George Washington's estate, Mount Vernon (see site report); our first President gave the land as a wedding gift to his foster daughter, Nellie Custis, when she married his favorite nephew and secretary, Lawrence Lewis.

Construction of the Georgian-style mansion, which was designed by Dr. William Thornton (who was the first architect of the Capitol), lasted from 1800 to 1805. The spacious sophistication of the plantation mansion contrasts with the house at Mount Vernon, which is much more like a farmhouse. From the porch at Woodlawn you can see Mount Vernon in the distance; it's said that Nellie Custis Lewis kept a tract of land between the two houses clear all the years she lived at Woodlawn so she could sit in her "catch-all" room on the second floor and look at her childhood home through a telescope.

In keeping with the standards of the National Trust for Historic Preservation, which maintains the plantation, all of the lovely furnishings in the house are from the Lewis' period and some of them are the pieces the family actually used. Of special interest are the music room with its pianoforte and two harps and the children's bedroom, well stocked with period toys.

After touring the house and visiting the exhibit area and gift shop in the basement, take the time to stroll through the handsome formal gardens, with a rest on one of the many shaded benches. If you want to walk the nature trails as well as view the mansion and its gardens, allow yourself at least two hours at Woodlawn.

Each year Woodlawn Plantation sponsors special events that require separate tickets for admission: a needlework exhibit is held in March; on a weekend in July the plantation is open in the evening for music, champagne, picnicking and dancing on the green; a quilt show in the fall; and a Woodlawn Christmas. Since these events are rescheduled each year, write or call (703) 780-4000 to find out the exact dates they'll be held.

Visit the Pope-Leighey House (see site report) while you're at Woodlawn; it's one of five houses on the East Coast designed by Frank Lloyd Wright.

WORTH NOTING

Carlyle House Historic Site, 121 N. Fairfax Street, Alexandria, VA 22314, (703) 549-2997. When John Carlyle, one of Alexandria's founding fathers, built his colonial mansion in 1751, the Potomac River lapped at the garden gate. Today the house is landlocked, bordered by modern row houses and a renovated factory. Because of restoration by the Northern Virgina Regional Park Authority, however, the grandeur of the house, if not its grounds, has been reinstated. While the furnishings of the house aren't Carlyle family pieces, they are representative of the period.

Christ Church, 118 N. Washington Street, Alexandria, VA 22314, (703) 549-1450. Christ Church, designed by James Wren and built in 1773, is typical of early Georgian church architecture, much like an English country church. The first Episcopal church in Alexandria, Christ Church served as the house of worship of General and Mrs. Washington as well as Robert E. Lee.

Colvin Run Mill, 10017 Colvin Run Road (5 miles west of Tyson's Corner on Rt. 7), Fairfax, VA 22030, (703) 759-2771. This water-driven wooden-geared mill sits alongside Difficult Run, which was in the nineteenth century a major transportation artery between the Shenandoah Valley and the port of Alexandria. An old-fashioned general store sells penny candy and flour ground by the mill. Often there are craft and wood-carving demonstrations.

George Washington's Grist Mill, 5514 Mount Vernon Memorial Highway, Alexandria, VA 22309, (703) 780-3383. George Washington had this grist mill built in 1770–1771; he took great interest in its operation and would walk from Mount Vernon to inspect it. Restored from 1932 to 1934 by the Civilian Conservation Corps, the mill is much the same as in Washington's day.

Lee-Fendall House, 429 N. Washington Street, Alexandria, VA 22314, (703) 548-1789. Some 37 Lees lived in this house from the time it was built in 1785 until 1903. Not surprisingly, the house reflects a variety of styles—Federal, Greek Revival and Victorian, which is how it is presented today. The interior is representative of upper-middle-class life from 1850 to 1900, including a fine collection of doll houses.

The Lyceum, 201 S. Washington Street, Alexandria, VA 22314, (703) 838-4994. The Lyceum, a brick-and-stucco Greek Revival–style house built in 1839, serves as Alexandria's history museum, exhibiting historic objects from the city's founding in 1749 to the present. The Lyceum also sponsors a variety of events, tours, lectures and musical performances. The staff can make hotel, campground and dinner reservations for you, help you plan an itinerary and inform you of special events throughout the state.

Pohick Church, 9301 Richmond Avenue, Lorton, VA 22079, (703) 550-9449. Both George Washington and George Mason were members of Pohick Church's building committee; Washington surveyed the site and drew the plans for the brick building and Mason designed the interior. The church was completed in 1774. A notable feature is the box pews, similar to those in English churches of the time; the boxed enclosures kept out drafts and retained the heat of footwarmers and hot bricks used by parishioners in winter.

Ramsey House, 221 King Street, Alexandria, VA 22314, (703) 838-4200. Ramsey House, the oldest house in Alexandria, serves as the city's Convention and Visitors Bureau. Most historians believe that this frame-over-brick structure was built in Dumfries in 1724 and moved to its present location in 1749–50 by William Ramsey, the city's first postmaster. The staff will provide you with a calendar of events listing house and garden tours, candlelight tours, walking tours, shopping information, and celebrations of historical events; they will also make group reservations for restaurants, hotels and entertainment.

Stabler-Leadbeater Apothecary Shop, 107 S. Fairfax Street, Alexandria, VA 22314, (703) 836-3713. The Apothecary Shop, founded by Edward Stabler, operated continuously as a pharmacy from 1792 to 1933. Included among the prominent customers of the shop were the Washington, Lee, Custis and Fairfax families. The Apothecary Shop museum, which opened in 1939, exhibits a collection of approximately 800 early hand-blown glass containers, antique mortars and pestles, scales, thermometers, the original account books and prescription files.

OLD TOWN RAMBLE

Founded in 1749 by Scottish merchants and named for John Alexander, a principal original landowner, Alexandria is today reminiscent of its colonial origins. Many of Virginia's most influential families settled around the new port city—among them the Washington, Lee, Mason and Fairfax clans. George Washington, then an apprentice surveyor, helped lay out many of the city's streets.

Alexandria thrived as a tobacco port; many merchants and sea captains built comfortable homes which survive today. Most of the streets in Old Alexandria are still lined with attached row houses that are flush with the sidewalks; behind many of these charming houses, out of view of the casual stroller and beyond earshot of the clatter of carriage on cobblestone, are lovely gardens and patios.

In Revolutionary days and through the mid-1800s, Alexandria was a political, commercial and cultural center in addition to its role as a leading seaport (surpassed in importance only by Boston). In 1846, Virginia successfully petitioned Congress to grant Alexandria back to the state, which, from the 1790s, had been an official part of the new nation's capital.

Alexandria was spared the destruction of the Civil War because Union troops occupied it from the first and cut it off from the rest of the South. Soon thereafter, however, the advent of the railroad caused Baltimore to become the dominant port in the area. With its economy slowed by the loss of commerce, Alexandria became a sleepy if genteel little city.

Only during the first administration of Franklin Roosevelt was the city rediscovered and appreciated for both its proximity to the capital city and its historic examples of Colonial, Revolutionary and Greek Revival styles of architecture. In the past 20 years, historic preservation groups have slowly restored the old sites, and the attention that they have paid to accurate historical detail today delights visitors.

Old Town—the restored center of Alexandria—lies roughly between Oronoco Street on the north, the Potomac River on the east, Gibbon Street on the south, and Washington Street on the west. The heart of the commercial development, which is quite charming, is King Street; start your tour here, at Ramsey House, which is the excellent tourist information center. Ramsey House also offers 1½-hour walking tours of the historic district; call (703) 838-4200 for times, which change throughout the year.

Old Town boasts many fine restaurants and shops. Check the shopping tips in Chapter 14, "Shopping/Galleries."

VIRGINIA VITTLES

It wasn't so long ago that you could not find a truly outstanding meal outside of the city, but, happily, that is no longer the case. Even the "restaurants with a view" have become gastronomically ambitious.

The best place to find moderately priced, convenient restaurants close to tourist attractions is Old Town Alexandria. King Street is the main attraction. You'll find everything from burgers to Creole, Greek and French cuisine. The Rosslyn-Clarendon-Ballston corridor in Arlington County is home to many inexpensive ethnic restaurants and suburban branches of downtown eateries. See Chapter 21, "Dining," for some specific Virginia recommendations.

11

NEARBY

MARYLAND

Glimpses into the past, portents of the future and events of the day will be found at different suburban Maryland points of interest. The only tie that binds these sites is the family car necessary to see just about all of them—they're scattered from 20 miles north to 16 miles south of downtown Washington, and virtually none is served by public transportation.

Historical sites include the National Colonial Farm, a working replica of a modest eighteenth-century plantation; Fort Washington Park, a fortress surviving from the 1820s; the C&O Canal, a national historic park celebrating canal life from the mid-1800s; Oxon Hill Farm, a functioning replica of a farm from the turn of the twentieth century; Clara Barton House, the restored home of the founder of the American Red Cross; the National Trolley Museum; and Glen Echo Park, an old-time amusement park that has been converted to offer creative leisure-time pursuits. NASA, the National Bureau of Standards and the Agricultural Research Center offer views of the government at work in space, in laboratories and on the land. Finally, Wheaton and Cabin John Regional parks let the whole family relax, exercise, picnic and play.

AGRICULTURAL RESEARCH CENTER   **(301) 504-8483**
Route 1, Beltsville, MD 20705
Hours: 8 A.M.–4:30 P.M. weekdays
       Closed holidays
Free Admission

P Free parking. Capital Beltway (I-495) to Exit 25 north (Route 1), or Exit 23; north on Kenilworth to Powder Mill; bear right on Powder Mill Road. The visitor center is in The Log House (Bldg. 302). The center is 15 miles northeast of Washington.

Picnic tables are available. There are a number of restaurants and fast-food operations along Route 1.

Special tours can be arranged in advance for schoolchildren, fifth grade and up, that concentrate on the animals. Call (301) 504-9484 to arrange a tour. New exhibits focus on science education, with particular emphasis on food and agriculture. A nature trail circles the lake at the visitor center.

Make arrangements two weeks in advance for group tours by calling (301) 504-9484.

The tour is taken on a wheelchair-accessible bus. The visitor center is fully accessible.

Arrangements can be made for a signing interpreter by calling (301) 504-9484 at least two weeks in advance.

A Guided tours are by appointment only (1½ hours). Call (301) 504-9484 or write: Visitor Center, Building 302, BARC-East, 10300 Baltimore Avenue, Beltsville, MD 20705.

The Agricultural Research Center of the U.S. Department of Agriculture covers more than 7,200 acres of experimental pastures, orchards, gardens, fields and woods, and has over 1,000 buildings, including research laboratories, greenhouses, barns, poultry houses, mechanical shops and other laboratories. The Beltsville ARC is the largest of some 130 research centers around the country. It houses the first National Education Center of the system, fulfilling the 1862 mandate for the Department of Agriculture when created during Lincoln's presidency. The center stresses environmental concerns—air, water, soil, plants and animals—and is the only federal facility to concentrate on plant and animal science education for the public. The folks from Beltsville were prime consultants to Disney World during the construction of the Kraft Pavilion.

You can call ahead to schedule a guided tour, which is given on an air-conditioned bus. We recommend the tour, since you'll learn about the experiments being conducted at the center, stop at some of the buildings and have someone to answer your questions. The tours are popular with farmers and foreign visitors but would be of interest to most people. Indeed, the staff has worked hard to make the center a fun, educational experience for all ages.

C&O CANAL NATIONAL HISTORIC PARK   (301) 299-3613
Great Falls
11710 MacArthur Boulevard, Potomac, MD 20854
Hours: Park: dawn to dusk
    Tavern Museum: 9 A.M.–5 P.M.
    Closed Thanksgiving, Christmas and New Year's
Free Admission

P Free parking in lot. From Washington, take Canal Road to its end; go left on MacArthur Boulevard. Take your first left, which is Falls Road; this leads to Great Falls Park.

Food concession open from mid-April to mid-October; picnic sites are available.

Recommended.

Groups can reserve the *Canal Clipper*, a mule-drawn boat, for day trips from April to October by calling (301) 299-3613.

Fully accessible. Both museum and rest rooms are accessible to someone in a wheelchair. Towpath is accessible but bumpy.

The Chesapeake and Ohio Canal, which stretches 184 miles from Georgetown to Cumberland, Maryland, is a great deal more successful today as a recreational experience than it ever was as a commercial venture. Constructed between 1828 and 1850, the canal was rendered obsolete—even before its completion—by the B&O Railroad, which was built concurrently. The aim of both projects was to link the abundant resources of the frontier with the cities and commercial ventures of the East, but the railroad accomplished this feat more cheaply and with greater speed. While the canal never achieved great economic success, it served as a conduit for grains, furs, lumber, coal and flour until it was destroyed by a flood in 1924.

Today the canal prospers as a National Historic Park. On the 12-foot-wide dirt towpath next to the canal, hikers, joggers, bikers and casual strollers all enjoy the park (see Chapter 15, "Outdoor Washington/Sports," for bike- and canoe-rental facilities). Wildlife abounds: we've spotted bald eagles, beaver, snapping turtles, families of Canada geese, snakes, osprey, indigo buntings and bass, to name a few. A footbridge to an island affords a spectacular view of the Great Falls.

At Great Falls, you can get a fine sense of life on the canal's barges.

The tavern, built circa 1830, has been turned into a lovely little museum. The museum also is the starting point for a 1½-hour mule-drawn boat trip on the *Canal Clipper;* on these trips, the park staff, dressed in period clothes, demonstrate typical canal tasks, such as guiding the mules and working the water locks, and lead the group in song. Tickets are $5 for adults, $3.50 for senior citizens and children 12 and under. Civic and educational groups can reserve the barge for daytime trips. Call (301) 299-2026 for the boat's schedule and group reservation information. The *Canal Clipper* runs from mid-April to mid-October, with weekend trips at 10:30 A.M., 1 P.M. and 3 P.M.

GODDARD SPACE FLIGHT CENTER (NASA) (301) 286-8981
Greenbelt, MD 20771
Hours: 10 A.M.–4 P.M. daily
Closed Thanksgiving, Christmas and New Year's
Free Admission

 Free parking. Capital Beltway (I-495) to Exit 22 (Greenbelt Road) north; bear right and follow signs to NASA.

 Recommended.

 Call (301) 286-3979 in advance to make arrangements for groups of 20 or more.

 Fully accessible.

 Tour objects can be handled.

 Call (301) 286-8981 or TDD (301) 286-8103 to arrange a special tour.

T Walk-in guided tours are given 11:30 A.M. and 2:30 P.M. daily.

At the Goddard Space Flight Center visitors center, you can see spacecraft and rockets and watch film clips of NASA's space feats. The guided tour takes you to view the NASA communications center as well as the Hubble Space Telescope Operations Control Center. From October to May on the second Saturday each month a NASA video is shown at 1 P.M. and Star Watch occurs at 7 P.M. On the fourth Sunday each month the Discover Goddard lecture series is held at 1 P.M. Local rocket clubs launch their models at Goddard on the first and third Sunday of each month from 1 to 2 P.M., weather permitting.

NATIONAL COLONIAL FARM   (301) 283-2113

3400 Bryan Point Road, Accokeek, MD 20607

Hours: 10 A.M.–5 P.M. Tuesday–Sunday
　　　　Closed Thanksgiving, Christmas and New Year's

Admission: Adults—$2   Children under 12—50¢   Family—$5 maximum

P Free parking. Capital Beltway (Route 95); take Exit 3A south (Indian Head Highway) for 10 miles; bear right on Bryan Point Road, continuing four miles to farm.

None on grounds. The Saylor Memorial Picnic Grove is adjacent to the visitor center.

Recommended. Seeing the farm in action will please children; demonstrations are given on weekends.

Group tours available. Make arrangements by calling (301) 283-2113.

Accessible. A vehicle is available for those with physical handicaps; call (301) 283-2113 to make arrangements.

Special tours for the visually impaired can be arranged by calling (301) 283-2113.

Special tours for those who are hearing-impaired can be arranged by calling (301) 283-2113.

T Walk-in guided tours are given on a casual basis, if a staff member is free.

The National Colonial Farm ushers you back to a modest Tidewater plantation of 1750; crops, livestock, agricultural methods, farm structures and farmers' garb are all from the mid-eighteenth century. Tobacco, corn, wheat, vegetables, fruits and herbs are grown; these crops provided both cash and food for the colonial farm family. A smokehouse, barn and kitchen are all open, and demonstrations of farm activities are given on weekends.

This lovely farm is operated by the Accokeek Foundation in cooperation with the National Park Service. It's situated across the Potomac River from Mount Vernon, George Washington's estate, about 15 miles south of downtown Washington. Consider combining your visit to the National Colonial Farm with a stop at Fort Washington Park, which is nearby (see "Worth Noting").

OXON HILL FARM (301) 839-1176
6411 Oxon Hill Road, Oxon Hill, MD 20021
Hours: 8:30 A.M.–5 P.M. daily
    Closed Thanksgiving, Christmas and New Year's
Free Admission

P   Free parking. Capital Beltway (Route 95); Exit 3A (Indian Head Highway) south; bear right onto Oxon Hill Road. The farm is on the right.

⚬   None on grounds. Picnic tables are available.

👪   Recommended. Kids will enjoy seeing farm tasks—milking cows and threshing wheat. They can also ride on the farm's hay wagon, plant corn and take part in other activities.

👨‍👩‍👧   Group tours for schools only. Call (301) 839-1176 to make arrangements.

♿   Call ahead at (301) 839-1176 to arrange to drive beyond the parking lot onto the farm. The farm, rest room, and visitors center are accessible; the phone is not.

👂   With notice, a signed tour can be arranged.

A   Call (301) 839-1177 to hear a recording of scheduled events.

T   No walk-in guided tours are given, but the friendly staff welcomes questions and conversations.

This delightful working farm, run by the National Park Service, is a replica of those in the Washington area at the turn of this century. The family cow is milked at 10:30 A.M. and 4 P.M.; the horse team plows the fields and hauls crops (you're welcome to hop aboard when the horses are pulling the hay wagon); and other farm animals are available for petting and observing. Check in at the visitors center when you arrive to ascertain the day's activities; they may include planting, harvesting, cooking, sheep-shearing, spinning or cider pressing, depending on the season. The farm's woodlot has a self-guided nature trail.

Consider combining your trip to Oxon Hill Farm with a stop at Fort Washington Park, which is nearby (see "Worth Noting").

WORTH NOTING

The hours of these sites vary widely; call before visiting.

Clara Barton National Historic Site, 5801 Oxford Road, Glen Echo, MD 20768, (301) 492-6245. The Clara Barton National Historic Site was home to Clara Barton, founder of the American Red Cross. Built in 1891 as a warehouse for the organization's supplies, the building was modified in 1897 and became Red Cross national headquarters and Barton's home. The charming dwelling is furnished with gifts Barton received from countries throughout the world in recognition of her work.

Fort Washington Park, Fort Washington, MD, (301) 763-4600. Fort Washington was originally built in 1808 to protect the new capital city from enemy intrusions up the Potomac River. During the War of 1812, however, the fort was destroyed by its own garrison to prevent British capture. A new fort was designed in the 1820s, and that garrison survives today. An explanatory film is shown in the visitors center, and occasional historic re-creations are staged.

Glen Echo Park, MacArthur Boulevard, Glen Echo, MD 20768, (301) 492-6229. Glen Echo Park began in 1891 as a National Chautauqua Assembly. Some of the Chautauqua structures survive, but most of the park activities take place in buildings from the park's next incarnation—an amusement park. Today the park offers creative leisure experiences for everyone, from arts-and-crafts classes to ethnic and folk festivals to a ride on a 60-year-old Dentzel carousel.

Mormon Temple, 9900 Stoneybrook Drive, Kensington, MD 20795, (301) 587-0144. Since its dedication in 1974, the Washington Temple of the Church of Latter-Day Saints has been closed to non-Mormons, but the visitors center and temple grounds are open to the general public. The visitors center's exhibits explain the church's history and doctrine, and display interior photos of the imposing temple. The 57 acres of grounds have won national landscaping awards and present lovely seasonal displays.

National Capital Trolley Museum, 1313 Bonifant Road, Wheaton, MD, (301) 384-6088. The small museum, filled with trolley memorabilia, is built in the form of an old train station. The trolleys, exhibited outdoors and available for rides, came from Austria, Germany and Washington.

Brookside Gardens, Wheaton Regional Park, Glenallen Avenue, Wheaton, MD 20902, (301) 949-8230. This 500-acre regional park offers a bonanza of recreational opportunities for the whole family: a large creative play area, picnic space, a small train, an ice rink, a nature center, tennis courts, hiking trails and the Brookside Gardens and Conservatory. The 50 acres of gardens are serenely beautiful, ranging from formal beds and fountains to a hillside of azaleas and rhododendrons to a Japanese pavilion overlooking a small pond. The Conservatory Greenhouse houses banana, cacao, bird-of-paradise, coffee bushes and many other exotic plants.

A DASH THROUGH ANNAPOLIS

Annapolis, an easy 30-mile drive from Washington, makes for a fun day-trip. First settled in 1649, Annapolis retains its impressive historic charm. This was a thriving center of political, commercial and social life in the eighteenth century, thanks to a booming tobacco trade. The commercial district now consists of gracious and carefully restored buildings facing brick-lined streets, a thriving collection of shops, eating spots and intriguing nooks and crannies.

Historic sites are plentiful. We suggest you first check in with the Visitors Information Center at 26 West Street (9 A.M.–5 P.M. daily) or its booth at the City Dock, (410) 268-TOUR, from April to October. Free brochures and maps are available. You may even want to park at the Navy-Marine Corps Stadium and take the shuttle bus to the nearby historic district, since parking is tight there. There is a nominal fee weekdays, and free parking on weekends at the lot.

Any visit to Annapolis should include the Naval Academy and the State House. The U.S. Naval Academy is open to visitors Monday to

Saturday, 9 A.M. to 4 P.M.; Sunday, 11 A.M. to 4 P.M. Guided tours ($3 for adults, $1 for children under 12) are given frequently from March 1 through Thanksgiving, and by appointment at other times; call (410) 267-3363. The State House is the oldest state capital building in continuous use in America. Free tours, given at 11 A.M. and 3 P.M. daily, begin in the restored Old Senate Chamber, where the Continental Congress met in 1783–84 when Annapolis was the nation's capital. The building is open 9 A.M. to 5 P.M. daily, except Christmas. Call (410) 974-3400 for more information.

There are three State Historic Buildings of interest: the Maritime Museum, an eighteenth-century building now serving as a colonial maritime history museum (77 Main Street, (410) 268-5576, open daily 9 A.M.–5 P.M.); The Barracks, restored to show how Revolutionary War soldiers lived (43 Pinckney Street, (410) 267-8149, open by appointment only); and The Tobacco Prise House, with exhibits of Maryland's historic tobacco trade, located in an eighteenth-century warehouse (4 Pinckney Street, (410) 267-8149, open by appointment only).

Annapolis boasts numerous historically and architecturally significant houses and mansions. The Hammond-Harwood House (19 Maryland Avenue, (410) 269-1714) is one of the country's finest examples of Georgian architecture; it was designed by William Buckland of Gunston Hall fame (see site report). Thomas Jefferson was apparently so impressed by its magnificent proportions and ornate decorative trim that he sketched it in his diary. Don't miss the William Paca House, its superb gardens, and the Historic Annapolis gift shop (186 Prince George Street, (410) 263-5553) or the magnificent gardens at the Chase-Lloyd House (22 Maryland Avenue, (410) 263-5553). The Shiplap House Museum (18 Pinckney Street, (410) 267-8149), open 10 A.M.–4 P.M. Monday to Saturday, and noon–4 P.M. Sunday, re-creates a tavern of the eighteenth century.

Annapolis features a variety of festivities and special events, such as the Marine Trades Exposition (April), the Maryland Seafood Festival (September) and the U.S. Sailboat and Power Boat Show (October). "Christmas in Annapolis" is a six-week-long celebration, and it includes an exhausting roster of events, from wreath-hanging and tree-lighting to candlelight touring of the State House to festive feasting.

James Michener, in his novel *Space,* called Annapolis "the most beautiful state capital in America . . . with an enchanting harbor right in the heart of town and small craft lining its shores." Alex Haley traced his roots here to Kunta Kinte's arrival by slave ship in 1767; look for the commemorative plaque by the dock.

To get to Annapolis, take New York Avenue, NW, out of Washington, which connects to Route 50.

Annapolis is a fine place to wine and dine. Nestled along the shores of the Chesapeake Bay, the town is, as you might guess, noted for its seafood. Even if you don't manage a full day in the town, we can certainly recommend Annapolis for a dinner, a stroll along the City Dock and some boat-watching.

Restaurants

Crate Cafe, 49 West Street, (410) 268-3600, moderately priced, with a convenient downtown location. Especially good for lunch. Make-your-own salads and sandwiches from broad selection of ingredients. *O'Brien's,* 113 Main Street, (410) 268-6288, has seafood, steaks, burgers, pasta, vegetarian fare, bar and dancing. *Old Towne Seafood Shoppe,* 105 Main Street, (410) 268-8703, offers absolutely fresh, inexpensive seafood in simple surroundings (no credit cards). Three bar/restaurants are located in Market Square, which encloses three sides of the Annapolis harbor: *Middleton's Tavern* at #2, (410) 263-3323; *McGarvey's* at #8, (410) 263-5700; and *Riordan's* at #26, (410) 263-5449. All are pleasant environments, convivial and relaxed.

Restaurants outside of downtown, but worth the effort: *Busch's Chesapeake Inn,* Route 50 between Annapolis and the Bay Bridge, (301) 261-2034; reservations recommended. This is an institution; it's a large place with an enormous selection of seafood, prepared just about any way you want it. *Steamboat Landing,* 4850 Riverside Drive, Galesville, (410) 867-4600, is a favorite of locals. It is situated on an old river steamboat and serves moderately expensive but excellent seafood. Tends to be extremely crowded on weekends, so reservations recommended.

Music

King of France Tavern, Maryland Inn, 16 Church Circle, (410) 263-2641, a pleasant spot with live jazz; cover. *O'Brien's,* 113 Main Street, (410) 268-6288, has dancing in a bar/restaurant setting. *Mum's Grill,* 136 Dock, (410) 263-3353, and *Armadillo's,* 132 Dock, (410) 268-6680, also feature live rock and folk.

Harbor/Bay Cruises

Chesapeake Marine Tours, City Dock, slip 20, (410) 268-7600, offers a narrated bay cruise, weather permitting, from mid-May to Labor Day, Wednesday to Sunday, at 1:30 and 3:30 P.M. Other cruises—from a daily 45-minute harbor tour offered every hour to a full-day Bay outing—are offered.

Walking Tours

Historic Annapolis, Old Treasury Building, State Circle, (410) 267-8149, provides a variety of walking tours, both standard and custom-designed. Their newest is an audio guide, narrated by Walter Cronkite, that can be rented at the Maritime Museum at 77 Main Street. Guided walking tours are also offered by Three Centuries Tours of Annapolis, (410) 263-5401, with tours departing at 9:30 A.M. from the Annapolis Waterfront Hotel from April to October and at 1:30 P.M. April to October from the City Dock Information Booth. From November to March, a walking tour is conducted on Saturday, starting at Gibson's Lodgings on Prince George's Street. Annapolis, being small and charming, lends itself nicely to walking tours.

A COOK'S TOUR OF BALTIMORE

Baltimore, about 35 miles north of Washington on I-95, has been undergoing an impressive rebirth. It's well worth a day-trip to have a look (or make a detour en route to or from Washington) to take in the lively harbor, wonderful ethnic food festivals, many sporting events and the general goings-on. We strongly suggest you call (410) 837-INFO to get an information packet on food, lodging and events. The Convention and Visitors Association runs an info booth at Harbor Place (open daily 10 A.M.–6 P.M.) and another at 300 West Pratt (open 9 A.M.–5:30 P.M. Monday–Saturday).

Many attractions* are clustered around the glass-enclosed pavilion of shops and restaurants known as Harbor Place. Make it your first stop—it's where most of the action is. A quick rundown of must-sees in this area includes the National Aquarium, a seven-level complex with 6,000 mammals, reptiles, fish, amphibians and birds in their

---

* Bear in mind that, unlike Washington, *everything* in Baltimore costs money—museums, exhibits. Be prepared to spend freely.

natural habitats. The aquarium has replicas of coral reefs, tropical rainforests and even a hands-on Children's Cove.

The World Trade Center has a 27th-floor observation level and museum for a stunning view of the area. Visitors are also welcome at the frigate U.S.S. *Constellation,* the oldest navy warship afloat. The Maryland Science Center and Davis Planetarium makes for an edifying—and fun—stop, too.

If you've got any energy left after touring these sites in the harbor area, Little Italy's array of wonderful ethnic restaurants is just a short walk away.

North from the harbor is Charles Street, the city's grand boulevard, lined with magnificent homes, shops, art galleries, antique shops and restaurants. The Museum of Art, near Johns Hopkins University, has one of the country's finest collections of works by Matisse. An impressive small museum deserving of a visit is the Walters Art Gallery, located at the George Washington Monument on Charles Street.

All in all, Baltimore has become a strong area attraction in its own right; do try to visit, and make sure to sample the fare.

MARYLAND RESTAURANTS

You will find clusters of reasonably-priced restaurants throughout the Maryland suburbs: Friendship Heights at the District line; Bethesda, which, at least in terms of restaurant choices, has become another "downtown"; Rockville, all along "the Pike," Route 355 (Wisconsin Avenue); and Silver Spring. See Chapter 21, "Dining," for some special recommendations.

12

A SHORT HISTORY
OF WASHINGTON

―――――

1608	Captain John Smith sails up the Potomac, probably as far as Little Falls above Georgetown.
1663–1703	All of present-day District acquired through grant or purchase by private landowners.
1751	Founding of Georgetown.
c. 1765	"Old Stone House" (3051 M Street, NW, in Georgetown) front portion built; one of the oldest buildings in D.C., now a historic-house museum.
1789	Georgetown University founded; first Catholic institution of higher learning in the United States and first university in Washington.
1790	The first Congress, sitting in New York, strikes a deal between New England and the South: the new government will assume the North's heavy war debts and the new capital will be in the South.
1791	Pierre Charles L'Enfant's plan for the city of Washington "unite[s] the useful with the commodious and agreeable" but he can't (or won't) produce a map. Andrew Ellicott and Benjamin Banneker (a free black) undertake survey.
1792	L'Enfant dismissed (dies in poverty, 1825).
	The White House begun in 1792 utilizing design of architect James Hoban, who won a competition over

several entries, including an anonymous one submitted by Thomas Jefferson.

1793   The Capitol begun in 1793, when George Washington lays the cornerstone using a silver trowel and with proper Masonic ceremonies. William Thornton (a doctor and amateur architect) wins design competition.

1797   "Chain Bridge" is the first bridge across the Potomac.

1799   Rhodes Tavern built at 15th and F streets; serves as home of L'Enfant.

1800   Mrs. John Quincy Adams arrives to find the Executive Mansion unplastered, short of firewood; hangs the family wash in the East Room.

    Library of Congress created by Act of Congress and founded with 3,000 books (possibly chosen by Jefferson); the Library is in the Capitol.

    Bill is presented in the House which would strip Washington residents of vote and representation in Congress.

1808   Washington's first black code (moderate by Southern standards) sets 10 P.M. curfew.

    Debate on moving capital from Washington rages in Congress. Congressmen decry the excessive living costs, innumerable inconveniences and the "debasement" of citizens willing to sacrifice their political freedom for pecuniary gain.

1812   First guidebook to Washington published.

1814   British burn White House and Capitol.

1815   Washington businessmen build "Brick Capitol" (current Supreme Court site) for Congress and end, for the moment, talk of moving the capital from Washington.

    Columbia Typographical Union formed, one of the first workingman's organizations in the U.S.

1820s   Washington is notorious for slave trade, but Congress refuses to grant city's request to bar trade from city.

1820   D.C. City Hall (451 Indiana Avenue, NW), George Hadfield, architect; 1916, reconstructed—stuccoed brick exterior replaced with limestone.

1853–63   Washington Aqueduct brings water from Great Falls, Maryland; water supply for Georgetown and D.C. had become critically inadequate, depending solely on natural springs, wells and rainwater cisterns for drinking as well as for fire fighting.

1857   Gallaudet College founded (as Columbia Institution for Deaf, Dumb, and Blind) through efforts of Jackson's Postmaster General Amos Kendall; campus designed by Frederick Law Olmsted. Edward Gallaudet heads school for next 53 years.

1858   Mathew Brady sets up photography studio in Gilman's Drug Store.

1859   Congressman Daniel Sickles, after learning of his wife's infidelity, shoots her lover, Philip Barton Key, son of Francis Scott Key, in Lafayette Park; he is acquitted amid courtroom cheers, convincing many of "the unparalleled depravity of Washington society," according to the *Star* newspaper.

1860s   Walt Whitman serves as a customs clerk, and tends to wounded soldiers in the building now housing the National Portrait Gallery, along with Louisa May Alcott (author of *Little Women*) and Clara Barton, founder of the American Red Cross.

1861   Inauguration of Abraham Lincoln; he comes into town quietly and possibly in disguise (there are threats of assassination) and stays at the Willard Hotel.

        Francis Preston Blair, Sr., editor of the *Washington Globe,* offers Robert E. Lee command of the Union Army on Lincoln's behalf; conversation takes place in Blair House, 1651 Pennsylvania Avenue, NW (built 1824).

Railroad bridges to the North are burned one week after Fort Sumter, leaving Washington isolated and nervous until Northern troops arrive.

Battle of Manassas—first great battle of the Civil War. Lincoln awaits news at Army headquarters in the Winder Building.

Julia Ward Howe, watching Union soldiers from the Willard Hotel, is inspired to write "The Battle Hymn of the Republic."

Washington's mayor refuses to take Union loyalty oath and is thrown in jail until he has a change of heart.

1862   Congress outlaws slavery in D.C.; the only place in the country where owners are legally compensated (but not above $300) if they will take the oath of allegiance to the Union; many refuse and leave town.

1863   Thomas Crawford's statue, "Freedom," placed on top of Capitol dome; Lincoln continues construction during Civil War as a symbol to the Union.

Municipal garbage carts begin regular rounds.

1864   General Jubal Early, with 15,000 Confederate troops, marches toward capital but is repulsed at Fort Stevens, only five miles from the White House.

1865   Lincoln's second inaugural ball; blacks take part for the first time; held in Patent Office (now the National Portrait Gallery), built 1849–67; largest government office building in the nineteenth century.

Lincoln is assassinated by John Wilkes Booth in Ford's Theatre (theater was later converted to government offices; front wall collapsed in 1893 killing 22 employees; restored 1964–68 as museum and theater).

Four people are hanged as Booth's conspirators in the courtyard of the Washington Penitentiary (built in 1826 and mostly razed by 1903, on site of present Fort McNair, 4th and P Streets, SW).

1867   Blacks get the vote in D.C.

Howard University is founded by General Oliver O. Howard, head of Freedmen's Bureau.

1868   Horace Greeley on Washington: "The rents are high, the food is bad, the dust is disgusting, the mud is deep, and the morals are deplorable."

1870s   Colonel Henry Robert, a District engineer commissioner, drafts *Robert's Rules of Order.*

1870   City Council prohibits racial discrimination in restaurants, bars, hotels and places of amusement.

Petitions in Congress from Midwest ask that capital be moved to Mississippi Valley, now the center of the country.

Laws against livestock running free within the city are to be enforced.

Prevost Paradahl, Napoleon III's minister to the U.S., shoots himself at the outbreak of the Franco-Prussian War; some surmise that the excessive heat of the town had unhinged his mind. Washington is not a popular post among foreign diplomats.

Washington Canal, mostly an open sewer, is covered by Constitution Avenue.

1871   Frederick Douglass comes to Washington to be an editor of the *New National Era,* Marshal of District, Recorder of Deeds, Minister to Haiti. First lives at 316–318 A Street, NE. In 1877 moves to a house on Cedar Hill, built 1855 (1411 W Street, SE), now preserved as a memorial to Douglass.

District Territorial Act provides an appointed governor, bicameral legislature (half elected), nonvoting delegate to Congress, and appointed Board of Public Works; three blacks, including Frederick Douglass, serve on Governor's Council.

"Boss" Alexander Shepherd and the Board of Public Works create a new Washington; plant trees, build sewers, pave streets, lay sidewalks, provide water facilities and parks, and spend money that isn't there.

1872   British Legation built near Dupont Circle (Connecticut Avenue and N Street, NW); first foreign-owned legation built in Washington; also the first significant structure built near Dupont Circle. Its location influenced development of area in late nineteenth century as most elegant residential area in Washington. Demolished in 1931, but portions incorporated in British Embassy today.

1874   Patrick Healy is first black man to head major white university (Georgetown).

Congressional investigation of Governor Shepherd and his buddies results in disgrace of territorial government and in its dissolution.

1875   Civil Rights Act forbids segregation in public places of entertainment, churches and cemeteries.

1875–76   Adas Israel Synagogue built at 6th and G streets, NW; oldest synagogue in Washington. Moved to 3rd and G streets, NW, when threatened with demolition (1969); now a museum.

1877   The Potomac floods; high water 10 feet at 17th Street.

Henry Adams comes to Washington to be "stable-companion to statesmen."

1878   The Organic Act strips the last vestiges of home rule from D.C., but acknowledges, for the first time, congressional responsibility to share equally with the local population the burden of expenses to maintain the capital city. Never mind that Congress has never once provided 50 percent of the city's funds.

President and Mrs. Hayes begin tradition of egg rolling for children on the White House Lawn on Easter Sunday.

Bathrooms built in the White House.

1880	John Philip Sousa becomes director of Marine Corps Band; gives concerts on White House and Capitol grounds.
	119 telephones in government offices.
1882	A newspaper estimates the personal fortunes of 17 senators at over $600 million (total city budget, 1881: $3.7 million). It is a common practice for congressmen and senators sitting on District committees to arrange to benefit financially from their legislation affecting the District.
1882–97	Redemption of Potomac Flats (filling in of tidal marshes).
1884	Belva Lockwood, Washington lawyer and first woman to be admitted to practice before the Supreme Court, is first woman to be nominated for President; she gets 4,149 votes.
	Aluminum capstone of Washington Monument is set in place.
1888–97	Library of Congress built at northeast corner of 1st Street and Independence Avenue.
1890	Electricity installed in the White House.
1891	Augustus Saint-Gaudens' sculpture "Grief" dedicated in memory of Mrs. Henry Adams in Rock Creek Cemetery.
1894	Coxey's Army of 300 unemployed marches to Washington where President Cleveland and Congress refuse to see them; Coxey is arrested for walking on the grass.
	Cairo Hotel, 1615 Q Street, NW, at 165 feet, is the tallest private building in the city; the debate it creates leads to imposition of height restrictions (1910); converted to apartments and then condominiums.
1896	First automobile driven down Pennsylvania Avenue.
1899–1901	Washington redesigned by Frederick Law Olmsted, Jr. (McMillan Commission), including park systems

and sites for the Lincoln and Jefferson memorials, Memorial Bridge, George Washington Parkway.

1904 — Theodore Roosevelt elected; swims in Potomac through floating ice.

1904–08 — District Building constructed southeast corner 14th and E streets, NW, Beaux Arts–style building housing municipal government of D.C.

1909 — Statue of Alexander Shepherd erected, first outdoor statue in honor of a native Washingtonian (removed without explanation in 1980 by Pennsylvania Avenue Development Corporation and supposedly next seen at Blue Plains Sewage Treatment Plant).

1911–12 — Mrs. Taft receives 2,000 cherry trees, a gift from the mayor of Tokyo, for planting around the Tidal Basin.

1912 — Griffith Stadium opens; President Taft is the first President to throw out the first ball.

President Taft's cow, Pauline, and sheep graze on White House grounds.

1921 — Wilson retires to private life at 2340 S Street, now a museum. He was the only President to retire to Washington.

1922 — At Lincoln Memorial dedication, blacks are relegated to a segregated section, across a road. Chief Justice Taft provides the weak defense that the arrangement was not "officially sanctioned."

1924 — C&O Canal, seriously damaged by storm, is closed as commercial waterway.

Washington Nats beat the New York Giants in the World Series; Walter Johnson pitches.

1928 — British embassy is first to be built on Embassy Row.

1932 — Bonus March: 10,000 jobless World War I veterans asking for immediate payment of bonus due in 1945; they camp out peacefully, but President Hoover sends MacArthur and the Army in with tear gas, bayonets, sabers and torches.

1935 Supreme Court building completed.

1939 The DAR refuses to let black singer Marian Anderson perform in Constitution Hall, so she sings at the Lincoln Memorial; the public outcry does much to advance the cause of civil rights.

1940 President Roosevelt issues executive order prohibiting racial discrimination in plants with defense contracts; represents the first Presidential action since the Emancipation Proclamation in 1863 to protect the rights of blacks. Action taken after A. Phillip Randolph, head of Brotherhood of Sleeping Car Porters, calls for march on D.C.

1943 Pentagon completed.

Jefferson Memorial opened, John Russell Pope, architect.

1950 Attempt on Truman's life by Puerto Rican nationalists in front of Blair House.

1963 March on Washington; Martin Luther King, Jr., delivers "I have a dream" speech to 200,000 at Lincoln Memorial.

1967 Reorganization Act establishes an appointed mayor and an elected nine-member city council.

Allen Ginsberg and several thousand protesters try to levitate the Pentagon; first of the large antiwar demonstrations.

1968 Riots follow assassination of Martin Luther King, Jr.

District residents vote in presidential election for the first time in 168 years.

1971 Walter Fauntroy is elected D.C.'s first representative in Congress in 100 years; nonvoting except in committee.

Texas steals the Washington Senators and makes them the Texas Rangers.

1972 Pandas arrive at the Washington Zoo.

1972   Pandas arrive at the Washington Zoo.

            Watergate break-in; five arrested in the Watergate
            while E. Howard Hunt watches from the Howard
            Johnson Hotel across Virginia Avenue.

1974   Richard M. Nixon resigns as President, the first ever
            to do so.

1975   District of Columbia Self-Government Reorganiza-
            tion Act provides an elected mayor and city council.

1976   University of the District of Columbia is founded.

            Metrorail service inaugurated.

            Washington serves as center of Bicentennial celebra-
            tion.

1981   Pershing Park opens as cornerstone of Pennsylvania
            Avenue Development Corporation's rebuilding of the
            "Avenue of Presidents."

1982   Vietnam Veterans Memorial dedicated.

1983   Convention Center opens.

            Redskins win the Super Bowl.

1986   Restored Willard Hotel opens.

1988   Navy Memorial opens at Market Square, 7th Street
            and Pennsylvania Avenue.

            Redskins win the Super Bowl again.

            Restored Union Station opens.

1989   Smithsonian Information Center opens in the Smith-
            sonian Institution Building (the Castle).

1991   Washington, D.C., bicentennial.

1992   Washington celebrates Columbus Quincentenary
            (500th anniversary of Columbus' arrival in America).

1993   Spring march brings several hundred thousand sup-
            porters of gay rights to Mall.

Historic accord signed by Israel and the Palestine Liberation Organization on White House lawn.

The issue of statehood for the District of Columbia comes to a vote in the House of Representatives. The measure is soundly defeated.

13

ENTERTAINMENT

LET US INTRODUCE YOU...

Washington's nightlife is concentrated in a few areas of town, with some lonesome surprises scattered here and there. Your best print resources for nightlife are the *Washington Post* Friday pull-out, "Weekend," which features reviews, lists, ads and more, and the *City Paper,* a weekly giveaway that can be found throughout the city.

Georgetown

The Grande Dame of Washington's entertainment venues, and still the best-known area of the city, is Georgetown. Sophisticated in part, trendy in part, old-style hippie in part, Georgetown can scratch just about any entertainment itch. It has excellent jazz clubs, nightclubs with rock bands, elegant ethnic or down-home restaurants and enough bars and saloons to satisfy the thirstiest sailor.

You can find live theater and both first-run and classic films. If your idea of entertainment runs to the more interpersonal, there are any number of spots to meet members of the opposite—or same—sex. In short, if you wander enough in Georgetown, you'll find it all.

Be prepared to spend money. Everything costs—and Georgetown merchants have a knack for making you want to buy something. Free street parking is hard to come by. In fact, parking along Georgetown's main streets—M and Wisconsin—is prohibited weekend evenings. Cars are towed. In clubs with live music, expect to pay a cover and a minimum. (And you may have to guard your drinks in bars with dancing. Many a customer has returned from a spin on the dance floor to find his half-full drink gone, and strangers at the table.)

The Georgetown area is geographically small, and it's crowded, especially on pleasant summer evenings and weekends. Narrow streets have many nighttime attractions crammed along them. Just walking the sidewalks on a weekend evening can be a form of entertainment in itself, or a sublime form of torture, depending on how claustrophobic you are.

A word of caution. Georgetown has been in recent years the subject of some local concern. The area has received extra police attention on weekend evenings, but money for police overtime has dried up, and extra patrols are in limbo. Local merchants are reporting an increase in incidents—purse snatching, fights among young people—and asking for reinstatement of the extra attention. The local citizens' group has asked the city to establish a special tax zone so that the residents and merchants can spend extra money on security and services. In the meantime be aware: this is a city, and things can happen. Exercise appropriate care.

Because of the intensive street traffic, many retail stores and boutiques stay open late at night. It is certainly possible to have dinner, dance the night away and, when you're done, still be able to buy a book, record or pair of jeans!

Georgetown attracts all types—young and old, straight and gay, black and white. But it is our feeling that Georgetown, except for a few expensive clubs, hotels and eateries, is preeminently a young person's place. Youth and high spirits dominate—at least at night.

Dupont Circle

The Dupont Circle area—Connecticut Avenue from the Washington Hilton to K Street—is experiencing a major boom. Some of the best, not just the most expensive, restaurants in town are here. Movie theaters are plentiful. And it is centrally located, easy to walk to from major hotels, and readily accessible by Metro (Farragut North and Dupont Circle stations).

As the city grows, it is becoming harder to define the borders of any area. To the west, Dupont Circle and Georgetown are spreading their wings toward each other—meeting in an area known as the "West End." In the past few years the West End has become a major entertainment center on its own, thus forming a seamless web of nighttime attractions from Key Bridge in Georgetown to Dupont

Circle. To the east, "gentrification" of previously run-down neighborhoods has pushed almost to 15th Street. The 17th Street corridor for three or four blocks north of P Street is a bustling new area, full of restaurants and cafés. To the north, up Connecticut Avenue, and 18th and 17th Streets, "Dupont Circle" is merging with Adams-Morgan.

Downtown

Cities are organic beasts. In the first edition of this guide, published in 1981, the old downtown (loosely defined as the area between the Capitol and the White House to the east and west, and Pennsylvania Avenue and K Streets, on the south and north, respectively) was dead, and almost buried. Businesses had followed the new office buildings to other areas of the city and suburbs; the age of the great downtown department stores was done; the elegant movie houses were fast disappearing; and the area was scarily deserted after 6 P.M. No more. The Pennsylvania Avenue Development Corporation, in concert with the District government and private developers, has engineered a revival of the area, with a combination of mixed-use development, tax breaks, and entrepreneurship. The process is by no means complete, and it still requires some self-confidence to venture out late at night, but the process is underway. Some of the trendiest bistros, hottest clubs, liveliest shopping, and best live theater will now be found in old downtown. If you are in a downtown hotel, you now have a real choice; you can stay in the neighborhood and walk to dinner and a night out, or you can migrate to other parts of the city or suburbs. And the quality of what you will eat and do is absolutely on a par with the rest of the city. Two of the spots sure to be hits with teenage kids are the just-opened chic club, *Planet Hollywood,* 11th and Pennsylvania Avenue, NW, (202) 783-7827, and the *Hard Rock Cafe,* 10th and E Streets, NW, (202) 787-7625.

Capitol Hill

Legislators and their staffs have long supplied Capitol Hill restaurateurs and pubkeepers with a good living, but in recent years new elements have been added to the scene. The residential neighborhoods surrounding the Capitol have been among the hottest markets for housing in the metropolitan area. Young professionals have moved in; the Metro has aligned the Hill with the rest of the city, encouraging non-Hill people to explore the neighborhood; and many older facilities—such as fresh-air markets and warehouses—have been renovated or recycled to new areas. As a consequence of this activity, a number of new enterprises have appeared, including restaurants, theaters and discos, catering to a diverse neighborhood market.

Historically, Hill entertainments have been discreet, not for the uninitiated. The legislators wanted it that way; no sense in letting stories leak back to the home district. By and large, the new businesses have followed this pattern. They do not advertise themselves over-much, so gay bars for men and women go virtually unnoticed—no big signs, no advertising; restaurants rely on word of mouth and night-clubs are small and expensive. In some ways, Capitol Hill is a town-within-a-city; it likes the rest of us, but is perfectly happy on its own, thank you.

Virginia Suburbs

Northern Virginia has grown up rapidly in the past half decade. Long a mystery to residents of Washington and Maryland, the northern Virginia suburbs were ignored by established restaurateurs and providers of nightlife. It took outsiders to wake the locals up to the enormous potential of a region rapidly becoming a mighty regional economic force. And nightlife has followed the money. You will find everything from elegant dining and opera to recycled-industrial-site bars and garage band clubs. There are more and more reasons to cross the river and explore the Virginia 'burbs, even if you are in town only for a short stay. Old Town Alexandria and the Clarendon/Ballston area of Arlington are the two close-in areas of concentrated nightlife activity. As a rule, however, except in clubs catering to a young crowd, Virginia nightlife tends to put itself to bed at an earlier hour than the city.

With its Federal architecture and cobbled streets, Old Town is a pleasant throwback—Georgetown without the frenzy. The city fathers (and mothers) like it that way. "Appropriate attire" here may be a notch or two up from the jeans and T's acceptable in Adams-Morgan, Dupont Circle, or Georgetown.

Clarendon/Ballston is an area just beginning to grow up as a nightlife center. Along Wilson Boulevard just west of Rosslyn (the cluster of high-rises just across the river from Georgetown), you will find clubs, many of the area's "best buy" ethnic restaurants, cinemas and live theater. The area is easily accessible by Metro or car, being maybe 10–15 minutes from downtown by either.

Maryland Suburbs

Bethesda, once a quiet bedroom community, is booming now, the result of Metro's arrival in the 1980s. Downtown Bethesda may now have the greatest concentration of restaurants outside of the city. You can park your car in a municipal lot, walk the streets, and take your choice of domestic or international cuisines, plain or fancy. Nightlife here tends toward the "family-style"—a meal, a movie, and an ice cream. There are a few clubs with live or recorded music, but if you are looking for a safe place, with every conceivable choice of food, and plenty of cinemas, you won't go wrong. Bethesda is accessible by Metro, and only 20–30 minutes from downtown by car or public transportation.

Wisconsin Avenue is the main drag leading into Bethesda from the city. From Georgetown to Bethesda, the avenue is a solid wall of shops, restaurants, cinemas, apartments, etc. Beyond Bethesda, Wisconsin Avenue becomes Rockville Pike, and from Rockville to Gaithersburg is nearly a seamless strip of consumer enticements.

LIVE MUSIC

While Washington is no Chicago for jazz or New York for rock, it has a live music scene that can keep you hopping or tapping all night long. In fact, the number of places where you can hear live music has grown so much that all we can do here is try to highlight some of the spots. We have attempted to pick out a wide variety of music—from new wave to classic jazz to hard-driving rock. The live-music scene being what it is, with changes in format, the appearance of new places and the disappearance of old ones, it's wise for you to check the local papers for a rundown of current happenings when you are actually in town. *City Paper* will have the most complete listings of live entertainment.

The Washington area has scads of free music, often presented under the auspices of local government. Again, check the newspapers on arrival.

Note: Categories can be misleading. Many clubs feature a variety of music over time. Our categories are provided to give you a rough idea of what you might expect.

Alternative/Folk/Acoustic/Country

Birchmere, 3901 Mount Vernon Avenue, Alexandria, (703) 549-5919. The Birchmere has moved away from straight country to include traditional folk as well. Many nationally known artists perform.

Dubliner, 4 F Street, NW, (202) 737-3773. Irish music, nightly.

Flanagan's, 7637 Old Georgetown Road, Bethesda, (301) 986-1007. Irish/folk.

Galaxy Hut, 2711 Wilson Boulevard, Arlington, (703) 525-8646. Mixed alternative, folk and rock, mostly weekends.

GW's, 1319 King Street, Alexandria, (703) 739-2274. Country/western, dancing, nightly.

Ireland's Four Provinces, 3412 Connecticut Avenue, NW, (202) 244-0860. Irish, nightly.

Kramerbooks & afterwords, 1517 Connecticut Avenue, NW, (202) 387-1462. Jazz, folk, Friday and Saturday.

Lone Star Grill, 1819 N. Lynn Street, Rosslyn, (703) 528-1823. Mostly country/western, weekends.

Mr. Smith's, 3014 M Street, NW, (202) 333-3104. Piano sing-along downstairs; acts upstairs.

Murphy's D.C., 2609 24th Street, NW, (202) 462-7171. Irish, nightly.

Tiffany Tavern, 1116 King Street, Alexandria, (703) 836-8844. Bluegrass, folk, Friday and Saturday.

Whitey's, 2761 Washington Boulevard, Arlington, (703) 525-9825. Rock, Saturday; blues, Sunday.

Jazz

Blues Alley, 1073 Wisconsin Avenue (rear alley entrance between K and M streets), (202) 337-4141. Washington's premier jazz showcase for a generation. Shows 8 and 10 nightly, plus a midnight show Friday, Saturday and Sunday. Cover. Creole cuisine on the dinner menu. Nationally known acts.

Brewbakers, 6931 Arlington Road, Bethesda, (301) 907-2600. Contemporary Jazz, Thursday through Sunday, mostly.

Busara, 2340 Wisconsin Avenue, NW, (202) 337-2340. Upstairs from a great Thai restaurant in upper Georgetown. Blues and jazz.

Dylan's, 3251 Prospect Street NW, (202) 337-0593. Mixed bag—folk to jazz to rock.

Henry Africa, 607 King Street, Alexandria, (703) 549-4010.

Kalorama Café, 2228 18th Street, NW, (202) 667-1022.

King of France Tavern, 16 Church Circle, Annapolis, (301) 263-2641. Often the venue for major names.

Marley's in the Henley Park Hotel, 926 Massachusetts Avenue, NW, (202) 638-5200. Friday and Saturday.

One Step Down, 2517 Pennsylvania Avenue, NW, (202) 331-8863. Thursday through Sunday.

International/Reggae/R&B/Rock/Dancing

Bayou, 3135 K Street, NW, (202) 333-2897, under the parkway in Georgetown. Local and national talent, rock to country to new wave. Cover and minimum varies.

Chelsea's, 1055 Thomas Jefferson Street, NW, (202) 298-8222. Persian, Wednesday and Sunday; Salsa, Thursday, Friday and Saturday.

Chief Ike's Mambo Room, 1725 Columbia Road, NW, (202) 332-2211. Beer to a young crowd and the incomparable DJ Stella Neptune weekends.

Club Asylum in Exile, 1210 U Street, NW. Grab bag. One of the new U Street clubs near the Metro. Thursday through Sunday.

Cowboy Café South, 2421 Columbia Pike, Arlington, (703) 483-3467. Western rock to eastern.

Crazy Horse Saloon, 3529 M Street, NW, (202) 333-0400. Bar bands, college crowd.

Déjà Vu, 2119 M Street, NW, (202) 452-1966. A large (capacity 2,000) emporium devoted to the oldies plus some new music.

15 Minutes, 1030 15th Street, NW, (202) 408-1855. A seriously ironic place which by night takes over a cafeteria. Nightlife on the cheap where the incongruous reigns. Live music most nights.

Fifth Column, 915 F Street NW, (202) 393-3632. Progressive dance club music, art gallery, lounge; new music, Sunday, Monday, Wednesday; European dance music, Thursday, Friday, Saturday.

Grog & Tankard, 2408 Wisconsin Avenue, NW, (202) 333-3114. R&B, rockabilly, nightly.

Hard Rock Café, 514 10th Street, NW, (202) 737-7625. DJ every night; college and tourist crowd. Open 11 A.M. for restaurant.

Ibex, 5832 Georgia Avenue, NW, (202) 726-1800. Live R&B dance music in the Marvin Gaye Room.

The Insect Club, 625 E Street, NW, (202) 347-8884. What can we say? The place is crawling with insects—a high-concept club where the decor does homage to our six-legged friends and so does the menu. The music is both live and recorded—a mix of progressive, Latin, R&B, hip-hop and more. Pool, too.

Kilimanjaro Restaurant-Nightclub, 1724 California Street, NW, (202) 328-3838. Sophisticated, cosmopolitan dining and entertainment. Music includes African, Calypso, Latin and American.

Nightclub 9:30, 930 F Street, NW, (202) 393-0930. Local and national bands, rock from the familiar to the far-out.

The Ritz, 919 E Street, NW, (202) 638-2852. Four-story, mixed music—R&B, fusion, some rock.

Roxy Restaurant, 1214 18th Street, NW (at Connecticut Avenue), (202) 296-9292. Dinner club with mixed styles—reggae, rock, blues; some local, some national acts. Also comedy.

Sports Fans, 3287 M Street, NW, (202) 338-7028. Sports fans, mostly a college crowd. House music by DJ.

Tornado Alley, 1139 Elkin Street, Wheaton, (301) 929-0795. "Roots" rock—R&B, country, Cajun. Live music, mostly weekends.

Tracks DC, 1st and M streets, SE, (202) 488-3320. Dancing and fun, for up to 3,000 people. Includes video room and volleyball court.

The Vault, 911 F Street, NW, (202) 347-8079. High energy DJ; 2 dance floors, in old bank. Wednesday to Saturday. Cover $4 to $7.

Zaxx, 6355 Rolling Road, Springfield VA (703) 569-2582. Some DJ, some live touring national and regional bands. Sunday is an "all ages dance." Claims the biggest light, sound, video show in North Virginia. Young crowd, teens and up.

Zei Club, 1415 Zei Alley (North of I Street between 14th and 15th), (202) 842-2445. A jolt to your brain—loud music, high-tech video, a basic approach to the differences between the sexes. Music live or taped every night.

Other

Brasil Tropical, 2519 Pennsylvania Ave, NW, (202) 293-1773. Live music of Brazil—lambada, samba, Friday and Saturday.

The Dandy, Zero Prince Street, Alexandria, (703) 683-6076. Luncheon and dinner cruises in climate-controlled riverboat, with taped music after dinner for dancing. Reservations essential.

F. Scott's, 1226 36th Street, NW, (202) 965-1789. Rock for the college crowd, Saturdays only.

Marquee Lounge, Shoreham Hotel, 2500 Calvert Street, NW, (202) 234-0700. A Washington landmark, former home of Mark Russell. Popular entertainment.

Nest at the Willard, 1401 Pennsylvania Avenue, NW, (202) 628-9100. Jazz in elegant surroundings.

Piano Bars/Lobby Music

Grand Hotel, 2350 M Street, NW, (202) 955-4404 or (202) 429-0100. One of the new luxury West End hotels.

Hyatt Regency Hotel, 400 New Jersey Avenue, NW, (202) 737-1234. Capitol View Room.

Ritz-Carlton, 2100 Massachusetts Avenue, NW, (202) 293-2100. Fairfax Bar.

Sheraton-Carlton, 16th and K streets, NW, (202) 638-2626. Allegro Bar.

COMEDY CLUBS

Chelsea's, 1055 Thomas Jefferson Street, NW, (202) 298-8222. The Capitol Steps, a witty and clever musical revue. Friday and Saturday.

Comedy Café, 1520 K Street, NW, (202) 638-5653. Varied schedule.

Garvin's Comedy Clubs. Multiple locations around the area, in the District, Maryland and Virginia. For information call (202) 298-7200.

Improv, 1140 Connecticut Avenue, NW, (202) 296-7008.

A note on comedy clubs: they tend to be ephemeral. If we, the authors, are lucky, the above-mentioned clubs will still exist on publication date. We don't make any promises for six months after that.

THE BAR SCENE

Many of the nightspots mentioned in "Live Music" above are also Washington's lively bars. Here are a few more, most of which do not offer live music. In Georgetown, the *River Club,* 3223 K Street, NW (202) 333-8118, has a long, elegant Art Deco bar that caters to the over-35 set, with a dance floor and sumptuous dining for those who have worked up an appetite. *Clyde's,* 3236 M Street, NW, (202) 333-0294, has developed a national reputation for its elegant decorations and respectable food. *Mr. Smith's,* 3104 M Street, NW, (202) 333-3104, is a casual and friendly place, and *Nathan's,* corner of M Street and Wisconsin Avenue, (202) 338-2000, has the best view of the passing parade on the busiest corner in town. *Champions,* "The American Sports Bar," 1206 Wisconsin Avenue, (202) 965-4005, is a jock hangout. It's the sort of place that sponsors 10K races, fitness contests and bikini contests. As we have noted earlier, wherever you go in Georgetown you can find something to suit your mood.

Dupont Circle and 17th Street above Massachusetts Avenue are chock-a-block with eateries/clubs/bars, catering to all tastes in food and companions. The newest downtown bar scene is happening around 14th and U streets—try *Andalusian Dog,* 1344 U Street, NW, (202) 986-6364, *State of the Union,* 1357 U Street, NW, (202) 588-8810, or *U-Topia,* 1418 U Street, NW, (202) 483-7669. At 1739 N Street, you'll find the *Tabard Inn,* (202) 785-1277, a country inn tucked into the heart of the city. Up 18th Street in Adams-Morgan, try *Café Lautrec*, 2431 18th Street, NW, (202) 265-6436. Down 19th Street from the circle is an endless array of bars, restaurants and discos. Work your way down to *Rumors,* 1900 M Street, (202) 466-

7378, for a breath of California ferns, or *The Sign of the Whale,* 1825 M Street, (202) 785-1110 and you still will not even have scratched the surface of this teeming area.

Up on Capitol Hill, you will find a relaxed crowd—lots of Hill staffers, and the occasional congressman or senator. Favorite hangouts include the *Hawk and Dove,* 329 Pennsylvania Avenue, SE, (202) 543-3300; *Duddington's,* 319 Pennsylvania Avenue, SE, (202) 544-3500; *Bistro le Monde,* 223 Pennsylvania Avenue, SE, (202) 544-4153; and the *Tune Inn,* 331½ Pennsylvania Avenue, SE, (202) 543-2725, called by many the best neighborhood bar in town.

Several area hotels have spectacular panoramic views of the city. *The Hotel Washington,* 15th Street and Pennsylvania Avenue, NW, (202) 638-5900, has a popular rooftop restaurant with what is acknowledged to be the best view from within the city. The *Marriott Key Bridge Hotel,* (703) 524-6400, in Rosslyn, just across Key Bridge from Georgetown, has a revolving rooftop restaurant, with a slowly changing view of the city and Virginia suburbs.

CLASSICAL MUSIC, BALLET AND OPERA

Coolidge Auditorium at the Library of Congress, 1st Street and Independence Avenue, SE, (202) 707-5502, hosts concerts by the resident string quartet using the library's invaluable collection of Stradivarius stringed instruments. In recent years, the Julliard Quartet has had this honor. Unfortunately, the auditorium is under repair until late 1995 or early 1996, but the concerts continue at the National Academy of Sciences. Concerts are given Friday nights, from October to May. Admission is on a first-come, first-served basis.

Corcoran Gallery of Art Auditorium, 17th Street and New York Avenue, NW, (202) 638-3211, is newly refurbished and will no doubt have music on a regular basis.

DAR Constitution Hall, 18th and D streets, NW, (202) 638-2661, is a cavern of a hall, owned and operated by the Daughters of the American Revolution. Less used than in past years (because of the Kennedy Center), Constitution Hall still attracts such visiting artists as Luciano Pavarotti. Accessible to wheelchairs.

East Garden Court at the National Gallery of Art, 6th Street and Constitution Avenue, NW, (202) 737-4215, is a handsome place, although the acoustics can be a bit spotty. The Gallery Orchestra, under George Manos, has been playing Sunday evening concerts (7 P.M.) for over 20 years. Season from September to June. Free admission.

The Folger Library has a Renaissance musical group that performs periodically.

The Kennedy Center (see "Theaters" for a full description of the facilities) is the principal site for classical music, opera and ballet, as the home of the National Symphony, and the Washington home for the New York City Ballet, the American Ballet Theatre and the Washington Performing Arts Society, which brings many orchestras, soloists and dance troupes to town.

Lisner Auditorium, 21st and H streets, NW, on the campus of George Washington University, (202) 994-6800, has been the home of the Washington Ballet, a fledgling dance company now receiving national attention for the efforts of its late gifted choreographer, Cho San Goh, and as the training ground for Amanda McKerrow, winner of the Gold Medal in Moscow in the summer of 1981. Lisner is a rather plain but well-constructed hall, with excellent sightlines and acoustics. Four wheelchairs can be accommodated at each performance.

The National Academy of Sciences, 2101 Constitution Avenue, NW, (202) 334-2436, offers free classical music in an acoustically superb hall.

Phillips Collection, 1600 21st Street, NW, (202) 387-2151, runs a chamber music series, Sunday afternoons at 5, from September to May. To wander among the French Impressionists and to bathe in music at the same time is a refreshing and relaxing experience.

The Smithsonian Institution museums have very active programs throughout the year. Each museum is responsible for its own schedule, and listings of current events will be posted at each museum. Often exhibits at the museums will generate special events. Budget uncertainties will cause substantial changes in programs, so check at each museum. For confirmation of all Smithsonian events, call (202) 357-2700.

The Smithsonian Performing Arts Division is designed around museum programs and offers a series of concerts, mostly by major names in American music and theater, as well as performance in dance, jazz ensembles, gospel groups and country music. Performances are given in various Smithsonian museums. The Performing Arts Division also sponsors the Twentieth Century Consort and the Smithsonian Chamber Players, who use antique instruments from the museum collection. Check local papers for details and prices, or call the Smithsonian at (202) 357-3030.

The Museum of American History has a variety of programs. Jazz workshops are held twice a month from fall to spring, Sunday afternoons in the Palm Court. The Smithsonian Chamber Orchestra offers two sets of concerts winter and spring. The Smithsonian String Quartet has a series of four concerts at the Renwick Museum. The Chamber Players uses old instruments from the Smithsonian's collection in the Hall of Musical Instruments at four sets of concerts.

The Black American Culture Program at the Museum of American History sponsors a series of major performance programs in jazz, gospel, dance and theater.

THEATERS

For convenience, we have divided area theaters into two groups—first, those theaters that present performances by either a resident or touring professional company of national stature or serve as the Washington home for national productions, and second, decidedly local companies, both professional and amateur. We also mention local children's theater.

Theaters survive on their ability to attract an audience. Any reasonably organized company will advertise itself extensively (or at least to the limit of its financial capability) during a run. Therefore, scan the local papers for announcements of what's playing, ticket prices, times of performances and, given the fluid nature of some theater productions in this city, where the theater is located. Again, we suggest checking the *Post, Washingtonian Magazine,* and *City Paper.*

Ticketplace, (202) 842-5387, located at Lisner Auditorium, 21st and H streets, NW, offers half-price tickets on the day of performance for most area theaters, including most music, dance and stage productions. The half-price tickets must be paid for in cash. Full-price tickets, for future performances, are also available and can be paid for with credit cards. For further information, write Ticketplace, c/o Cultural Alliance, 410 8th Street, NW, Suite 45, Washington, D.C. 20005.

There are a number of ticket brokers in town. Brokers buy up blocks of seats and resell them for what the market will bear. Prices will vary for shows, and among brokers. Try Premiere Theatre Seats, 1-800-969-9991 and (703) 533-1600; Ticket Finders, 1-800-356-7983 and (301) 513-0300, and Top Centre, 1-800-673-8422 and (301) 585-0046. Brokers may not have tickets for all shows or all theaters but, on the other hand, may have tickets for shows that are "sold out" at the box office. The ticket brokers also handle special events and sporting events, both locally and nationally.

Ticketmaster, (202) 432-7328, is agent for a variety of shows that come to town—rock concerts, reviews, etc.—and work out of multiple locations around the city. Ads will direct you to them for specific shows.

A note to students, senior citizens, people with disabilities and military personnel E-4 and below: the Kennedy Center and National Theater offer discounts on tickets. Discounts vary with the size of group, length of run and so on. For information, call the group-sales number, where listed, or the main number given. People with handicaps should also refer to Chapter 18, "Tips for Visitors with Disabilities."

ARENA STAGE
6th Street and Maine Avenue, SW

Information: (202) 554-9066
Charge-A-Ticket: (202) 488-3300
Group Sales: (202) 488-4380

 Fully accessible.

 Interpreters for some performances; earphones for people who are hard of hearing. Phonic Ear. Call for dates.

 Audio described performances for each run. Call for dates.

This is actually three theaters under one roof. The Arena Stage is a theater-in-the-round with its own repertory company of national stature. New plays by major playwrights often have their premiere here;

old standards are often given new life. The Kreeger Theatre is a proscenium stage in a smaller, more intimate setting. The Old Vat Room often presents one-man shows and small-cast reviews.

FORD'S THEATRE
511 10th Street, NW

Information: (202) 347-4833
Ticket Master: (202) 432-7328
Group Sales: (202) 638-2367
TTY: (202) 347-5599

 Fully accessible.

 Each run has a minimum of two interpreted performances. Call (202) 347-4833 for dates.

 Each run has a minimum of two audio-described performances. Call for dates.

The theater in which Lincoln was shot is now the site of many dramatic plays, musical shows, reviews and dance. Touring companies often appear.

THE JOHN F. KENNEDY CENTER FOR THE PERFORMING ARTS

Information & Tickets for all Theaters: (202) 467-4600
2700 F Street, NW

TTY: (202) 416-8524
1-800-444-1324
Offices: (202) 416-8000

 Fully accessible. For questions and assistance call (202) 416-8727 or TTY (202) 416-8728.

 A wireless infrared listening enhancement system is available in all theaters. Signed performances are offered in each run.

 Audio-described performances are offered.

The Kennedy Center is not only a complex for the performing arts, it is a major tourist attraction on its own. An extensive description of the building and its furnishings is in the "Foggy Bottom" section of Chapter 7. The center now houses six locations for the arts, each with a different purpose. Taken together, they form the most complete arts center in the city, rivaling Lincoln Center in New York City and the South Bank arts complex in London. On any given day you can feast on a wide assortment of cultural goodies. Ample parking is usually available in the underground garage for $5 or at two nearby apartment complexes—the Watergate, 600 New Hampshire Avenue, NW, and Columbia Plaza, 2400 Virginia Avenue, NW. For evening and weekend performances a free shuttle bus service is available from Columbia Plaza. One hour free parking is allowed at the center for ticket buyers before 6 P.M.; be sure to get ticket stamped at box office. Here is a brief summary of what you may find at the center:

Concert Hall

Designed for concert performances, the hall hosts a wide variety of performers from jazz to pop, and serves as the principal stage for visiting orchestras and soloists. The Concert Hall is the home of the National Symphony, which presents a full season from September to June and summer concerts elsewhere in the city.

Opera House

More opulent and somewhat smaller than the Concert Hall, the Opera House offers opera, dance and musicals.

Eisenhower Theater

This is the Kennedy Center stage for plays and small reviews. Original productions and Broadway-bound shows often make their first appearance here; this is a comfortable and rather intimate house.

Terrace Theater

A gift of the Japanese people, the Terrace is an attempt to provide a showcase setting for new dance, experimental theater, chamber music, soloists, and small musical reviews in an intimate theater with professional facilities.

Theater Lab

Theater Lab provides two functions to the Kennedy Center—as a small stage (it has been the home for the past four years for *Shear Madness,* a satirical review, still going strong on an open run), and as the educational arm, offering productions for, and with, children, summer drama classes and productions for school groups.

American Film Institute Theater　　　**Box Office: (202) 785-4600**

A bow in the direction of the cinematic arts, the institute runs a never-ending series of films, each presented only one night, in a small, rather tacky (for the Kennedy Center, anyway) room off the Hall of Nations. Talk is that a new screening room will be constructed soon.

NATIONAL THEATER　　　**Information: (202) 628-6161**
1321 E Street, NW　　　　　　**Telecharge: 1-800-447-7400**
　　　　　　　　　　　　　　Group Sales: (202) 628-6166

 Fully accessible.

 Special amplification earphones. Signed, interpreted performances scheduled for each run.
 Audio-described performance for each run.

Washington's oldest continuously operating theater (founded 1835), the National is now under the booking management of the Shubert Organization. As the National is free now to compete directly for top bookings with the Kennedy Center (under whose management the theater operated for several years), Washington will likely enjoy a boom in topflight shows. Free theater and music are presented in the Helen Hayes Gallery on Monday nights; call (202) 783-3372 for information and reservations. Special note for parents: the National is conducting a series of Saturday-morning entertainments for kids, including mime, magic and music. Call (202) 783-3372 for information.

THE SHAKESPEARE THEATRE
450 7th Street, NW

Tickets: (202) 393-2700
Group Sales: (202) 628-5770
TDD: (202) 638-3863
Offices: (202) 547-3230

 Fully Accessible.

 For the hearing impaired, amplified headsets are available; at least one performance each run will be signed.

 For the visually impaired, one performance will be audio-described.

The troupe that formed the Folger Shakespeare Theatre moved into a brand-new theater in downtown Washington in 1992. It is a state-of-the-art facility, seating 450, with a horseshoe-shaped stage. The company will present four productions each season, three by Shakespeare. The Theatre also presents two weeks of free "Shakespeare-in-the-Park" at Carter Barron Amphitheater every June. The company has attracted many New York and Hollywood actors and actresses to its usually well-received productions.

WARNER THEATER
13th & E streets, NW

Tickets: (202) 783-4000
Offices: (202) 628-1818

 Accessible.

 Sound enhancement devices available.

The Warner just completed a three-year, $7 million renovation, restoring the 1,980-seat theater to its original 1920s glory, but with a state-of-the-art light and sound system, and vastly improved backstage capabilities. The Warner hosts short-run Broadway productions, concerts, including pop, jazz, rock and world music, and dance.

LOCAL THEATERS

It is the nature of local theater to defy classification. Indeed, some considerable energy is expended in modern theater to achieve that very situation. So, much as we would like, we cannot, in some cases that follow, give you a very clear picture of what it is each of the theaters listed actually does. Your best bet is to consult local papers for reviews of the current shows. Bear in mind that many of the small theaters are in recycled buildings. Limited budgets do not often permit the construction of facilities with access for people confined to wheelchairs, or modern rest rooms or efficient air-conditioning systems. If you are concerned with any of these issues, you should call the theater and check.

A final word on local theater: some, maybe many, of the companies listed here may have disappeared, or been renamed, or moved, by the time this book is published. The best guide to the local theater scene is the daily paper.

Folger Library, 201 East Capitol Street, (202) 504-7077. The original Folger troupe has moved downtown but a new group is still performing Shakespeare in the Library's re-created Globe Theatre.

Gala Theater, 1625 Park Road, NW, (202) 234-7174. A bilingual theater troupe, performing in English and Spanish on alternate nights.

Hartke Theater, Catholic University of America, Harwood Road, NE, (202) 319-5367. The respected home of CUA college dramatics. Several cuts above your ordinary college fare.

Olney Theater, Route 108, Olney, MD, (301) 924-3400. A professional summer theater offering old favorites.

Roundhouse Theatre, 12210 Bushey Drive, Silver Spring, MD, (301) 217-3300. A Montgomery County–sponsored professional theater that often performs at local festivals as well as in its home—a converted elementary school.

Source Theater Company, 1835 14th Street, NW, (202) 462-1073. One of the long-term survivors, presenting new American works, often of a challenging nature.

Studio Theatre, 14th and P streets, NW, (202) 232-3300. A company that has introduced many new works to Washington audiences.

Washington Project for the Arts, 400 7th Street, NW, (202) 347-8304. A young, experimental, changing arts organization that seeks to incorporate and integrate the arts—from music and dance to video and three-dimensional art.

Woolly Mammoth, 1401 Church Street, NW, (202) 393-3939. The productions of this small company have met with rave reviews.

CHILDREN'S THEATERS AND ATTRACTIONS

Adventure Theater, Glen Echo Park, Glen Echo, MD, (301) 320-5331. Performances Saturday and Sunday, 1:30 and 3:30 P.M. Group rates; reservations recommended.

B&O Railroad Station Museum, Main Street and Maryland Avenue, Ellicott City, MD, (301) 461-1944. Admission fee. Tuesday to Sunday, 11 A.M. to 4 P.M. Station house (c. 1831) with authentic model of the 13 miles of the original system.

BARNSTORM! The Barns at Wolf Trap Farm Park, 1624 Trap Road, Vienna, VA, (703) 255-1827. On Saturdays at 11 A.M. and 1 P.M., October through May, performers ranging from folksingers to mimes, storytellers and puppeteers regale youngsters.

Bob Brown Puppet Productions, 1415 South Queen Street, Arlington, VA, (703) 920-1040. Performances at various theaters around town. A professional and highly competent, sophisticated and entertaining troupe. Catch them if you can.

Discovery Theater, Smithsonian Institution, Arts and Industries Building, 900 Jefferson Drive, SW, (202) 357-1300. See site report for details.

National Theater, 1321 E Street, NW, (202) 783-3370. The National conducts a series of Saturday-morning entertainments for kids, including mime, magic and music.

The Puppet Company, Glen Echo Park, Glen Echo, MD, (301) 320-6668. Midweek and weekend performances.

Washington Dolls' House and Toy Museum, 5236 44th Street, NW, (202) 244-0024. Admission fee. Tuesday to Saturday, 10 A.M. to 5 P.M. Sunday, noon to 5 P.M. This wonderful private museum, founded by author and dollhouse authority Flora Gill Jacobs, exhibits antique dollhouses, dolls and other toys from all over the world.

DINNER THEATERS

Burn Brae, 3811 Blackburn Road, Burtonsville, MD, (301) 384-5800. Broadway musicals. Full-course dinners from varied menu. Tickets from $22 to $33. Group rates. No smoking. Fully accessible.
PERFORMANCES:

	Open	*Dinner*	*Show*
Tuesday to Sunday	6 P.M.	6:15 P.M.	8 P.M.
Wednesday matinee	11 A.M.	11:15 A.M.	12:45 P.M.
Sunday matinee	10:30 A.M.	10:45 A.M.	12:15 P.M.

Lazy Susan, Route 1, Woodbridge, VA, (703) 550-7384. Musicals. Varied buffet menu with many home-style dishes. Tickets from $27 to $30. Group rates. Theater and rest room accessible. Separate smoking section.
PERFORMANCES:

	Open	*Dinner*	*Show*
Tuesday to Saturday	6 P.M.	7 P.M.	8:30 P.M.
Sunday	5	6	7:30

Toby's, South Entrance Road, Columbia, MD, (301) 596-6161. Musicals. Buffet with varied entrées, salads and desserts. Tickets from $27 to $32. Group rates. Theater accessible. Accessible rest room.
PERFORMANCES:

	Open	*Dinner*	*Show*
Tuesday to Saturday	6 P.M.	6:15 P.M.	8:15 P.M.
Sunday	5	5:15	7:15
Sunday matinee	10:30 A.M.	10:30 A.M.	12:30 P.M.

West End, 4615 Duke Street, Alexandria, VA, (703) 370-2500. Broadway musical comedies. Tickets from $27 to $34. Table service, American cuisine. Accessible. Group rates for 20 or more. No smoking.
PERFORMANCES:

	Open	*Dinner*	*Show*
Tuesday to Sunday	5:30 P.M.	6 P.M.	8 P.M.
Sunday and Wednesday matinee	11:30 A.M.	noon	2 P.M.

OUTDOOR MUSIC AND PAVILIONS

Carter Barron Amphitheater, 16th and Kennedy streets, NW, (202) 426-0486. Theater and rest room accessible.

A 4,500-seat open amphitheater, owned by the National Park Service and leased to local entrepreneurs and promoters, Carter Barron presents a varied program of popular entertainments.

Merriweather Post Pavilion, Columbia, MD, 1-800-551-7328. The pavilion offers a summer season of mostly popular music, including rock and roll, folk and jazz. Located about 45 minutes from D.C. up Route 29.

Wolf Trap Farm Park, 1624 Trap Road, Vienna, VA, (703) 255-1800. Group Sales: (703) 255-1851. Theater and rest room accessible.

A gift to the nation by a generous benefactor, Catherine Jouett Shouse, Wolf Trap is one of the loveliest settings for a summer's evening of entertainment. Through the season—which goes from early June to early September—one can enjoy the widest possible array of entertainment. The Metropolitan Opera, a bluegrass music festival, the National Symphony, Bill Cosby, the Alvin Ailey Dance Theater and many, many more have delighted the more than 500,000 people a season who come to enjoy not only the performance but the acres of grassy slopes for serene picnicking. Wolf Trap hosts an International Children's Festival every August.

From October through May, a variety of entertainments takes place in The Barns at Wolf Trap. Folk singers, jazz performers and chamber musicians can be seen on a varying schedule of Friday and Saturday nights in this more intimate setting. Wolf Trap also runs a lively series of programs for children at The Barns and on the grounds.

FREE MUSIC AND THEATER

Throughout the year, but especially during the warm months, residents and visitors are treated to a wide variety of free music and entertainment. The various armed forces bands—Army, Navy, Air Force and Marine Corps—can be found somewhere around the city almost every day. Regular performances are given on the West Terrace of the U.S. Capitol, at the Jefferson Memorial, The White House Ellipse, the U.S. Navy Memorial and the Marine Barracks (8th and I streets, SE). Reservations are required for the Marine evening parades, and should be made in advance by calling (202) 433-6060. The list of organizations sponsoring free music and entertainment is ever-changing, but the following have participated substantially in the past few years:

Arlington County Parks and Recreation Department, various locations in Arlington throughout the summer.

Carter Barron Amphitheater, 16th and Kennedy streets, NW.

D.C. Government Summer in the Parks Program, various locations around the city.

Folger Shakespeare Library, 201 E. Capitol Street.

Foundry Shopping Mall, Georgetown, summer jazz series.

Glen Echo Park, Maryland; folk and ethnic music.

Kennedy Center, a varied program of seasonal music at Christmastime and free kids' series throughout the year.

Library of Congress, 1st Street and Independence Avenue, SE.

National Gallery of Art, Constitution Avenue at 6th Street, NW.

National Symphony, summer concerts on the West Terrace of the Capitol and on the Mall.

National Theater, 1321 E Street, NW. Free music and theater, Monday nights. Free entertainment for children, Saturday mornings.

Smithsonian Institution, most museums.

Washington Cathedral, Massachusetts Avenue at Wisconsin Avenue, NW.

Free music will be announced and promoted through the local papers. The "Calendar of Events" in the *Washingtonian* magazine is a good source of information as is "Weekend," the *Washington Post* Friday supplement.

MOVIE THEATERS

The grand movie palaces may all have been torn down, and first-run films fled to the suburban multiscreen theaters, but Washington can still boast of many well-run movie houses, including first-run, second-run and classic film houses. Check the local papers, especially the "Style" section of the daily *Post* and the pullout "Weekend" section of the Friday *Post,* for complete movie listings.

A theater that might escape your attention is the **American Film Institute Theater,** Kennedy Center, (202) 785-4600. The AFI runs series of all kinds: stars, directors, love stories, westerns, etc. Usually there are two shows per day, an early show, between 5 and 6 P.M., and another between 8 and 9 P.M. The only drawback to AFI is that films come and go in a single day.

The **Pickford Theater** at the Library of Congress shows films and television programs from the library's collection—the largest in the world—four nights a week. Performances are free, but reservations are required. Call (202) 707-5677. The library also publishes a quarterly schedule.

Good areas for movies are Georgetown and the West End, with about 15 screens in close proximity; Dupont Circle with over 10 screens within walking range; upper Northwest, along Wisconsin Avenue, where you will find more than 20 screens within a 10-minute drive of each other; and the malls, where you can usually find multi-screen theaters.

BOAT RIDES

The *Dandy,* Zero Prince Street, Alexandria, VA (703) 683-6076. Luncheon and dinner cruises in a climate-controlled riverboat, in the tradition of Parisian restaurant-riverboats. With a low profile, the *Dandy* can go under all the Potomac bridges. Weekday luncheon cruises 11:30 A.M. to 2 P.M., $25.00. Saturday luncheon 12:30 to 3 P.M., $27.00. Sunday Champagne luncheon 12:30–3 P.M., $29.00. Evening cruises every night 7 to 10 P.M. Sunday–Thursday, $47; Friday, $50; Saturday, $55. Group discounts for 20 or more available on selected cruises. The menu includes beef, fish, poultry and vegetarian.

Spirit of Washington. Pier 4, 6th and Water streets, SW, (202) 554-8000.

Evening Dinner Cruise. Boards 6:30 P.M. daily. Dinner and dancing until 10 P.M.; $28 weekdays, $32 Fridays and Saturdays.

Moonlight Party Cruise. Departs 11 P.M. Friday and Saturday in season; $14 per person. Live bands, snacks and cocktails.

Lunch Cruise. Thursday, Friday and Saturday, departs at noon, returns at 2 P.M.; $17 per person weekdays; $20 Saturday. Sunday Brunch Cruise. Departs 1 P.M., returns at 3 P.M., $20 per person.

City Lights Cruise. Sunday nights 8 to 10 P.M. Arlington/Georgetown shoreline; $8 per person.

Mount Vernon. Departs daily in season at 9 A.M. and 2 P.M.; one-hour-45-minute stopover at Mount Vernon. Adults $11.25, children 2 to 11, $7; does not include Mount Vernon admission.

The Admiral Tilp gives 50-minute waterfront cruises of Alexandria, leaving from the dock at North Union and Cameron streets (behind the Torpedo Factory). The *Tilp* has a highly variable schedule, so call (703) 548-9000 for information, but in general, it leaves on the hour most days (closed Monday). The cost in 1993 was $6 for adults, $5 for seniors and $4.00 for children ages 2–12.

AMUSEMENT PARKS

King's Dominion, Doswell, VA 23047, (804) 876-5000. Located 75 miles south of Washington on Interstate Route 95. Entrance fees (1993) $24.95 for 7 and up. $16.95 3–6, and free for two years and under. Seniors over 55, $19.95. Open weekends from late March to Memorial Day, daily from Memorial Day through Labor Day and weekends through mid-October. High season hours 9:30 A.M. to 10 P.M. A single ticket is good for all rides.

King's Dominion is a massive amusement park designed for a full day of experiences. It offers many rides, daily live shows (including national headliner acts), and a variety of food options, from fast-food kiosks to sit-down restaurants. In 1993, Days of Thunder, a racing simulator, was added. In 1992, Hurricane Reef, a multi-ride water park, opened. The Anaconda—a twist-and-turn-you-upside-down roller coaster—was the big 1991 news. Other locally famous rides are White Water Canyon, Diamond Falls, Haunted River, Sky Pilot and a batch of hair-raising roller coasters, including Shock Wave, Grizzly, and Rebel Yell. There are also plenty of attractions for little kids— Hanna-Barberaland, the Scooby-Doo roller coaster and play areas with climbing apparatus, slides, chutes, and ball bounce, etc.

Wild World, 13710 Central Avenue, Mitchellville, MD 20716, (301) 249-1500. Capital Beltway (I-495) to Exit 15A or 17A, to Route 214 east (Central Avenue) 4 miles, park on left. The 1993 entrance fee was $18.99 for adults and kids 9 and older, $14.99 for children 3 to 8 and $12.99 for seniors over 62. The park is free to children 2 and under. Open daily Memorial Day to Labor Day. Hours: 10:30 A.M. to approximately 10 P.M.

Major attractions: large wave pool, swimming, rides, shows.

Major rides: roller coaster called Wild One, the only wooden roller coaster on the East Coast; Rampage and Rainbow Zoom, water rides. New in 1990 were Rafter's Run, a double-inner tube water ride, and Paradise Island, a large activity pool surrounded by a lazy river for tubing. Under new ownership in 1992, the park has begun a five-year program of major improvements.

Shows: four major shows daily, including song and dance revue, puppets and others, to be announced.

Food: pizza, hamburgers, hot dogs, chicken, ribs, shrimp, Mexican, barbecue.

Play area for kids includes climbing apparatus, slides, ball bounce.

14

SHOPPING/

GALLERIES

Washington shopping opportunities are vast—whether you're looking for a major purchase or just a few trinkets. As the federal city, Washington is home to a variety of government and nonprofit cultural organizations that sell unusual and often reasonably priced goods. At the same time, during the 1970s and 1980s, nationally known retailers suddenly discovered the area and descended to tap its affluent residential and tourist market. Yet the city is still down-to-earth enough to support countless street vendors.

You name it, and chances are you'll find it in Washington. Streets are lined with clothing and gift shops, bookstores, jewelry and antique stores, galleries and restaurants. Upscale shopping malls dot the landscape, often housing the city's most exclusive shops.

While we note gift shops and special finds in the *Guide*'s site reports, this chapter gives an overview of shopping opportunities, pointing you in the general direction of places to buy and highlighting out-of-the-ordinary wares. Although there are plenty of things to do in Washington without even going near a store, you'll probably want to sample the fare and bring a piece of your visit back home.

FEDERAL FINDS

The *Smithsonian Institution* shops are consistently interesting, offering a changing variety of special exhibit-related merchandise as well as a stable collection of museum-based goods. Shoppers can find gems, astronaut freeze-dried ice cream, hand-crafted dinnerware, African artifacts and robots among the endless treasures for sale. The *Guide*'s individual site reports will alert you to shopping opportunities in various parts of the Smithsonian.

The *Indian Craft Shop,* tucked away in the Department of the Interior Building at 18th and C streets, NW, has a wonderful selection of jewelry, rugs, baskets, pottery and other handicrafts made by Native Americans. Since the shop is in a government building you'll have to sign in; the hours are Monday to Friday, 8:30 A.M. to 4 P.M. In addition, a branch has opened in the Georgetown Park Mall.

The *Library of Congress* sells cards, exhibition catalogs and posters, recordings and other items based on its vast collection of Americana. The photographs here are a real find. You can buy a copy of a photograph by Walker Evans, Charles H. Currier or Dorothea Lange for rock-bottom prices. Explore the shop and lobby display areas thoroughly; often there are examples of regional crafts for sale, including rag rugs and basketry (see site report).

The *Government Printing Office* bookstore sells nearly all of the literature the federal government prints for the public on everything from national parks to foreign affairs, Social Security, cooking, health and fish diseases. You can also pick up copies of the daily *Congressional Record* and *Federal Register,* as well as patriotic and nature posters. Everything is reasonably priced. Located near Union Station, at 710 North Capitol Street, NW (between G and H streets), it may not be worth a trip unless you're looking for something special. You can call (202) 783-3238 to order a particular item, and GPO can send it to you. The general bookstore number is (202) 275-2091. The *United States Government Bookstore* offers many of the same titles, posters and maps at a more convenient location: 1510 H Street, NW.

While the next two suggestions aren't under the auspices of the federal government, they offer similar high-quality goods.

The *National Trust for Historic Preservation* shop, located at 1600 H Street, NW, (202) 842-1856, has a large selection of books on architecture and historic preservation, as well as gifts such as glass, ceramic and silver objects, dolls, T-shirts, ties, stationery and posters. Some are reproductions while others are modern interpretations of traditional crafts.

The shop at the *Corcoran Gallery,* 17th Street and New York Avenue, NW, has a variety of unusual cards and other stationery items, art books and posters and slides. A few special items made by gifted hands are usually available. On a recent visit we found exquisite glassware, hand-painted pillows and unique jewelry.

The shop at the *National Building Museum,* 401 F Street, NW, (202) 272-7706, offers a fine collection of architecture-inspired clothing, gifts, jewelry, posters, books, cards and more, in a newly remodeled and very handsome store.

DEPARTMENT STORES

You'll find a staggering variety of stores in Washington. The major home-grown department stores are Hecht's, a large department store with a full line of clothing, accessories and furniture; and Woodward & Lothrop, affectionately dubbed "Woodie's," which has a wide variety of clothing, furniture and household items. Hecht's and Woodie's have main stores downtown and are also located in various shopping centers and malls throughout the area. Several large retailers from other parts of the country are here, too, such as Bloomingdale's, Neiman Marcus, Lord & Taylor, Saks Fifth Avenue, Nordstrom and Macy's. Filene's Basement opened two branches in the fall of 1993, one at Connecticut Avenue and DeSales Street, NW, and another at Mazza Gallerie, in Friendship Heights.

STREET VENDORS

Pounding the pavement may provide an afternoon's amusement, as well as fill your shopping needs. The sidewalks in certain areas around town are transformed into bazaars, as eager street vendors set up shop. The goods piled high on their tables run the gamut, including baskets, purses and briefcases, Chinese canvas shoes, clothing, plants, framed posters and prints, crafts and, of course, food.

The best area for street shopping is the corridor around Connecticut Avenue and K Street, NW; the scene continues along Connecticut Avenue toward Dupont Circle.

The Mall, too, becomes a cacophony of street vendors, particularly on bright, warm days. The trailers here offer T-shirts, postcards and other souvenirs, as well as snacks. We found the best T-shirt prices in town here.

The Capitol Hill lunch crowd is usually greeted by some local vendors, especially along Independence Avenue, SE, between 2nd and 4th streets.

Georgetown also boasts a lively commercial street scene. Vendors sell T-shirts, crafts, jewelry and more. They generally won't pack up their goods until late, so plan to stroll and browse after dinner.

MAIN SHOPPING AREAS

There are several main shopping areas where you can simply window shop or join the hustle and bustle of Washingtonians in hot pursuit of a purchase.

Downtown

The *F Street Plaza,* between 7th and 14th streets, NW, has been the heart of the Downtown shopping area for years, and it has undergone a recent rejuvenation. Here you can shop at *Woodward & Lothrop,* which has direct access from the Metrorail stop at Metro Center. If you're traveling aboveground, Woodie's is at 10th and 11th streets, NW, between F and G streets. *Hecht's* glittery new flagship store—the only urban free-standing department store built in this country since World War II—is located at 12th and G streets, NW.

The Shops at National Place stretch between F Street and Pennsylvania Avenue in the 1300 block, bringing pizzazz to the refurbished National Press Building. Over 85 shops and eateries offer a full array of goods, from computerized clock radios to lacy underpinnings and Chinese fast food to complete seafood dinners. The shops connect to the elegant lobby of the new Marriott Hotel.

A block down Pennsylvania Avenue is yet another stunning renovated retail space, *The Pavilion at the Old Post Office.* The shopping is less serious here, with knickknacks and casual jewelry stores outweighing clothing operations, but eating possibilities vary from snack to sumptuous. (You might also want to take the elevator to the top of the 315-foot clock tower for a great view of the city. Tours start from the elevator on the stage level.)

After years of neglect and more years of bad planning and fiscal mismanagement, Washington's grand railroad terminal, Union Station, has been beautifully reborn—this time as a railroad/Metro station combined with a major urban shopping/dining mall. Some judge the restoration to have produced one of the country's finest interior spaces. Several significant retailers are present—The Limited, Cignal, Brookstone, Nature Company, Ann Taylor—and more than 100 others, including small retailers selling a variety of handmade and other unusual merchandise. Cafés and five major restaurants complete the space, along with a food court featuring varied cuisines and a nine-screen movie house.

Georgetown

Georgetown offers a smorgasbord of amusement, among which are its shops, which range from chic and expensive to urban and grungy. Art and antique stores cater to all tastes and price capabilities. The neighborhood has long been a mecca for restaurants, including all the major cuisines of the world—European, Asian, Latin American, good old American and modern, mesclun American. Your best bet here is to walk, exploring and discovering.

Along M Street:

Save the Children Craft Shop, 2803 M Street; handmade crafts from around the world.

American Hand, 2906 M Street; stunning ceramics and wooden pieces, jewelry and architect-designed dinnerware, serving pieces and kitchen implements.

Antiques, 31st Street above M Street; several antique shops.

Canal Square, 1054 31st Street; a collection of galleries selling international art, artifacts and antiques.

earl allen, 3109 M Street; elegant dresses, suits and sweaters for women.

Urban Outfitters, 3111 M Street; casual, trendy clothes and toys for adults and kids; brightly colored plastic housewares.

door store, 3140 M Street; assemble-it-yourself furniture.

Banana Republic, M Street at Wisconsin Avenue; safari-, tropics- and Egyptian-inspired clothing for urban adults with adventure in their hearts.

United Colors of Benetton, M Street at Wisconsin Avenue; larger than most of this chain, this store offers a range of trendy apparel for women.

Georgetown Park, 3222 M Street; Washington's largest mall, this is a fancy neo-Victorian collection of almost 100 shops and restaurants. A number of Georgetown's most elegant retailers moved here when it opened in 1981. Some examples of the stores include

Abercrombie & Fitch, Ann Taylor, Carroll Reed, Conran's, F. A. O. Schwarz, The Gallery of History (historic documents), *Godiva Chocolatier, Mark Cross, Polo/Ralph Lauren, The Sharper Image,* and the *Indian Craft Shop.*

Laura Ashley, 3213 M Street; women's clothing, fabrics and accessories in the English-country tradition.

Georgetown Leather Design, 3265 M Street; brand-name leather goods and their own designs.

Dean & De Luca, 3276 M Street; NYC's posh grocer complete with café.

Along Wisconsin Avenue:

Pirjo, 1044 Wisconsin Avenue; chic and unique clothing and jewelry for women.

Pleasure Chest, 1063 Wisconsin Avenue; erotica in a nonthreatening environment. Adults only.

Red Balloon, 1073 Wisconsin Avenue; toys, clothes and other children's goodies.

The Coach Store, 1214 Wisconsin Avenue; fine leather accessories.

Olsson's Books and Records, 1239 Wisconsin Avenue; an excellent selection of discounted books and tapes.

Boogie's Diner and Retail, 1229 Wisconsin Avenue; clothing for the young and young-at-heart surrounded by a 50's-style restaurant/ diner upstairs.

Britches, 1247 Wisconsin Avenue; local chain of fine menswear. Other branches along Wisconsin Avenue cater to the more casual dresser.

Georgetown Court, 3251 Prospect Street; a small, exclusive mall of 25 shops, galleries and restaurants.

The Nature Company, 1323 Wisconsin Avenue; globes, minerals, binoculars, chimes, toys, games, posters, T-shirts, books—all with a focus on nature.

Commander Salamander, 1420 Wisconsin Avenue; an emporium of the latest punk regalia.

Appalachian Spring, 1415 Wisconsin Avenue; lovely, high-quality regional handcrafted items.

Moda, 1510 Wisconsin Avenue; designer men's clothing including Giorgio Armani and Missoni.

Watergate/Les Champs

The Watergate Complex, at the intersection of Virginia Avenue, NW, and Rock Creek Parkway, offers ample opportunities for conspicuous consumption. From the choicest of chic to South American handicrafts to the famous Watergate pastries, it's all here.

Connecticut Avenue

The Connecticut Avenue corridor from K Street to Dupont Circle aims primarily for a well-heeled professional clientele. *Burberry's* (1155 Connecticut Avenue), *Bally of Switzerland* (1020 Connecticut Avenue) and *Louis Vuitton* (1028 Connecticut Avenue) share the promenade with numerous jewelry stores. The less-than-wealthy will feel right at home here, as well, in a variety of lower-ticket shops, especially Filene's Basement (1133 Connecticut Avenue). *Eddie Bauer* is around the corner on M Street for urban campers.

Connecticut Avenue in the area of Dupont Circle is far less imposing and more eclectic. *Americana West Galleries* (1630 Connecticut Avenue) showcases contemporary and traditional Native American and western art and handicrafts. The *News Room* (1753 Connecticut Avenue) sells domestic and foreign periodicals and T-shirts. *Kramerbooks & afterwords* (1517 Connecticut Avenue) reflects the cosmopolitan atmosphere of the neighborhood in its bookstore/café—a delightful combination of fiction and fettuccine. Numerous other shops invite extensive browsing.

Friendship Heights/Chevy Chase

Friendship Heights marks the District-Maryland border at Wisconsin and Western Avenues, NW, and it's easily reached by Metrobus and Metrorail. You can find lots of department stores and fine specialty shops in a spacious setting, with the diversity and selection of city shopping but the convenience offered by suburbia. The area features the *Chevy Chase Shopping Center, Mazza Gallerie,* and *Chevy Chase Pavilion.* Offering cream-of-the-crop merchandise, Mazza Gallerie's 50-plus shops include *Neiman Marcus,* the famous, extravagant Texas specialty store; *Kron Chocolatier; Pierre Deux,* featuring its own handblocked French provincial fabrics and accessories. *Woodward & Lothrop* is next door on Wisconsin Avenue, and *Lord & Taylor* is genteelly tucked behind Mazza Gallerie on Western Avenue. *Gucci* and *Saks-Jandel* (expensive dresses and furs) reside in elegance a bit farther up Wisconsin Avenue, with *Saks Fifth Avenue* across the street.

Old Town, Alexandria

Just across the Potomac in Alexandria, Virginia, there's a charming enclave of historic sites, restaurants, galleries and small shops selling clothing, antiques, housewares, crafts and gifts for the discriminating shopper. *The Winterthur Museum Store,* 207 King Street, has a lovely selection of decorative furnishings and gifts. *Thos. Moser Cabinetmakers,* 601 S. Washington Street, offers distinctive handcrafted furniture. *Gilpin House Book Shop,* at 208 King Street, is good for a browse, too, particularly in the children's room. *John Davy Toys,* a block behind King Street at 301 Cameron Street, is filled with classic and unusual playthings; it's the stuff of sweet nostalgia, as well. *Frankie Welch,* at 305 Cameron Street, designs her own sportswear and accessories for women.

Other Shopping Prospects

International Square at 18th and K streets, NW (Farragut West Metro), offers international variety from 40 shops, restaurants and a food court. Most notable: *Sidney Kramer Books,* a well-rounded bookstore dealing with the "businesses" of Washington—politics, defense, economics—with excellent travel, kids and fiction sections as well, in a beautifully designed setting.

Tower Records, 2000 Pennsylvania Avenue, NW, has an astonishing array of records, tapes and compact discs in every musical style, from every corner of the globe; it's open 9 A.M. to midnight, 365 days a year.

The Farrell Collection, 2633 Connecticut Avenue, NW, sells a glorious selection of handcrafted items, from fine ceramic dishes and wooden objects to one-of-a-kind pieces of jewelry and designer birdhouses.

Foxhall Mall, 3301 New Mexico Avenue, NW, is a small, upscale collection of galleries and shops, including *New Conceptions,* a choice maternity clothing store; *Just So,* a children's boutique, and *Jackie Chalkley Fine Contemporary Crafts,* an elegant and pricy emporium of designed clothing, jewelry and ceramics (also at the Willard Collection and in Friendship Heights).

The primary shop of interest in Chevy Chase is the *Cheshire Cat Children's Book Store,* a well-stocked and fun haven for kids, which offers mini-concerts and author get-togethers.

Bethesda, Maryland, along Wisconsin Avenue has become the region's center of Oriental rug galleries.

Shopping Malls

Washington is ringed by suburban shopping centers and malls, and there are several particularly outstanding ones. *White Flint,* an upscale complex of about 115 stores, including *Bloomingdale's* and *Lord & Taylor,* is in Rockville, Maryland, about a half-hour drive or Metro ride from Downtown. It's not far from the Capital Beltway (I-495); take Exit 34 north (Rockville Pike) and you'll see White Flint in about 1.5 miles. *The Fashion Centre at Pentagon City* is the newest entry in the mall game, and it's a winner. Four stories of shops, specialty stores and eateries look onto a bright 70-foot atrium. *Nordstrom* and *Macy's* keep company with 120 quality retailers that can satisfy every shopper's needs and dreams. Metro to Pentagon City, or take the Pentagon City exit from I-395 or Army-Navy Drive in Arlington. *Tyson's Corner,* in McLean, Virginia, features *Bloomingdale's, Nordstrom, Woodward & Lothrop, Hecht's* and about 140 other shops, restaurants and movie theaters. *The Galleria at Tyson's II* rivals its neighbor across the street with *Macy's, Saks Fifth Avenue* and over 100 other elegant entries. This is about a 10-mile drive from Washington; take either the George Washington Parkway or the Capital Beltway to Route 123, Old Chain Bridge Road. The shopping center is at the intersection of Routes 495, 123 and 7. *Springfield Mall,* in Springfield, Virginia, has some more moderately priced stores among its 180 stores. The large department stores here are *Montgomery Ward* and *JC Penney.* To get to the Springfield Mall, take the Capital Beltway (I-495) to I-95 south and follow signs to Franconia. *Fair Oaks,* a shopping center in Fairfax, Virginia, has five major department stores—*Sears, JC Penney, Hecht's, Woodward & Lothrop* and *Lord & Taylor*—as well as 200 shops and restaurants. The best way to get there is to take the Capital Beltway (I-495) to Interstate 66 west and exit at Route 50 west.

For truly dedicated bargain hunters, a foray to *Potomac Mills Mall* is in order; about 250,000 shoppers make the trip each week. In fact, *Potomac Mills* has surpassed Colonial Williamsburg as Virginia's most popular tourist attraction. The mall boasts over 200 stores and restaurants, with more to come in 1994. All the retail outlets are discount stores, offering clothing (from designer to casual) for all the family, shoes, furs, furniture, records, cosmetics and dinnerware. The banner store is *IKEA,* an immense Scandinavian furniture and housewares retailer selling assemble-it-yourself furniture at astonishingly low prices. Take I-95 south for 20 miles to Exit 52 (Dale City). Bear right to Potomac Mills Road; take a right to Gideon Road and another right into the mall.

While Metrobus and Metrorail serve suburban areas, an excursion to a shopping mall is much easier and quicker with a car. Most mall stores are open 10 A.M. to 9:30 P.M., Monday to Saturday, and some stores are open Sunday, noon to 5 or 6 P.M.

ART GALLERIES

Artists from the city, metropolitan area and region are well represented in over 100 commercial art galleries in the Washington area. A few galleries have broadened their scope to the national scene as well. With few exceptions, District galleries emphasize twentieth-century works, and many specialize in contemporary art.

Local artists have voiced resentment at a lack of support for their work in the Washington area: they are in "competition" of sorts with pieces exhibited in the national museums here; serious art collectors are lured away by New York's dazzle and proximity; the remaining art-buying public is quite cautious and conservative. Despite this, District galleries (as well as a few notable suburban exhibit spaces) give vibrant display to a wide range of artistic talent, and a new generation of collectors is appreciative of home-grown art.

For years, the city administration and the Pennsylvania Avenue Development Corporation have attempted to make the 7th Street corridor the center of the art world, but supporting development has lagged far behind ambitious plans. Most galleries that had been lured by the initial promises have departed 7th Street to join their colleagues in the Dupont Circle area. The area north and west of Dupont Circle is ripe with town houses converted into gallery space, as well as some notable museums (the Phillips Collection and the Textile Museum, as well as others detailed in Chapter 8, "Northwest"). Another cluster of fine galleries is in Georgetown; a few other notables are scattered elsewhere (as listed below).

An excellent publication essential to the serious viewer of art is *Galleries: A Guide to Washington Area Art Galleries,* published monthly and available free in most galleries.

The list below highlights some of the area's best galleries:

Dupont Circle

Addison/Ripley Gallery, Ltd., 9 Hillyer Court, NW 20008, (202) 328-2332. American contemporary art.

Affrica, 2010½ R Street, NW 20009, (202) 745-7272. Museum-quality traditional African arts.

Baumgartner Galleries, Inc., 2016 R Street, NW 20009, (202) 232-6320. Primarily local contemporary artists.

District of Columbia Arts Center, 2438 18th Street, NW 20009, (202) 462-7833. A noncommercial alternative arts center committed to supporting local artists, complete with exhibit and performance space. Call for performance and exhibit schedules.

Foundry Gallery, 9 Hillyer Court, NW 20008, (202) 387-0203. Cooperative gallery showing contemporary art by members and guest artists.

Gallery K, 2010 R Street, NW 20009, (202) 234-0339. Contemporary American artists.

Jane Haslem, 2025 Hillyer Place, NW 20009, (202) 232-4644. Twentieth-century American paintings, prints and works on paper.

Jones Troyer Fitzpatrick Gallery, 1710 Connecticut Avenue, NW 20009, (202) 328-7189. Contemporary Washington artists in all media, and photography by American photographers.

Kathleen Ewing Gallery, 1609 Connecticut Avenue, NW 20009, (202) 328-0955. Nineteenth- and twentieth-century photography.

Studio Gallery, 2108 R Street, NW 20008, (202) 232-8734. Cooperative gallery of area artists.

St. Luke's Gallery, 1715 Q Street, NW, (202) 328-2424. Oils, prints, and drawings by European old masters, seventeenth- to nineteenth-century English watercolors and mural and fresco paintings.

The Tartt Gallery, 2017 Q Street, NW 20009, (202) 332-5652. Nineteenth- and twentieth-century photography, and contemporary painting and sculpture.

Touchstone Gallery, 2009 R Street NW, 20009, (202) 797-7278. Cooperative gallery of area artists.

Georgetown

Adams Davidson Galleries, 3233 P Street, NW 20007, (202) 965-3800. Nineteenth- and early twentieth-century American art.

Shogun Gallery, 1083 Wisconsin Avenue, NW 20007, (202) 965-5454.

Japanese woodblock prints, both contemporary and from previous eras.

Hollis Taggart Gallery, 3241 P Street, NW 20007, (202) 298-7676. Nineteenth- and twentieth-century American paintings.

7th Street

David Adamson Gallery, 406 7th Street, NW 20004, (202) 628-0257. Contemporary American paintings, sculpture and works on paper.

Mahler Gallery, 406 7th Street, NW 20004, (202) 393-0780. Works in all media, but with special emphasis in works on paper, from regional artists.

Washington Project for the Arts, 400 7th Street, NW 20004, (202) 347-4813. An artist-directed, multidisciplinary (visual, media, literary, performing and book) arts organization that provides progressive artists (local, national and international) with work and exhibit space as well as funding. Artist support includes residency programs, commissions and the introduction of new art to the community. Call for exhibit and performance schedules.

Zenith Gallery, 413 7th Street, NW 20004, (202) 783-2963. Art and crafts by area and national artists.

Other D.C. Areas

Franz Bader Gallery, 1500 K Street, NW 20005, (202) 393-6111. Contemporary sculpture, paintings, works on paper and furniture by area artists.

Sansar, 4200 Wisconsin Avenue, NW 20016, (202) 244-4448. Contemporary American furniture and other fine wooden pieces.

Very Special Arts Gallery, 1331 F Street, NW, 20004, (202) 628-0800. Near Metro Center (downtown), this gallery is non-profit and proceeds benefit artists with disabilities.

Suburbs

Buffalo Gallery, 127 S. Fairfax Street, Alexandria, VA 22314, (703) 548-3338. Native American and Western art.

Capricorn Galleries, 4849 Rugby Avenue, Bethesda, MD 20814, (301) 657-3477. Contemporary American realist paintings, drawings, sculpture and prints.

Glass Gallery, 4720 Hampden Lane, Bethesda, MD 20814, (301) 657-3478. Glass artworks.

Torpedo Factory Art Center, 105 N. Union Street, Alexandria, VA 22314, (703) 838-4565. Originally a factory that manufactured torpedos during both world wars, the building has been renovated to house galleries and artists' studios. Many art media and crafts are represented.

15

OUTDOOR
WASHINGTON/
SPORTS

Ever since Pierre L'Enfant first designed the federal city in 1791, green parks, open spaces and natural woodlands have been an integral part of the essence of Washington. To this day, Washington has one of the highest ratios of parks to residents among urban areas in the U.S.

The city is literally riven with large, natural, open spaces on which still stand virgin timber, native wildflowers and hundreds of varieties of trees and shrubs. While many areas, such as Rock Creek Park and Great Falls Park, are best appreciated by repeat visits, they are also accessible to the casual visitor for the simple pleasures of walking and looking, or more active enjoyment, such as jogging, biking and horseback riding.

In this chapter we shall list, and in some cases briefly describe, a full range of outdoor activities—from gardens to golf, from active participant sports to spectator sports. These lists are by no means complete; entire books have been devoted to Washington's parks alone. Rather, we have tried to concentrate on those activities and attractions that are most accessible and appealing to the visitor. The various park authorities listed at the end of this chapter can provide much additional information.

As a guide to appropriate clothing for outdoor Washington, here are average high and low temperatures for each month of the year in the D.C. area.

Month	High	Low
January	43°F	27°F
February	46	28
March	55	35
April	67	45
May	76	55
June	84	64
July	88	69
August	86	67
September	80	61
October	69	49
November	57	38
December	45	29

Other sporting opportunities are within a day's drive of Washington, including ocean beaches, downhill and cross-country skiing and white-water rafting. For details, contact the information offices (all in D.C.) of the following states: Delaware, Maryland, Virginia, West Virginia and Pennsylvania.

PICNICKING

Washingtonians are, by nature, a sedentary species; it is not unusual, therefore, that picnicking is far and away the most popular outdoor activity in the capital city. Not only is it popular, but it is extremely simple in Washington: much of the downtown area is one big picnic site. Some of the more popular areas are:

The Mall
Constitution Gardens
Pershing Park
Lafayette Park
Farragut Square
Dupont Circle
The banks of the Potomac—from Thompson's Boat Center to Memorial Bridge and in East and West Potomac parks

A bit farther out:

Rock Creek Park—Military Road area, Beach Drive, Glover
Road. Phone (202) 673-7646 for reservations for large picnic
areas.
Great Falls Park—both Maryland and Virginia sides.
The banks of the Anacostia River.
Wolf Trap Farm Park—before show (see Chapter 13,
"Entertainment").
Any of the county regional parks, such as Wheaton, Cabin
John, Burke Lake.

Carry-outs, delicatessens, street food vendors and small grocery stores
are found throughout the city, so handy picnic food is nearby. Check
our recommendations in Chapter 3 through 10 for the best of the
takeouts.

GARDENS

As you explore Washington's monuments and museums, you'll undoubtedly walk through or around many of the gardens listed below.
Some of these parks are sufficiently interesting to warrant their own
reports, and more extensive descriptions are elsewhere in the *Guide,*
as noted.

Brookside Gardens. See Wheaton Regional Park site report in Chapter 11, "Nearby Maryland." Fifty acres of flowers, shrubs and trees
with particularly fine displays of azaleas, roses and flowering bulbs.
Other attractions include a Japanese pavilion, a large greenhouse of
exotic flora and a Braille garden.

Circles and Squares. A few of the nicest of these parks in Northwest
are:

Dupont Circle—Connecticut Avenue at P Street
Farragut Square—K Street between Connecticut Avenue and
17th Street
Lafayette Square—16th and H streets, opposite the White
House
McPherson Square—15th and K streets
Rawlins Park—E Street between 18th and 20th streets

Washington's circles and squares, while the bane of the driver unfamiliar with their traffic flow, are an unending delight to the stroller. Administered both by the National Park Service and the District government, the various "vest-pocket" parks show an array of seasonal flowers, bulbs and flowering shrubs through the entire year. Washingtonians have come to watch carefully for the change of displays, because most of the bulbs are discarded after one season and given away to passersby on request!

These areas are a good place to examine the locals, who come out of their office burrows at lunch to bask in the noonday sun.

The D.C. Highway Department has almost completed the process of creating curb cuts for wheelchairs and bikes in most downtown areas. At present, most circles and squares are wheelchair-accessible.

Constitution Gardens. Dedicated in May 1976, these Mall gardens are some 50 acres of rolling, tree-shaded lawns with a six-acre lake as a focal point. A footbridge leads to a one-acre island in the shallow lake. Designed principally for walking, jogging and picnicking, the gently contoured hills have paved pathways and are planted with over 5,000 trees, including oak, maple, dogwood, elm, crabapple and nearly 100,000 other plants. Constitution Avenue between 17th and 23rd streets, NW. Open all year. Wheelchair-accessible.

Dumbarton Oaks. See site report in Chapter 7, "Georgetown/Foggy Bottom/The West End." Grand formal gardens—beds, fountains, pools, paths, stairways, nooks and crannies—on the Dumbarton Oaks estate.

Floral Library. A small wedge of blossoms between the Tidal Basin and the Washington Monument, the Floral Library presents a myriad of tulips in spring and annuals in summer and fall. Independence Avenue at the Tidal Basin. In bloom from spring to fall. Wheelchair-accessible.

Franciscan Monastery Grounds. See site report in Chapter 9, "Other D.C. Areas." Lovingly tended grounds, with reproductions of Holy Land shrines.

Gunston Hall. See site report in Chapter 10, "Suburban Virginia." Formal gardens of plants and flowers grown in colonial days, complete with ancient boxwood hedges.

Hillwood Museum Gardens. See site report in Chapter 8, "Northwest." Japanese and formal European gardens, rhododendron-lined paths, greenhouse with 5,000 orchids on the former estate of Marjorie Merriweather Post.

Kenilworth Aquatic Gardens. See site report in Chapter 9, "Other D.C. Areas." Spectacular displays of waterlilies, lotus and other water-loving plants, and riverside wildlife as well.

Kensington Orchids. Not a public garden, but a commercial concern. Still, if you are an orchid fancier, you will not have a better opportunity to examine so many varieties of orchids in one place: 3301 Plyers Mill Road, Kensington, MD 20895, (301) 933-0036. Capital Beltway (Route 495); take Connecticut Avenue north exit. Turn right on Plyers Mill Road to 3301. Open daily, 8 A.M. to noon, 1 to 5 P.M. Free admission. Wheelchair-accessible.

Kenwood, Maryland, Cherry Trees. A strictly seasonal but spectacular drive-through attraction. Cuttings and grafts from the Tidal Basin cherry trees have been added to native wild cherries for over 50 years. The results are stunning. When in flower, the trees turn Kenwood, an exclusive (and, of course, expensive) community, into a fairyland; gaudy but unforgettable: 5500 block of River Road, Bethesda, Maryland. Turn into Kenwood at Dorset Avenue.

Lady Bird Johnson Park–Lyndon Baines Johnson Memorial Grove. Imagine one million daffodils in bloom, followed by 2,700 pink-and-white dogwoods. Breathtaking! Lady Bird Park, dedicated in 1968 as thanks for her efforts to beautify the country, is located on what used to be called Columbia Island, the Virginia end of the Memorial Bridge. A handsome, 15-acre grove of white pine, dogwoods, azaleas and rhododendron form the natural background for the large Texas granite memorial to LBJ at the south end of the park. When visiting the LBJ Memorial and Lady Bird Park, be sure to note the handsome and graceful "gulls and waves" monument between the parkway and the Potomac. It is a memorial to Navy and Merchant Marine personnel, sculpted by Ernesto Begni del Piatta, and dedicated in 1934. George Washington Memorial Parkway at Arlington Memorial Bridge. Open all year. Wheelchair-accessible.

Meridian Hill Park. Meridian Hill overlooks downtown Washington with vistas to the Potomac and Anacostia rivers and the hills of Virginia. It's in close architectural harmony with the ornate marble "palaces" of 16th Street just north of the park. Meridian Hill Park shows both French and Italian influences—French, in the long promenades and a mall with heavy borders of plants that occupy the flat upper part; and Italian, in the opulent use of water, in falls, in jets and in the handsome cascade of 13 falls of graduated size leading down the slope of the park. Located at 16th and Euclid streets, NW, two miles north of The White House. We must add a cautionary note: as beautiful as the park is, it has become, unfortunately, a haven for drug users and street people. You should consider going only with others, and during daylight hours. Open all year. Limited wheelchair accessibility due to hilly terrain and many steps.

Mount Vernon Grounds. See site report in Chapter 10, "Suburban Virginia." Grounds of the beloved estate of our first President, complete with colonial flower and vegetable gardens.

National Arboretum. See site report in Chapter 9, "Other D.C. Areas"; 415 acres of gardens, trees, shrubs, overlooks and ponds, and a spectacular collection of bonsai in the Japanese pavilion.

United States Botanic Gardens. See site report in Chapter 5, "Capitol Hill." A lush conservatory with an incredible array of plants.

Washington Cathedral Grounds. See site report in Chapter 8, "Northwest." Rose and medieval herb gardens, perennial and yew walks, and wildflowers along a woodland path.

Washington Temple of the Church of Latter-Day Saints Grounds. See site report in Chapter 11, "Nearby Maryland." Award-winning gardens of annuals, perennials, trees and shrubs give year-round displays.

White House Grounds. See site report in Chapter 6, "Downtown." These spectacular, well-manicured plantings are open to the public on very limited occasions.

Woodlawn Plantation. See site report in Chapter 10, "Suburban Virginia." Old-fashioned roses, boxwood and assorted colonial plants in a classic garden painstakingly restored by the Garden Club of Virginia. Wooded nature trails.

HIKING—WOODLAND TRAILS

Serene woodland trails can crop up in the most unlikely places in Washington. You can be in snarling, rush-hour, downtown traffic one minute, and the next find a quiet byway where cars and noise and time don't exist. Some of the nicest trails can be found right in the middle of the city.

Many of the trails will be found cheek by jowl with the garden parks, so this section will overlap with the preceding list of gardens.

Hiking

Rock Creek Nature Center, 5200 Glover Road, NW, (202) 426-6829, is the focal point of a variety of outdoor activities and educational programs for children and adults. The center is open 9 A.M. to 5 P.M. Tuesday through Sunday. Groups are welcome, by reservation. The center is ramped, and rest rooms are accessible. The same basic activities are offered on a regular schedule, mostly on weekends—check when you get there.

> 1 P.M.—Children's Planetarium presentation. Ages 4 and up. Film and show, 35 minutes.
>
> 3 P.M.—Nature walk, a 45-minute guided walk. (Many self-guided walks of greater length start in the area of the center.)
>
> 4 P.M.—Adult Planetarium show. Ages 7 and up. A longer, more comprehensive version of the 1 P.M. show, designed for older children and adults. Presentation lasts 45 minutes to an hour.

Other special programs are announced in the National Park Service publication, *Kiosk* (see Chapter 3, "Planning Ahead").

C&O Canal Historic Park. From Georgetown to Cumberland, Maryland: 184.5 miles. For a history and description of the canal, see site report in Chapter 11, "Nearby Maryland."

Georgetown. Pleasant walking anywhere. This segment of the canal tends to be crowded with bikers, joggers and strollers from its terminus in Georgetown for several miles upstream. The National Historic Park that contains the canal abounds in wildlife: beaver, fox, squirrel, raccoon, woodchuck, muskrat, great blue heron, waterfowl and woodpeckers—hairy, yellow-bellied sapsucker, red-bellied and pileated. The list could go on and on. Many old stands of trees remain—majestic beech, oak, maple, willow, sycamore. In the spring the redbud are a handsome sight—splotches of purple among the white and pink dogwood.

Barge Trips along the C&O Canal. A fun and unusual outdoor activity is to tour the historic C&O Canal aboard a horse-drawn boat in 1876 style. The 90-minute tour is narrated by guides dressed in period costume. Tours are offered mid-April to mid-October, on Wednesdays, Thursdays and Fridays at 1 and 3 P.M., and on Saturdays and Sundays at 10:30 A.M., 1 and 3 P.M. Call (202) 472-4376 or (202) 653-5844 for further information. We advise you to call well in advance to make arrangements, especially if touring as a large group.

Billy Goat Trail. This four-mile trail can be accessed from the parking lot across from Old Angler's Inn on MacArthur Boulevard. The trail, which is steep and rocky, offers a remarkable variety of terrain, vistas, flora and fauna.

Great Falls. Great Falls, Maryland, is the site of the Great Falls Tavern, now a museum describing life on the old canal. Since Hurricane Agnes in 1977, the scenic overlooks on the Maryland side have been seriously diminished. Better views of the falls can be obtained from the Virginia side. Good walking trails on both sides of the Potomac.

Woodland Trails

Rock Creek Park. The park has 15 miles of hiking trails. Bridle paths may also be used for hiking. Maps can be found at the Visitor Information Center on Beach Drive near Military Road, or at the Park Headquarters at the Nature Center. Nice hikes can be combined with visits to the Nature Center, Planetarium and the stables within the park.

Montrose Park. Next to Dumbarton Oaks and Rock Creek Cemetery, Montrose Park is a genteel place. A clay tennis court with a gazebo, a playground and a field make up the upper portion of the park facing R Street, and a lovely woodland path comprises the lower portion. The path goes through to Massachusetts Avenue, near the Naval Observatory.

National Arboretum. This is not exactly rough woodlands, but handsomely constructed paths show off many varieties of trees, shrubs and wildflowers, in season.

Woodend Nature Trail. Located at the headquarters of the Audubon Naturalist Society of the Central Atlantic States, 8940 Jones Mill Road, Chevy Chase, MD 20815, (301) 652-9188, the trail is part of a 40-acre estate bequeathed to the society. The mansion, by the way, was designed in the 1920s by John Russell Pope, architect of the National Gallery of Art and the Jefferson Memorial, and is a fine example of Georgian-revival domestic architecture. The estate is a haven for wildlife in the middle of suburban development, and counts among its residents some 29 species of birds, many small mammals and a family of red foxes. The society is extremely active in educational programs for schoolchildren, and organizes numerous outings in and around the Washington area. The society operates a bookshop at Woodend. The house and grounds (except the trail) at Woodend are accessible.

Regional Parks. All of the surrounding counties in Maryland and Virginia maintain parks with good hiking trails. For information, contact the various park authorities; addresses are listed at the end of this chapter.

For information and activities, serious hikers and backpackers should contact The Potomac Appalachian Trail Club (703) 242-0965.

JOGGING

Washington is well designed for the casual or serious runner; the wealth of the city parks gives joggers a wide choice of nice runs. Most of the better jogging areas are relatively flat, but with considerable visual interest. Many of the paths are centrally located, close to major hotels and other attractions, so a morning or evening run will not interfere with other events of the day.

The center of Washington jogging is the heart of the city—the Mall (packed-dirt paths), Ellipse and Tidal Basin (paved pathways). You can start virtually anywhere in this area, and jog in comfort, with only moderate traffic to impede you, and with relatively little need for a specific route in advance. The *Ellipse,* the park south of The White House, is just about a half mile around. An *Ellipse–Washington Monument* route is approximately 1.5 miles around from The White House, down 17th Street, around the edge of the monument grounds, and back up the other side of the Ellipse to your starting point. You can arrange longer runs by adding the Lincoln Memorial or some part of the Mall itself—from 14th Street all the way down to the steps of the Capitol (approximately 1.25 miles each way).

Rock Creek Park is a natural jogging area. Tree-shaded and usually 10 degrees cooler than the rest of the city, it is an oasis in the worst of the Washington summer heat and humidity. A nice run of about four miles would start where Rock Creek Parkway crosses under Connecticut Avenue. Head north in the park to Peirce Mill and retrace your steps. Along Rock Creek Parkway, starting at Cathedral Avenue, by the Shoreham Hotel, you will find a *Parcourse trail.* It has 18 stations, and is about 1.5 miles long.

Starting in Georgetown, the *C&O Canal Towpath* is perhaps the best single running surface in downtown Washington. A wide, packed-dirt trail, the towpath is home to runners, bikers and walkers, all of whom enjoy the serenity and beauty of this historic waterway. The National Park Service has erected mile posts all along the route up to Great Falls, so pace yourself as you run to your heart's content.

Hook up with the *Mount Vernon Bike Path* starting from the Lincoln Memorial, by taking the bridge across the Potomac (using the left sidewalk) and bearing left in Virginia. The paved path goes all the way to Mount Vernon, 15 miles or so downriver, but the best running is to the airport and back, a run of about 7.5 miles.

A run along the *Tidal Basin* and through *East Potomac Park* is another option. Starting from the Jefferson Memorial, head down either side of Ohio Drive, make the loop at the end of the park; continue past the Jefferson Memorial on the way back to take in the Tidal Basin loop, running under the beautiful cherry trees. This route is a must if you happen to hit D.C. when the trees are in bloom, but the crowds will cut down your speed.

BICYCLING

While in theory—and law—the bicycle has the same claim to the roadway as a motorized vehicle, urban cycling is still dangerous. We do not recommend bikes as a general means of transportation around Washington, although many residents bike regularly. The area abounds in good bike trails, however, many of which are the same as the jogging trails in the preceding section.

For the serious biker, the Potomac Area Council of American Youth Hostels and the Washington Area Bicyclist Association have coauthored the *Bicycle Atlas to the Greater Washington Area,* sold at bookstores or obtained direct from WABA, 1819 H Street, NW, #640, Washington, D.C. 20006, (202) 872-9830.

Bike rentals are reasonable. Try:

Thompson's Boat Center, Virginia Avenue at Rock Creek Parkway, D.C., (202) 333-4861. Standard bikes, mountain bikes, some equipped with child-carrier seats. $6/hour, $20/day. Hours: 6:30 A.M. to 7 P.M. weekdays, 8 A.M.–6 P.M. weekends.

Fletcher's Boat House, Canal and Reservoir roads, D.C., (202) 244-0461. Single-speed and kids' (20-inch) bikes. $3/hour, $10/ day, two-hour minimum. Hours: 9 A.M. to 7 P.M.

Swain's Lock Boat House, 10700 Swains Lock Road, Potomac, MD, (301) 299-9006. Standard, 3-speed, kids', tandem bikes; some standards are equipped with child-carrier seats. $5.25/ hour, $11.60/day. Hours: 10 A.M. to 7 P.M. daily.

Proteus Bikes, 7945 MacArthur Boulevard, Cabin John, MD, (301) 229-5900. All types of bikes for adults and kids, $9/hour, $30/day, $45 weekend deal (Friday morning to Monday afternoon). Hours: 11 A.M.–8 P.M. Monday-Friday; 9 A.M.–6 P.M. Saturday; 10 A.M.–5 P.M. Sunday.

Some of the best bikepaths are:

Arlington Cemetery–Lincoln Memorial–Rock Creek Parkway. A five-mile stretch, most easily accessed at Thompson's Boat Center along Rock Creek Parkway. You can bike either uptown toward the zoo, or downtown to Lincoln Memorial and across

Memorial Bridge to Arlington Cemetery (where you can connect to the Mount Vernon bikepath).

Upper Rock Creek Park. An 11-mile run from Beach Drive at
Tilden Street to East-West Highway in Chevy Chase, Maryland.
Several additional paths lead off of Beach Drive—explore
Glover Road, Oregon Avenue and Bingham Drive. Follow
signs. Level throughout. Bikes-only on the roadway Sundays, 9
A.M. to 5 P.M.

Mount Vernon Bikepath. Previously described.

C&O Canal Towpath. Previously described.

BOATING

Canoes, Rowboats and Paddle Boats

Canoes and rowboats are available for rental on the C&O Canal and
the Potomac River. The river can be very tricky; heed the advice of
the boatmen carefully.

Rentals at: *Thompson's Boat Center; Fletcher's Boat House; Belle
Haven Marina* (see "Sailboats"); *Swain's Lock Boat House* (see "Bicy-
cling" for addresses and phone numbers); *Jack's Boats,* 35th and K
streets, NW (under the Whitehurst Freeway), (202) 337-9642. At all
locations canoes and rowboats will run around $20 a day. Rowing
shells and sailboats—14-foot Phantoms—are available at Thompson's
Boat Center for $13/hour (certification required). Paddle boats are
available for rent at the Tidal Basin; it's a fun way to see the area.

Boat Rides

C&O Canal—The mule-drawn barges, *Canal Clipper* and *Georgetown,* offer 1½-hour excursions back to the nineteenth-century
canal life. The *Georgetown* leaves from The Foundry at 30th and
Thomas Jefferson streets, one-half block below M Street. The
Canal Clipper begins its voyage at Great Falls Park (see "C&O
Canal" in Chapter 11, "Nearby Maryland"). The barges run from
mid-April to mid-October, and schedules, while variable, will undoubtedly include 10:30 A.M., 1 P.M. and 3 P.M. trips on the weekends. Additional trips on weekdays and a 5 P.M. excursion Sundays
are often available. The cost on either boat is $5 for adults, $3.50

for seniors and children 12 and under. For further details, call (202) 472-4376 *(Georgetown)* or (301) 299-2026 *(Canal Clipper).*
Potomac River—See Chapter 13, "Entertainment," for a description of Potomac River rides.

Sailboats

The Potomac is not a premier sailing river, but rentals are available at:

Washington Sailing Marina—George Washington Memorial Parkway south of National Airport, (703) 548-9027. Sunfish, Designer Choice sloops, and Island 17s.

Belle Haven Marina—George Washington Parkway south of Alexandria. (703) 768-0018. C&C 34-footers, Flying Scots, Sunfish, Hobie Cats, windsurfers, canoes, and ocean kayaks.

If you want a first-rate sailing experience, spend a day on the Chesapeake Bay out of Annapolis. A good place for information, lessons and charters is the Annapolis Sailing School, (301) 267-7205. The Chesapeake Bay Yacht Racing Association, P.O. Box 1989, Annapolis, MD 21404, has a complete list of yacht clubs.

TENNIS

If you read the columns of Art Buchwald, you are aware of how important a role tennis plays in the lives of the ruling class. The surrounding jurisdictions have responded to this need with alacrity, building scores of courts throughout the area. Complete lists with addresses available at the phone numbers listed.

Alexandria, Parks Division, (703) 838-4343. 28 courts at 15 locations; six lighted. Open all year.

Arlington, (703) 358-4747. 98 courts at 29 locations; reserved courts for fee at Bluemont and Bancroft parks.

District of Columbia, (202) 673-7646. 144 outdoor, 60 lighted at 45 locations; open all year, permit required; charges at three locations: Hains Point, (202) 554-5962; Peirce Mill, (202) 723-2669 and 16th and Kennedy streets, NW, (202) 722-5949. Pay courts are both hard and soft; fees range from $8 to $16/hour depending on season and time of day. Indoor courts under bubbles at Hains Point during winter, (202) 485-9880.

Fairfax County, (703) 246-5700. 110 courts, 60 lighted; fee charges at four sites; reservations required at fee courts.

Montgomery County, 235 free outdoor courts; courts turn over on the hour. Indoor pay courts at Wheaton Regional Park, (301) 495-2525, and Cabin John Park, (301) 469-7300; spot time usually available.

Prince George's County, (301) 699-2415. 210 free courts at 90 locations, 45 with lights. Fees charged at two locations; call for information.

City of Rockville, (301) 424-8000. 34 courts, 15 lighted.

GOLF

District of Columbia. Two nine-hole courses and one 18-hole course at Hains Point, (202) 554-7660. Two nine-hole courses at Rock Creek Park, (202) 882-7332.

Maryland. 27-hole course, championship level at Northwest Park, (301) 598-6100; 18-hole course at Needwood, (301) 948-1075.

Virginia. Burke Lake Park, Fairfax, (703) 323-1641; Greendale, Alexandria, (703) 971-6170.

Surrounding counties run other public links. Call the parks department in the area you are interested in for further information. Reservations a few days in advance are usually recommended. Club rentals almost always available.

ICE SKATING

Several winters in the past decade, Washington has been treated to the unusual sight of a completely frozen Potomac River. Naturally, this has occasioned several attempts to make use of the river as an ice-skating rink or winter stock-car track. The local authorities have not been amused. But they have provided several legitimate outlets for winter sports fever.

District of Columbia. Besides the C&O Canal, on which skating is rarely allowed due to the uncertain nature of the ice, the Reflecting Pool, in front of the Lincoln Memorial, and the lake in Constitution Gardens are likely spots for good skating. An artificial rink—the *Sculpture Garden Outdoor Rink*—has been constructed between 7th and 9th streets, NW, and will appear at the right time of year. The *Federal Home Loan Bank Board* Building (on 17th Street, just below Pennsylvania Avenue, NW) has a small rink favored by a downtown lunch crowd, like Rockefeller Center. *Pershing Park,* carved out of what used to be Pennsylvania Avenue from 13th to 15th streets, NW, has a shallow pond used as a rink. *Fort Dupont Park* at 37th Street and Ely Place, SE, has a superior facility that is underutilized. Skate rentals are available at all facilities.

Maryland. *Wheaton Regional Park,* (301) 649-2250, and *Cabin John Regional Park,* (301) 365-0585, both have good artificial rinks. Skate rentals available.

Virginia. *Mount Vernon District Park,* (703) 768-3222, has an artificial rink. Skate rentals available.

HORSEBACK RIDING

District of Columbia:

Rock Creek Park Horse Center
Military Road and Glover Road, NW
(202) 362-0117
Open all year. Call for rates and availability.
The center does a lot of work with handicapped children; call if special services are desired.

Maryland:

Wheaton Park Stables (in Wheaton Regional Park)
1101 Glenallen Avenue, Wheaton
(301) 622-3311
Open all year. Trails, ring.

Polo fans, take note: On Sunday afternoons in spring, summer and fall, polo matches are held on the Lincoln Memorial Polo Field located on Ohio Drive, between the Lincoln Memorial and the Tidal Basin. Local teams play one another and visiting teams from other parts of the United States and overseas. Call the National Park Service, (202) 426-6700, for information.

PLAYING FIELDS

Here, as in every part of the country, find a school and you have found a playing field, usually more than one. Amateur, but reasonably serious, ballplayers—baseball, soccer, volleyball—find their way to the playing fields around the Lincoln Memorial and West Potomac Park. Established league games may prevent you from just fooling around when you want to, but pickup games usually can be found early evenings and weekends, when a league game is not scheduled.

SWIMMING

Local waters: not highly recommended. All local rivers and streams are polluted to a greater or lesser degree. Stick to the pools.

If your hotel or motel does not have a pool, seek out the various free, public pools.

District of Columbia. Nineteen outdoor pools. Call (202) 576-6436 for information.

Capitol East Natatorium. Indoor pool, 635 North Carolina Avenue, NE, (202) 724-4495.

Montgomery County. Six pools with differing restrictions. Call Aquatics Division, (301) 217-6840. In 1990, the county opened Montgomery Aquatic Center (301) 468-4211, at 5900 Executive Boulevard, Rockville, a world-class facility with an Olympic-size pool, diving area and an exciting 70-foot water slide.

Prince George's County. Eight pools, indoor and outdoor. The major center is Allentown Road Aquatic Center, Camp Springs, (301) 449-5567, with a complex of three outdoor and two indoor pools.

Alexandria. Seven pools. Admission charged. Call (703) 838-4343 for details.

Arlington. Three indoor/outdoor pools. Call (703) 358-4747 for details.

Fairfax. Five pools. Call (703) 941-5000 for details.

Good beaches are within an hour's drive of the area; the closest is Sandy Point State Park, located off Route 50, just west of the Bay Bridge. Ocean beaches are at least a three-hour drive, and often involve heavy traffic. Local radio stations broadcast beach weather and traffic reports.

SPECTATOR SPORTS

Baseball. Washington has lost two major-league baseball teams in the past 30 years—to Minneapolis and to Texas. Now some cynics say neither team was a major loss, but then, those folks probably don't care for apple pie either.

Baseball is still available, though.

The Baltimore Orioles play out of Oriole Park at Camden Yards, a handsome, old-fashioned ballpark close to Baltimore's Inner Harbor, one hour from downtown D.C. The stadium opened in the 1992 season to great critical acclaim. New stadiums attract large crowds. Tickets for the O's are at a premium. Get yours early. Tickets are available at the Orioles ticket office at 914 17th Street, NW (202) 296-2473; or from Ticketcenter, (410) 481-7328.

Basketball. The Washington Bullets, former NBA champs, play out of the USAir Arena. Tickets, available through the USAir Arena box office, (301) NBA-DUNK, run from $11 to $27. The USAir Arena is located off the Beltway (Route 495), accessible from either Exit 32 or 33. Good signs will lead you to the arena.

University of Maryland, a member of the Atlantic Coast Conference, offers a topflight brand of college basketball at Cole Field House. Call (301) 454-2123 for information, (301) 454-2121 for tickets. Perennial Big East Powerhouse, Georgetown, plays its home games at the USAir Arena. Call (301) 350-3400 for ticket and schedule information.

Football. The Washington Redskins have sold out RFK Stadium for the past decade. The waiting list for season tickets is years, so tickets are just not available except at considerably more than face value through ticket brokers. See theater section in Chapter 13, "Entertainment," for names and phone numbers.

Tickets are usually available, however, for local college teams. The Maryland Terrapins play at the College Park campus; call for ticket information at (301) 454-2121. The Naval Academy in Annapolis and Howard University in Washington also field competent teams. Check the paper for details of home games.

Hockey. Washington Capitals at the USAir Arena. Call Ticketmaster, (202) 432-7328. Tickets from around $10 to $20.

Horse Racing. One or another of the area tracks is usually in season. Check local papers for details. Buses are usually available from various locations in the Washington area to the tracks in season. Ask for details if you call. Local sports pages will normally carry ads for bus services, as well.

Harness:
Rosecroft Raceway—Oxon Hill, Maryland, (301) 567-4000
Del Marva Downs—Berlin, Maryland, (301) 641-0600

Thoroughbred:
Bowie Race Course—Bowie, Maryland, (301) 262-8111
Laurel Race Course—Laurel, Maryland, (301) 725-0400
Pimlico Race Course—Baltimore, Maryland, (301) 542-9400
Shenandoah Downs—Charleston, West Virginia, (304) 725-2021

Steeplechase:
Steeplechase is a seasonal happening in both Virginia and Maryland. Four major events occur in the spring: the Fair Hill meeting, the Maryland Hunt Cup, the Virginia Gold Cup and the Middleburg Hunt Cup. In autumn, Middleburg, Montpelier and Fairfax hold major meets. Check the papers for details.

16

ON THE TOWN
WITH CHILDREN

Washington can be an especially exciting and fun place for a family vacation. There are lots of unusual, interesting things for kids to do. A word to the wise, though: plan your trip—and each day—well so you can keep inconvenience and annoyance to a minimum. Good times await.

Throughout the *Guide,* you'll find useful information for planning your family trip. Each site report includes a key symbol communicating valuable information regarding that site's appropriateness for children. For each of the sites in this book, we advise whether or not it's recommended for children and highlight special offerings for them. We're brutally honest, too, noting those sites the kids are sure to find boring. If there is no kids' entry in the key, assume there's nothing special for the younger set. Chapter 15, "Outdoor Washington/ Sports," and the "Calendar of Annual Events" section include information that will help you plan your family visit. Chapter 13, "Entertainment," lists children's theaters and attractions. In addition to this chapter, the *Guide* offers a wealth of information to ensure a terrific visit.

Logistics first. As you plan where to stay, please be aware that many hotels offer family rates. Chapter 22, "Hotels," presents a comprehensive listing of where to stay in the area. It also notes whether an indoor or outdoor pool is available—an amenity that makes kids happy no matter what. That chapter also includes a broad selection of all-suites hotels. Often these are no more expensive than traditional hotel rooms, and they offer a great deal more space and comfort as well as the convenience of eating in. As you're deciding where to stay, we strongly advise that you carefully consider the hotel's proximity to your touring destinations. The savings offered by the bargain hotel across town or in an outlying area may be more than offset by the expense and aggravation of having to traverse great distances throughout your visit. Your budget may be better served by a slightly more expensive hotel choice convenient to the major sites of interest, as well as to the Metrorail system. Metro offers a special Family Pass for weekend use (see Chapter 2, "Getting To and Around Town," for details).

We enthusiastically recommend Metro throughout the *Guide;* from personal experience we can report that kids find riding the Metro great fun. The stations are futuristic: gleaming and new, with waffle-walled, pressed-concrete structures; flashing lights warning of approaching trains; mechanized ticket systems and, often, an exceptionally long escalator ride, in itself a treat.

While Washington has more free sites to visit and things to do than any other city we can think of, some attractions do charge admission. In these cases there are often reduced rates for children, which we note in the site report. In any event, it never hurts to ask.

For those times you require baby-sitting services, we suggest you consult the concierge at your hotel.

While dining on the town can become exceedingly expensive, you can keep the family budget by seeking out some reasonably priced options noted in the *Guide.* Washington has many, many delis, cafés, ethnic restaurants and fast-food spots. In recent years, a number of food courts have appeared on the scene, and we think they're terrific. You can't beat the variety of food, the speed, convenience and cost, plus they're usually lively and fun. Our favorites are at Union Station (1st Street and Massachusetts Avenue, NE), the Pavilion at the Old Post Office (12th Street and Pennsylvania Avenue), The Shops at National Place (13th Street and Pennsylvania Avenue), Connecticut Connection (Farragut North Metro stop), Metro Market (18th and I streets, NW), Georgetown Park (Wisconsin Avenue and M Street) and various shopping malls. While touring the Smithsonian, enjoy lunch in the cafeterias/restaurants in the Air and Space Museum and the National Gallery of Art.

There's a full menu of things going on for kids in metropolitan Washington. In addition to making good use of this *Guide,* don't overlook other helpful resources about town. The *Washington Post* contains a helpful weekly feature called "Saturday's Child" that highlights special activities for family fun; look for it in the Friday "Weekend" supplement.

SITES FOR KIDS

See site reports throughout the *Guide* for additional information. Note the key symbol specifically for kids.

The Mall
Smithsonian Information Center in the Smithsonian Institution Building (the Castle). Make this your first stop before you begin touring, no matter what—even if you've been to Washington before and feel you know your way around. This new center is the cats pajamas. Kids will adore the interactive videos and the highlighted wall maps orienting them to the city's attractions. You can plan your touring in the best-informed fashion: video monitors note each site's special offerings for children.

National Air and Space Museum. The museum is chock-full of fascinating exhibits, including a walk through Skylab, a simulated moon landing, the Starship *Enterprise* and the U.S.S. *Smithsonian* aircraft carrier. The planetarium and theater are wonderful for kids, although the youngest set may find the IMAX movies overpowering and scary. The gift shop offers loads of enticing delights, sure to require an advance on weeks of allowance.

National Museum of Natural History. Many popular exhibits mesmerize children, including the Discovery Room, which offers hands-on exhibits and games, and the Insect Zoo, where visitors can actually hold three types of insects, as well as observe a beehive, an ant colony and a tarantula feeding. Outside is a life-size dinosaur model named Uncle Beazley.

National Museum of American History. This museum is practically bursting with exhibits that will fascinate kids, including early autos, racing cars and bicycles, as well as a new permanent exhibition on the information age. Demonstration centers present an array of engrossing topics.

Arts and Industries Building. Discovery Theater presents changing programs by dancers, actors, singers and mimes. Reservations and tickets required; call (202) 357-1500. Outside, an old-time carousel is fun for kids.

Bureau of Engraving and Printing. Kids love this tour where they can see money being printed, but beware of the long waits, especially during the busy spring and summer seasons.

National Archives and Records Service. The Exhibition Hall has a permanent display of the Declaration of Independence, the Constitution and the Bill of Rights. Older children may enjoy undertaking a project researching the family background.

Jefferson, Lincoln and Vietnam Veterans Memorials and Washington Monument. *All* must-sees!

Capitol Hill

Capital Children's Museum (Admission fee) Clearly the one place in town dedicated just to kids. We wholeheartedly recommend this stop where kids can learn about all sorts of things, in a most hands-on fashion. A helpful mural advises how best to tour the museum according to the time you have available. The museum offers a wonderful range of free seasonal activities on weekends; call (202) 543-8600 for a schedule.

National Postal Museum. This brand new museum has been designed with kids and families in mind. Many hands-on exhibits, videos, computer games, and The Discovery Center, as well as the museum's relatively small size, make the postal museum eminently kid-accessible.

Navy Yard (Navy Museum, Marine Corps Museum and Museum Annex). A great place for kids, since they can run around and play. Kids especially enjoy the old and modern submarines housed here, as well as the Navy destroyer open for touring at the pier.

Union Station. Shops particularly appealing to kids include *The Nature Company,* a potpourri of rocks and minerals, inflatable creatures and other amusing and educational gifts based on the mother-nature theme; *The Great Train Store,* which is a collection sure to delight any train buff; and a variety of colorful and well-stocked boutiques. The National Trust for Historic Preservation's tour may be of interest to older children, and the food court here is sure to please.

U.S. Capitol. A must-see for older children, whether it be a tour of the hallowed halls or a view of the House or Senate in session from the Visitors Gallery.

Downtown
FBI (J. Edgar Hoover Building). Tours featuring gangster paraphernalia, a fingerprint lab and a marksmanship demonstration help make this one of Washington's most popular attractions. However, the wait in line may be tedious and tax even the most eager and patient family.

Ford's Theatre and the House Where Lincoln Died. Older children will enjoy seeing the setting of Lincoln's assassination and the objects relating to it, including John Wilkes Booth's diary.

National Aquarium. This is the oldest aquarium in the country, and while not nearly as big or glitzy as the National Aquarium in Baltimore, it is still an absorbing place to visit. Young kids will especially like the tiny hands-on tidal pool.

National Geographic Society Headquarters. The organization that publishes that captivating magazine, *National Geographic,* has created dramatic displays complete with interactive videos detailing the society's exciting exploratory missions. Great fun for kids.

The Pavilion at the Old Post Office. We highly recommend a stop at this beautifully restored site. Not only will kids enjoy the diversion of interesting shops, a bustling food court and frequent lively entertainment, but the tour of the clock tower is a real highlight. From the 315-foot observation deck you'll see terrific views of Washington and also have the chance to see the Congress Bells.

Saturday Morning at the National. Free entertainment for children in the lobby of the restored National Theater. Shows include singing, tap dancing and puppet shows.

Tech 2000 (Admission fee). The newest attraction on the touring scene is just wonderful for kids. They'll love the hands-on interactive video that includes video-painting for younger children and action-packed simulations for older kids.

The White House. Not to be overlooked, of course, but the long wait may prove tiresome.

Georgetown/Foggy Bottom/The West End
Georgetown. An excursion here will delight kids who enjoy exploring interesting little boutiques and shops.

John F. Kennedy Center for the Performing Arts. On Saturdays there are often free entertainment programs for kids, including dance, plays, music and puppets. Call (202) 467-4600 for information.

Northwest
National Zoological Park. The zoo is bound to be a favorite with kids, especially ZOOlab and HERPlab for explorations of a variety of animals and reptiles. BIRDlab invites visitors to look closely at feathers, nests and eggs and to find out what birds eat. A beautiful park, the zoo is also pleasant even for those not overly interested in animals.

Washington National Cathedral. This imposing site appeals to kids, generally, and special tours can be arranged. On Saturdays, hands-on family activities are offered, including stone carving and stained-glass production; call (202) 537-2930 for information. Call (202) 537-2934 for information on medieval workshop.

Note: Suburban Maryland and Virginia offerings may be worthwhile primarily for visitors (or residents) near the area. With the city so rich in attractions, we recommend that visitors do Washington's sites first.

Suburban Virginia
Arlington National Cemetery. Older children, especially history buffs, will enjoy strolling among the graves of famous soldiers. The highlight of your visit with kids will most likely be the Changing of the Guard.

Claude Moore Colonial Farm at Turkey Run. A wonderful introduction to life of a rural, eighteenth-century farm family. Kids can watch re-created farm activities, including cooking over a log fire, planting buckwheat and growing tobacco. Domesticated animals roam the farm.

Gunston Hall Plantation. The nature trail appeals to kids, as does the introduction to everyday plantation life in the eighteenth century.

Nearby Maryland
C&O Canal National Historic Park. Outdoor activities abound. Kids will really like the mule-drawn barge rides down the canal.

NASA. The Goddard Space Flight Center features spacecraft and rockets for the enthusiast who has already explored every nook and cranny of the Air and Space Museum.

National Capital Trolley Museum. The trolley memorabilia may interest kids, but the real attraction here is the trolley ride through the countryside.

National Colonial Farm. A lovely farm demonstrating the ways of mid-eighteenth-century farm life.

Oxon Hill Farm. A working farm full of activities, as practiced at the turn of the century.

PHONE NUMBERS OF SPECIAL INTEREST TO KIDS

Capital Children's Museum	(202) 543-8600
Dial-A-Story	(202) 638-5717
Sampler of Week's Events	(202) 737-8866
Smithsonian Skywatcher's Report	(202) 357-2000
Smithsonian	(202) 357-2020

17

ADVICE

TO GROUPS

The key to all successful group visits to Washington is careful advance planning. In this chapter, we have included some tips to help in this process. Be sure to read Chapter 3, "Planning Ahead," for additional considerations when making your plans.

For groups, it is especially important to cover *every* phase of the trip in the preplanning process. A group is a cumbersome thing: it moves slowly and reacts badly to adverse situations. The more careful and complete the pretrip planning, the less likely that your visit can be ruined by misadventures.

It is never too early to begin the planning process. The group's ability to undertake certain tours, see a special site or meet with the particular person of most importance to the group depends on the availability of the specific resource at the precise time of the trip. Many thousands of groups come to Washington each year, bringing literally millions of visitors. Your group is just a droplet in the downpour. Many groups are repeatedly disappointed by the failure of their plans to materialize because of someone's "prior commitments." Proper advance planning can make *your* request the "prior commitment."

The second major concern of a group is the careful allocation of available funds. Too many times, a group will try to save money in ways that could result in unpleasant experiences for the group. In a group tour small matters—timing, locations, meal arrangements—take on exaggerated significance. For example, even though a group may come to the city with its own bus and driver, it may make sense to hire *another* bus and driver, or a step-on guide, who is thoroughly familiar with the city streets. Unfamiliarity with the geography, parking regulations and traffic patterns may mean missed appointments and destroyed mealtimes.

Being a city whose principal business is tourism, Washington is abundantly supplied with professionals. Take advantage of their experience. If you are interested in a "standard" tour of the principal tourist attractions, there are numerous services which will satisfy your needs. They include:

Capitol Events, (703) 461-3838, offers tours of all major museums, monuments, and memorials, plus a special Washington-by-Night tour of the illuminated monuments with refreshments and hors d'oeuvres served on board.

Gray Line/Gold Line. one of the largest bus companies in the area, offers a full line of scheduled sightseeing tours in and around the region, plus charter services to any destination a bus can go. Among the daily tours are an all-day tour (1993 Prices: Adult: $36. Child: $18) including Mount Vernon, Alexandria, Arlington Cemetery, and the City; Monticello/Thomas Jefferson Country ($50); Williamsburg overnight (from $118); Black Heritage ($18/$9), four hours; Two-Day Grand Tour ($60/$30); Harpers Ferry/Gettysburg ($40/$20), 10 hours; Washington After Dark ($20/$10), three hours; and a variety of half-day or full-day public building tours ($18–30/$9–18). All trips begin at Gray Line's Union Station terminal, with pickups at major hotels, and drop offs as close to hotels as possible. Gray Line also offers a multi-lingual four-hour sightseeing excursion with commentary in French, Spanish, German, Italian, and Japanese ($26.50/$14). Charters of 47-seat passenger deluxe coaches, 25-seat executive coaches, and 22-seat mini-buses are available. For information on all services, and reservations call 1-800-862-1400, or locally (301) 386-8300 or (202) 289-1995.

Guide Service of Washington, 733 15th Street, Suite 1040, NW, Washington, D.C. 20005, (202) 628-2842, provides step-on guide service, in 20 major languages, including French, Spanish, German, Italian, Chinese, Japanese, and Arabic. Step-on service runs approximately $100 for a half-day tour with English-speaking guides, $110 for a single foreign language and $115 for multilanguage (the prices are $150, $160, and $175 for full-day tours). The Guide Service guide will meet a group at its hotel; guides are thoroughly familiar with the area and can direct bus drivers.

If you are interested in more specialized services, you may do well to contact the Guild of Professional Tour Guides (202)298-1474, a membership organization of more than 200 licensed guides, each of whom has at least 10 years' experience. The Guild is not a hiring service, but will refer callers to individual guides or companies that can fulfill your specific requirements. The Guild list includes speakers of 15 foreign languages, plus signers.

Capitol Entertainment, (202)636-9203, offers, in addition to tours of the standard sites, an African-American History Tour of Washington, which includes the Frederick Douglass National Historic Site, Lincoln and LeDroit Parks, and the Howard University area.

Washington has several competent firms that will organize your group's visit from top to bottom, if need be.

Heritage Tours, Ltd., 1331 P Street, NW, Washington, D.C. 20005, (202) 822-9542, will custom design tours for any size group. It offers in-town tours as well as day trips to Annapolis, Williamsburg, Baltimore and the Pennsylvania Dutch country. For children's programs, Heritage provides three adults per coach. The company recently introduced a service providing complete packages of points of Jewish interest, including tours and Kosher meals. Heritage promises that if any tour is canceled because of insufficient registration, the organization is under no financial obligation.

Washington, Inc., 1225 19th Street, NW, Washington, D.C. 20036, (202) 828-7000, is run by a knowledgeable group that organizes not only group tours, but social extravaganzas and special events for the political, social and corporate communities. Their programs are imaginative, thoroughly planned and of the highest quality.

Washington, Inc., will arrange a press conference for your group—and the audience asks the questions of a panel of well-known and well-informed people. If you need a "military" band, they can provide one—up to 45 musicians in splendid scarlet uniforms.

The company boasts a long list of corporate clients and trade associations that have used their services during corporate meetings and conventions. The fees are not inconsiderable, but the growing list seems to indicate value received.

National Fine Arts Associates, 4801 Massachusetts Avenue, NW, Suite 400, Washington, D.C. 20016, (202) 966-3800, offers a broad array of complete tour packages, and many unique tours as well. The principal business of the firm, as their name suggests, is art-related. Their clients include conventions, historical societies, museum groups from all over the country, college students and alumni associations.

All the Fine Arts guides are art professionals, with advanced degrees in art history. Many, in fact, are teachers and professors.

A variety of historic house tours are offered in Washington and the surrounding counties of Maryland and Virginia. Such tours may include private homes not ordinarily opened to tourists. Personalized limousine tours, while quite expensive, can provide an intimate and luxurious means by which to see the city. National Fine Arts asks that you write or call as far in advance of your visit as possible.

Every year, thousands of buses with school groups aboard parade through the city. One of the largest organizers of junior and senior high school trips to Washington is *Lakeland Tours,* 2000 Holiday Drive, Charlottesville, VA 22901, (804) 296-9100 or 1-800-999-7676. Lakeland, a group travel agency, specializes in tours of Washington. One recent year it brought over 40,000 students to town. The company will tailor a program for any size group, with each tour priced according to the specific program. Lakeland's tours are accompanied by a company escort, as well as its own sightseeing guides.

In addition to student tours, Lakeland has had experience with every kind of group, including senior citizens, foreign exchange students and handicapped visitors.

A major wholesaler of Washington tours is *Washington Group Tours,* 1110 Vermont Avenue, NW, Suite 407, Washington, D.C. 20005, (202) 955-5667 or 1-800-424-8895. Working almost exclusively through airlines and travel agents (but accessible directly, too), Washington Group Tours handles all nature of groups—students, affinity organizations, seniors, handicapped. An affiliate company specializes in smaller conventions, up to 250, making all necessary arrangements—from the technical requirements of the convention itself to sightseeing tours and entertainment.

Commercial tour companies have several distinct advantages: by booking a large volume of business, with hotels, theaters, etc., they can sometimes deliver services at a lower price than might otherwise be available, or offer considerably expanded services at the same price you would ordinarily expect to pay. Second, familiarity with the city prevents disasters. Experience eliminates bad hotels, restaurants and entertainments. A reputable firm can offer some peace of mind and the assurance of a smooth visit.

If your group chooses not to use a local company to plan some part or all of the itinerary, consult your local travel agent, but take into account the various components of a successful trip: transportation, lodging, sightseeing, eating and entertainment.

TRANSPORTATION

Several alternatives have been mentioned previously: hiring a local bus company or a step-on guide, or the use of existing facilities, such as Tourmobile or Old Town Trolley Tour. It bears repeating that local drivers will get the group around the city faster and more safely than drivers unfamiliar with the streets. In Chapter 2, "Getting To and Around Town," we have listed a few of the local companies offering bus or trolley tours. They will all be pleased to provide a vehicle for a group, so call or write ahead for charter information.

If you are part of a bus tour group, you will want your driver to have a copy of "Tour Bus Operations in Washington, D.C.," a brochure describing regulations, licensing information, parking enforcement and more, available by writing or calling the D.C. Committee to Promote Washington, 1212 New York Avenue, NW, Suite 200, Washington, D.C. 20005, (202) 724-4091.

LODGING

Finding a suitable hotel for a large group can be a problem. Use Chapter 22 "Hotels," for basic information as to size, rates and services. During peak season—April to August—some hotels may be unable to handle, or even be dismissive of, group business. But, as with the rest of the country, Washington is currently in the middle of a business downturn, and so hotels may find they have more rooms to let go at bargain rates for groups. In general, the downtown hotels have been less interested, and suburban hotels more interested, in group business.

Route 1, or Jefferson Davis Highway, at Crystal City just across the Potomac and next to National Airport has several hotels that welcome groups. They include the Hospitality House, Crystal City Marriott, Stouffer's National Center and the Quality Inn. Motels along the New York Avenue corridor (Route 50) also cater to groups, including such hotels as the Holiday Inn. The Alexandria Tourist

Council, 221 King Street, (703) 838-4200, will assist groups with many aspects of their plans.

Among in-town hotels, the Washington Hilton, a very large hotel, has proved itself accommodating to groups of all kinds; it is so constructed as to be accessible to large numbers of buses for easy loading and unloading. Surprisingly, few hotels, even the new ones, are well designed for this purpose.

If any members of your group are handicapped, be sure to read Chapter 18, "Tips to Visitors with Disabilities." In addition, Chapter 22, "Hotels," highlights accessibility in hotels.

A final word about lodging: when making reservations, do so as far in advance as possible, and reconfirm two weeks before departure. Be sure to ask, when making reservations, whether the hotel has "quads"—that is, rooms that can accommodate four beds. Where applicable, four to a room can be a real dollar savings—the $80 room becomes, effectively, the $20 room, a real bargain in Washington.

SIGHTSEEING

In planning a schedule of sites, refer to Chapter 20, "Washington on the Run," which outlines one-, two-, and three-day tour schedules that are feasible, whether for an individual or a group. When your itinerary is established, read the site reports and take note of any possible problems for your group. For example, you might not think to consider that the congressional galleries are not open to children under 6, or that the Capitol subway cars are off-limits to kids under 12, unless accompanied by an adult.

Large groups may find it easier to break into small groups, visiting the same sites on different schedules, or different places according to differing interests. The smaller the group, the easier problems are to overcome, and the fewer problems that will arise.

Take advantage of the special services accorded groups in both the Capitol and the Smithsonian, as well as other sites.

At the Capitol, your congressman or senator can help set up your group visit. Groups using the Capitol cafeterias must have written permission for the time and size of the group. Your congressional office can arrange it. Special rooms can be reserved through your congressmen and luncheon lectures arranged. Musical groups are permitted to perform on the Capitol steps, with written permission, also acquired through your congressional office. Requests for musical performances should be made well in advance.

EATING

Washington has literally thousands of options for satisfying hunger pangs during the sightseeing day, but unless a group plans carefully, it may find itself a long way from *any* kind of food.

Breakfast is best taken care of in or around the hotel. Once your touring day is under way the possibilities expand. Many area restaurants and carry-outs will prepare box or bag lunches, plain or fancy, at an agreeable price. Downtown, try *The Dutch Treat,* 1710 L Street, NW and 818 15th Street, NW, (202) 296-3219, for gourmet fare. On Capitol Hill, try *The American Café,* 227 Massachusetts Avenue, NE, (202) 546-7690. If you are housed in one of the major hotel areas, other carry-outs can be found in the neighborhood.

Cafeterias are almost invariably quick and inexpensive. Government cafeterias are one of the great bargains in town. Try the Madison Building at the Library of Congress after 12:30 P.M.; it's big, with good food and a fabulous view; the National Gallery of Art, also quite handsome, and the assorted Smithsonian cafeterias (see site reports for addresses and hours) are also good bets. On the Hill, you can arrange to eat at the House Office Building cafeterias, or the Senate Office Building, or the Capitol itself.

Commercial cafeterias vary markedly in quality. The following are centrally located facilities, large enough to handle groups, and serve respectable food:

The White House		
Connection	1725 F Street, NW	(202) 842-1777
Sholl's Colonial	1990 K Street, NW	(202) 296-3065

The Pavilion at the Old Post Office, 1100 Pennsylvania Avenue, NW, (202) 289-4224, has a "meal-deal" for groups—$5.50 will buy a meal, soda and dessert at any of the Pavilion's food stands. Write ahead or go to the management office, balcony level.

The tourism director at *Union Station* will arrange food for groups with two weeks' notice. Call (202) 289-1908 for information.

Outside of downtown, the shopping malls offer a variety of eating possibilities. See Chapter 14, "Shopping/Galleries," for addresses of the area malls. Some nearby malls that have decent cafeterias include the Crystal City Mall, Tyson's Corner, Springfield and White Flint.

It is important to call ahead to restaurants, even the cafeterias listed above, and let them know when you want to arrive, how many are in your group and how you intend to pay, as individuals or on a single check.

Visitors in groups can descend en masse to several festival food halls; choices within are virtually unlimited and fast, whether you want to carry food out or eat there. Most of the seats may be packed at lunch, so avoid the crunch by lunching either early or late. Best bets are: *International Square,* 1825 I Street, NW; *The Shops at National Place,* 1300 Pennsylvania Avenue, NW; *Connecticut Connection,* Farragut North Metro stop, red line, underground at Connecticut Avenue and L Street, NW; and *Union Station,* 50 Massachusetts Avenue, NE.

Another possibility is fast food. The major fast-food chains operate in large numbers of in-town locations. Look in the white pages for chains.

ENTERTAINMENT

Almost without exception, whatever an individual can do at night, so can a group. The possibilities are limited only by imagination and budgets. Obviously, groups must plan well in advance for limited-seating facilities, such as theaters and concert halls. At the Kennedy Center, group reservations may have to be made up to a year in advance to assure block seating. Most theaters, even movie theaters, offer group discounts, and we have noted such discounts in Chapter 13, "Entertainment." If in doubt, call and ask.

The Washington area has numerous excellent dinner theaters; many groups have found them to be ideal for evenings out. Other popular group activities include evening cruises of the Washington Boat Lines (see Chapter 15, "Outdoor Washington/Sports") and nighttime bus tours of the monuments, offered by most city bus tour companies.

USEFUL PHONE NUMBERS

Washington D.C. Convention and Visitors Association 1575 I Street, NW	(202) 789-7000
Better Business Bureau	(202) 393-8000
1012 14th Street, NW	Complaints: (202) 393-8020
U.S. Capitol; House of Representatives; U.S. Senate	(202) 224-3121
Alexandria Convention and Visitors Bureau	(703) 838-4200

18

TIPS
FOR VISITORS
WITH DISABILITIES

WASHINGTON'S ACCESS RATING

In facilities, design and provision of services, Washington rates about average in consideration of the needs of disabled people. In some regards, however, the capital city ranks well above many other urban centers; the Metrorail system, the public-service sector, the Smithsonian Institution and the National Park Service are most notable in the plans and provisions for the treatment of visitors who have disabilities.

Metro, Washington's subway system, was designed in compliance with federal laws enacted in the 1960s and 1970s that prescribed accessibility standards. In general, stations and trains are well designed, and careful thought has been given to the best ways of providing optimal services to the extremely varied population of users. A more detailed discussion of services keyed to specific disabilities will follow.

For several reasons, the service sectors dealing with the general public—bus drivers, waiters, ticket sellers, retail clerks, cab drivers and so forth—are somewhat more enlightened than their counterparts in other cities in their dealings with people who have disabilities. Washington has been a good job market for folks with disabilities; the federal government dominates and its influence is so enormous that many employers have hired with equal employment opportunities firmly in mind. People with disabilities, therefore, have been better integrated into the work force than in most places in the U.S., and so are quite visible and mobile. One result has been the education through experience of service-sector employees in meeting the needs of people with impairments to their mobility, vision and hearing, as well as other disabilities. In addition, a multitude of consumer-oriented organizations founded by and for people with disabilities have their national headquarters in Washington and have developed programs for training people who deal directly with the public in how they can best provide services to the organizations' constituencies.

The Smithsonian and the National Park Service are exemplary in the facilities, exhibits, programs and tours they have developed to make the national treasures in their domain accessible to and enjoyable for people with disabilities. Guards and guides have been trained to deal with the problems faced by people with specific disabilities. With advance notice, both organizations will conduct special tours with oral or sign interpreters or tours designed for the visually impaired for practically every site under their jurisdiction. To make arrangements for these tours, call the Smithsonian Accessibility Coordinator at (202) 786-2942 or TDD (202) 786-2414, or call the specific museum of interest to you between 9 A.M. and 5 P.M. daily; call NPS on the Mall at (202) 426-6841. The Smithsonian also publishes a guide for disabled visitors called *Smithsonian Access,* which details museum services and facilities designed for those with disabilities. This is available at the Smithsonian Institution Building (the Castle) or by mail from the Visitor Information Associates Reception Center, Smithsonian Institution Building, Smithsonian Institution, Washington, D.C. 20560. In addition, an excellent orientation video on the Smithsonian is on view at the Castle; the monitor is at a convenient height for those in wheelchairs and captions are provided for those with hearing disabilities.

The most important piece of advice for a Washington visitor with disabilities is to ask: ask at information desks, ask museum guards, docents or anyone else connected with a site what specifically has been designed or can be experienced thoroughly by someone with your disability. We also recommend that you call ahead to recheck details that you will depend on for your visit; it would be a sad waste of energy to set off to see a particular exhibit or gallery only to discover that it has been phased out.

Beyond these points, Washington will probably present no greater challenges than you face in your daily life. If you do need assistance in some realm, Washington is home to any number of national and local consumer-oriented organizations of people with disabilities that may be able to offer advice and assistance. We've listed these organizations, addresses and phone numbers at the end of this chapter.

METROBUS AND METRORAIL

The Metrobus and Metrorail systems offer substantial (50–60 percent) fare discounts and priority-seating arrangements to people with disabilities. For fare discounts you must obtain a Handicapped Identification Card. Since it's a rather complex process to get such an identification card, your visit should be of some length to justify the effort. Pick up an application at a Metro sales outlet, or call (202) 962-1245 and they will send you one. The application must be completed by a licensed physician; you then take the application to the ID Office on the lobby level of Metro Headquarters, 600 5th Street, NW, from 7:30 A.M. to 3:30 P.M. on weekdays. An identification card with a photograph will be issued to you. If this is an inconvenient location, IDs are periodically issued in other locations throughout the Metropolitan area; call (202) 962-1245 for places and schedules.

To ride Metrorail at a discounted rate, a special farecard is needed; it is available with a Handicapped Identification Card at Metro outlets and many area banks (call (202) 637-7000 for specific locations). The farecard can then be used in the automatic fare-collection equipment at every Metro station, charging you half the rush-hour fare to your destination, not to exceed $1.40.

An invaluable guide to Metro services is the pamphlet "Senior Citizens and People with Disabilities Metro System Guide"; call (202) 637-7000 to get one.

THEATER TICKETS

The Kennedy Center theaters and the National Theater offer people with disabilities half-price seats at most performances. At the Kennedy Center, half-price tickets are available for any performance if you purchase tickets before a show begins its run; after that, half-price tickets can be purchased on the day of performance only, and since the number of discounted tickets is limited, none may be available for the most popular shows. To qualify for the discount, you must present a letter from a doctor to receive a Kennedy Center Disability

Identification Card (call (202) 416-8340); this card will enable you to acquire discounted tickets by mail or by Instacharge over the phone (the purchase must still be accomplished before the show begins its run).

At the National, you must purchase your tickets at the box office with some documentation of your disability. You may also send someone to purchase your tickets in advance, but they must also bring proof of your disability. Discounted tickets are limited in number and not offered for all performances; check on availability by calling (202) 628-6161 well in advance of the dates you want.

FOR THOSE WITH LIMITED MOBILITY

Getting Around Town

The Metrorail system has been designed to be accessible to wheelchair users, and it works well toward that purpose. Each station is serviced by an elevator; it must be noted, however, that the elevators are not always operating. Call (202) 962-1825 to check the status of elevators at particular stations before you set off on your trip. Elevator locations are noted below:

Addison Road	Main entrance
Anacostia	Main entrance
Archives-Navy Memorial	North of Pennsylvania Avenue, west of 7th Street, NW
Arlington Cemetery	Memorial Drive
Ballston	NW corner of Fairfax Drive
Benning Road	Main entrance
Bethesda	Main entrance
Braddock Road	Main entrance
Brookland-CUA	Main entrance
Capitol Heights	Main entrance
Capitol South	Main entrance
Cheverly	Main entrance
Clarendon	Main entrance
Cleveland Park	East side of Connecticut Avenue north of Ordway Street, NW
College Park-U. of Maryland	Faces parking lot

Court House	Wilson Boulevard, between Veitch and N. Wayne streets
Crystal City	Main entrance
Deanwood	Main entrance
Dunn Loring	Main entrance
Dupont Circle	SW corner of Connecticut Avenue and Q Street, NW
Eisenhower Avenue	Main entrance
Eastern Market	Main entrance
Farragut North	NE corner of Connecticut Avenue and K Street, NW
Farragut West	NW corner of 18th and I streets, NW
East Falls Church	Main entrance
Federal Center SW	Main entrance
Federal Triangle	Main entrance
Foggy Bottom-GWU	Main entrance
Fort Totten	Main entrance
Friendship Heights	SE corner of Wisconsin Avenue near Jennifer Street, NW
Gallery Place-Chinatown	SE corner of 7th and G streets, NW
Greenbelt	Faces parking lot
Grosvenor	East side of Rockville Pike, between Montrose Avenue and Tuckerman Lane
Huntington	Both entrances
Judiciary Square	South side of F Street between 4th and 5th streets, NW
King Street	Main entrance
Landover	Main entrance
L'Enfant Plaza	SW corner of Maryland Avenue and 7th Street, SW
McPherson Square	SW corner of 14th and I streets, NW
Medical Center	Main entrance
Metro Center	NE corner of 12th and G streets, NW
Minnesota Avenue	Main entrance
Mount Vernon Square-UDC	SW corner of 7th and M streets, NW
National Airport	Main entrance—a courtesy van is available between the terminal building and Metro station

Navy Yard	Main entrance
New Carrollton	West of Garden City Drive, north of John Hanson Highway
Pentagon	Shopping concourse
Pentagon City	East side of Hayes Street between Army-Navy Drive and 15th Street
Potomac Avenue	Main entrance
Prince George's Plaza	Main entrance
Rhode Island Avenue	Main entrance
Rockville	Main entrance
Rosslyn	East side of N. Moore Street, between 19th Street and Wilson Boulevard
Shady Grove	Somerville Drive, north of Route 355
Shaw-Howard University	NE corner of 7th and S streets, NW
Silver Spring	South side of Colesville Road between East-West Highway and 2nd Avenue
Smithsonian	NW corner of 12th Street and Independence Avenue, SW
Stadium Armory	East side of 19th Street between C and Burke streets, SE
Takoma	Main entrance
Tenleytown-AU	East side of Wisconsin Avenue north of Albemarle Street, NW
Twinbrook	Main entrance
Union Station	Entrance to Amtrak Terminal
U Street-Cardozo	SE corner of 13th and U streets, NW
Van Ness-UDC	West side of Connecticut Avenue, south of Veazy Street
Vienna	Main entrance
Virginia Square-GMU	Main entrance
Waterfront	Main entrance
West Falls Church	Main entrance
West Hyattsville	Main entrance
White Flint	East side of Rockville Pike at Marinelli Road
Woodley Park-Zoo	SW corner Connecticut Avenue and Woodley Road, NW

The Metrobus fleet has more than 200 buses that are equipped with wheelchair lifts or have the capacity to "kneel" to facilitate boarding. Both types of buses are regularly scheduled on some routes (call (202) 637-7000 for route information). In addition, you can schedule a lift-equipped bus on any other route by calling (202) 962-1825—TDD (202) 638-3780—before 3 P.M. a day in advance. Unfortunately, this specialized service has not been absolutely reliable. Often users have waited from one to three hours for the special buses, and have been stranded when the lifts have failed to work (the lifts are checked each day before the buses leave on their routes).

To complement its regular service, Tourmobile operates a van equipped with wheelchair lift for the same cost as a regular ticket. The van makes all the Mall stops and waits for its passengers to return. Because of the popularity of this service, two or more parties may be grouped together, necessitating the coordination of pickup times. Reservations must be made at least a day in advance by calling (202) 554-7020.

Taxis around town are very good about transporting people with wheelchairs, as long as the chairs are collapsible. Expensive van service is available for people with motorized and noncollapsing wheelchairs; a one-way trip in town may cost more than $30.

Around the Mall and Downtown, most street corners have curb cuts, but other areas of the city (notably Georgetown) are woefully lacking. The Mall paths have hard-packed dirt surfaces which may be tiring for a wheelchair user to negotiate for any distance.

Office Buildings

Most federal buildings and new private office buildings are accessible to people in wheelchairs, but many structures in the city are still inaccessible. If you don't have specific information about your destination's entrance and facilities, definitely call ahead to ascertain their status. The Hubert H. Humphrey Building, a Department of Health and Human Services facility, is a model in design for people with disabilities (complete with talking elevator) but unfortunately most of the city lags far behind.

Hotels

Hotels in Washington have been termed marginally accessible by several wheelchair users. Even the newer hotels may not have bathrooms with wide enough doors to permit access. We've noted in Chapter 22, "Hotels," which facilities term themselves accessible; when you make your reservations, be sure to double-check—ask for actual door widths and availability of grab bars to be certain you'll be comfortable.

Some other considerations when choosing your hotel: distance from the center of town, ease of catching cabs at that location, accessibility to eating facilities in or near the hotel.

Shopping

The Shops at National Place, The Pavilion at the Old Post Office and Georgetown Park, as well as the major suburban shopping malls, are all equipped with ramps or at-grade entries and internal elevators. See Chapter 14, "Shopping/Galleries."

Restaurants

Often restaurants seem to offer a trade-off between accessibility and quality; the best eating establishments seem to be above or below street level. If you do find a good restaurant that you can get into, almost certainly there will be no accessible rest room. Georgetown has a good number of street-level restaurants and carry-outs; unfortunately, as we have mentioned, the lack of curb cuts may require someone in a wheelchair to travel a half a block to get to an alley entrance—and then he or she will be faced with heavy traffic when crossing the street. In warm weather, outdoor cafés abound and are quite accessible, since they are at street level. Other good bets are hotel restaurants, although some have been designed on differing levels to satisfy the architect's artistic sensibilities. The rule of thumb: call ahead.

Theaters and Movies

We note in Chapter 13, "Entertainment," which theaters are accessible to people in wheelchairs. Always call ahead to reserve a space and to alert the theater staff of your arrival. Local movie theaters are usually accommodating as well, but call ahead to check on the specific house since many are quite small.

FOR THOSE WITH VISUAL IMPAIRMENTS

Getting Around Town

The Metrorail system represents a major hurdle for those who are blind or visually impaired: the farecard machines are entirely visual. Each station, however, has an information kiosk and attendant who will assist you in paying your fare and entering the system. A special handrail stretches from the mezzanine to escalator entrance. The platform edge is of a differing rough texture from the smooth platform, although the contrast is not dramatic enough to be truly helpful, and several tragic accidents have occurred involving people who were visually impaired. Trains and stops are announced on loudspeakers (although the speakers have been known to fail).

For those with visual disabilities, Washington's street system can be baffling. While the streets are laid out on a square grid, avenues are on the diagonal, creating numerous circles and triangles at street/ avenue intersections.

On the Mall, we strongly recommend the Tourmobile to provide a narrated circuit tour of Washington's major points of interest.

Restaurants

Some restaurants in Washington have menus prepared in Braille; call the particular restaurant you are interested in to see if they offer this service. Since restaurant prices and offerings change so frequently, these special menus may be out-of-date.

Communications

If you have one, bring a small radio with you to tune in on local news and events. The *Washington Ear,* a closed-circuit radio station, broadcasts continually; volunteers read local and national newspapers as well as current best-sellers. Call (301) 681-6636 for information.

Many sites have recorded messages of activities; check Chapter 3, "Planning Ahead," for a short listing.

Entertainment

Martin Luther King, Jr., Library in D.C., (202) 727-2142, records on cassette tapes the *Washingtonian* magazine, an excellent local periodical that lists current entertainment and museum shows. These tapes, which lag about one month behind the current issue, are offered free of charge.

The *Washington Ear* offers "Dial-in-Newspaper," a recording of *The Washington Post* (everything except the classifieds). Via a touch-tone phone, any section of the newspaper can be accessed. "Style" and "Weekend" list all current entertainment. Call (301) 681-6636 to access this service. In addition, the Kennedy Center has a recorded listing of their current offerings as well as what's coming up. Call other theaters directly to see what's showing while you're in town.

Several area theaters offer the "phonic ear" service, provided by the *Washington Ear;* those with visual impairments may borrow earphones that, in addition to the dialogue, broadcast a description of the play's action. Theaters with this service include the Kennedy Center, Arena Stage, National Theater, Olney Theater, Roundhouse Theater, Adventure Theater and the National Air and Space Museum's IMAX movies, *To Fly* and *The Dream Is Alive.* Call the theater to arrange for this service; it's not offered at every performance, so check before purchasing tickets.

The Kennedy Center also has cassette recordings of program notes; those with visual impairments can borrow headphones to hear these comments before symphonic performances.

The central YMCA, at 17th Street and Rhode Island Avenue, has originated "Project Venture," a Saturday-morning program of physical activities for the visually and/or physically handicapped. Volunteers participate in one-on-one activities, which can include jogging, calisthenics, weightlifting and swimming in the Y's facility, as well as bike trips and picnics. You do not need to be a Y member to participate. Call (202) 862-9622 for information.

The Sites

Recall that many of Washington's points of interest offer special tours for people with visual disabilities; refer to the site descriptions for specific instructions on how to arrange for these tours. Even if no special service is listed, call the site to see if they can accommodate your special needs.

A Braille map of the Mall area can be found in the Smithsonian Information Center in the Castle.

FOR THOSE WITH HEARING IMPAIRMENTS

Communications

A number of Washington organizations and services have special numbers to call for use with telecommunication devices for the deaf (TDD). We note these numbers at the end of this section. In addition, many public places (airports, train stations, bus stations and some hotels and museums) are equipped with special well-marked amplifying telephones; some also have TDDs alongside the usual phones. TDDs are located in Metro stations on the mezzanines; pick up the key from the station manager.

Entertainment

Several theaters in Washington are equipped with headphones for use by people with hearing impairments; they include the Kennedy Center, National Theater and Arena Stage. They offer sign interpreters for some plays. Check Chapter 13, "Entertainment," for phone numbers.

Many Washington movie theaters show topflight foreign films with subtitles. In addition, the array of Washington entertainment often includes mime, ballet and other dance and gymnastics.

The Sites

Many of Washington's points of interest give special tours with sign language or oral interpretation for people with hearing impairments. Refer to the site reports for specific instructions on how to arrange for these tours. If special tours aren't available, but tours for the general public are given, notify the tour guide of your disability so that he or she can place you at the front of the group for easier hearing or lipreading. Most sites will also accommodate groups that bring their own interpreter.

Gallaudet College

Gallaudet is the world's only accredited liberal arts university for deaf and hard of hearing persons; current enrollment is 2,200 students. Tours of the campus and visits to "Gallaudet: A Legacy and a Promise," a multimedia exhibit on deafness, can be arranged by calling (202) 651-5050 (voice and TTY), or by writing the Visitors Center, Gallaudet University, 800 Florida Avenue, NW, Washington, D.C. 20002.

SPECIAL NUMBERS FOR THE HEARING-IMPAIRED
(V-VOICE T-TDD)

Emergency Numbers

D.C. Police & Fire Emergency	911 T
Montgomery County Police, Fire and Rescue	911 or (301) 762-7619 T
Alexandria Police Emergency	911 T

Transportation
Call individual carriers for information.

Metrobus/Metrorail Information	(202) 638-3780 T

Tourist Sites
U.S. Capitol

House	(202) 225-1904 T
Senate	(202) 224-4049 T
Kennedy Center (tickets)	(202) 416-8524 T
Smithsonian Institution Information for the Deaf	(202) 357-1729 T
National Park Service—National Capital Regional Headquarters	(202) 619-7159 T

Information on Arlington House, C&O Canal, Clara Barton House, Claude Moore Colonial Farm, Ford's Theatre, Frederick Douglass Memorial Home, Lincoln Memorial, Oxon Hill Farm, Old Post Office, Old Stone House, Peirce Mill, Thomas Jefferson Memorial, Vietnam Memorial, Washington Monument

NATIONAL ORGANIZATIONS

Disabilities in General
National Organization on Disabilities
910 16th Street, NW
Suite 600
Washington, D.C. 20006
(202) 293-5960 voice
(202) 293-5968 TDD

Information Protection and Advocacy Center for Handicapped
  Individuals, Inc.
4455 Connecticut Avenue, NW
Suite B100
Washington, D.C. 20008
(202) 966-8081
(202) 966-2500 TDD

D.C. Center for Independent Living
1400 Florida Avenue, NE
Washington, D.C. 20002
(202) 388-0033 V/T

Mobility Impairments
National Easter Seal Society
1350 New York Avenue, NW
Suite 915
Washington, D.C. 20005
(202) 347-3066
(202) 347-7385 TDD

National Rehabilitation Association
633 S. Washington Street
Alexandria, VA 22314
(703) 836-0850
(703) 836-0849 TDD

Paralyzed Veterans of America
801 18th Street, NW
Washington, D.C. 20006
(202) 872-1300
(202) 416-7622 TDD

National Spinal Cord Injury Association
National Capital Area Chapter
Spinal Cord Hot Line and Information Referral Service
250 Hungerford Drive
Suite 115
Rockville, MD 20850
(301) 424-8335

Disabled American Veterans Association
807 Maine Avenue, SW
Washington, D.C. 20024
(202) 554-3501 V/T

Blind and Visual Impairments
Columbia Lighthouse for the Blind
1421 P Street, NW
Washington, D.C. 20005
(202) 462-2900

American Council of the Blind
1155 15th Street, NW
Suite 720
Washington, D.C. 20005
(202) 467-5081 or 1-800-424-8666

Blinded Veterans Association
477 H Street, NW
Washington, DC 20001-2694
(202) 371-8880

Hearing Impairments
National Association of the Deaf
814 Thayer Avenue
Silver Spring, MD 20910
(301) 587-1788
(301) 587-1789 TTY

Telecommunications for the Deaf, Inc.
8719 Colesville Road
Suite 300
Silver Spring, MD 20910
(301) 589-3786
(301) 589-3006 TTY

Registry of Interpreters for the Deaf, Inc.
8719 Colesville Road
Suite 310
Silver Spring, MD 20919
(301) 608-0050 voice and TTY

American Society for Deaf Children
814 Thayer Avenue
Silver Spring, MD 20910
1-800-942-2732

Alexander Graham Bell Association for the Deaf, Inc.
1537 35th Street, NW
Washington, D.C. 20007
(202) 337-5220 voice and TDD

Deafpride, Inc.
1350 Potomac Avenue, SE
Washington, D.C. 20003–4412
(202) 675-6700 voice and TTY

Otis House–National Health Care Foundations for the Deaf
1203 Otis Street, NE
Washington, D.C. 20017
(202) 832-2660 voice and TDD

Self-Help for Hard of Hearing People
7800 Wisconsin Avenue
Bethesda, MD 20814
(301) 657-2249 voice and TDD

Gallaudet College
Kendall Green
Washington, D.C. 20002
(202) 651-5000 voice and TDD

Many services and facilities for deaf and hearing-impaired people are
located at Gallaudet; they include:

National Information Center on Deafness
(202) 651-5051 voice
(202) 651-5054 TDD

National Center for Law and the Deaf
(202) 651-5373 voice and TDD

Kendall Demonstration Elementary School
(202) 651-5031 voice
(202) 651-5636 TDD

Model Secondary School for the Deaf
(202) 651-5466 voice and TDD

19

A WELCOME

TO INTERNATIONAL

VISITORS

Washington attracts more than 1.4 million international visitors annually, and the number is growing. The city, the East Coast's newest gateway for international business and vacation travelers, is now recognized worldwide as an exciting, cosmopolitan capital city with first-class hotels, restaurants, theater, nightlife and unparalleled scenic beauty.

Currently, the top inbound markets include Canada, Japan, the United Kingdom, France, Germany, Italy and Australia.

While Americans have a well-deserved reputation for their lack of linguistic ability, even the non-English-speaking visitor will do just fine, thanks to a variety of services and publications available.

SPECIAL SERVICES

Washington, D.C., Convention
and Visitors Association Services

The Washington, D.C., Convention and Visitors Association assists international travelers in planning a business or vacation trip to the nation's capital. Write to the address below for a variety of free literature, including a visitor map, a quarterly "Calendar of Events" brochure, a "Washington's Accommodations" (hotel/motel) guide and a "Washington Dining & Shopping" guide.

They also publish a comprehensive "Welcome to Washington" brochure/map in English, Japanese and German.

Washington, D.C., Convention & Visitors Association
1212 New York Avenue, NW
Washington, D.C. 20005
(202) 789-7000

The International Visitors Information Service (IVIS)

The International Visitors Information Service (IVIS) devotes itself to assisting international visitors. The staff here is eager to help with your visit; write, call or stop by. They stock a plethora of brochures and other useful information, including a good selection in German, French, Spanish, Italian and Japanese, as well as English. Literature is also available on other likely destinations, such as Baltimore and Annapolis; Maryland, Virginia and New York; highway maps and assorted materials from state tourist offices.

If you write well in advance of your visit, IVIS will send you a few helpful brochures. Friends or family members in the United States helping with arrangements for international visitors can, for a small fee, obtain a large packet of tourist information.

IVIS maintains a telephone Language Bank that provides assistance in virtually any language (expertise in 45 languages available). Call them at (202) 939-5566, 6 A.M. to 11 P.M., seven days a week. The office is open 9 A.M. to 5 P.M., Monday to Friday.

International Visitors Information Service
1623 Belmont Street, NW
Washington, D.C. 20009
(202) 939-5566

Travelers Aid Society of Washington

The Travelers Aid Society maintains information desks at all three Washington airports and Union Station. Assistance is offered 24 hours a day for such problems as lost money, searching for someone who was to pick you up and other similar difficulties. The organization, found throughout the country, has its main Washington office at 512 C Street, NE, (202) 546-3120.

The Smithsonian Information Center

This brand-new, ultramodern Smithsonian facility is an absolute must for every visitor to Washington (see site report). It includes computer monitors listing the day's Smithsonian events, a 20-minute orientation video, electronic wall maps wired to highlight 100 attractions throughout Washington and interactive videodisc stations that index museum attractions by date and areas of interest.

Users can access videodisc information in six languages in addition to English—Arabic, Chinese, French, German, Japanese and Spanish. Striking another, albeit more traditional, international note are the flags of 159 nations. The center is open every day, except Christmas, 9 A.M. to 5:50 P.M.

Smithsonian Information Center
1000 Jefferson Drive, SW
Washington, D.C. 20560
(202) 357-2700, TDD 357-1729

Museum Tours in Foreign Languages

All Smithsonian museums have foreign-language brochures for self-guiding tours. In addition, the Hirschhorn provides taped tours, and the National Gallery of Art has guided tours, all in a variety of languages. See Chapter 4, "The Mall," for phone numbers, as advance notice will usually be required for guided tours. While many museums do not indicate whether foreign-language tours are available, it never hurts to call in advance to see if a special tour can be arranged. Don't hesitate to ask; where available, the service will be provided with enthusiasm.

The Washington Visitor Information Center

Operated by the Washington, D.C., Convention and Visitors Association, the Visitor Information Center is a one-stop shopping resource for free brochures, maps and advice. The center is open 9 A.M. to 5 P.M., Monday to Saturday throughout the year, and 11 A.M. to 3 P.M. Sundays in the summer. It is located in the shops next to the Willard Inter-Continental Hotel, at 1455 Pennsylvania Avenue, NW, (202) 789-7000.

CURRENCY EXCHANGE

The three airports have currency exchange desks. Many larger Washington banks offer currency exchange services, although not at all branches; banking hours in the U.S. are usually 9 A.M. to 3 P.M. weekdays (sometimes later on Friday); a few have Saturday hours. Frequently, Washington hotels will exchange currency for guests.

Thomas Cook exchanges currency at Union Station on Capitol Hill (202) 371-9219; in Georgetown Park at 3222 M Street, NW, (202) 338-3325; and downtown at 1800 K Street, NW, (202) 872-1233.

American Express provides international financial and travel services from more than 10 offices in the metropolitan area. Their main office is downtown at 1150 Connecticut Avenue, NW, (202) 457-1300, open 9 A.M. to 6 P.M., Monday to Friday.

MULTILINGUAL SIGHTSEEING

A number of major area attractions offer free brochures in foreign languages (available through IVIS). These include the White House, the John F. Kennedy Center for the Performing Arts, the Library of Congress and the Smithsonian Institution Complex. The Smithsonian publishes an informative brochure in Arabic, Chinese, French, German, Japanese and Spanish, free upon request; write to the Smithsonian Information Center, Smithsonian Institution, Washington, D.C. 20560. The National Park Services also publishes materials in foreign languages.

Washington's modern and efficient subway system offers free Metro maps in English, French, German, Spanish and Japanese; call (202) 939-5566.

Guide Service of Washington, Inc., offers groups and individuals custom-designed tours of Washington and the surrounding areas conducted by step-on guides. Tours are available for half-day, full-day, evening and multiday excursions in 20 languages. Contact Guide Service of Washington, Inc., 733 15th Street, NW, Suite 1040, Washington, D.C. 20005, (202) 628-2842.

EMBASSIES

Nearly 150 countries are represented by embassies in Washington. Most embassies are located along Massachusetts Avenue between Sheridan and Observatory Circles, NW, and are found in the Washington telephone directory under "Embassy."

International visitors may want to locate and visit their country's embassy in Washington for educational and practical purposes.

ADVANCE PLANNING

Air

Many international carriers offer unlimited air-travel packages to the U.S., with widely varying fares, depending on your point of departure, the time of year, your age and the relationship of the participating travelers. Given the ordinary cost of air travel today, the fare is a great bargain. Check with various airlines to see if they offer anything that might be relevant to your travel plans.

Bus

Greyhound-Trailways offers international visitors the Ameripass, good for travel anywhere in the U.S. and Canada. In 1993, the costs were around $200 for seven days, around $300 for 15 days, and around $400 for 30 days. Call 1-800-231-2222 for the full details of the current program. Spanish-language assistance is available at 1-800-531-5332.

Rail

Amtrak has an International USA Railpass, available overseas, or in Washington, at its ticket offices at Union Station and 1721 K Street, NW. The Railpass is available in 15-day or 30-day lengths, for peak (summer months) and off-peak periods, and for travel throughout the country, or for just the Eastern Region (all destinations east of the Mississippi River) or Western Region. Adult and children (2–11) fares are available. Under twos travel free. In 1993 the peak-period 15-day nationwide adult fare was $308/child fare $154; 30 days— $389/$195. Off-peak fares are about $100 lower for adults, $50 lower for children, and the regional fares are a little more than half the nationwide fare. Call Amtrak at 1-800-USA-RAIL (872-7245) for full details and fares, or write Amtrak International, 400 N Street, NW, Washington, D.C. 20001.

BOOKS AND NEWSPAPERS

A few bookshops in town stock foreign-language materials. Near Dupont Circle, one of the major international centers in town, there are several such shops. *The News Room* (1753 Connecticut Avenue, NW, (202) 332-1489) carries foreign magazines, periodicals and newspapers. *B and B Newsstand* (2621 Connecticut Avenue, NW, (202) 234-0494) also stocks a wide selection of foreign periodicals. Downtown, *Waldenbooks* (17th and G streets, NW, (202) 393-1490) and *Sidney Kramer Books* (1825 I Street, NW, (202) 293-2685) both have a good selection of foreign- and English-language dictionaries.

POST OFFICES

U.S. post offices, unlike their European counterparts, do not house telephone and telegraph facilities. They are strictly for mail. Stamps purchased at post offices cost face value, but will cost more than face value if purchased at vending machines, drugstores or hotels.

SOME AMERICAN CUSTOMS

Tipping. Gratuities are not ordinarily added automatically to restaurant bills. A gratuity of 15 to 20 percent, depending on the quality of service, is expected. A bartender will expect the same gratuity as a waiter, for bar service. Tipping a maître d'hôtel is optional. Airport, train station and hotel porters will expect a tip of 50¢ to $1 per bag. Hotel maids should receive a $2 per day gratuity. Taxi drivers are not always tipped in Washington, but a gratuity of 10 to 15 percent for polite service and careful driving ought to be forthcoming. Theater and movie-house ushers, unlike in Europe, are not tipped, nor are hotel-desk clerks (except for unusual services provided), gas-station attendants, or store clerks. Hotel doormen are tipped, usually 50¢ to $1, for hailing a taxi. In parking lots, a 50¢ tip for retrieving a car is acceptable; for valet parking, $1–$2 is appropriate.

Dress Codes. Americans are by nature an informal people. In recent years, many restaurants have relaxed dress requirements, but more expensive restaurants may require jacket and tie for men. Shorts are not appropriate attire in many expensive to moderate establishments. For foreign guests, native attire is always appropriate.

20

WASHINGTON

ON THE RUN:

ONE-, TWO- AND THREE-DAY
TOURS AND SPECIALIZED TOURS

Anyone with limited time and unlimited energy can still "see" Washington, though it will be a panoramic view rather than a closeup study. Whether you are a part of a group tour or in town for a business convention, there's enough variety in the nation's capital to satisfy any sightseeing appetite.

Limited time means, however, that you must plan your sightseeing carefully in advance, taking in the attractions you want to see in one area of town before heading off to another. Keep in mind that some sites, such as the White House, are open only during limited periods, and may require tickets.

In the following short tour suggestions, we have tried to highlight the major attractions. Your own interests may lead you to eliminate some of the sites we suggest, or add others more suited to your own taste. We have, therefore, summarized many of the tourist sites listed by *interest area;* this book will give you all the information you need to put together your individualized tour of the city and its environs.

DAY ONE

White House: Guided tours, which must be arranged well in advance through your senator or representative, begin at 8 A.M. For regular tours in summer, the White House ticket booths on the Ellipse are open from 8 A.M. till noon; the tours throughout the year begin at 10 A.M.

Tourmobile circuit of **Mall:** stay on for the 90-minute ride.

Smithsonian Information Center (the Castle): orient yourself to the full range of capital offerings.

Lunch at **National Gallery of Art** or **National Air and Space Museum.**

Smithsonian Museum(s) of your choice: most popular are National Air and Space Museum and National Museum of Natural History.

Vietnam Veterans Memorial.

Georgetown dinner and stroll: the extent of your walk will be a true test of your strength.

Washington Monument: short lines and romantic view at night— April to Labor Day.

DAY TWO

U.S. Capitol: take tour.

Supreme Court.

Library of Congress.

Lunch in **Union Station.**

Smithsonian Museum(s) of your choice.

Dinner in Northwest or Downtown.

Dupont Circle—19th Street stroll; or

Nighttime entertainment (see Chapter 13, "Entertainment"): theater, music, dance, etc. In summer, many entertainment options are free.

DAY THREE

Smithsonian Museums or **National Memorials** or **National Archives:** take the morning to fill in the Mall attractions you may have missed or devote morning to **Holocaust Museum.** Picnic lunch on the Mall, or catch lunch at the **Pavilion at the Old Post Office.**

If you don't have a car . . .

Ford's Theatre and the **House Where Lincoln Died.** Try the **FBI** (check to see how long the wait will be before you get in line).

Dinner in Northwest.

Nighttime entertainment.

Or, via Tourmobile or your own car . . .

Arlington National Cemetery, Arlington House

Mount Vernon

Old Town, Alexandria: as time and energy permit, visit sites of interest and stroll about.
Dinner in Old Town.

Or via your own car . . .
Embassy Row
Washington National Cathedral
National Zoo
Dinner in Northwest.

MAJOR ATTRACTIONS ARRANGED BY INTEREST AREA

The American History Tour

Mall . . . Arts and Industries Building . . . National Museum of American History . . . Jefferson Memorial . . . Lincoln Memorial . . . Washington Monument . . . National Archives

Capitol Hill . . . Capitol building . . . Library of Congress . . . Supreme Court

Downtown, Georgetown and Northwest . . . Anderson House . . . DAR Museum . . . Ford's Theatre/House Where Lincoln Died . . . National Portrait Gallery . . . The Octagon . . . Decatur House . . . Historical Society of Washington, D.C.

Suburbs . . . Alexandria . . . Civil War battlefields . . . colonial farms: Oxon Hill, Claude Moore Colonial Farm, National Colonial Farm . . . Fort Washington . . . Mount Vernon . . . Sully Historic House . . . Woodlawn Plantation . . . Gunston Hall Plantation . . . Lee-Fendal House . . . Clara Barton House

The Art Tour

Mall . . . Freer . . . Hirschhorn . . . National Gallery of Art . . . *National Museum of American History . . . National Museum of African Art . . . Arthur M. Sackler Gallery

Downtown and Northwest . . . Corcoran . . . National Museum of American Art . . . National Portrait Gallery . . . Phillips Collection

* Indicates museum with special emphasis on arts and crafts.

. . . *Renwick . . . *Textile Museum . . . National Museum of Women in the Arts . . . Museum of Modern Art in Latin America

Commercial Art Galleries . . . Dupont Circle west and north to Columbia Road . . . Georgetown . . . 7th Street between D and E streets, NW

The Garden Tour
See Chapter 15, "Outdoor Washington/Sports," for a complete, alphabetical guide to Washington's gardens and woodlands.

Washington . . . U.S. Botanic Gardens . . . Dumbarton Oaks . . . Hillwood . . . Kenilworth Aquatic Gardens . . . Enid A. Haupt Gardens (at the Sackler Museum) . . . Washington National Cathedral . . . Tudor Place . . . National Arboretum . . . Old Stone House

Suburbs . . . Brookside Gardens . . . The Historic Houses and Plantations
Remember: if you are visiting the city in April, you may catch the White House Garden Tour or the Georgetown Garden Tours. In September the White House Gardens open once again.

The Historic Home Tour
Washington . . . Anderson House . . . Frederick Douglass House . . . Hillwood . . . The Octagon . . . Old Stone House . . . Sewall-Belmont House . . . Woodrow Wilson House . . . Historical Society of Washington, D.C. . . . Tudor Place . . . Dumbarton House . . . Decatur House . . . Walk through Georgetown

Suburbs . . . Arlington House . . . Carlyle House . . . Clara Barton House . . . Colonial Farms . . . Gunston Hall . . . Lee's Boyhood Home . . . Lee-Fendall House . . . Mount Vernon . . . Ramsay House . . . Sully Historic House . . . Woodlawn Plantation

The Afro American History Tour
Washington . . . Frederick Douglass House . . . National Archives . . . National Museum of African Art . . . Bethune Museum-Archives . . . Anacostia Museum

* Indicates museum with special emphasis on arts and crafts.

The Military History Tour

Washington . . . Air and Space Museum . . . National Archives . . . National Guard Memorial (no site report): One Massachusetts Avenue, NW, (202) 789-0031; 9 A.M. to 4 P.M. daily except weekends and holidays; exhibits of the American Militia and National Guard through 200 years of service . . . National Museum of American History . . . Navy Yard . . . Vietnam Veterans Memorial . . . U.S. Navy Memorial

Virginia . . . Arlington National Cemetery . . . Civil War battlefields . . . Fort Washington Park . . . Marine Corps Memorial . . . Old Guard Museum at Fort Myer (no site report): Building 249, Fort Myer, (202) 692-9721; 10 A.M. to 4 P.M. Tuesday to Saturday; weapons and infantry items dating back to the Revolutionary War.

Maryland . . . Baltimore . . . Fort McHenry . . . Lightship *Chesapeake* . . . S.S. *Torsk* . . . U.S.S. *Constellation* . . . U.S. Naval Academy in Annapolis

The Natural History Tour

Washington . . . C&O Canal . . . Museum of Natural History . . . National Aquarium—Department of Commerce . . . National Geographic Society . . . National Zoo . . . Theodore Roosevelt Island . . . Rock Creek Nature Center

Suburbs . . . Great Falls Parks . . . National Aquarium—Baltimore Inner Harbor . . . Regional Parks—Cabin John and Wheaton . . . Woodend—Audubon Naturalist Society

The Religious Tour

Catholic . . . Franciscan Monastery . . . National Shrine of the Immaculate Conception . . . St. Matthew's Cathedral (no site report), Rhode Island Avenue at Connecticut Avenue, NW

Protestant . . . Christ Church . . . Pohick Church . . . St. John's Church . . . Washington National Cathedral

Jewish . . . B'nai B'rith . . . Lillian and Albert Small Jewish Museum . . . U.S. Holocaust Memorial Museum

Other . . . Islamic Center . . . Mormon Temple

The Science Tour

Washington . . . Air and Space Museum . . . Arts and Industries Building . . . INTELSAT . . . National Geographic Society . . . National Museum of American History . . . Naval Observatory . . . Walter Reed Medical Museum

Suburbs . . . National Aquarium in Baltimore . . . Beltsville Agricultural Research Center . . . Maryland Science Center—Baltimore Inner Harbor . . . NASA—National Aeronautics and Space Administration, Greenbelt, MD

21

DINING

We have tried, in this chapter, to provide a very brief survey of the kinds of food you will find in the Washington area. We have concentrated on the restaurants more conveniently located for tourists-on-the-go. You will not find a vast selection of suburban Maryland and Virginia restaurants, although the 'burbs are full of excellent restaurants in all price ranges and representing all cuisines.

If you're the kind of person who enjoys exploring the unknown and want to peek at menus while taking in the town, you have many good choices for strolling. The Dupont Circle area of downtown has at least 100 restaurants in a five-block radius, including every imaginable ethnic cuisine. Adams-Morgan has become the city hot spot for inexpensive and moderate ethnic fare. And the people-watching is great. Of course Chinatown is designed for exactly this kind of restaurant shopping—there are perhaps 40 restaurants in a three-block stretch. The one block of Connecticut Avenue at Calvert Street, close to the Sheraton and Shoreham hotels, is wall-to-wall restaurants, as are the several blocks of the same avenue above the zoo, up to Porter Street. (We'll sneak in a mention of a restaurant you would never find on your own, Csiko's, a classic, high-ceilinged, white-tableclothed, strolling gypsy-violined Hungarian restaurant—shades of the '30s, in a grand old apartment house at 3601 Connecticut Avenue, (202) 362-5624. $.)

Farther afield, Bethesda, Maryland, has tempted many Downtown restaurateurs to set lures for the ex-urban yuppies. And it's working—there are now over 100 places to choose from. Park and walk, though many of the restaurants are "reservation only." The Virginia suburbs offer several choices: Old Town, Alexandria, has scores of varied restaurants set among the historic buildings. The Wilson Boulevard strip in Arlington has become the area's "little Saigon," with many family-run Vietnamese restaurants, along with Cambodian, Thai and more. Rosslyn, while not an attractive place to walk (it's a barren set of high-rise office canyons), does have many restaurants, and a few very good ones.

Our choices are heavily weighted toward inexpensive and moderate dining. What Washingtonians call "moderate" would be at the high end in most communities. We have, however, included some of our favorite expensive Italian and French restaurants. With the opening of so many moderately priced restaurants, it is not necessary to spend exorbitant amounts of money to have a peak dining experience. After all, you can't eat the marble and mahoghany.

We have tried, also, to provide illustrations of many of the dozens of varied cuisines from all over the globe that are available in this area. Unfortunately, space does not allow us to cover them all. Rest assured, though, that whatever your fancy, you can find it here.

Virtually all restaurants will accept credit cards now, but policies do change, and it pays to check. Calling ahead will also give you the opportunity to make reservations. The least expensive restaurants are least likely to accept reservations. Many moderately priced restaurants also do not accept reservations. We have not included days of operation or hours, as we have found, to our dismay, that they do change over time, so we again provide the advice: call ahead.

Our final word on District dining is: be adventuresome. The nation's capital is an international metropolis and each nationality and ethnic group proudly presents its cuisine for the enjoyment of others. Take up the invitation.

Key to Price

Includes dinner for two, complete with appetizer, entrée, dessert, drink, tax and tip (15–20 percent for good service is the going rate now).

$	Inexpensive	Under $40
$$	Moderate	$40–$70
$$$	Expensive	$70–$100
$$$$	Very Expensive	Over $100

CAPITOL HILL/SOUTHWEST

America American $$
50 Massachusetts Avenue, NE (Union Station)   (202) 682-9555

This restaurant lives up to its name—colorful, dynamic, energetic and spunky. The unique decor includes backlit maps of the states that have spawned America's unusually sensible yet remarkably fun approach to food. Here you'll find regional specialties from across the country, ranging from Santa Fe club sandwiches to shrimp jambalaya. Among the artfully interpreted pizzas and main entrées are offerings rich in sweet nostalgia—peanut butter and jelly sandwiches and, sure enough, Fluffer Nutters.

Bistro le Monde   French bistro and American $
233 Pennsylvania Avenue, SE   (202) 544-4153
A bright, new addition to Capitol Hill, Bistro le Monde offers light French bistro food, as well as a full selection of burgers and pizza. In addition to early weekday breakfasts, Bistro le Monde prides itself on hearty brunches, Saturday and Sunday. This neighborhood hangout, at lunch and after work, is jammed with the congressional staffers who work nearby; it's abuzz with political chatter.

Cafe Berlin   German $$
322 Massachusetts Avenue, NE   (202) 543-7656
Cafe Berlin is one of the few good German restaurants in Washington. Count on it for a homey, no-frills selection of such Bavarian standards as Wiener schnitzel, sauerbraten and goulash. People rave about the potato pancakes (smooth and full-flavored) and the tempting strudels (light pastry and not excessively sweet). Set in a cozy town house, Cafe Berlin spreads outdoors in nice weather for a lively European feel.

La Colline   French $$
400 North Capitol Street, NW   (202) 737-0400
If it were smaller and better decorated, La Colline would command the high prices charged by its exalted French counterparts downtown. The food is every bit as good, better in some cases; heavy on the substance here and not so much on the style. This large restaurant serves careful and professional presentations of French bistro food and is very sensibly priced, particularly the three-course, price-fixed dinner. Menus vary daily, with a strong emphasis on seafood. Its Capitol Hill location makes for good people-watching and a slightly clubby atmosphere.

Le Rivage   French $$
1000 Water Street, SW   (202) 488-8111
Washington's Southwest waterfront has, for the most part, catered to huge packs of tourists, often on buses and without many dining options. Le Rivage is the best of the bunch. Serving classic French food and specializing in seafood, this restaurant makes good use of its waterfront site. Diners on the

open terrace are rewarded with a gorgeous panoramic view of the Washington Monument and the nearby marina on the Potomac. This is a good stop for the pretheater, price-fixed dinner, en route to the Arena Stage, some two blocks away.

Sfuzzi Italian $$$
50 Massachusetts Avenue, NE (Union Station) (202) 842-4141
In this Union Station hot spot, the pizzas, pastas, seafoods and desserts are well-prepared and presented, having been perfected in sister restaurants in Dallas and New York. The decor is postmodern, with original frescoes covering ceilings and walls. Downstairs is more casual; upstairs provides a more formal setting.

GEORGETOWN/FOGGY BOTTOM/WEST END

Austin Grill Tex-Mex $$
2404 Wisconsin Avenue, NW (202) 337-8080
The most authentic Tex-Mex cuisine in the area. The dining room is noisy and crowded, but the food—from the hot, hot chicken wings to the smoked-pork enchiladas and grilled shrimp—is done up right. The margaritas are famous around town, as is the chocolate-lover's dessert—a warm, almond-topped Ibarra chocolate brownie.

Bamiyan Afghani $
3320 M Street, NW (202) 338-1896
(also 300 King Street, Alexandria, VA)
Afghan food may not be among the most common ethnic offerings, but this is a good choice for interesting, filling and reasonably priced fare. Try all the appetizers—every one is delicious, from the ravioli-like *aushak* to the deep-fried *bulanee*.

Busara Thai $$
2340 Wisconsin Avenue, NW (202) 337-2340
You could go for the decor alone—little pools of colored light shine down on laquered tables in the dining rooms; the small, sleek bar looks like it stepped off a Hollywood set; the charming rear courtyard invites you to test the Washington weather. But, go for the food—it's modern Thai, with hints of Western influences. If you are in a group, you will want to try a variety of appetizers, while at the same time leaving room for the extensive and consistently excellent main dishes. We have especially enjoyed the pad thai and various fiery shrimp dishes.

El Caribe Latin American $$
3288 M Street, NW (202) 338-3121
(also 1828 Columbia Road, NW, and 8130 Wisconsin Avenue, Bethesda,
  MD)
At El Caribe you'll find piquant satisfaction in the paella, roast pork and black
beans and rice. This is the Georgetown outpost of our old favorite Adams-
Morgan restaurant where years and experience have melded into reliably
delicious Latin food.

Enriqueta's Mexican $
2811 M Street, NW (202) 338-7772
That which passes for Mexican food at the countless haciendas that dot the
land won't be found here. Enriqueta's has been serving *authentic* Mexican
fare since long before the Mexican food craze. In this tiny Georgetown
restaurant you'll find dishes with a tantalizing chile and chocolate molé sauce.
Enriqueta's is also known for its baked peppers stuffed with pork and glazed
with a spicy fruit sauce. Don't miss the potent and tasty margaritas. Lively
and often noisy, this is a charming little place done up in bright fiesta garb.

Foggy Bottom Cafe American $$
924 25th Street, NW (in the River Inn) (202) 338-8707
This New American-style restaurant is a reliable and fun haunt. By day it's
sunny and cheering; by night this is a great stop before or after theater,
especially the nearby Kennedy Center. The menu is eclectic and contains
some unusual interpretations of popular dishes. Sunday brunch is deservedly
popular.

La Chaumière French $$$
2813 M Street, NW (202) 338-1784
Although most restaurants would hardly want to be likened to a comfortable
pair of old shoes, we just can't help ourselves. With apologies, then. La
Chaumière is a most informal and inviting place with its country French
decor and soothing fireplace. In the Paris bistro tradition, La Chaumière
serves reliable French classics with daily specials. A diverse wine list, too,
makes this an all-around pleasing respite from the fervor of dining in the
1990s.

Las Pampas Argentine $
3291 M Street, NW (202) 333-5151
This small but attractive Argentine restaurant rounds out the area's ethnic
offerings. As in Buenos Aires, the specialties are steaks and whole chickens.
Parillada, a mixed grill with steak, sausage, kidneys, and sweetbreads, is
showily finished at your table.

Madurai Indian $
3318 M Street, NW (202) 333-0997
Even those who normally insist on meat, seafood or poultry at every meal will
be happy at Madurai. Not that you'll get any of that center-of-the-plate
protein here, but the vegetable curries are so splendid, you'll simply forget.
Curries here capture the best of what they were meant to be—concoctions
blending spices into alluringly complex flavors. Lunch and dinner on Sunday
is all-you-can-eat for a mere $6.95 (as of this writing); it's worth it for the
breads alone.

Morton's of Chicago American $$$
3251 Prospect Street, NW (202) 342-6258
Who says people don't eat meat anymore? Hardly! Morton's, a Chicago-based
restaurant recently expanded to other cities, serves up some of the best beef
in town. Porterhouse steaks and prime rib are hearty and tender. First class
all the way . . . and be prepared to pay. Also, do know that this is an extremely
busy and noisy place. Best to arrive early and still be prepared to wait at the
bar.

Old Glory American $$
3139 M Street, NW (202) 337-3406
A new entry in the BBQ stakes, serving up excellent ribs and brisket with a
table-top choice of six different (all good) sauces. The side dishes—biscuits,
slaw, beans, fries, potato salad and more—are all up to the mark. Lots of beers
on tap—including root for the kids. Surprisingly, there is a lot on this menu
for veggie lovers.

Paolo's Italian $$
1303 Wisconsin Avenue, NW (202) 333-7353
Paolo's works magic with its wood-burning pizza oven. Their pizzas are
inventive and delicious. Our favorite is with four white cheeses, roasted red
peppers, fresh thyme and smoked salmon, yet the more traditional pizzas are
just thrilling, too. In addition to pizzas, Paolo's serves up a full selection of
pasta and full-fledged entrées. This is a hot place, in the center of Georgetown.
In warm weather, they fling open the glass front and transform the restaurant
into a lively sidewalk café.

Sushi-Ko Japanese $$
2309 Wisconsin Avenue, NW (202) 333-4187
Washington's first sushi bar (1978) is still our favorite, even after all these
years of the sushi fad. Somehow their seafood always seems the freshest,
thanks, in good measure, to the crowd sure to be found here. For those who

don't eat raw tidbits no matter how artfully done up, Sushi-Ko offers a small selection of tempura, teriyaki and soup.

Tony & Joe's Seafood Place   Seafood $$
3000 K Street, NW (Washington Harbor)   (202) 944-4545
Tony & Joe's Seafood Place is a fine choice for fresh seafood. It's a huge and appealing restaurant, run by the owners of the ever-popular haunt in upper Northwest called The Dancing Crab. Smart and sleek, the decor is after an old-time fish market, complete with blue-and-white tile floors. Occupying a big chunk of Washington Harbor, a very, very toney mixed-use development, Tony & Joe's features lovely views of the Potomac and a nice river walk for after-dinner strolling.

Zed's   Ethiopian $
3318 M Street, NW   (202) 333-4710
While the dining room is charmless, the food is excellent. In addition to the standard stews (called *wats* and *alechas*), and the Ethiopian version of steak tartare (*kifto*), Zed's offers up several signature dishes—beef simmered with yellow split peas, and beef with collard greens. For their bread (*injera*), Zed's uses flour from *teff*, a high-grade millet, which results in a fine, light and flavorful bread.

DOWNTOWN

Bacchus   Middle Eastern $$
1827 Jefferson Place, NW   (202) 785-0734
Bacchus is a small Lebanese restaurant on a charming side street that became so popular that it expanded to bigger quarters in the suburbs (see Bacchus-Bethesda). The quality of the food in both is comparable, and it is excellent. While the main dishes are delicious (kebabs, chicken breasts, marinated lamb and rice), the appetizers are out of this world and a splendid meal can be put together with bits of this and that. The hummus and baba ghanoush are wonderfully fresh, perfectly spiced, as are the homemade sausage, kibbe, kafta—in fact it's difficult to find a dish we wouldn't recommend.

Bice   Italian $$$
601 Pennsylvania Avenue, NW (entrance on Indiana Avenue)   (202) 638-2423
There are only a few places in D.C. where money *and* power come together so publicly for inspection. The food may have lost a step or two since its opening in 1991 but Bice still delivers with better-than-average (and very

genuine) Italian cuisine, a handsome (and very elegant) dining room, and still reasonable prices. The home made sausages, roasted duck breast, quail with porcini mushrooms, and the varied selection of pastas are all worth trying.

Bombay Club   Indian $$
815 Connecticut Avenue, NW   (202) 659-3727
We loved everything about Bombay Club, from the atmosphere (unpretentiously elegant, human-scale comfortable, with a touch of the exotic) and the service (friendly, polite, knowledgeable) to the delightful selection of Indian classics. It was difficult to get beyond appetizers to the main course but worth the gustatory effort; one of the main courses is a sampler of many dishes, each spiced to perfection and distinct in its appeal. The prawns were perfect—marinated and grilled to a succulent crispness.

Cafe Mozart   German $$
1331 H Street, NW   (202) 347-5732
In the heart of old downtown lies a real gem. This German deli-restaurant is a delightful throwback to Washington life in days gone by. The atmosphere is straightforward and sensible—who needs more? The food is what we come back for—seemingly endless quantities of hearty Bavarian food and the most delicious pastries and desserts downtown.

Capitol City Brewing Company   American $$
1100 New York Avenue, NW   (202) 628-2222
The first of DC's "brew-pubs," featuring a variety of brewed-on-site beers and ales. The pub has become a hot spot for mid-week late afternoon meeting-and-greeting, and is just as lively on weekend nights. Beyond the beers is a quite decent menu, starting with excellent burgers and moving on to grilled chicken breasts, ribs, and chops. For heat-lovers, there is several-alarm chili, "fireworks" shrimp, and sausage with a kick.

Dixie Grill   American $
518 10th Street, NW   (202) 628-4800
Southern cooking is one of the newest Washington food trends. The Dixie Grill is truly "down home," with pine banquettes and the traditional red-checkered tablecloths. The food is also traditional, from fried catfish and meatloaf to black-eyed peas and fried okra. Anyone homesick for the taste of youth may find it among the several dozen regional and local soft drinks from all over the South. There are pool tables upstairs.

Dominique's   French $$
1900 Pennsylvania Avenue, NW   (202) 452-1126
Wading through Dominique's menu can be an overwhelming task—they offer *everything,* from rattlesnake on down, in all sorts of combinations (pre-theater

specials can be delicious bargains). Service is expert, and staff suggestions are usually accurate and quite helpful. The seafood is fresh and perfectly cooked, and desserts can be continentally divine.

Duke Zeibert's American $$
1050 Connecticut Avenue, NW (202) 466-3730
Devotees consider this *the* quintessentially Washington restaurant. Power brokers abound—starting with Duke himself. It's a vast, modern dining room, a men's club of sorts and, if the truth be told, best left to the insiders. Food in this power spot is largely meat and seafood, adequate but certainly not outstanding.

Le Lion d'Or French $$$$
1150 Connecticut Avenue, NW (202) 296-7972
Our final downtown French entry is the definition of haute cuisine. Elegant yet experimental (without being nouvelle), Le Lion d'Or is a classic expensive French restaurant. The service is professionally unobtrusive and the food is grand, rich with sauces and layers of fresh, perfectly seasoned ingredients. This is the perfect spot for the last blowout meal before returning home.

Los Planes de Renderos Mexican $
908 11th Street, NW (202) 347-8416
Very simple, very good Mexican food served up in a coffee shop setting. The high quality and low prices draw crowds.

Morrison-Clark Inn Nouvelle American $$$
Massachusetts Avenue at 11th Street, NW (202) 898-1200
This beautifully restored inn in the middle of the city of Washington is a real treat, both aesthetically and culinarily. The ingredients are fresh, combined in interesting fashion and served in quite adequate portions. The veal and beef dishes are exceptional, cooked to juicy perfection, served with unusual yet complementary sauces and exquisite vegetables.

Occidental American $$$
Occidental Grill American $$
1475 Pennsylvania Avenue, NW (Willard Complex) (202) 783-1475
The Occidental Grill is a tempting, clubby spot. Washington through and through, it features endless photographs of the luminaries who frequented the original restaurant. Steeped in elegance, you'll find a fine selection of burgers, various and sundry specialties and desserts. Its formal sibling, The Occidental, offers an impressive dining experience. From the stately Presidential portraits at the entrance to the striking views of the Washington Monument, this is truly a capital place. The food is stylized—an inventive interpretation

of Modern American cooking. It's outstanding in every way, including the price.

Old Ebbitt Grill American $$
675 15th Street, NW (202) 347-4801
The Old Ebbitt is the most grand of saloons. The rich woods and the brass fixtures must surely be polished as often as diners blink for them to gleam so. Beyond the impressive setting, this is a grill serving traditional American fare. Of course, the burgers are fine, but the ambitious menu stretches well beyond. Consider this for an after-dinner drink or for a post-theater supper; it's a lively late-night stop.

Red Sage American $$
605 14th Street, NW (202) 638-4444
Red Sage arrived in D.C. with a grand splash—about $5 million dollars were spent on a largely handcrafted Southwestern decor, bread ovens were imported from France, and special lockers were built for aging beef and smoking hams and house sausage. The cuisine is "modern Western," creatively blending organic foods with Native American and Southwestern influences. A great place to see, and be seen.

CHINATOWN

China Inn Chinese $
631 H Street, NW (202) 842-0909
At China Inn, longevity makes a statement; Chinatown's oldest restaurant is also among its best. A long menu offers a wide variety of Cantonese food in a spacious setting. Be experimental; almost every new dish is a delight. If you've designated one night for Chinese food, and high spice is not a primary goal, China Inn is your best bet. Dim sum are served daily.

Hunan Chinatown Chinese $
624 H Street, NW (202) 783-5858
A limited but excellent menu offers delicious, attractive food in a clean and modern setting.

Mr. Yung's Chinese $
740 6th Street, NW (202) 628-1098
Mr. Yung's exhaustive menu offers everything, and there is probably not a dish to disappoint. A relative newcomer on the Chinatown scene, this restaurant has perhaps the widest selection of noodle dishes, and they are delectable. Dim sum is also excellent.

Tony Cheng's Seafood Restaurant   Chinese $$
619 H Street, NW   (202) 371-8669
The newest of Tony Cheng's restaurants offers fresh (pick them while they're
still swimming) seafood cooked in a variety of methods and Chinese regional
cuisines with good results.

NORTHWEST

Dupont Circle

Childe Harolde   American $
1610 20th Street, NW   (202) 483-6700
The upstairs restaurant is casual and warm, with rich wood finishes and
Edwardian decor. The menu is broad—burgers and steaks, fish and chops,
salads and sandwiches. Portions are honest, and the food consistent. The
downstairs bar serves the same food in a pub atmosphere, with one of the
District's best jukeboxes in the background.

Donna Adele   Italian $$
2100 P Street, NW   (202) 296-1142
Recently transformed into a significant Italian restaurant, Donna Adele offers
each day a new selection of inventive pastas, meats, and seafood. In this
pleasant and polished atmosphere, the staff is attentive and helpful, contribut-
ing to a most enjoyable dining experience. The grilled veal chop was well-
seasoned and attractively presented. While prices are not cheap, Donna Adele
is less expensive than most of Washington's other authentic Italian kitchens.

Galileo   Italian $$$
1120 21st Street, NW   (202) 293-7191
This Northern Italian restaurant has a big reputation; its popularity has made
possible a recent move to much larger quarters. Galileo has always been
admired for the strength of its "primi"—hot and cold antipasti and pastas.
The tortellini are melt-in-your mouth magnificent; grilled meats and fresh fish
are also winners. The homemade desserts are as much a pleasure to the eye
as to the palate.

iRicchi   Rustic Italian $$$$
1220 20th Street, NW   (202) 835-0459
iRicchi serves the food of rural Tuscany—hearty, simple, utterly fresh and
designed to be eaten in three or four small courses, rather than a single huge
entrée. Try the peasant soup—ribollita—a combination of slabs of bread with
white beans, carrots, zucchini and chard, eaten at room temperature. Rabbit,
goat, quail will all appear in season. The grilled meats are one of the restau-

rant's strong suits. And if you have never tried risotto, here is the place to do it. The restaurant is a bit crowded and noisy, but the atmosphere is thick with anticipation, so it's not unpleasant but rather a shared culinary experience.

Iron Gate Inn Middle Eastern $$
1734 N Street, NW (202) 737-1370
Typical Near Eastern offerings—baba ghanoush, hummus, eggplant, stuffed grape leaves, stuffed cabbage, kebabs. The food is decent but not overwhelming. What is outstanding is the setting: a grape-arbored courtyard, an oasis in the city. For a summer evening you can imagine you are someplace else— the birds, the stars, the trees and leaves and perfectly acceptable food.

Kramerbooks & afterwords American $
1517 Connecticut Avenue, NW (202) 387-1462
4201 Wilson Boulevard, Arlington, VA (703) 524-3900
This bookstore/café combination offers a full menu, from sandwiches and salads to pastas and grilled fish and chicken. The accent is often on the Southwest, and the nacho plate is among the best around. Full bar, with an emphasis on a broad selection of American and European wines and beers. Try the smooth and satisfying ice cream drinks. Great desserts, most made in house. Open all night on the weekends (in DC), until the wee hours the rest of the week.

Lucie French $$$$
2015 Massachusetts Avenue, NW (202) 939-4250
The portrait of Lucie, wife of the French impressionist Maurice Utrillo, hangs in the entryway, and the restaurant decor follows the color scheme of the portrait—simple, refined and modern. The all-fresh food is haute, but designed for modern "nouvelle" palates, and the menu changes with the seasons. Hot and cold hors d'oeuvres, fish, meats, poultry. Prices at lunch are moderate but push up at night. Chef James Papovich was named 1990 Washington Chef of the Year by his peers.

Nora American $$$
2132 Florida Avenue, NW (202) 462-5143
Since 1979, owner/chef Nora Pouillon has been serving organic meats, vegetables and fruits to an increasingly appreciative audience. The Clinton administration has made Nora a star, with everyone from the first family on down discovering just how good healthy food can be. The menu changes daily, based on what's available to meet Nora's standards, but will always include vegetarian dishes, meats and fish. The homemade ice cream and desserts may not be classified as "health foods," but they are sinfully good.

Pan Asian Noodles & Grill Thai $$
2020 P Street, NW (202) 872-8889
As the name suggests, this moderately priced restaurant serves several Asian cuisines—Malaysian, Thai, Chinese. Noodles are the star, served in scores of ways—in soups, floating in sauces, soggy, dry. The surroundings are Dupont Circle–modern—informal, lively and colorful.

Pesce Seafood $$$
Two of DC's star chefs, Jean-Louis Palladin (*Jean-Louis* and *Palladin* both at the Watergate Hotel) and Roberto Donna (*Galileo, iMatti* and *Il Radicchio,* 1509 17th Street, NW) have joined forces to create a seafood café and market. You can pick out your meal at the counter and it will be on your plate in short order—grilled simply or sauteed and accompanied by an elegant sauce. The prices are moderate at lunch, and go up sharply at night.

Star of Siam Thai $
1136 19th Street, NW (202) 785-2839
This new entry is considered among the best Thai restaurants in town and has popularized Thai curries, which unlike their Indian counterparts are light and not oily. The curry heat is tamed by coconut milk. Green are the tamest; the red, yellow, and Muslim curries are more powerful. Try also the broad noodles served with beef, broccoli and baby corn.

Vincenzo Italian/Seafood $$$$
1606 20th Street, NW (202) 667-0047
Competition for recognition as the "best" Italian restaurant has only driven Vincenzo to greater glory. The restaurant was recently expanded, adding dozens of tables in a charming enclosed courtyard. Vincenzo does fish better than just about anyplace else. Simple fish, grilled mostly, but so fresh and so delicately finished that you may change your notion of what fish is all about. The pastas lean to seafood as well—with crab, lobster, shrimp, mussels. With the exception of the wine, everything, breadsticks to desserts, are made in-house.

Adams-Morgan/Connecticut Avenue

Adams-Morgan Spaghetti House Italian $
2317 18th Street, NW (202) 265-6665
If the kids are complaining about your exotic choices, take yourself off to the Spaghetti House; it's cheap and the kids will recognize every dish—spaghetti (of course), pizza, ravioli, lasagne, manicotti and some special Parmesan dishes. A sure winner.

Café Atlantico Latin American/Caribbean $
1819 Columbia Road, NW (202) 575-2233

For early drinks or an island-inspired meal, this small but trendy café is the right spot. Chili biscuits with black bean dip greet you, followed by cod or yucca fritters and entrees including jerk chicken, grilled fish, and pork dishes, served with plenty of rice and vegetables.

Cities American/Latin/Asian $$
2424 18th Street, NW   (202) 328-7194
The fun of Cities is that every four months the entire restaurant is remodeled and the menu completely changed to reflect the cuisine of the new city, or regional, theme. We haven't a clue as to what you'll find as you read this guide—except that the place will be fun to look at—sort of unreconstructed-warehouse-modern with the stage designer's knack of setting the scene with a few well-chosen props—and the food will be inventive and good.

Fish, Wings & Tings Latin American/Caribbean $
2418 18th Street, NW   (202) 234-0322
This bright, colorful, jazzy place would be at home in Soho. Order at the counter and be served at one of a dozen tables. The food is spicy; the tempo upbeat. Try the homey fish soup, grilled or fried fish (whatever's in season) served with a topping of sauteed onions and peppers, chicken wings in a ginger/curry sauce, sweet and sour pineapple or Jamaican barbecued chicken. The goat curry is famous, as is *ital,* a curried mixture of veggies that goes well with the rice.

iMatti Italian $$
2436 18th Street, NW   (202) 462-8844
This entry from Roberto Donna's stable has the look, feel, and price range of a simple trattoria, but the menu is lengthy and often ambitious. You won't go wrong with the pastas or any of the fishes. Do leave room for dessert—all are house-made and terrific.

Khyber Pass Afghani $
2309 Calvert Street, NW   (202) 234-4632
We never tire of sending people to try the cuisine of Afghanistan; everyone raves. It is a cross between Middle Eastern, with its kebabs and yogurt sauces, and north Indian, in the form of fried, vegetable-stuffed pastries. You should not pass up *aushak,* raviolis stuffed with scallions and topped by a sauce of ground beef, mint and yogurt. The sauteed pumpkin is marvelous, honest.

La Plaza Latin American $$
1847 Columbia Road, NW   (202) 667-1900
Both Spanish and Latin American cooking hold places on the menu at this homey, pleasant, comfortable, quiet restaurant. La Plaza was a neighborhood

restaurant long before Adams-Morgan exploded with food competition, and the deep roots show. Food is fresh, simply prepared (country cooking rather than effete city stuff) and attentively served.

Lavandou   French $$
3321 Connecticut Avenue, NW   (202) 966-3002
Tucked away in Cleveland Park, Lavandou may well figuratively transport you to Provence, a region celebrating basic, hearty, well-prepared food. Colorful and often garlicky, the soups and appetizers are excellent. Provençal stew is a traditional winner.

Lebanese Taverna   Middle Eastern $
2641 Connecticut Avenue, NW   (202) 265-8681
It's hard to get past the appetizers in this comfortable neighborhood restaurant—a meal can easily be made of standard Lebanese finger foods as well as more unusual offerings such as spinach turnovers and garlicky cauliflower. Entrees deserve attention, too; lamb, chicken, and pilaf dishes predominate.

Meskerem   Ethiopian $
2434 18th Street, NW   (202) 462-4100
Washington has a dozen or so Ethiopian restaurants. Meskerem has been among the most successful; it tones down the hottest of native dishes for American sensibilities, and it has built a pleasant environment to suit the locals. Ethiopian food is traditionally eaten by scooping food into *injera,* a spongy bread. You will find various *wats* (spicy stews, with currylike sauces) and alechas (cold vegetable salads), *kitfo* (steak tartare), lots of vegetarian dishes based on the wats and a variety of salads.

Mixtec   Mexican $
1792 Columbia Road NW   (202) 332-1011
Mixtec's tacos al carbon are its calling card—corn tortillas to be filled with sizable portions of beef or pork, sauced with a variety of (potent) salsas, folded and eaten like a serving of moo shu pork. You can also find more familiar fare: burritos, enchiladas, chicken mole, fajitas.

Petitto's   Italian $$
2653 Connecticut Avenue, NW   (202) 667-5350
Pasta is the foundation of much of the menu—scores of sauces: vegetarian, meat, shellfish and more—adorn the various noodles—fat, thin, flat, round, with holes, curled. The homemade desserts are worthy of keeping a corner of your stomach available.

Thai Taste   Thai $
2606 Connecticut Avenue, NW   (202) 387-8876

Close to the convention hotels, Thai Taste is a good introduction to the peppery food of Thailand, as they tone it down a bit and give it a familiar Chinese twist. Among its specialties are duck with mixed veggies, steamed whole fish with preserved plums and beef with chili and coconut milk.

SUBURBAN MARYLAND

Bacchus-Bethesda   Middle Eastern $$
7945 Norfolk Avenue, Bethesda, MD   (301) 657-1722
This popular, bustling restaurant maintains an elegant air despite shoulder-to-shoulder dining; the delectable variety of Middle Eastern fare makes the crowd bearable. While the main dishes are delicious (kebabs, chicken breasts, marinated lamb and rice), the appetizers are out of this world and a splendid meal can be put together with bits of this and that. The hummus and baba ghanoush are wonderfully fresh, perfectly spiced, as are the homemade sausage, *kibbe, kafta*—in fact it's difficult to find a dish we wouldn't recommend.

Crisfield I & II   Seafood $$
I—8012 Georgia Avenue, Silver Spring, MD   (301) 589-1306
II—8606 Colesville Road, Silver Spring, MD   (301) 588-1572
Crisfield is a Chesapeake Bay fishing village—and the food at both Crisfield restaurants is pure Tidewater: fish and shellfish broiled, sauteed or fried. Don't stray from the local dishes—they're grand, right down to the crispy french fries and sweet, light cole slaw. Crab-stuffed shrimp and flounder, steamed shrimp, imperial crab, crab Norfolk and plump, juicy oysters—on the half shell, fried, stewed—they can't be beat anywhere in the Washington area. Crisfield I—no credit cards or reservations; closed Mondays; diner decor. II takes cards and is more upscale.

Foong Lin   Chinese $
7710 Norfolk Avenue, Bethesda, MD   (301) 656-3427
Foong Lin, offering the cuisines of several regions of China, has the air and comfort of a neighborhood restaurant with food well above standard in quality. The food is beautifully and deliciously prepared, and while seafood (whole steamed fish and stuffed scallops are excellent) and noodles (Singapore rice noodles and Shanghai pan-fried noodles are memorable) are especially good, most other dishes shine as well (try the crispy Yulan fried chicken).

La Ferme   French $$$
7101 Brookville Road, Chevy Chase, MD   (301) 986-5255
Not to be dismissed as simply a neighborhood place, this. La Ferme is an inviting, country-style restaurant serving reliable, classic French food. People

rave about the hot dessert soufflés. Garden dining is an especially appealing experience.

Louisiana Express American $
4921 Bethesda Avenue, Bethesda, MD (301) 652-6945
This small, unassuming place serves up authentically vigorous Cajun cuisine, from po'boys to jambalayas and gumbos, all in ample portions at very modest prices.

Old Angler's Inn American $$$
10801 MacArthur Boulevard, Potomac, MD (301) 299-9097
Modern American (and usually quite inventive) cuisine combines nicely with country-like setting of this old stone building close to the C&O Canal about 12 miles from Georgetown. Meats from foie gras to lamb, seafood from lobster to fresh fish—all prepared with an eye to unusual flavor combinations and pleasing visual presentation. Especially romantic if you arrive early on a fall or winter's evening and have a drink in the lounge by the fireplace.

Pines of Rome Italian $
4709 Hampden Lane, Bethesda, MD (301) 657-8775
A good, old-fashioned neighborhood Italian restaurant with excellent, simple dishes is a great find, and the crowds at Pines of Rome attest to this fact. Good veal, delicious white and red pizza, crispy fried zucchini, zippy tomato-sauced standards are the best menu items. Go early—no reservations are accepted.

Rio Grande Cafe American (Tex-Mex) $$
4919 Fairmont Avenue, Bethesda, MD (301) 656-2981
Perhaps the best Tex-Mex eatery in the entire Washington area, Rio Grande cooks up regional standards with homemade flair—fajitas, a variety of tacos, chiles rellenos—and adds dishes not often encountered in other Washington Tex-Mex establishments—broiled quail, superb grilled shrimp, frogs legs. The whimsically decorated warehouse setting is *always* crowded, and reservations aren't accepted, so go early or be prepared to drink your share of margaritas at the popular bar while you wait.

NORTHERN VIRGINIA

Angkor West Cambodian $
6703 Lowell Avenue, McLean, VA (703) 893-6077
Spicy Asiatic cuisine—delicious curries, noodle soups and spicy-hot seafood and meat dishes.

East Wind Vietnamese $$
809 King Street, Alexandria, VA (703) 836-1515
An excellent representation of Vietnamese cuisine, offering a grand variety of soups, appetizers and meat dishes, with accompanying fish and spicy sauces.

L'Auberge Chez Francois French $$$
332 Springvale Road, Great Falls, VA (703) 759-3800
But for the fact it's Virginia, this feels (and tastes) like the real thing—a French country inn. The aura is as wonderful as the food; dinner here is indeed a special event. Good crusty breads, stews, pâtés, homemade sausage, casseroles—these are the best offerings. The desserts are splendid. Weekend reservations must be made weeks in advance—try a weeknight. You must have a car to get to the restaurant; it's truly in the country (far suburbs anyway).

Nizam's Middle Eastern $$
523 Maple Avenue W, Vienna, VA (703) 938-8948
As in most Middle Eastern restaurants, lamb and eggplant are stars here, particularly the doner kebab (marinated lamb slices cooked together over a spit). The meats are grilled, baked and braised expertly, the casseroles are flavorful and the service is polite and attentive.

Queen Bee Vietnamese $
3181 Wilson Boulevard, Arlington, VA (703) 527-3444
Queen Bee is among the best Vietnamese restaurants in the Washington area. An extensive menu gives the diner a full appreciation of the range of Vietnamese cooking. Noodle soups will make a delicious meal in themselves, but then you would miss out on the delicate appetizers and superb main courses. We are partial to anything made with pork or shrimp. The spring rolls are superb.

Red Hot & Blue American (BBQ) $
1600 Wilson Boulevard, Arlington, VA (703) 276-7427
Barbecued ribs and pulled pig sandwiches at Red Hot & Blue drive the crowds crazy with delight (that's why they'll wait so long for tables—one hour is not unusual for dinner). The best in the Washington area. A tip: order some carry-out as soon as you arrive—and eat it as an appetizer while you wait outside on the building sidewalk plaza.

Tachibana Japanese $$
4050 Lee Highway, Arlington, VA (703) 528-1122
Always busy—a good sign for lovers of sushi, for the fish is invariably fresh. The chefs make a wide variety of sushi, and are always willing to discuss what

is freshest or unusual. *Nigiri* (the oblong balls of rice with *wasabi* and fish), *maki* (sushi rolls), and more. For non–sushi eaters, the tempura are excellent, as are the *nabemono,* stews served in pots.

RESTAURANTS BY CUISINE

Afghani

Bamiyan Afghan	$	Georgetown
Khyber Pass	$	Northwest

American

America	$$	Capitol Hill/Southwest
Austin Grill	$$	Georgetown/Foggy Bottom
Capitol City Brewing Company	$$	Downtown
Childe Harolde	$	Northwest/Dupont Circle
Cities	$$	Northwest/Adams-Morgan
Dixie Grill	$	Downtown
Duke Ziebert's	$$	Downtown
Foggy Bottom Cafe	$	Georgetown/Foggy Bottom
Kramerbooks & afterwords	$	Northwest/Dupont Circle & Arlington, VA
Le Bistro Monde	$	Capitol Hill/Southwest
Louisiana Express	$	Maryland
Morrison-Clark Inn	$$$	Downtown
Morton's	$$$	Georgetown/Foggy Bottom
Nora	$$$	Dupont Circle
Occidental	$$$	Downtown
Occidental Grill	$$	Downtown
Old Angler's Inn	$$$	Maryland
Old Ebbitt Grill	$$	Downtown
Old Glory	$$	Georgetown
Red, Hot & Blue	$	Virginia
Red Sage	$$	Downtown
Rio Grande Cafe	$$	Maryland, Virginia

Cambodian

Angkor West	$	Virginia

Chinese

China Inn	$	Downtown
Foong Lin	$	Maryland
Hunan Chinatown	$	Downtown
Mr. Yung's	$	Downtown
Tony Cheng's Seafood	$$	Downtown

Ethiopian

Meskerem	$	Northwest/Adams-Morgan
Zed's	$	Georgetown

French

Dominique's	$$-	Downtown
L'Auberge Chez Francois	$$$	Virginia
La Chaumière	$$$	Georgetown
La Colline	$$	Capitol Hill/Southwest
La Ferme	$$$	Maryland
Lavandou	$$	Northwest/Cleveland Circle
Le Lion d'Or	$$$$	Downtown
Le Rivage	$$	Capitol Hill/Southwest
Lucie	$$$$	Northwest/Dupont Circle

German

Cafe Berlin	$$	Capitol Hill
Cafe Mozart	$$	Downtown

Indian

Madurai	$	Georgetown
Bombay Club	$$	Downtown

Italian

Adams Morgan Spaghetti House	$	Northwest/Adams-Morgan
Bice	$$$	Downtown
Donna Adele	$$	Northwest/Dupont Circle
Galileo	$$$	Northwest/Dupont Circle
iMatti	$$	Adams-Morgan
iRicchi	$$$$	Northwest/Dupont Circle
Paolo's	$$	Georgetown
Petitto's	$$	Northwest

Pines of Rome	$	Maryland
Sfuzzi	$$$	Capitol Hill/Southwest
Vincenzo	$$$$	Northwest/Dupont Circle

Japanese

| Sushi-ko | $ | Georgetown |
| Tachibana | $$ | Virginia |

Latin American/Mexican/Caribbean

Café Atlantico	$	Northwest/Adams-Morgan
El Caribe	$$	Northwest/Adams-Morgan
Enriqueta's	$	Georgetown
Fish, Wings & Tings	$	Northwest/Adams-Morgan
La Plaza	$$	Northwest/Adams-Morgan
Las Pampas	$	Georgetown
Los Planes de Renderos	$	Downtown
Mixtec	$	Northwest/Adams-Morgan

Middle Eastern

Bacchus	$$	Downtown
Bacchus Bethesda	$$	Maryland
Iron Gate Inn	$$	Northwest/Dupont Circle
Lebanese Taverna	$$	Connecticut Avenue/Adams-Morgan
Nizam's	$$	Virginia

Seafood

Crisfield I & II	$$	Maryland
Pesce	$$$	Dupont Circle
Tony & Joe's Seafood	$$	Georgetown
Tony Cheng's Seafood	$$	Downtown
Vincenzo	$$$$	Northwest/Dupont Circle

Thai

Busara	$$	Georgetown
Pan Asian Noodles	$$	Northwest
Thai Taste	$	Northwest

Vietnamese

| East Wind | $$ | Virginia |
| Queen Bee | $ | Virginia |

22

HOTELS

Washington has over 50,000 rooms for visitors to the city. You can undoubtedly find whatever kind of accommodation best suits you—from a budget motel to a quaint bed and breakfast, a suburban highrise hotel to a downtown historic inn. Our job is to point out better-than-adequate representatives of the many different kinds of accommodations in various parts of the city and surrounding suburbs. None of the hotels, motels or inns mentioned here has paid any fee to be listed. We have tried to list reasonably convenient facilities offering what every traveler has the right to expect—safety and cleanliness. Should your experiences at any of these hotels not meet these standards, we would appreciate knowing about it.

We have included, in this new edition, many "all-suites" hotels. The growth of this segment of the hospitality industry is a great boon to traveling families, offering accommodations priced comparably to first-rate hotels but providing considerably more space, more beds and the opportunity to save money on meals.

Further assistance for lodging is easily obtained. The Washington, D.C., Convention and Visitors Association, 1212 New York Avenue, NW, Suite 600, Washington, D.C. 20005, (202) 789-7000, can supply you with a brochure listing various kinds of accommodations by region and budget. The brochure does not, however, contain photographs or descriptions, but, like this *Guide,* simply provides basic information through a key system. WCVA also publishes two brochures on summer and holiday hotel packages, available at the number above. The D.C. Committee to Promote Washington publishes a booklet called "Washington D.C. Weekends," a descriptive pamphlet on hotel deals offered all year. Call 1-800-422-8644.

Several companies are knowledgeable brokers to area hotels and can help match your needs to specific lodgings. They can offer extensive descriptions and often have access to special rates. (Often rooms booked for conventions or meetings go unclaimed, and hotels make them available at the last minute at substantial discounts: the brokers will be told, and you can benefit.) Their services are paid for by the hotel and are free to you. Try Washington, D.C. Accommodations, 1-800-554-2220, and Capitol Reservations, 1-800-847-4832. Both promise personalized service for individuals, groups and corporate travel.

BED & BREAKFASTS

The B&B movement is gaining strength in the U.S. It used to be that B&Bs were thought to be just a European experience, but you can get the same homey flavor right here in your nation's capital, and often save a lot of money, too. Two services dominate the Washington market:

The Bed & Breakfast League, Ltd./Sweet Dreams & Toast, P.O. Box 9490, Washington, D.C. 20016, (202) 483-9191, homes and apartments in the District, Maryland and Virginia. Rates will range from around $35 for a single with a shared bath, to over $100 for a double with a private bath. A two-night minimum stay is required, and a nonrefundable deposit is requested. The League will provide descriptions and an application on request. The office is closed on weekends, federal holidays and for two weeks around Christmas and New Year.

Bed & Breakfast Accommodations, Ltd. P.O. Box 12011, Washington, D.C. 20005, (202) 328-3510, Fax (202) 332-3885, private homes, apartments, guest houses and inns. In 1992, rates ranged from $40 to $225 for single occupancy, and $50 to $225 for double occupancy. Call, fax, or write for detailed information on the rooms, hosts, locations, and rates.

HOTEL LISTINGS

Hotels are divided into five groups by price. The categories are broad, and you may well find rooms priced both somewhat below and above the ranges listed here. Always be bold enough to ask for the "Best rate" available for your stay. The broad categories will, however, give you an idea of what to expect: plain or fancy, and in-between. The classifications are:

Budget—under $60 (for a double occupancy room)
Moderate—between $60 and $100
Expensive—between $100 and $150
Luxury—between $150 and $200
Super luxury—over $200

Users of previous editions will note a small change in the way in which we present our hotel listings. We have expanded our descriptions and condensed the basic information, using a simple key system. Here is the key to the key system.

Rates

G   Group rates available. Usually group rates are available only for a significant number of rooms, a minimum of, say, five or ten, and are subject to availability. In high season—from March to July—group rates may be higher than at other times, or not available at all. Make your reservations as far in advance as your plans (or the hotel) will permit.

W   Weekend rates available. As many hotels make their living principally off business travelers, they find they have rooms aplenty on the weekends. Weekend discounts can be substantial, and may often include such bonuses as free parking and a complimentary meal. Ask.

F   Family rates available. Some hotels are rather snooty about "family rates," thinking that people will imagine a roadside motel if it is used. Nonetheless, all but the fanciest hotels catering to a business clientele offer a substantial discount, or free lodging, for children in the same room as parents. Some may charge if an extra bed is required. Some hotels have a limit on the number of persons allowed to occupy a single room or suite.

We do not provide the specifics of these special rates: they vary with season and hotel occupancy rates.

Services/Amenities

EX   Exercise/health facility (* indicates off premises)

FP   Free overnight parking for guests

HC   Equipped rooms for the physically impaired

IP   Indoor swimming pool

K   Kitchenette available (* indicates only some rooms equipped)

M   Minibar/refrigerator in room (* indicates only some rooms equipped)

NSF   No smoking floor available

NSR   No smoking rooms available

OP   Outdoor swimming pool

PP   Pay parking in hotel lot

R   Restaurant on premises

WC   Public areas wheelchair-accessible

BUDGET (UNDER $60)

Allan Lee Hotel   2224 F Street, NW   (202) 331-1224; 1-800-462-0186
85 rooms.   Services: PP.   Metro: Foggy Bottom-GWU (3 blocks).
A no-frills, slightly seedy urban high-rise hotel whose primary charms are its price and location. It is within walking distance of the State Department, World Bank, George Washington University, the White House, Washington Monument, Vietnam Memorial and Kennedy Center.

Braxton Hotel   1440 Rhode Island Avenue, NW   (202) 232-7800
62 rooms.   Services: PP.   Metro: McPherson Square (6 blocks).
A downtown facility, close to the Convention Center and downtown office buildings, which underwent a complete renovation in 1993.

Connecticut-Woodley   2647 Woodley Road, NW   (202) 667-0218
15 rooms.   Rates: F.   Services: PP.   Metro: Woodley Park (½ block).
A modest, nicely appointed guest house across the street from the Sheraton, a block from the Shoreham, close to good restaurants and uptown attractions—the zoo and the National Cathedral. A brisk 10-minute walk to Dupont Circle. Extended stay rates available.

International Youth Hostel   1009 11th Street, NW   (202) 737-2333
Accommodates 300.   Services: HC, PP, WC.   Metro: Metro Center (3 blocks).
In the hostel tradition, rooms and bathrooms are same-sex shared (although some family rooms may be available from November through February). Cooking facilities available.

MODERATE ($60–$100)

American Inn of Bethesda   8130 Wisconsin Avenue, Bethesda, MD
(301) 656-9300; 1-800-323-7081
75 rooms.   Rates: G, W, F(16).   Services: FP, NSR, OP, R, WC, HC.
Metro: Bethesda (2 blocks).
An older high-rise motel that was completely renovated in 1989. Easy access to NIH, walk to Metro. Good shopping and restaurants in Bethesda. Cable TV. Complimentary continental breakfast.

The Carlyle Suites 1731 New Hampshire Avenue, NW (202) 234-3200;
1-800-964-5377
170 suites. Rates: G, W, F. Services: EX*, FP. Metro: Dupont Circle
(2 blocks).
Dupont Circle is Washington's equivalent (or as close as it gets) to New
York's West Village—hip, lively, heterogeneous, full of nightlife. The Suites
are in the middle of it, close also to Downtown offices and within walking
distance to many attractions, short Metro ride from others. The Suites occupy
a converted apartment building with Art Deco styling inside and out. Rooms
are generously sized.

Days Inn Connecticut Avenue 4400 Connecticut Avenue, NW (202)
244-5600; 1-800-325-2525
155 rooms. Rates: G, W, F(18). Services: PP, HC, NSF, WC. Metro:
Van Ness (2 blocks).
A plain but more-than-adequate hotel (renovated in 1988) located in upper
northwest, close to the zoo, National Cathedral, UDC, Chevy Chase, Friendship Heights; 10 minutes by Metro to downtown. Free continental breakfast.

Holiday Inn of Silver Spring 8777 Georgia Avenue Silver Spring, MD
(301) 589-0800; 1-800-HOLIDAY
230 rooms. Rates: G, W, F(18). Services: EX, FP, HC, NSF, OP, R,
WC. Metro: Silver Spring (3 blocks).
What you expect from Holiday, in downtown Silver Spring. Hotel van will
provide free pickup and drop-off at Metro and area tourist attractions.

Hotel Harrington 11th & E streets, NW (202) 628-8140;
1-800-424-8532
275 rooms. Rates: G, F(16). Services: PP, HC*, NSF, R, WC. Metro:
Metro Center (1 block).
A venerable, family-owned Downtown high-rise hotel. The surroundings are
modest, but the staff prides itself on being friendly. Popular with Europeans
and families. Walking distance to Mall, museums, Capitol Hill. This area of
downtown is a bit run-down but is undergoing rehabilitation and renovation.

Howard Johnson Motor Lodge 2601 Virginia Avenue, NW (202)
965-2700; 1-800-654-2000
192 rooms. Rates: G, W, F(12). Services: FP, M, NSF, OP, R.
Metro: Foggy Bottom-GWU (2 blocks).
Made famous in the Watergate scandal, located directly across the street from
the Watergate complex. Within walking distance to the White House,
Georgetown, the West End and Kennedy Center. Convenient to all sites by
Metro.

Inn at Foggy Bottom Hotel   824 New Hampshire Avenue, NW   (202)
  337-6620; 1-800-426-4455
95 rooms.   Rates: G, W, F(12).   Services: NSF, PP, R, K*.   Metro:
  Foggy Bottom-GWU (1 block).
Renovated in 1990, this small high-rise inn is around the corner from the
Howard Johnson. Guests have access to GWU's Smith Center—an athletic
complex with tennis courts, racquetball, swimming, weights.

Kalorama Guest Houses
Kalorama Park: 1854 Mintwood Place, NW   (202) 667-6369
Woodley Park: 2700 Cathedral Avenue, NW   (202) 328-0860
50 rooms in 4 houses.   Rates: G.   Services: FP (limited, by reservation)
These small "pensiones" are located in quiet residential neighborhoods, in
converted townhouses. With a total of 50 guest rooms and suites, each distinc-
tively furnished in a turn-of-the-century style, complimentary continental
breakfast, afternoon sherry in the parlor, and live-in managers, these charming hotels make every effort to give guests a sense of coming "home" after
a day of sightseeing or work. Choose between the bustle of the multiethnic
Adams-Morgan district (Kalorama) or the quieter confines of the zoo area.
The Woodley Park facility is closer to a Metro. Singles with shared bath as
low as $40; suites up to $115.

Normandy Inn   2118 Wyoming Avenue, NW   (202) 483-1350;
  1-800-424-3729
74 rooms.   Rates: G, W.   Services: M*, NSF, PP, WC, HC*.   Metro:
  Dupont Circle (5 blocks).
This modern inn offers a complimentary afternoon tea. Located in Kalorama,
a very pleasant part of town with handsome old apartment buildings and large
residences. Free wine and cheese Tuesday 5:30–7 P.M.

Rosslyn Westpark Hotel   1900 North Fort Myer Drive, Arlington, VA
  (703) 527-4814; 1-800-368-3408
308 rooms.   Rates: G, W, F(18).   Services: EX, FP, HC, IP, WC, R,
  NSF.   Metro: Rosslyn (1 block).
A member of the Best Western chain, this hotel completed a top-to-bottom
renovation in 1991. Rosslyn, just across the river from Georgetown, is very
convenient to all city sites, by Metro or car, and offers great nighttime views
of the city.

Savoy Suites Hotel   2505 Wisconsin Avenue, NW   (202) 337-9700;
  1-800-944-5377
150 rooms & suites.   Rates: G, W, F(18).   Services: FP, HC, K*, NSF,
  EX*, R, WC.   Metro: Tenley (1 mile).

At the top of Georgetown, on one of the highest points of the city, close to the National Cathedral and a quick bus ride downtown (stop is across the street). Completely renovated in 1992 with Art Deco touches. Free shuttle to Metro.

Skyline Inn Best Western   South Capitol & I streets, SW   (202) 488-7500; 1-800-528-1234
203 rooms.   Rates: G, W, F(18).   Services: FP, NSR, OP, R, HC.
Metro: Capitol South (5 blocks).
A close-in hotel, within walking distance of Capitol Hill destinations. Not fancy but decent, having undergone a major renovation in 1989–90.

Tabard Inn   1739 N Street, NW   (202) 785-1277
40 rooms.   Services: EX*, R, K*.   Metro: Dupont Circle (2 blocks).
N Street is reminiscent of Manhattan side streets in the '60s off Fifth—tree-shaded, handsome town houses, sophisticated and urban. The Tabard fits in nicely, with its quirky decoration in the lobby and funky guest rooms, some of which have shared baths. Free passes to the YMCA a block away—pools, racquetball, Nautilus, etc. Complimentary continental breakfast. In 1993, a room with shared bath could still be had for under $60.

Windsor Park Hotel   2116 Kalorama Road, NW   (202) 483-7700; 1-800-247-3064
43 rooms.   Rates: G, W, F.   Metro: Dupont Circle (5 blocks).
A very plain, European-type hotel in one of the most lovely sections of town, close to major convention hotels—Hilton, Shoreham, Sheraton Park. Within walking distance to Dupont Circle. Complimentray continental breakfast.

EXPENSIVE ($100–$150)

Anthony Hotel   1823 L Street, NW   (202) 223-4320; 1-800-424-2970
99 suites.   Rates: G, W.   Services: EX*, R, PP, HC, WC.   Metro: Farragut North or Farragut West (1 block).
This midtown hotel underwent extensive renovation in 1989. All suites, the hotel is very convenient to Downtown offices, within walking distance of the White House, Georgetown, Dupont Circle. Health club facilities are two blocks away.

Bellevue Hotel   15 E Street, NW   (202) 638-0900; 1-800-327-6667
138 rooms.   Rates: G, W, F(18).   Services: FP, M*, NSF, R, EX*, HC.
Metro: Union Station (2 blocks).
Completely renovated from top to bottom in 1990, the hotel couldn't be more convenient to Capitol Hill and the Mall. Popular with Europeans.

Best Western New Hampshire Suites Hotel   1121 New Hampshire
  Avenue, NW   (202) 457-0565; 1-800-762-3777
75 suites.   Rates: G, W, F(18).   Services: EX*, K, PP.   Metro: Dupont
Circle (3 blocks), Foggy Bottom-GWU (3 blocks).
All suites, complimentary "English sideboard" breakfast. Within walking
distance of Downtown, Dupont Circle, Georgetown. Renovation completed
in 1990.

The Capitol Hill   200 C Street SE   (202) 543-6000; 1-800-424-9165
152 suites.   Rates: G, W, F(18).   Services: EX*, K, NSR, PP.   Metro:
Capitol South (2 blocks).
This all-suites hotel is one block from the Capitol. Free morning paper,
continental breakfast. Access to nearby exercise facility (fee). Complete renovation in 1990.

Channel Inn   Maine Avenue & 6th Street, SW   (202) 554-2400;
  1-800-368-5668
100 rooms.   Rates: W, G, F(12).   Services: FP, OP, R, WC.   Metro:
L'Enfant Plaza (5 blocks).
Washington's waterfront hotel, completely renovated in 1990. Close to Capitol Hill, the Mall, Arena Stage, Washington Design Center. The southwest
quadrant of the city was virtually leveled during the 1960s urban renewal
boom and is only now regaining some character and life. The area is safe and
convenient. Houses the quite good seafood restaurant, Pier 7.

Days Hotel Crystal City   2000 Jefferson Davis Highway, Arlington, VA
  (703) 920-8600; 1-800-325-2525
247 rooms.   Rates: G, W, F(18).   Services: FP, NSF, OP, R, WC.
Metro: Crystal City (1 block).
An upgraded Days Inn, often mentioned as a friendly and efficient host to
small meetings and group tours. Free shuttle bus to National Airport. Close
to Pentagon, offices and shopping at Crystal City and Pentagon City, and a
short hop to city sites.

Doubletree Hotel   300 Army-Navy Drive, Arlington, VA   (703)
  892-4100; 1-800-848-7000
633 rooms.   Rates: G, W, F(18).   Services: EX, HC, IP, M*, NSF, PP,
R, WC.   Metro: Crystal City, Pentagon City.
Formerly called the Holiday Inn–Crowne Plaza, the hotel is a block from the
new Pentagon City mall (Nordstrom's, Macy's and lots of upscale shops).
Convenient to the Pentagon.

Embassy Square Suites 2000 N Street, NW (202) 659-9000;
1-800-424-2999
250 suites. Rates: G, W, F(16). Services: HC, OP, PP, R, WC.
Metro: Dupont Circle (2 blocks).
Just off Dupont Circle toward downtown, the hotel is built around a green
courtyard and pool. All rooms have VCRs, and a rental library is at the desk.
Free continental breakfast. Free morning paper.

Georgetown Dutch Inn 1075 Thomas Jefferson Street, NW (202)
337-0900; 1-800-388-2410
47 suites, 9 penthouses. Rates: G, W, F(14). Services: FP, K, M, HC,
WC. Metro: Foggy Bottom-GWU (7 blocks).
The Inn displays all the charms of Georgetown—narrow streets, close to the
C&O Canal, a few paces from excellent shopping and dining. The Inn was
fully renovated in 1992.

Georgetown Suites 1111 30th Street, NW (202) 298-7731
100 suites. Rates: G, W. Services: K, PP. Metro: Foggy Bottom-
GWU (5 blocks).
In the heart of Georgetown close to the C&O Canal. Daily, weekly, monthly
rates. Studio, 1BR, 2BR suites. Parking subject to availability.

Holiday Inn Georgetown 2101 Wisconsin Avenue, NW (202) 338-4600;
1-800-HOLIDAY
296 rooms. Rates: G, W, F(18). Services: EX, HC, NSF, OP, PP, R,
WC. Metro: None within easy walking distance.
Close enough to Georgetown to qualify for the name, but far enough away
to avoid the worst of the traffic and noise. Overlooks Rock Creek Park in the
back. Close to National Cathedral. Total overhaul completed in fall 1993.

Lombardy Hotel 2019 I Street, NW (202) 828-2600; 1-800-424-5486
125 rooms/suites. Rates: G, W, F(16). Services: EX*, HC, K*, M,
NSR, R, WC. Metro: Farragut West (3 blocks).
A converted apartment building in the heart of Downtown, facing Pennsyl-
vania Avenue, convenient to the World Bank, GWU, Kennedy Center, the
White House.

Morrison-Clark Inn Massachusetts Avenue & 11th Street, NW (202)
898-1200; 1-800-332-7898
54 rooms/suites. Rates: G, W, F. Services: PP, NSF, R, WC. Metro:
Metro Center—11th & G exit (5 blocks).
This beautifully restored inn bills itself as Washington's only "historic inn,"
its buildings dating back to the mid-nineteenth century (the buildings served

for years as the Soldiers & Sailors Club). The Inn recently built a new section. All rooms are handsomely decorated either in Early American or tropical wicker, but no two are exactly alike. We're not wild about this section of town, but it is close to the Convention Center and downtown sites, and the area is undergoing rapid gentrification. The restaurant, serving distinctive American cuisine, is superb. Free continental breakfast.

One Washington Circle One Washington Circle, NW   (202) 872-1680; 1-800-424-9671
151 rooms. Rates: G, W, F(18). Services: K, M, OP, PP, R, WC.
  Metro: Foggy Bottom-GWU (2 blocks).
Most rooms are suites in this apartment/hotel close to the Kennedy Center, the West End, Georgetown, and Downtown. Renovated in 1990. Excellent restaurant: West End Cafe.

Quality Hotel Central 1900 Connecticut Avenue, NW   (202) 332-9300; 1-800-842-4211
149 rooms. Rates: G, W, F(18). Services: EX*, PP, HC, NSF, OP, R, M, WC. Metro: Dupont Circle (3 blocks).
Reopened in fall 1992 after a complete overhaul, this hotel offers great convenience—close to Dupont Circle, and excellent shopping and dining.

The River Inn 924 25th Street, NW   (202) 337-7600; 1-800-424-2741
128 suites. Rates: G, W, F(12). Services: EX*, K, NSF, PP, R, WC.
  Metro: Foggy Bottom-GWU (1 block).
All-suites hotel in a quiet, sophisticated atmosphere, with such touches as coffee grinders supplied with fresh beans in the 1BR suites. Close to the State Department, Kennedy Center, Vietnam and Lincoln memorials.

Sheraton City Center Hotel 1143 New Hampshire Avenue, NW   (202) 775-0800; 1-800-526-7495
351 rooms. Rates: G, W, F(18). Services: EX*, HC, M, NSF, PP, R, WC. Metro: Dupont Circle (3 blocks), Foggy Bottom-GWU (3 blocks).
Renovated completely in 1989, the hotel (the former Ramada Renaissance) is halfway between Dupont Circle and the West End, convenient to most everything by foot or Metro.

State Plaza Hotel 2117 E Street, NW   (202) 861-8200; 1-800-424-2859
215 suites. Rates: G, W, F(16). Services: K, PP, WC, NSF. Metro: Foggy Bottom-GWU (3 blocks).
All suites, every one with a full kitchen as this is another converted apartment house. Spacious, great location very close to Constitution Gardens, the Viet-

nam and Lincoln memorials and all sites along the Mall. The Sunday brunch in the Garden Cafe is all Russian food.

LUXURY ($150-$200)

Barcelo Washington Hotel   2121 P Street, NW   (202) 293-3100;
   1-800-223-0880
297 rooms.   Rates: G, W, F(17).   Services: EX, HC, M, NSF, OP, PP,
   R, WC.   Metro: Dupont Circle (2 blocks).
Occupying what was once an apartment building, this hotel changed ownership in the fall of 1993, and is currently undergoing renovation. All guest rooms have been redecorated. The hotel restaurant, The Rock Creek Cafe, will also be renovated by winter of 1993.

The Canterbury Hotel   1733 N Street, NW   (202) 393-3000;
   1-800-424-2950
99 suites.   Rates: G, W, F(16).   Services: EX*, HC, K, NSF, PP, R,
   WC.   Metro: Dupont Circle (2 blocks).
On the same street as the Tabard Inn (see Moderate), a quiet, tree-lined cityscape street. The suites are handsomely, and expensively, furnished with some four-poster beds, antiques and rich fabrics.

Dupont Plaza Hotel   Dupont Circle at New Hampshire Avenue, NW
   (202) 483-6000; 1-800-421-6662
310 rooms.   Rates: G, W, F(14).   Services: HC, NSF, PP, R, WC, M.
   Metro: Dupont Circle (1 block).
Right on Dupont Circle (but the quiet side), a rather plain but well-run facility with ample-sized rooms. Renovated in 1992.

Embassy Suites Hotels   1-800-EMBASSY
Washington: 1250 22nd Street, NW   (202) 857-3388   Metro: Foggy
   Bottom-GWU (4 blocks).
Crystal City: 1300 Jefferson Davis Highway, Arlington, VA   (703)
   979-9799   Metro: Crystal City (2 blocks).
Tysons Corner: 8517 Leesburg Pike, Vienna, VA   (703) 883-0707
232–318 suites.   Rates: G, W.   Services: EX, HC, IP, M, NSR, PP, R,
   WC.
All the Embassy Suites are built to the same specifications. You can expect a clean, inviting facility, with all rooms opening onto a corridor overlooking the sunny, enclosed atrium. Free full breakfast and beverages in the late afternoon.

The Georgetown Inn   1310 Wisconsin Avenue, NW   (202) 333-8900;
1-800-424-2979
95 rooms.   Rates: G, W, F(14).   Services: NSF, PP, R.   Metro: None
within easy walking distance.
Right on Georgetown's main drag, it puts you in the heart of the liveliest
nightlife in the District. Was at one time one of the fancier hotels in the
city. Complimentary continental breakfast. Renovated top to bottom in
1992.

Guest Quarters   1-800-424-2900
801 New Hampshire Avenue, NW   (202) 785-2000
2500 Pennsylvania Avenue, NW   (202) 333-8060
101–123 suites.   Rates: G, W, F($15 ea. addl.).   Services: EX*, K, NSF,
OP, PP, WC.   Metro: Foggy Bottom-GWU (2 blocks from each).
All-suites hotels, a few blocks away from each other in the Foggy Bottom
area, close to Georgetown, Kennedy Center and Downtown. Health facilities
two blocks away include Nautilus, free weights, Lifecycles.

Henley Park Hotel   926 Massachusetts Avenue, NW   (202) 638-5200;
1-800-222-8474
96 rooms.   Rates: G, W.   Services: EX*, M, NSF, PP, R.   Metro:
Gallery Place (3 blocks).
This handsomely refurbished Tudor-style, former apartment house is a personal, business-oriented hotel offering complimentary limousine service
around the District. It's convenient to the Convention Center (2 blocks) and
Downtown.

Hotel Washington   15th Street & Pennsylvania Avenue, NW   (202)
638-5900; 1-800-424-9540
350 rooms.   Rates: G, W, F(14).   Services: EX, HC, R, PP, M*, NSF,
WC.   Metro: Federal Triangle (2 blocks).
A venerable hotel, with a restaurant that offers a great nighttime view of
Washington, within sight of the White House and Washington Monument.
Guest room renovations completed in 1990.

Marriott Crystal City   1999 Jeff Davis Highway, Arlington, VA   (703)
413-5500; 1-800-228-9290
340 rooms.   Rates: G, W, F.   Services: EX, HC, IP, NSF, PP, R, WC.
Metro: Crystal City.
Not to be confused with any of the other Marriotts—Key Bridge, Crystal
Gateway, JW Marriott, Washington, etc. Shuttle to National Airport, excellent with groups. 1989 renovation.

Mayflower Stouffer Hotel 1127 Connecticut Avenue, NW (202)
347-3000; 1-800-468-3571
658 rooms. Rates: G, W, F(18). Services: EX, HC, NSR, PP, R, M*,
K*, WC. Metro: Farragut North (1 block).
A Washington landmark since 1925, recently the beneficiary of extensive
refurbishing (which, incidentally, uncovered some 1930s landscape murals by
Edward Lanning). Its long, ornate lobby from Connecticut Avenue to 17th
Street is a classic of hotel architecture. The hotel provides passes to the nearby
YMCA (fee).

Omni Shoreham 2500 Calvert Street, NW (202) 234-0700;
1-800-THE-OMNI
770 rooms. Rates: G, W, F(12). Services: EX, NSF, OP, PP, R.
Metro: Woodley Park (1 block).
A leading convention site, billing itself as a "resort in the city," as it has tennis
courts, several swimming pools (including a kid's wading pool) and extensive
new exercise facilities. A handsome view from rear rooms overlooking Rock
Creek Park. Continuing room renovation since 1988.

Pullman Highland Hotel 1914 Connecticut Avenue, NW (202)
797-2000; 1-800-424-2464
105 rooms. 40 suites. Rates: G, W, F(14). Services: EX*, OP*, NSF,
PP, R. Metro: Dupont Circle (3 blocks)
This converted apartment building is the only French-owned hotel in the city,
part of the Sofitel chain. Each room has a studio. All staff is bi-lingual, and
the entire enterprise has an air of understated elegance. Highly rated restaurant.

Stouffer's Concourse Hotel 2399 Jeff Davis Highway, Arlington, VA
(703) 418-6800; 1-800-HOTELS1
388 rooms. Rates: G, W, F(18). Services: EX, HC, IP, M*, NSF, PP,
R, WC. Metro: Crystal City (2 blocks).
Complimentary van service to and from National Airport, Metro and Mall.
In Crystal City area, close to Pentagon.

Washington Hilton & Towers 1919 Connecticut Avenue, NW (202)
483-3000; 1-800-HILTONS
1154 rooms. Rates: G, W, F. Services: EX, HC, M*, OP, PP, R, NSF,
WC. Metro: Dupont Circle (3 blocks).
A major convention hotel; outdoor tennis courts.

Washington Vista 1400 M Street, NW (202) 429-1700; 1-800-223-1146
399 rooms. Rates: G, W, F. Services: EX, M, NSF, PP, R, HC, WC.
Metro: McPherson Square (4 blocks).

Although atriums are commonplace, the Vista's 14-story garden atrium is particularly pleasing. Rooms completely refurbished in 1993. Executive floor available.

Wyndham Bristol Hotel 2430 Pennsylvania Avenue, NW (202) 955-6400; 1-800-822-4200
240 rooms and suites. Rates: G, W, F(18). Services: K, NSF, PP, R, EX*, WC. Metro: Foggy Bottom-GWU (2 blocks).
Another converted apartment building, this time with a distinctly British tone. Elegantly outfitted, each room has a four-poster bed. The Bristol Grill restaurant is noted for its mesquite-prepared meats.

SUPER-LUXURY (OVER $200)

ANA Hotel 2401 M Street, NW (202) 429-2400; 1-800-262-4683
416 rooms. Rates: G, W, F(18). Services: EX, HC, IP, M, NSF, PP, R, WC. Metro: Foggy Bottom-GWU (3 blocks).
One of several luxury hotels in the West End, the ANA (originally the Westin Hotel) is more charming than opulent, and is built around a lovely courtyard garden. The Executive Club Floor offers a wide range of services to guests. The Fitness Center is one of the best in the city (fee). The guest rooms were recently renovated.

The Capital Hilton 16h & K streets, NW (202) 393-1000; 1-800-HILTONS
549 rooms. Rates: G, W, F. Services: EX, M, NSR, PP, R, HC, WC. Metro: Farragut North (3 blocks), McPherson Square (3 blocks).
A 40-year institution two blocks from the White House. Major business hotel, completely renovated several years back, nearly halving the number of rooms, making them among the most spacious in town.

Embassy Row Hotel 2015 Massachusetts Avenue, NW (202) 265-1600; 1-800-424-2400
196 rooms. Rates: G, W, F(16). Services: EX*, M*, NSR, OP, PP, R, HC, WC. Metro: Dupont Circle (1 block).
A refined atmosphere catering to the international clientele found at nearby embassies. Health facilities two blocks away include Nautilus, Lifecycle, sauna, whirlpool. A full renovation of guest rooms and public areas began in August 1993.

The Four Seasons Hotel 2800 Pennsylvania Avenue, NW (202)
342-0444; 1-800-332-3442
197 rooms. Rates: G, W, F(18). Services: EX, HC, IP, M, NSF, PP,
R, WC. Metro: Foggy Bottom-GWU (4 blocks).
One of the area's most respected elegant hotels. Afternoon tea and champagne
brunch are popular features. The weekend packages may be, for most, the
only affordable way in which to enjoy this most gracious of hotels.

The Grand 2350 M Street, NW (202) 429-0100; 1-800-848-0016
262 rooms including 30 suites. Rates: G, W, F(16). Services: EX, HC,
M, NSF, OP, PP, R, WC. Metro: Foggy Bottom-GWU (5 blocks).
A member of the Concord group of hotels, the Grand caters to a multina-
tional clientele. Privacy reigns here, with extraordinary attention paid to a
guest's needs—from plush terry robes to meeting special dietary requirements.

Grand Hyatt 1000 H Street, NW (202) 582-1234; 1-800-233-1234
907 rooms. Rates: G, W, F(18). Services: EX, HC, IP, M, NSF, PP,
R, WC. Metro: Metro Center.
Directly across the street from the Convention Center, the Hyatt contains all
the traditional Hyatt touches—marble, water, multitiered lobbies, helpful
amenities in the rooms.

Hay-Adams Hotel 800 16th Street, NW (202) 638-2260;
1-800-424-5054
143 rooms. Rates: G, W. Services: EX*, HC, M, NSF, PP, R, WC.
Metro: Farragut North (1 block).
If you want to be close to the seat of power, you can't do better than the
Hay-Adams, with rooms overlooking Lafayette Square and the White House.
The exceptionally handsome stone facade wraps an intimate, personal hotel,
where you can expect the highest level of competent service, and particularly
good food in all of the hotel's restaurants.

Jefferson Hotel 16th & M streets, NW (202) 347-2200; 1-800-368-5966
100 rooms. Rates: G, W, F(12). Services: EX*, M, NSF, PP, R, HC,
WC. Metro: Farragut North (3 blocks).
One of the finest small hotels in the area, with an eighteenth-century English
style. The restaurant is superb; the service in all arenas quiet, dignified and
polished. Fitness facilities through the University Club (fee) across the street.

Loew's L'Enfant Plaza 480 L'Enfant Plaza East, SW (202) 484-1000;
1-800-223-0888
372 rooms. Rates: G, W, F(14). Services: EX, HC, I/OP, M, NSF,
PP, R, WC. Metro: L'Enfant Plaza.

The hotel is placed amid an environment of office buildings and concrete plaza, but the location, close to the Mall, is ideal for sightseeing. The hotel is modern and efficient, and has not only the pools to amuse kids, but a complete game center and VCRs in rooms. Renovated in 1990.

Madison Hotel   15th & M streets, NW   (202) 862-1600; 1-800-424-8577
353 rooms.   Rates: G, W.   Services: EX*, M, NSF, PP, R, HC, WC.
Metro: McPherson Square (2 blocks).
Long the standard for Washington's luxury hotels, the Madison now has stiff competition, and is thus undergoing extensive renovation. Each room is individually and eclectically furnished, often with the owner's oriental objets d'art. Free passes to the nearby YMCA.

Sheraton-Carlton Hotel   16th & K streets, NW   (202) 638-2626;
1-800-325-3535
200 rooms, 15 suites.   Rates: G, W, F(18).   Services: EX, HC, M, NSF,
PP, R, WC.   Metro: McPherson Square (1 block).
The complete 1991 renovation of this landmark two blocks from the White House was overseen by Mrs. Rose Narva (whose influence is also seen at the Jefferson and Hay-Adams hotels). The hotel has been returned to its 1926 glory, all glass, glitter and opulence. Guest rooms are plush, with every amenity.

Sheraton Washington   2660 Woodley Road, NW   (202) 328-2000;
1-800-325-3535
1,500 rooms.   Rates: G, W, F(18).   Services: EX, HC, M*, NSR, OP,
PP, R, WC.   Metro: Woodley Park (1 block).
A major convention hotel, with large meeting rooms and facilities to match. Convenient to zoo, Dupont Circle.

Watergate Hotel   2560 Virginia Avenue, NW   (202) 965-2300;
1-800-424-2736
235 rooms.   Rates: G, W, F(18).   Services: EX, HC, IP, K*, M, NSF,
PP, R, WC.   Metro: Foggy Bottom-GWU (1 block).
Part of the Watergate complex, close to Kennedy Center, overlooking the Potomac. Elegant touches and considerate service are trademarks of this establishment. Home to Jean-Louis, an haute-cuisine French restaurant.

Willard Inter-continental Hotel   1401 Pennsylvania Avenue, NW   (202)
628-9100; 1-800-327-0200
365 rooms.   Rates: G, W.   Services: EX, HC, M, NSF, PP, R, WC.
Metro: Federal Triangle (1 block).

This Beaux Arts structure was saved from the wrecker's ball and lovingly (and expensively) re-created to its nineteenth-century high-Victorian glory. Red plush velvet and mirrors abound. The Willard Room restaurant is highly regarded. The term "lobbyist," referring to the political favor-seekers who gathered here to exchange gossip, was coined in Peacock Alley. A block from the White House, within walking distance of the Mall.

CALENDAR OF ANNUAL EVENTS

Check newspapers for special events while you're in town. Also call the following numbers to check on what's happening when you're in Washington:

Smithsonian Special Events Office	(202) 357-2284
National Park Service	(202) 485-9666
Alexandria Tourist Council	(703) 838-4200
Washington, D.C., Convention and Visitors Association	(202) 789-7000

January

Opening of Congress

Inauguration and festivities (every four years)

Martin Luther King, Jr.'s, Birthday celebration, January 15, (202) 727-6306

Birthday celebrations of Light-Horse Harry Lee and Robert E. Lee at Lee's Boyhood Home, Alexandria, VA, (703) 548-1789

Washington Antiques Show, Omni Shoreham Hotel, (202) 234-0700

February

Lincoln's Birthday celebration at Lincoln Memorial, February 12, (202) 485-9666

Washington's Birthday celebration at Washington Monument, February 22, (202) 485-9666

Washington's Birthday parade, Alexandria, VA; nation's largest (703) 838-4200

George Washington Birthnight Ball and Buffet, Gadsby's Tavern, Alexandria, VA, (703) 838-4200

George Washington Classic 10K Run, Alexandria, VA, (703) 438-4200

Revolutionary War Encampment, Fort Ward, VA, (703) 838-4848

Washington International Boat Show, Washington Convention Center, (202) 789-1600

Chinese New Year, Chinatown (may be in January, depending on Chinese calendar)

Washington Boat Show, Convention Center, (703) 569-7141

March

Cherry Blossom Festival and Parade (may be in April, depending on cherry trees), (202) 485-9666

St. Patrick's Day parade, Constitution Avenue

St. Patrick's parade (2nd Saturday), Alexandria, VA, (703) 838-4200

Festival of St. Patrick, Paul VI Institute for the Arts, (202) 347-1450

Smithsonian Kite Festival, Washington Monument Grounds, (202) 357-2284

U.S. Botanic Garden Spring Flower Show, (202) 225-8333

Tour of the Defenses of Washington. Fort Ward, VA, bus tour of Washington's Civil War forts, (703) 838-4848

Kite Festival, Gunston Hall, Lorton, VA, (703) 550-9220

Spring Flower Show, U.S. Botanic Gardens, (202) 225-8333

Easter sunrise services, Arlington National Cemetery (may be in April), (703) 692-0931

Easter Egg Roll, White House (may be in April), (202) 456-7041

Flower and Garden Show, Convention Center, (703) 569-7141

April

Imagination Celebration of the Performing Arts (for children), Kennedy Center, (202) 467-4600

White House Garden Tour, (202) 456-7041

Georgetown House Tour, (202) 338-1796

Georgetown Garden Tour, (202) 333-4953

Old Town House and Garden Tour, Alexandria, VA, (703) 848-4200

Jefferson's Birthday celebration, Jefferson Memorial, April 13, (202) 485-9666

Shakespeare's Birthday celebration, Folger Library, (202) 544-7077

Washington International Film Festival, (202) 727-2396

Ringling Brothers/Barnum and Bailey Circus, (202) 546-3337

Washington Craft Show, (202) 357-2700

Wings and Things Aviation Open House, Paul Garber Air and Space Annex, Suitland, MD, (202) 357-2627

Gross National Parade, Georgetown

Spring Fair, Audubon Naturalist Society, (301) 652-9188

DC Film Festival, various locations, (202) 727-2396

American College Theater Festival, Kennedy Center, (202) 416-8850

May

Washington National Cathedral Fair, (202) 537-6200

Irish Festival, Glen Echo Park, MD (Memorial Weekend Sunday), (301) 492-6282

Festival of the Building Arts, National Building Museum, (202) 272-2448

Goodwill Embassy Tour, (202) 636-4225

Kemper Open Pro-Am Golf Tournament, (301) 469-3737

Memorial Day—National Symphony free concert, Capitol grounds; Jazz Festival, Alexandria, VA, (703) 838-4686; services at Tomb of the Unknowns, Arlington National Cemetery, (703) 692-0931

Andrews Air Force Base Air Show, (202) 981-6681

Georgetown Garden Tour, (202) 333-4953

Preakness Stakes, Pimlico Race Course, (410) 542-9400

June

Washington Folk Festival, Glen Echo Park, MD (first weekend in June), (301) 492-6282

Dupont-Kalorama Museum Walk Day (first Saturday), (202) 387-4062

Waterfront Festival, Alexandria, VA (second weekend), (703) 549-8300

Mostly Mozart Festival, Kennedy Center, (202) 467-4600

Military Band free concerts, June through August, Capitol, Sylvan Theater, U.S. Navy Memorial, (202) 524-0830

Folk Life Festival, Smithsonian Institution, Mall, (202) 357-2284

July

Fourth of July—Fireworks and celebration, Mall; National Symphony free concert, Capitol grounds; Marine Band concert, Wolf Trap Park, (703) 255-1916

Folk Life Festival, Smithsonian Institution, Mall, (202) 357-2700

Alexandria Birthday celebration, Alexandria, VA (second Saturday), (703) 838-4686

Civil War Living History Day, Fort Ward, VA, (703) 838-4848

Virginia Scottish Games and Gathering of Clans, Alexandria, VA, (703) 838-4200

Grand Prix Tennis, Rock Creek Park

Bastille Day Waiters Race, Dominique's Restaurant, (202) 452-1132

Soap Box Derby, Capitol Hill, (301) 670-1110

Latin American Festival, Washington Monument grounds, (202) 319-1340

August

1812 Overture, U.S. Army Band, Washington Monument grounds, (202) 696-3718

Maryland State Fair, Timonium, MD, (301) 252-0200

Lollipop Concert, U.S. Navy Band, Sylvan Theater (third Thursday), (202) 433-2394
Christmas in August, Air Force Band, Sylvan Theater, (202) 433-2394
Howard County Fair, Fairgrounds, (410) 442-1022
Arlington County Fair, (703) 358-6412
Montgomery County Fair, Fairgrounds, (301) 926-3100

September
Labor Day, National Symphony free concert, Capitol grounds
White House Garden Tour, (202) 456-7041
Alexandria House Tour, (703) 838-4200
International Children's Festival, Wolf Trap Park, (703) 255-2916
Star-Spangled Banner, Georgetown Anniversary
Caribbeana, Fonda del Sol Visual Arts Center, (202) 483-2777
Adams-Morgan Day
James Madison Birthday celebration, The Octagon, (202) 638-3105
Constitution Day commemoration, National Archives, (202) 501-5215
Antique Car Show, Gunston Hall, Lorton, VA, (703) 550-9220
Washington National Cathedral Open House, (202) 537-6200
Eighteenth-Century Fair, Market Square, Alexandria, VA, (703) 838-4200

October
White House Garden Tour, (202) 456-7041
Celebration of Lafayette's visit, Lee's Boyhood Home, (703) 838-4200
Opening Ceremony of Supreme Court (first Monday), (202) 479-3000
War Between the States Chili Cookoff, Alexandria, VA, (703) 836-7449
U.S. Navy Birthday concert, Kennedy Center, (202) 433-2394
International Gold Cup Horse Races, The Plains, VA, (703) 347-1215
Ghost Tours, Alexandria, VA, (703) 838-4200
Washington International Horse Race, Laurel, MD, (301) 725-0400
Washington International Horse Show, Capitol Center, (301) 840-0281

November
Colonial Craft Fair, Decatur House, (202) 673-4030
Marine Corps Marathon, Iwo Jima Memorial
Armistice Day Celebration, Woodrow Wilson House, (202) 387-4062
Veteran's Day ceremony, Arlington National Cemetery and Vietnam Veterans' Memorial
Many, many Christmas craft fairs, continuing through December

December
Candlelight tours (second Friday and Saturday)—Lee's Boyhood Home; Gadsby's Tavern, Carlyle House, Lee-Fendall House, Woodlawn Plantation, (703) 838-4200

Evening candlelight tour, White House, (202) 456-7041

Caroling and *Messiah* sing-along, Kennedy Center, (202) 254-3600

Scottish Christmas Walk, Alexandria, VA, (703) 838-4200

Historic Caroling, Gunston Hall, Lorton, VA, (703) 550-9220

Christmas Pageant of Peace, Lighting of the National Christmas Tree, The Ellipse

Annual Christmas Program, Wolf Trap Park, (703) 944-6066

Festival of Music and Lights, Mormon Temple, (301) 587-0144

New Year's Eve Celebration, Pavilion at the Old Post Office, (202) 289-4224

INDEX

ABOUT THE AUTHORS

JUDY DUFFIELD has been a devoted fan of Washington since her arrival in the area more than twenty years ago. In past years she has been a teacher and an editor for a variety of concerns—a national consulting firm, the D.C. government, and a federally funded project. She and Bill Kramer are the parents of Jacob and Michael, now attending public school.

BILL KRAMER is a native Washingtonian. He is the owner of several bookstores in Washington: Kramerbooks & afterwords, the bookstore/cafés mentioned in the *Guide,* and Sidney Kramer Books, a professional and technical bookstore. He is married to Judy Duffield.

CYNTHIA SHEPPARD, originally from the Boston area, contracted Potomac fever at a tender age. She has worked in government, publishing and business in Washington. Although she now lives in Massachusetts, she often returns to her adopted second home.